94-3247

Organizations
on the Couch

Manfred F. R. Kets de Vries
and Associates

Organizations on the Couch

Clinical Perspectives on Organizational Behavior and Change

 Jossey-Bass Publishers

San Francisco   •   Oxford   •   1991

HD
58.7
.07468
1991
X

ORGANIZATIONS ON THE COUCH
Clinical Perspectives on Organizational Behavior and Change
by Manfred F. R. Kets de Vries and Associates

Copyright © 1991 by: Jossey-Bass Inc., Publishers
350 Sansome Street
San Francisco, California 94104
&
Jossey-Bass Limited
Headington Hill Hall
Oxford OX3 0BW

Library of Congress Cataloging-in-Publication Data

Organizations on the couch : clinical perspectives on organizational
behavior and change / Manfred F. R. Kets de Vries and associates. —
1st ed.
p.   cm. — (The Jossey-Bass management series)
Includes bibliographical references and index.
ISBN 1-55542-384-1
1. Organizational behavior. 2. Psychology, Industrial.
3. Executives. I. Kets de Vries, Manfred F. R. II. Series.
HD58.7.07468   1991
158.7—dc20   91-15877
                                                    CIP

Manufactured in the United States of America

The paper in this book meets the guidelines for
permanence and durability of the Committee on
Production Guidelines for Book Longevity of
the Council on Library Resources.

Credits are on page 408.

JACKET DESIGN BY WILLI BAUM

FIRST EDITION

Code 9186

The Jossey-Bass Management Series

*To my mentors
at different life stages:
Jonas, Abraham,
Sudhir, and Maurice*

Contents

ix

Contents

Preface

Increasing international competition and rapid technological change have magnified expectations about organizational performance and adaptation. Deregulation and the globalization of our postindustrial society are putting an enormous amount of pressure on organizations. Changes in political alliances and orientations, such as those recently occurring in Eastern Europe, offer a host of new opportunities. In response to the new challenges, a plethora of models of organizational analysis and decision making have come to the fore. Unfortunately, in spite of all these up-to-date management technologies and techniques, disasters such as the nuclear explosion at Chernobyl, the Exxon *Valdez* oil spill, or the loss of the NASA shuttle *Challenger* still seem to be inevitable. Notwithstanding systematic analysis of possible contingencies, in all these instances something went terribly wrong.

If we have learned anything from these incidents, it is that in each case too little attention was paid to the human processes associated with the decision-making models. All too often, the element of human psychology has been excluded from seemingly very sophisticated designs, or it has received superficial consideration.

Background

In organizational research, attention has traditionally focused on telling executives how to do things correctly by creating models for rational analysis. The reality of the situation often requires a very different approach. To understand what makes for successful organizational performance, it is advisable to pay attention to the quirks and irrational processes that are part and parcel of individual behavior. Given that human error is inevitable, it is vital to consider how to deal with processes *outside* the recommended models; to gain insight into both conscious and unconscious behavior, rational and irrational actions; and to understand better the *real* nature of the interface between individuals and organizations. The authors of *Organizations on the Couch* set out to do this. The book has grown out of the contributors' shared interest in bringing human beings back into the organization, in demonstrating the importance of the clinical paradigm for a more commonsense understanding of organizational functioning.

The pioneers in this field have been taking this approach for many years. Management scholars such as Abraham Zaleznik, Harry Levinson, and Elliott Jaques have made important contributions to the psychodynamic understanding of organizations. Their writings provided the stimulus for the first International Symposium on Applied Psychoanalysis and Organizations, which was organized by Michael Hofmann of the Wirtschaftsuniversität of Vienna and took place in the summer of 1980 at the Grundlsee in Austria. A further impetus came from Leopold Gruenfeld, who organized a number of conferences under the auspices of Cornell University. These various symposia eventually led to the founding of the International Society for the Psychoanalytic Study of Organizations (ISPSO), whose annual meetings have been attended by an ever-increasing number of scholars and practitioners interested in the subject.

My purpose as editor of *The Irrational Executive: Psychoanalytic Explorations in Management* (1984) was to bring together articles by leading psychoanalytically oriented management theorists and clinicians interested in organizations. By that time it had become clear to me that although important work was being done on this subject in various parts of the world, the published material was scattered about in highly diverse journals aimed at equally diverse audiences. *The Irrational Executive* attempted to give greater visibility to the clinical approach to organizational analysis. Critical reaction to the book was positive and encouraging.

Things have not stood still since then. Numerous publications centering on the clinical paradigm have appeared, including many articles in mainstream management journals. A burgeoning interest in topics such as leadership, corporate culture, family business, organizational stress, and career dynamics has helped to account for this. People have begun to realize that the use of the clinical paradigm can provide a greater insight into these often very vexing issues.

Audience

Given all these developments, I felt that the time had come once more to draw together in one place the work of the small but growing group of management theorists. The present volume introduces the work of a good number of leading scholars interested in the clinical approach to organizational analysis. *Organizations on the Couch* will probably have five major audiences. First, the book will help human resource management professionals to design organizations that work and to introduce more realistic organizational systems and structures. Second, for students of management, the book will provide a deeper understanding of human motivation and action within organizations. It will help in identifying the paradoxical rationale behind irrational behavior and consequently will further the development of more realistic models of organizational functioning. Third, the insights the book offers will benefit management consultants, improving their effectiveness in handling organizational diagnosis, intervention, and change processes. Fourth, mental health professionals, such as industrial and organizational psychologists, organizational sociologists, industrial social workers, occupational psychiatrists, and clinical organizational psychologists, will be able to use ideas presented here to assist their clients in lessening irrational behavior and stress in organizations. The fifth important audience for this book will be enlightened business practitioners who want to deepen their understanding of organizational decision making, culture, leadership style, organizational stress, and the general interface between individuals and the organization. The central aim of this book is to promote better understanding of the use and applicability of the clinical paradigm.

Overview of the Contents

The introductory chapter sets the stage for the observation that executives are not necessarily logical beings but are prone to irrational behavior that can seriously affect organizational processes. To help understand the rationale behind the irrationality, I introduce the clinical paradigm, along with a case study as an aid in decoding the organizational "text."

Organizations on the Couch is divided into five parts. Part One centers on conceptual frameworks for analyzing organizations. In Chapter One, Laurence J. Gould explores the relation of psychoanalytic theory and practice to the working group and organizational consultation. He makes a distinction between type 1 practice, which utilizes the technical procedures and methods of psychoanalysis, and type 2 practice, which uses psychoanalytic theory as a guide for various intervention methods and procedures not necessarily restricted to psychoanalysis. Gould gives examples of these various practices and discusses the implications of a psychoanalytically based organizational psychology. Harry Levinson, in Chapter Two, offers a comprehensive framework (derived from psychoanalysis, sociology, and systems theory) for systematically diagnosing organizations and deciding on possible means of intervention. Detailed information is given on how to obtain and organize the collected material, prepare a report, and feed it back to the organization. In Chapter Three, taking the leader as his point of departure, Laurent Lapierre demonstrates the value of the clinical approach. He shows how case histories and fictional works can be used as research tools for understanding the extent to which intrapsychic "fantasies" contribute to specific management and leadership practices.

Part Two focuses on leadership, a critical component of organizational life. Abraham Zaleznik, in Chapter Four, sheds light on what is wrong with contemporary corporate life and differentiates between leaders and managers. Managers focus on process, while leaders are interested in substance, in imaginative ideas. He makes a plea for bringing true leadership back to organizations. In Chapter Five, I comment on the vicissitudes of becoming a CEO, paying particular attention to issues such as transference and power. I describe a number of reasons for the addictiveness of power and conclude the chapter by listing some ways of dealing with the pressures of leadership. Alain Noël, in Chapter Six, undertakes an observational study of three CEOs that demonstrates the causality between intention and strategic action. He suggests that a "magnificent obsession," latent in each of his subjects' activities and preoccupations, appears to be the element common to whatever activities they undertake.

In Part Three, we shift our attention to group processes. Susan C. Schneider, in Chapter Seven, considers boundary management from the perspective of the individual, the family, the group, and the organization. With a case example she highlights the fact that proper boundary management is essential to effective organizational functioning. In Chapter Eight, Michael A. Diamond compares three regressive and psychologically defensive work groups to a nonregressive one, discussing psychodynamic features to highlight the differences between the groups. He suggests that the balance between the needs for independence and belonging will determine healthy or regressive group response. Basing their observations on a case study of an oil refinery, Larry Hirschhorn and Donald R. Young (Chapter Nine) describe how groups in organizations may develop specific "social defenses" as a way of containing work anxiety. These social defenses come to the fore in the form of particular relationships, procedures, and organizational rituals.

Part Four covers the question of organizational character. In Chapter Ten, Danny Miller and I examine the links between executive personality, corporate culture, strategy, and structure.

We establish a typology of five potentially dysfunctional leadership styles and organizational structures—suspicious, depressive, dramatic, compulsive, and detached—and describe the characteristics associated with each. Howell S. Baum, in Chapter Eleven, discusses the way in which bureaucracy discourages responsibility. Drawing on two case histories, he reveals the underlying psychological character of bureaucratic organizations. Using the concept of the organizational ideal, Howard S. Schwartz (Chapter Twelve) indicates how, because of faulty superego development, organizational participants can move away from reality toward a world of fantasy. He illustrates this phenomenon using the National Aeronautics and Space Administration as a case example.

Part Five concentrates on organizational consultation and change. It begins with a chapter by James Krantz and Thomas North Gilmore (Chapter Thirteen) that elucidates the impact of projective identification on the consulting relationship. Krantz and Gilmore explain the parallelism between the dynamics within consultancy teams and those of client systems. They point out that understanding this form of repetition can be invaluable in gleaning data about the client system and in furthering the process of intervention and change. In Chapter Fourteen, Roderick Gilkey, building on Erik Erikson's ideas about the eight ages of man, provides a conceptual framework for understanding the psychodynamic upheavals caused by mergers and acquisitions. Drawing on data gathered from a two-year study of successful postmerger practices, he describes a number of specific intervention strategies introduced to alleviate the pain of adjustment for employees in the new "blended corporate family." In Chapter Fifteen, Isabel Menzies Lyth explains the psychoanalytic clinical method. With the help of case examples, she demonstrates the extent to which the approach can be of use to the consultant. She also explores the question of what makes for organizational health.

Finally, in Chapter Sixteen I call attention to areas of convergence and divergence in the various chapters and speculate about future directions of the clinical approach to organizational analysis.

Acknowledgments

I would like to thank all the contributors for the ideas that made the publication of this book a reality. The International Society for the Psychoanalytic Study of Organizations provided the initial forum for many of the ideas presented here. The assistance of Donald Levine, the society's chairman, was invaluable. I would also like to thank Laurent Lapierre, whose imaginative "Fantasies and Leadership" conference, held at the Ecole des Hautes Etudes Commerciales in Montreal in 1986, afforded further stimulating exploration of the clinical paradigm. I would like to express my appreciation to the Department of Research at INSEAD, particularly the past and present associate deans, Yves Doz, Ludo Van der Heyden, and Charles Wyplosz, for their support for this work. I am indebted to Diane Mitchell of the same department for generously coming to my aid every time the need arose. I would like to thank my secretary, Ranu Capron, for keeping me organized, and to express my appreciation to Lee Guarino for typing the manuscript with infinite care. Last but not least, let me express my deep gratitude to my research associate, Sally Simmons, for assisting me in the editorial process. Without her help the book would not have been the same.

Paris, France   Manfred F. R. Kets de Vries
September 1991

The Authors

Manfred F. R. Kets de Vries holds the Raoul de Vitry d'Avaucourt Chair of Human Resource Management at the European Institute of Business Administration (INSEAD) in Fontainebleau, France. He did a doctoral examination in economics (Econ. Drs., 1966) at the University of Amsterdam and holds an M.B.A. degree (1968) and a D.B.A. degree (1970) from the Harvard Business School. In 1977 he undertook psychoanalytic training at the Canadian Psychoanalytic Institute and was certified to practice psychoanalysis by the Canadian Psychoanalytic Society and the International Psychoanalytic Association. He is a practicing psychoanalyst. He is also a founding member of the International Society for the Psychoanalytic Study of Organizations and a member of its steering committee. He has held professorships at McGill University, the Ecole des Hautes Etudes Commerciales de Montréal, and the Harvard Business School. Kets de Vries's main research interest is the interface between psychoanalysis, dynamic psychiatry, and international management. Other areas of interest to him are leadership, career dynamics, organizational stress, family business, organizational diagnosis, intervention, and change. Kets de Vries is the author or coauthor of many books, including *Power and the Corporate Mind* (1975, 1985, with A. Zaleznik), *Organizational Paradoxes: Clinical Approaches to Management* (1980), *The Neurotic Organization: Diagnosing and Changing Counterproductive Styles of Management* (1984, 1990, with D. Miller), *Unstable at the Top: Inside the Troubled Organization* (1987, with D. Miller), and *Prisoners of Leadership* (1989). He is the editor of *The Irrational Executive: Psychoanalytic Studies in*

Management (1984), and coeditor of the *Handbook of Character Studies* (1991, with S. Perzow). In addition, more than eighty of his scientific papers have been published as chapters in books or as articles. He serves on a number of editorial boards. He is also a newspaper columnist. Kets de Vries's books and papers have been translated into ten languages. He has been a regular consultant on organizational design and strategic human resource management and has done executive development work with many U.S., Canadian, European, and Asian companies.

Howell S. Baum is professor of planning in the Department of Urban Studies and Planning at the University of Maryland, College Park. He received his B.A. degree (1967) from the University of California, Berkeley, in political science; his M.A. degree (1968) from the University of Pennsylvania in American civilization; and his M.C.P. (1971) and Ph.D. (1974) degrees from the University of California, Berkeley, in city and regional planning. He has written *Planners and Public Expectations* (1983), *The Invisible Bureaucracy* (1987), and *Organizational Membership* (1990). He is a founding member of the International Society for the Psychoanalytic Study of Organizations and a member of its steering committee.

Michael A. Diamond is professor of public administration and chair in the College of Business and Public Administration at the University of Missouri, Columbia. He received his B.A. (1976), M.A. (1978), and Ph.D. (1981) degrees from the University of Maryland, College Park, all in government and politics. His many published works bridging psychoanalysis, groups, and organizations have appeared in journals such as *Administration & Society, Political Psychology, Journal of Management Studies, Human Relations, Organizational Dynamics, The Social Science Journal, Personnel Journal,* and *Public Administration Quarterly*. In 1987 he received the Harry Hall Trice Faculty Research Award from the College of Business and Public Administration at the University of Missouri, Columbia. He is an active organizational consultant and cofounder and chair of the International Society for the Psychoanalytic Study of Organizations.

Roderick Gilkey is associate professor of organization and management at Emory Business School and assistant professor of psychiatry at Emory Medical School in Atlanta. He received an M.Div. degree (1971) from Harvard University and A.B. (1968), A.M. (1975), and Ph.D. (1977) degrees from the University of Michigan in clinical psychology. In his clinical work he has specialized in the treatment of executives and their families. His research interests center on leadership and negotiation, managing change, and postmerger management. He has conducted numerous executive education programs in the United States, Europe, and Asia for *Fortune* 500 companies.

Thomas North Gilmore is vice president of the Wharton Center for Applied Research, an independent consulting firm. He is adjunct associate professor in the Health Care Systems Program at the Wharton School and senior fellow at the University of Pennsylvania's Leonard David Institute of Health Economics. He received his A.B. degree (1966) from Harvard in Roman history and literature and his M.A. degree (1970) from the University of Pennsylvania in architecture. He has written extensively on issues of organization, management, and leadership and is the author of *Making a Leadership Change: How Organizations and Leaders Can Handle Leadership Transitions Successfully* (1989). He is a founding member of the International Society for the Psychoanalytic Study of Organizations and teaches organizational development and consultation at the William Alanson White Institute in New York City.

Laurence J. Gould is professor of psychology and director of the Psychological Center in the clinical psychology doctoral program at the City University of New York. He received his B.A. degree (1958) from the University of Michigan in psychology and his M.A. (1961) and Ph.D. (1965) degrees from the University of Connecticut, also in psychology. He was a National Institute of Mental Health postdoctoral fellow in psychology at Yale University (1966). He is a 1984 graduate of the William Alanson White Institute and director of its program on organizational development and consultation. Gould is a

founding member of the International Society for the Psychoanalytic Study of Organizations, past president and fellow of the
A. K. Rice Institute, and a principal of the firm Gould Krantz
White, Organizational Consultation. He has written and lectured extensively on leadership, the organization of health and
service settings, models of organizational consultation, professional development, and organizational and training dilemmas
in service enterprises.

Larry Hirschhorn is a principal with the Wharton Center
for Applied Research, an independent management consulting
company. He received his B.A. degree (1967) from Brandeis
University and his Ph.D. degree (1971) from the Massachu-
setts Institute of Technology in economics. He was a Woodrow
Wilson Fellow in 1968 and received a Rockefeller Foundation
Fellowship in the humanities in 1978. He is the author of nu-
merous articles and three books, including *The Workplace Within:
Psychodynamics of Organizational Life* (1988) and *Managing in the
New Team Environment* (1990). He is a founding member of the
International Society for the Psychoanalytic Study of Organi-
zations and is on the faculty of the program on organizational
development and consultation at the William Alanson White
Institute in New York City. He is also a member of the Organizational Development Network and the A. K. Rice Institute.
He consults extensively in the areas of organizational development and design and the application of new technologies to fac-
tories and offices.

James Krantz is assistant professor at the Yale School of
Organization and Management and a principal in the organizational consulting firm of Gould Krantz White. He received
his B.A. degree (1974) from Wesleyan University in economics and philosophy and his Ph.D. degree (1986) from the Wharton School of the University of Pennsylvania in social systems
sciences. He has been on the faculties of Yale, Wharton, and
Columbia. Krantz has written and lectured on the unconscious
background of group and organizational life, consultation practice and theory, emerging conceptions of work and collaboration
in postindustrial society, dilemmas of structuring organizational

innovation, and changing patterns of authority and leadership in emerging organizations.

Laurent Lapierre is associate professor of management and leadership at the Ecole des Hautes Etudes Commerciales de Montréal. He has been the general manager of a university cultural center and of one of the foremost theater companies in Quebec. He holds three bachelor's degrees (1962, 1964, and 1968) from the Université Laval, in arts, pedagogy, and history, respectively; an M.B.A. degree (1975) from the Ecole des Hautes Etudes Commerciales de Montréal; and a Ph.D. degree (1984) from McGill University. He is a founding member of the International Society for the Psychoanalytic Study of Organizations and a member of its steering committee. He has also served as editor-in-chief of *Gestion: Revue Internationale de Gestion.*

Harry Levinson is president of the Levinson Institute, clinical professor of psychology in the Department of Psychiatry, Harvard Medical School, and the head of the Section on Organizational Mental Health, Massachusetts Mental Health Center. He received both his B.S. degree (1943) and his M.S. degree (1947) from Emporia State University in education; and his Ph.D. degree (1952) from the University of Kansas in clinical psychology. He is the author of numerous works, among them *The Great Jackass Fallacy* (1973), *Executive Stress* (1964), *Organizational Diagnosis* (1972), *Executive* (1981), and *CEO* (1984, with S. Rosenthal). He is a founding member of the International Society for the Psychoanalytic Study of Organizations and a member of its steering committee.

Isabel Menzies Lyth took her M.A. degree at St. Andrews University in economics and experimental psychology. She then undertook psychoanalytic training with the British Institute of Psychoanalysis and qualified as a psychoanalyst in 1954. She is a member of the British Psychoanalytical Society, a fellow of the British Psychological Society, and an honorary fellow of the Australian Institute of Social Analysis. She was a lecturer in economics at St. Andrews University from 1939 to 1945. In 1945 she joined Civil Resettlement Headquarters, an army unit concerned with the resettlement in civilian life of returning British prisoners of war. From 1946 to 1954 she was a full-time member of the staff of the Tavistock Institute of Human Relations in London. In 1954 she became a part-time consultant at the Tavistock Institute and worked part time as a psychoanalyst. She has been on the training staff of the British Institute of Psychoanalysis since 1959. From 1950 on, she has been involved in consultancy and teaching overseas with the World Health Organization and a number of psychoanalytic societies. Her main publications are collected in two volumes, *Containing Anxiety in Institutions* (1988) and *The Dynamics of the Social* (1989).

Danny Miller is research professor of management at the Ecole des Hautes Etudes Commerciales de Montréal and visiting professor at McGill University and the University of Alberta. His Ph.D. degree (1976) from McGill University is in management policy; he also holds an M.B.A. degree (1970) from the University of Toronto and a B. Comm. degree (1968) from Sir George Williams University. Miller's main research interests are the formulation of competitive business strategies, organizational change and development, the decline of once-great corporations, and the impact of chief executives on their organizations. His most recent book is *The Icarus Paradox: How Exceptional Companies Bring About Their Own Decline* (1990); his other books include *Organizations: A Quantum View* (1984, with P. H. Friesen), *The Neurotic Organization: Diagnosing and Changing Counterproductive Styles of Management* (1984, with M.F.R. Kets de Vries), and *Unstable at the Top: Inside the Troubled Organization* (1987, with M.F.R. Kets de Vries). More than fifty of Miller's scientific papers have been published as book chapters or journal articles. He serves on the editorial boards of *Administrative Science Quarterly, Academy of Management Journal, Organization Science, Strategic Management Journal,* and *Industrial Crisis Quarterly.*

Alain Noël is associate professor of business policy and international management at the Ecole des Hautes Etudes Commerciales de Montréal, where he is also a managing partner of the Centre d'Etudes en Administration Internationale (Center

for International Business Studies). He received his B.A. degree
(1969) from l'Université de Montréal in liberal arts and a B.A.A.
degree (1974) in business administration and an M.B.A. degree
(1976) from the Ecole des Hautes Etudes Commerciales de Montréal. After several years of consulting practice, he completed
a Ph.D. degree (1984) at McGill University in management. His
current research and consulting activities focus on the strategic
intentions of CEOs facing the newly emerging trading blocks
(Canada–United States, the European Economic Community,
and Eastern Europe). His articles have been published in journals such as the *Strategic Management Journal* and *Gestion.*

Susan C. Schneider is associate professor of organizational
behavior at INSEAD in Fontainebleau, France. She holds a B.A.
degree (1971) from the University of Michigan in psychology and
both her M.A. (1973) and Ph.D. (1976) degrees from Adelphi
University in clinical psychology. She was a practicing psychologist for several years in the public sector. Her research deals
with "organizational sense making," that is, how organizations
process and interpret information. Her teaching interests focus
on national and corporate culture. Schneider has published in
*Organization Studies, Human Relations, Human Resource Management,
Human Systems Management,* and *Political Psychology.* She is a founding member of the International Society for the Psychoanalytic
Study of Organizations, a member of its steering committee,
and a board member of the Standing Committee on Organizational Symbolism and Corporate Culture.

Howard S. Schwartz is associate professor of organizational
behavior at Oakland University in Rochester, Michigan. He
received his B.A. degree (1965) from Antioch College in philosophy and did graduate work in philosophy at the University
of Pittsburgh and the University of California, San Diego. His
Ph.D. degree (1980) is from Cornell in organizational behavior.
Schwartz is interested in the psychodynamics of organizational
totalitarianism and decay and in the causes of organizational disasters. His publications include *Narcissistic Process and Corporate
Decay: The Theory of the Organization Ideal* (1990).

Donald R. Young has been working in the petroleum industry for nearly a decade, developing programs in support of employee health and well-being, including organizational consultation, substance abuse programs, and a wide range of employee assistance services. He received his B.A. degree (1952) from Southwestern College (Kansas) in social science, his M.A. degree (1958) from Northwestern University in psychology, and his Ed.D. degree (1962) from the University of Pennsylvania in marriage and family therapy. Prior to his employment in the petroleum industry, he both taught and practiced marriage and family therapy at a variety of institutions, including the Menninger Foundation and the University of Pennsylvania, and as a founding member of the Marriage and Family Consultation Center in Houston, Texas, was in private practice, as well.

Abraham Zaleznik is the Konosuke Matsushita Professor of Leadership, emeritus, at the Harvard Graduate School of Business Administration. He holds a B.A. degree (1945) from Alma College in economics, an M.B.A. degree from Harvard University, and a D.C.S. degree (1951), also from Harvard, in commercial sciences. He is known internationally for his research and teaching in the field of social psychology in the business setting and for his investigations into the distinguishing characteristics of managers and leaders. A graduate of the Boston Psychoanalytic Institute, he is certified by the American Psychoanalytic Association as a clinical psychoanalyst. He is the author of numerous award-winning articles and has published thirteen books, the most recent being *The Managerial Mystique* (1989) and the *Executive's Guide to Motivating People* (1990).

Organizations
on the Couch

Introduction: Exploding the Myth That Organizations and Executives Are Rational

Manfred F. R. Kets de Vries

The classic management theory of rational organizational action—that human beings can be managed solely around logical means-ends models of organization—is giving rise to an increasing amount of unease. Many students of organizational life have been seriously disillusioned by the gap between their expectations of how decision making takes place and their observation of what actually happens. The lack of resemblance to the dictates of rational action has made some students of organizations realize how simplistic many of their concepts are.

In numerous empirical attempts to study organizations there has been a lack of scientific imagination, a tendency to overlook much of the real data. The intrinsic richness of the material has been lost. In many instances we are left with superficial descriptions that neglect the underlying factors that could help explain managerial and organizational behavior. We are reminded of a comment attributed to Thoreau: "It is not worth going round the world to count cats in Zanzibar."

1

Many of these studies clearly ignore subjectively determined self-interest and motivation. While management science talks about rational choices, many observers and practitioners of organizational life have come to understand that the "irrational" personality needs of the principal decision makers can seriously affect the management process. If these needs are not taken into consideration, it is only to be expected that many management models will fail to work.

Interestingly enough, until very recently students of organizations were extremely reluctant to use clinical concepts taken from psychoanalysis and dynamic psychiatry. There are a number of possible reasons for this. Those antagonistic to the use of clinical concepts maintain that what cannot be directly observed does not exist. This presupposition omits one of the centerpieces of psychoanalytic thought, that is, unconscious motivation. For others, investigation of the real reasons for certain actions and behaviors can become psychologically disturbing — such probing may arouse a host of defensive reactions. We are familiar with the tendency of first-year medical students to discover in themselves all the symptoms of every new disease being studied. To prevent disturbing thoughts from coming to the surface, many students of organizational processes find it much safer to operate at a superficial level and stick to the obvious and banal. Moreover, the desire for a "quick fix" in organizational intervention means that for many people psychodynamic formulations only complicate life, and they do not like the implication that their quick-fix solutions are more often than not completely illusory. We know all too well that suppressing symptoms rarely has a lasting effect — news that is unfortunately not welcomed by those who receive it.

In spite of these barriers to the clinical approach, however, an increasing number of participants in organizational life have come to accept the fact that there *are* limitations to logical decision making, that extrarational forces *can* strongly influence leadership, group functioning, and organizational strategy, structure, and culture. Recognition of the existence of cognitive and affective distortions helps us to identify the extent to which unconscious fantasies and out-of-awareness behavior affect decision making and management practices in organizations.

There is a substantial body of knowledge to support the contention that organizational leaders are not necessarily rational, logical, sensible, and dependable human beings. Quantities of research show that executives are prone to a fair amount of irrational behavior. Given the impact leaders have on their environment, organizations are not spared. Within them (as with all human endeavors) we find both irrationality and intentional destructiveness. Clinical investigation shows that many organizational problems originate in the private, inner world of an organization's senior executives — in the way they act out their conflicts, desires, fantasies, and defensive structures (Zaleznik, 1966, 1989; Jaques, 1970; Levinson, 1981; Zaleznik and Kets de Vries, 1985; Baum, 1987; Hirschhorn, 1988; Kets de Vries, 1989). As the science of the irrational, psychoanalysis is ideally placed to provide new insights into organizational functioning.

The Clinical Paradigm

The use of psychoanalytic concepts outside a purely clinical context is not new. In his writings Freud devoted some attention to societal issues, questioning the nature of religion, civilization, and war. He also contributed to the study of group behavior by emphasizing the peculiar nature of the identification processes that take place between leaders and followers. Unfortunately, apart from some comments about the army and the church, Freud said very little about the nature of organizations and work. In one of his rare reflections on this topic, he viewed work not only as a way to neutralize human drives but also as a means of binding the individual to reality. He emphasized the role of sublimation and examined the relationships between work and creativity.

Since Freud, clinical knowledge has greatly expanded, contributing to the advancement of psychoanalysis. At present, psychoanalysis can be looked at as a *method of investigation* of language, action, and imaginary productions such as dreams, fantasies, and delusions. It can be seen, too, as a *therapeutic method* distinguished by interpretation of resistances, wishes, and transference reactions. Finally, psychoanalysis is also a *set of psychological and psychopathological theories* that systematize the data collected through the psychoanalytic method of investigation and treatment. These three orientations make psychoanalysis a rich source of understanding of life in organizations.

Furthermore, psychoanalytic theory has become increasingly complex, integrating drive psychology, neurology, ethology, information theory, child development, ego psychology, cognition, family systems theory, self-psychology, and object relations theory. This has enabled the development of a more general psychology. At the same time, the application of psychoanalytic concepts to the social sciences has become more widespread. With this evolution, and given the importance of work to overall mental functioning, students of organizations have begun to realize the value of applying the psychoanalytic method to an organizational setting. The main working premise is the role of unconscious motivation in explaining human action and decision making.

Psychoanalytic models of the mind are now being used to clarify life in organizations and to deal with issues concerning career, individual and organizational stress, corporate culture, leadership, entrepreneurship, and family businesses. Psychoanalytic conceptualizations have proved helpful to the better understanding of the behavior of groups (Bion, 1959). Resistance to change and intervention have been looked at in a new light. It is now recognized that individual defensive processes operate throughout organizational life and may become integrated in the social structure of the organization, affecting strategy (Jaques, 1955; Menzies, 1960; Kets de Vries and Miller, 1984). Processes such as affectionate reactions, aggression, control, and dependency have been viewed in an organizational context. Metapsychological constructs such as ego, id, superego, and ego ideal have been introduced, indicating the importance of fantasy, anxiety, envy, shame, and guilt and illustrating the relationship of these concepts to ambition and goal-directed behavior.

The "clinical approach," with its premise of *not* taking for granted what is directly observable, has been helped by contributions from other fields. For example, Clifford Geertz (1973), an anthropologist, has continuously advocated the search for deep, underlying structures. He has urged that we should go beyond the obvious and superficial. Geertz presents his argument by distinguishing between "thin description" and "thick description." The first approach typifies traditional studies that concentrate on what is merely observable and a simple relating of facts. Thick description, however, is interpretive. Like literary criticism it involves an iterative process of analysis that seeks out the basic significance of events. It searches for a theme that can explain a myriad of facts. Thick description is, in Geertz's words (1973, p. 20), "guessing at meanings, assessing the guesses, and drawing explanatory conclusions from the better guesses."

Such an approach involves the study of "texts," which can be viewed as groupings of interrelated elements — all types of data containing messages and themes that can be systematized. This requires the analysis of "a multiplicity of complex conceptual structures, many of them superimposed or knotted into one another, which are at once strange, irregular, and inexplicit, and which we must continue somehow to grasp and then to render" (Geertz, 1973, p. 10). In decoding texts, significance is extracted from interrelated factual, cognitive, and affective units constructed out of experiences. The observer looking for meaning becomes a sort of translator and cryptographer, transforming different levels of understanding.

In studying organizations we can interpret their "texts" through the analysis of organizational artifacts: managerial statements, writings, and observable behavior (Kets de Vries and Miller, 1987). The "text" implicit in a specific strategic decision, choice of a particular interpersonal style, or type of organizational structure gives clues to what life in that organization is all about. A further dimension is added if we are alert to underlying themes, meanings behind the metaphors used by managers, reasons for the selection of certain words, and implications of certain activities (Barley, 1983; Martin, 1982; Riley, 1983). The ability to distinguish between the signifiers and the signified (Saussure, [1916] 1966) and understand the underlying messages (hidden agendas) can help scholars and managers identify the crucial orientations and assumptions that influence organizational life, an important step toward clarification, diagnosis, and intervention. Recognizing the ways in which intra-

psychic processes affect decision making will make for a more
complex and more authentic description of organizational life.
This can direct the executive toward more effective problem solving and creative leadership.

The following case study will clarify this process of organizational "textual analysis" in action. It illustrates how the personalities of the members of the dominant coalition can affect
corporate culture, strategy, and structure (Kets de Vries and
Miller, 1984, 1986; Kets de Vries, 1989). However, the reader
should bear in mind that the material presented here is only
a preliminary analysis and not the final reading of the case.

Hollywood in the Alps

The Vocatron Corporation was set up about fifteen years ago
by Stephan Muller. (All names in this case study have been disguised.) Muller believed that there was a niche in the market
for private vocational training programs, particularly for younger people. His hunch proved to be right, and over the years
the company had steadily expanded. Muller had branched out
from his home base in Denmark and set up sales subsidiaries
in most European countries, the United States, Canada, and
Australia. Almost all of his fifty regional sales offices were run
by women, who were usually in their twenties or early thirties.
Most of the selling took place by telephone and through home
visits. For tax reasons, Muller had very recently decided to move
the head office from his home country to Switzerland.

I was asked to visit Vocatron by a friend who was a principal in a consulting firm. He explained that he was somewhat
vexed by the problems at Vocatron and hoped that a second
party would help him understand what was really going on in
the company. He thought my experience with entrepreneurs
and family businesses would be helpful.

Vocatron's head office commanded a spectacular view of
snowcapped mountains. The small parking lot in front of the
building was full of Porsches and Mercedes — and a splendid red
Ferrari that stole the show. Once past the heavy security at the
entrance, the visitor discovered an opulent interior with white

wall-to-wall carpeting and modern paintings and sculptures, including a Henry Moore. An attractive secretary pointed out a fitness center with sauna, whirl bath, and swimming pool.

We waited for ten minutes before being greeted by Stephan Muller. The president was very well, if conservatively, dressed and seemed young for his age. His height, bushy eyebrows, and penetrating stare left a lasting impression. His manner of speaking was obviously that of a man used to giving orders.

Muller explained that all was not well with Vocatron. Growth had leveled off and profits had been declining. After a rapid increase in the number of sales offices, subsidiary development had been put on ice for the last year and a half. He attributed these new circumstances to the fact that his top-management group had become seriously overextended.

The president explained what he expected from us: He wanted us to find a way for the company to continue the growth pattern of the past, eliminating the bottleneck caused by what he felt was a scarcity of top-management talent in the company. For that purpose, arrangements had been made for us to interview his top-management team and some of the more experienced subsidiary directors. He also wanted us to assess his son David, who had been working for the company for the last two years. He wanted to know if his son had top-management potential and could eventually become his successor. He mentioned as an aside that he had heard rumors that had sown doubts about his son's competence.

The interviews quickly revealed a number of problematic issues. The directors of the subsidiaries, who were specially flown in for the occasion, turned out to be a deeply disgruntled group. These young women were very unhappy about the way their careers were progressing. At first, working for Vocatron had seemed very glamorous. They had had early responsibility, excitement, adventure, and travel. But as the years passed, the glamour had gradually worn off.

We were astonished to discover that none of the female directors had ever been at the new head office before. Communication took place by phone, fax, letter, or personal visits from senior management. Comparing the modest conditions under which she worked with the opulence of head office, one of the directors commented, "This place is unbelievable, it's like Hollywood in the Alps!" During her visit, this particular woman made several attempts to see the president. She was prevented from doing so by his secretary, who consistently maintained that he had gone out for a business meeting. The president had, however, been seen in the office. We learned that Muller had made promises about this woman's future career that had come to nothing, although she had apparently been running the most profitable subsidiary for the last ten years. A previous attempt to pacify her by giving her a sports car as a bonus seemed to have met with only partial success. While we were present, in an angry attempt to get through the president's door, this woman "accidentally" spilled a cup of black coffee on the immaculate, deep-piled white carpet.

There is no need to dwell on this personal symbolic act. What is more important is that the feelings of this director were shared by most of the others. The common complaint was that they all felt stuck in their present position. When they had joined Vocatron in their early twenties, it had seemed exciting and challenging to set up a sales office in a foreign country. Over time, however, the long hours and only average salaries had killed the spirit of adventure. Since most of the selling took place in the evening, and there was a lot of pressure to perform, their social life had been seriously affected. None was married or had a long-term stable relationship. Indeed, the only relationships they appeared to have were with some of the men from head office who made regular visits to monitor their performance. Many complained of stress symptoms and had repeatedly been put on medication and even been hospitalized. The major criticism was that career progress stopped with the position of director of a sales subsidiary. No woman had ever been promoted to head office.

A close inner circle of all-male executives, many of them old school friends of Stephan Muller, ran the head office. Some of the directors compared this group to the KGB because of the control systems they used to monitor sales performance. When asked why they did not leave, the subsidiary directors replied they did not know where to go. Many of them had left their home countries long ago and felt no sense of belonging anywhere — their only sense of being part of something was the ambience created by Vocatron. They felt that the people at head office would look after them, whatever the circumstances.

During the interviews, some of these subsidiary directors talked about David Muller, the president's son. According to them he was incompetent and without his father would never have got on in business. They drew their conclusions from his behavior during internships at three of the sales subsidiaries and cited incidents illustrating what a disaster he had been.

This view of David rather surprised us. He had come across as a thoughtful individual when we interviewed him and he was well trained, with both law and business degrees. However, when talking to him, we had detected a certain amount of ambivalence toward his father, who gave him impossible assignments, never praised him for work well done, kept checking up on everything he did, and chastised him in public.

Although it may have been premature at this stage of the consultation, at a further meeting with Stephan Muller, we asked him why, given his own assessment of the need for more top-management talent in his company, he did not do the obvious thing and select the most capable subsidiary directors for promotion to head office? Muller reacted with astonishing violence. He became very agitated and then stiffened up, saying, "Impossible! Women have only limited capabilities and running a sales office is as far as they can go." According to him, having women in senior positions at head office would seriously disrupt the general atmosphere. He then said, rather wistfully, "Wouldn't it be nice if only I could get rid of all these older women in a pleasant way. They were all right when they were younger but they turned into such bitches later on!"

In contrast to the female subsidiary directors, the four male executives who made up Muller's inner circle at the head office seemed to be quite happy working at Vocatron. They shared their boss's perception of women, believing that it would be very disruptive to have them at head office in anything other than secretarial positions. In their opinion these particular women needed continuous surveillance, otherwise they would begin to act irresponsibly. Then they jokingly said, with an obvious sexual innuendo, that they knew how to keep their subordinates in line.

This group of executives seemed to be quite satisfied with the existing reward structure. Further prompting revealed, however, that at Vocatron bonuses were given rather haphazardly. One of the executives had once gone to Muller saying that he needed a yacht and, surprisingly enough, in due course he received it.

An organizational consultant is something of a detective. We try to decipher and interpret what is going on in the world around us. As "code breakers" we are constantly bombarded with different kinds of information; sometimes we understand its meaning, sometimes we are at a loss, and sometimes we fail to realize that an important piece of evidence is being presented. In every situation, however, our task is to make sense of things, to get behind the surface and disclose the underlying significance. Inevitably, we engage in interpretative acts. This becomes a reiterative process: Every interpretation brings up new associations and leads to new interpretations. Thus, there will never be complete closure.

This visit to the company's head office and the interviews with the key players provided us with a preliminary "text." It was now up to us to translate the signs, to find the rationale behind all this irrational behavior. We had to be literate enough, however, to make sense out of the text that was presented. If scholars of organizations and executives want to understand their world, they must pay attention to the subtleties of the text. They must interpret the way in which the stories unfold, and assemble the fragments into a coherent whole. They will have to find the hidden meanings, motives, and consequences behind acts, decisions, and social behavior.

During a subsequent dinner with the president, we learned more about his background. He was an only child and he had not been happy growing up. A key event of his childhood had been his father's leaving home when Stephan was only five years old. His father had moved to another country, where he had started a new family. His son had not seen him since.

Muller described his mother as an irresponsible, unreliable individual who went through an endless series of short-lived love affairs. He felt that his father's departure had really changed her. He cherished a few early memories of family togetherness. Later on, his tactics for survival at home had been to minimize his stays there. He spent most of his time with a close circle of friends, some of whom now worked for him. The interest shown in him by an uncle who regularly took him on excursions had helped to overcome his feelings of desertion by his father. His uncle had provided some kind of stability.

Muller explained that his own marriage had not been successful. He and his wife had not divorced, but they lived separate lives. Although it had never been explicitly stated, his wife was aware that he had had (and maybe still had) a number of mistresses.

After some prompting about stress symptoms, the president said that at times he had stomach problems. He also complained about recurrent nightmares, describing one where he would dream that he was cornered by a horrible-looking witch who would jump on his back and almost choke him. He would begin to scream, which woke him up.

This dinner conversation helped put some of the irrational patterns prevailing in the company into perspective. An essential aspect of the organizational "text" obviously had to do with Muller's relationship to women. In his inner world, he had developed some kind of mental block vis-à-vis women following the experiences he had had as a child. Women seemed to him to be dangerous, unreliable, and untrustworthy. In order for him to keep the upper hand, they had to be played off against one another and kept down, otherwise chaos would prevail. So, by re-creating his childhood situation within his organization, he and his small "band of brothers" could keep things in order and prevent this from happening. And he knew all too well what chaos meant, given the "messes" he had experienced when growing up.

In his company, the president had managed to create a sort of folie à deux situation, in that his key executives had begun to share his strange feelings about women (Kets de Vries, 1979). They did not have much choice — if they thought differently they would be asked to leave. Muller had made it clear that "fickle" women could never become part of the inner circle. Every kind of behavior was permitted in order to keep women in line, including sexual manipulation. The origins of this way of thinking were not hard to find: After all, his mother had provided a negative role model as far as sexual relationships were concerned.

The organizational consequences of the president's behavior were predictable. A strong paranoid streak ran through the company; a fight-flight culture prevailed. Not only was there a "war" going on with the competition, another "war" was taking place within the company, and the adversaries were the women. They were hired for the *purpose* of being continuously put down, in order to master the anxiety of the president and others who had absorbed his ideas. With this kind of attitude there was obviously a lack of trust and a considerable amount of secrecy between the inner circle and the others. Information was a much-sought-after commodity, with the sales subsidiaries usually kept in the dark. In spite of its irrational nature, this formula had worked for many years. Only now, *because of its success*, had it begun to crack at the seams.

As might be expected, these management practices were causing tremendous anger and bitterness on the part of the women in the company. In spite of the perks, they eventually came to feel that they had given the best years of their lives to Vocatron. They had been molded into workaholics with no consideration given to their private lives. And what could have been a major "pacifier" — a top job at head office — would pass them by. The accumulated result of the irrational practices at Vocatron was a demotivated group of sales directors, overextended head office executives, stagnation in sales, and a decline in profits.

How did this state of affairs affect the president's son, David? It is quite possible that he became the victim of displacement activities when he was sent to the subsidiaries to learn the rules of the trade. He may have been a scapegoat for the disgruntled group of directors, who may have been trying to "kill" the father through the son. Apart from this "displaced parricide," we should not rule out a problematic father-son relationship. Did David ever really have a chance of joining the "band of brothers" that surrounded his father? Would they be willing to accept such an interloper? Could it be that the father, because of his unresolved problems with his own deserting father, projected his sense of responsibility for that occurrence onto his son? Maybe, because he had not been able to keep his own father, sons unconsciously became "bad" for him. Perhaps he had set up his own son and sent him on an impossible mission. Unconsciously, he may have given him assignments that were insurmountable. Of course, the other side of this Oedipal drama could be that his son may have been rebelling, unwilling to submit to his father's wishes and thus consciously or unconsciously playing the role of the incompetent.

Finally, there is the way the consultant is perceived by Stephan Muller. Will he turn into the "good uncle" of Muller's childhood, or will he become the deserting father or even the irresponsible and unreliable mother? Or will he play all of these characters at once, or in turn? Muller's future reactions toward the consultant will tell.

Our interpretation of the "text" of "Hollywood in the Alps" has really only just started. The few inferences proposed represent the proverbial tip of the iceberg. Longer-term interaction with the key players will be needed to succeed in validating some of these conjectures. We should bear in mind here that acting is another form of remembering. More data about the past will help us understand the present better and give counsel for the future.

The story of "Hollywood in the Alps" illustrates how, by putting an organization "on the couch," we can find a rationale for what would otherwise come across as highly irrational action and behavior. In this case, the intrapsychic fantasies of the key powerholder turned out to be the catalyst for a series of highly unusual management practices.

Freud and the Semantics of Desire

For Freud the "semantics of desire" became the basis for understanding a text. He developed a theory aimed at revealing the

messages hidden in manifest statements and the desires implicit
in these messages. He wished to understand the resistances
against expressing these desires in order to comprehend better
the patient's basic fears and needs. Freud's early work on dreams
is illustrative. He was trying to solve the riddle of dreams,
to discover the hidden logic of their processes. In his magnum
opus, *The Interpretation of Dreams* ([1900] 1962, p. 671), he claimed
that "the dream-work is only the first to be discovered of a
whole series of unconscious, hidden psychical processes, responsible for the generation of hysterical symptoms, of phobias,
obsessions, and delusions. Condensation and, above all, displacement are invariable characteristics of these other processes
as well."

The themes and symbols that result from an individual's
subjective experience create an evolving series of "signifiers"
through the processes of displacement (the transference of emotions from the original idea to others) and condensation (two
or more images combine to form a composite image) under the
influence of social forces. Certain signifiers come to be preferred
over others. These become manifest and recur in social interactions. What initially may have been a purely subjective experience becomes a "text" more readily open to interpretation
by others, particularly in a clinical setting. We have observed
in the Vocatron case that, like the structural anthropologist, the
clinical investigator becomes a code breaker or interpreter. He
or she "listens with the third ear," searching for hidden meanings in texts and looking for the unconscious ideas and fantasies that underlie manifest experience.

In the psychoanalytic setting, the task is to re-create or
reexperience the thought of the creator of the "text." In principle, at least, it is possible to enter into a dialogue. We realize
that the text will deepen if we reexperience the author's thoughts
and check our empathic understanding (Devereux, 1978; Lacan,
1978; Levine, 1980; Watson, 1976). To do this, there must be
an effort to understand the individual's past, to examine his or
her personal history for clues regarding current behavior.

A major device for understanding the meaning of text in
a psychoanalytic setting is the interpretation of transference (Gill,

1982; Greenson, 1967; Kets de Vries and Miller, 1984; Racker, 1968). Briefly, transference is a process whereby attitudes that developed early in life are repeated in the present. Thus the transference reactions that appear in the psychoanalytic dialogue, the kind of feelings the person evokes in the other, can be considered as additional text, confirming or disconfirming other "textual" information about a person. This additional text provides clues about the person's past and facilitates the recognition of fundamental themes and important defenses, since these will often be acted out when the patient reacts to the analyst as though he or she were a key figure from the past.

There is, however, a difference between the work of a psychoanalyst in a consulting room and that of an organizational consultant: The psychological contract tends to be different. In a psychoanalytic relationship the analysand is there for the long haul; he or she is involved in a continuing exploratory journey to learn more about the self. Time factors tend to become more-or-less irrelevant. By contrast, the client usually wants quick results from consultancy. In most instances the luxury of a long-term learning commitment is not really an option. So in some ways consultancy work can be likened to clinical intervention "on the run." In spite of all these disadvantages, however, consultants have one advantage: Unlike psychoanalysts, they can observe their clients in their natural environment. They can visit the places where they operate. Through conversations with superiors, subordinates, friends, and family members they can check some of their conjectures.

We should also note that the psychoanalyst tries to make conscious what is unconscious. (We have only to remember the famous dictum from Freud's *New Introductory Lectures,* "Where id was, there ego shall be.") Clinically trained consultants often arrive at more realistic and durable interventions using their understanding of unconscious processes but without necessarily making the unconscious conscious, given the different psychological context within which they operate. Basically, there is usually much less opportunity for clarification, confrontation, and working through in consultation (Kets de Vries and Miller, 1984; Zaleznik, 1987).

Rules of Interpretation

Putting organizations on the couch involves a search for central themes in apparently unstructured processes. The patterns, ideas, or sentiments that surface often appear to explain many phenomena. We use the notions of compression and underlying structure—the idea that much surface complexity can be explained by an underlying organizing theme. This was suggested by Geertz (1973, 1983), Lévi-Strauss (1955, 1969), and the proponents of hermeneutics (Palmer, 1969; Radnitzky, 1973).

We must look for elements that are not only logically central but that have deep, perhaps unconscious, emotional significance (see Freud, [1900] 1962, [1920] 1955; Greenson, 1967; Lacan, 1978). The emotional components that motivate an organizational text are crucial to its decoding. These components are best understood by some form of "historical" analysis. Finding out about the individual actors, their past, and their current modes of interaction can disclose information about their aspirations, goals, and fears and can explain their behavior. This involves dialogue.

Obviously, to tease out deeper structures, a *process* of discovery rather than a single stab at explanation is necessary. Initial conjectures must be tested against reality as it is perceived by others. Informal predictions are made, based on initial insights, and these are compared to what actually happens or are tested to determine if they can explain other parts of the "text" (Kets de Vries and Miller, 1984). Interpretation is a dynamic, iterative, and interactive process that may bring insights but rarely provides any final, unitary solution. The tentative conjectures or explanations that evolve are made more concrete and operational and are checked against other aspects of the situation or against events to come. The importance of dialogue, reformulation, historical analysis, tentative explanation, and modification cannot be overemphasized.

In interpreting organizational texts, the rule of *thematic unity* comes first. When we analyze an organizational story we try to shape the different observations into an interconnected, cohesive unit. In the case of Vocatron, we found the unifying theme of the unreliability and limited capabilities of women; consequently, women were denied greater responsibilities and had to be carefully monitored.

Second, we are engaged in *pattern matching,* looking for structural parallels, for a "fit" between present-day events and earlier incidents in the history of an individual or organization. We are watching out for revealing repetition (Geertz, 1973; Spence, 1982). To turn to Vocatron again, the president of the company consistently transferred his childhood situation into the present. For example, his remark that women turn into "bitches" when they get older is probably very closely related to his childhood perception of his mother's behavior before his father left. His re-creation of his childhood situation with the "band of brothers" is another indication. Pattern matching is based on the tendency each of us has to become entangled in displacements in time. Instead of *remembering* the past, we may *misunderstand* the present in terms of the past and relive the past through our present actions. We often react to important individuals and situations as if these were figures or incidents from the past (Greenson, 1967). What might have been an appropriate reaction at one time now turns out to be transparently anachronistic. This is what is referred to as "transference" in psychoanalysis.

Third, interpretation must be guided by the rule of *psychological urgency* (Freud, [1920] 1955; Lacan, 1978). The challenge is to identify a pervasive relationship pattern (Luborsky, 1984; Luborsky, Crits-Cristoph, Minz, and Auerbach, 1988). The assumption behind this rule is that somewhere in the text it is always possible to identify the most pressing need or needs. In our case study, it was the need of the president to settle a score with women, to get even for the wrongs he had experienced at the hands of his mother. He wanted to be free from domination, to assert himself, and to impose his will on others. His agitation at the idea of breaking the vicious circle in the company by giving the female directors more responsibility was highly revealing. He clearly saw this as opening the way to being controlled by women. The need to assert oneself and the preoccupation with getting even pulsated throughout the company, because it was shared by the other executives. When we play organizational detective, then, it is important to note the persistence, enthusiasm, regularity, pervasiveness, and emotions surrounding decisions, interactions, and pronouncements.

Finally, there is the rule of *multiple function*. Depending on the psychological urgency of the matter at hand, a part of the text can have more than one meaning and can be looked at from many different points of view (Waelder, 1936). Sometimes organizational resistances and defensive processes stand out. At other times the key dynamics may be related to how organizational participants manage aggression or affectionate bonds. Processes centered around shame and guilt can also become important. To complicate matters even further, these issues may all play a concurrent role and may occur at the individual, interpersonal, group, and organizational levels (Geertz, 1973, 1983; Kets de Vries and Miller, 1987). It is thus necessary to seek out meaning at multiple levels and to determine the individual and organizational roots and consequences of actions and decisions.

Interpretation is at the center of work in organizations. Researchers and executives are inevitably involved in a continual dialogue with other actors in the organization. They must search for basic themes and configurations in their text, finding meaning in what at first glance may seem random or insignificant. Text, as we have indicated, must be viewed in context for true decoding to take place. The rules just outlined — thematic unity, pattern matching, psychological urgency, and multiple function — are useful clues in the search for continuity and connection. They disclose patterns that can be woven into a unified gestalt, revealing a matrix that helps to explain the psychodynamics of organizational life.

References

Barley, S. R. "Semiotics and the Study of Occupational and Organizational Cultures." *Administrative Science Quarterly*, 1983, *28*, 393–413.

Baum, H. S. *The Invisible Bureaucracy*. New York: Oxford University Press, 1987.

Bion, W. R. *Experiences in Groups, and Other Papers.* London: Tavistock, 1959.

Devereux, G. *Ethnopsychoanalysis.* Berkeley: University of California Press, 1978.

Freud, S. "Beyond the Pleasure Principle." In J. Strachey (ed. and trans.), *The Standard Edition of the Complete Psychological Works of Sigmund Freud.* Vol. 18. London: Hogarth Press, 1955. (Originally published 1920.)

Freud, S. "The Interpretation of Dreams." In J. Strachey (ed. and trans.), *The Standard Edition of the Complete Psychological Works of Sigmund Freud.* Vol. 5. London: Hogarth Press, 1962. (Originally published 1900.)

Geertz, C. *The Interpretation of Cultures.* New York: Basic Books, 1973.

Geertz, C. *Local Knowledge.* New York: Basic Books, 1983.

Gill, M. *Analysis of Transference.* Vol. 1: Theory and Technique. New York: International Universities Press, 1982.

Greenson, R. R. *The Technique and Practice of Psychoanalysis.* New York: International Universities Press, 1967.

Hirschhorn, L. *The Workplace Within: Psychodynamics of Organizational Life.* Cambridge, Mass.: MIT Press, 1988.

Jaques, E. "Social Systems as a Defence Against Persecutory and Depressive Anxiety." In M. Klein, P. Heimann, and R. E. Money-Kyrle (eds.), *New Directions in Psychoanalysis.* London: Tavistock, 1955.

Jaques, E. *Work, Creativity, and Social Justice.* New York: International Universities Press, 1970.

Kets de Vries, M.F.R. "Managers Can Drive Their Subordinates Mad." *Harvard Business Review,* 1979, *57,* 125–134.

Kets de Vries, M.F.R. *Prisoners of Leadership.* New York: Wiley, 1989.

Kets de Vries, M.F.R., and Miller, D. *The Neurotic Organization: Diagnosing and Changing Counterproductive Styles of Management.* San Francisco: Jossey-Bass, 1984.

Kets de Vries, M.F.R., and Miller, D. "Personality, Culture, and Organization." *Academy of Management Review,* 1986, *11,* 266–279.

Kets de Vries, M.F.R., and Miller, D. "Interpreting Organizational Texts." *Journal of Management Studies,* 1987, *24* (3), 233–248.

Lacan, J. *The Four Fundamental Concepts of Psychoanalysis*. New York: Norton, 1978.

Lévi-Strauss, C. "The Structural Study of Myth." *Journal of American Folklore*, 1955, *68*, 428–444.

Lévi-Strauss, C. *The Raw and the Cooked*. New York: Harper & Row, 1969.

Levine, R. A. *Culture, Behavior, and Personality*. New York: Aldine, 1980.

Levinson, H. *Executive*. Cambridge, Mass.: Harvard University Press, 1981.

Luborsky, L. *Principles of Psychoanalytic Therapy*. New York: Basic Books, 1984.

Luborsky, L., Crits-Christoph, P., Minz, J., and Auerbach, A. *Who Will Benefit from Psychotherapy?* New York: Basic Books, 1988.

Martin, J. "Stories and Scripts in Organizational Settings." In A. H. Hastorf and A. M. Iren (eds.), *Cognitive Social Psychology*. New York: Elsevier/North-Holland, 1982.

Menzies, I. "A Case-Study in the Functioning of Social Systems as a Defence Against Anxiety: A Report on a Study of the Nursing Service of a General Hospital." *Human Relations*, 1960, *13*, 95–121.

Palmer, R. *Hermeneutics: Interpretation Theory in Schleiermacher, Dilthey, Heidegger, and Gadomer*. Evanston, Ill.: Northwestern University Press, 1969.

Racker, H. *Transference and Countertransference*. New York: International Universities Press, 1968.

Radnitzky, G. *Contemporary Schools of Metascience*. Chicago: Regnery, 1973.

Riley, P. "A Structuralist Account of Political Culture." *Administrative Science Quarterly*, 1983, *28*, 414–437.

Saussure, F. de. *Course in General Linguistics*. (C. Bally and A. Sechehaye, eds.; W. Baskin, trans.) New York: McGraw-Hill, 1966. (Originally published 1916.)

Spence, D. P. *Narrative Truth and Historical Truth*. New York: Norton, 1982.

Waelder, R. "The Principle of Multiple Function." *Psychoanalytic Quarterly*, 1936, *5*, 45–62.

Watson, A. "Understanding a Life History as a Subjective Document: Hermeneutical and Phenomenological Perspectives." *Ethos,* 1976, *21,* 95–181.

Zaleznik, A. *Human Dilemmas of Leadership.* New York: Harper & Row, 1966.

Zaleznik, A. "The Case for Not Interpreting Unconscious Mental Life in Consulting in Organizations." Paper presented at annual meeting of the International Society for the Psychoanalytic Study of Organizations, Oct. 1987.

Zaleznik, A. *The Managerial Mystique: Restoring Leadership in Business.* New York: Harper & Row, 1989.

Zaleznik, A., and Kets de Vries, M.F.R. *Power and the Corporate Mind.* (Rev. ed.) Chicago: Bonus Books, 1980.

PART ONE

New Perspectives on Organizations

1

---•◆•◆•---

Using Psychoanalytic Frameworks for Organizational Analysis

Laurence J. Gould

It may be said that within psychoanalysis the application to organizational life began with Freud's ([1921] 1955a) consideration of the church and army. He linked ([1911–1915] 1958) certain dynamic aspects of these organizations to his earlier hypotheses regarding the origins of social process and social structure — namely, the primal horde. While Freud never directly pursued this line of thought, other than generally in his later sociological works ([1927] 1961b, [1930] 1961a, [1939] 1964), there is by now a rapidly growing and impressive body of literature on psychoanalytic conceptions of organizational behavior (for example, Baum, 1987; Bion, 1959; Hirschhorn, 1988; Jaques, 1951, 1955; Kernberg, 1979, 1984; Kets de Vries, 1984; Kets de Vries and Miller, 1984; Lawrence, 1979; Levinson, 1972a, 1972b; Menzies, 1960, 1988, 1989; Miller, 1976; Miller and Gwynne, 1972; Miller and Rice, 1967; Rice, 1958; Trist and Murray, 1990; Zaleznik, 1967, 1984). However, despite this rich and abundant interest, there has been little work on developing techniques and methodologies for the practice of organizational consultation that derives from these conceptions. The reasons are numerous and can be briefly adumbrated.

Compared to clinical psychoanalysis, psychoanalytic organizational psychology is still in its infancy. Furthermore, many

25

of those interested in applying psychoanalytic viewpoints to their organizational consultation work are not clinicians, much less psychoanalysts. Hence, such practitioners usually have little knowledge of, or direct experience with, the sorts of technical issues, questions, and dilemmas that are at the heart of psychoanalytic organizational consultation work, and indeed the majority have little experience working with groups of any sort, to say nothing of large formal organizations. In consequence, the different backgrounds and experiences of psychoanalytically trained clinicians and organizational practitioners have a counterpart in the almost nonexistent area of psychoanalytic practice and technique in group and organizational work settings.

A related factor is the strong and pervasive intrapsychic and narrowly interpersonal (dyadic and triadic) biases of psychoanalysis — even among many of those who practice psychoanalytic group psychotherapy! Therefore, transindividual psychoanalytic methods and perspectives have at best been slow to develop. Another issue is the rather marked differences in the culture of psychoanalytic clinical practice compared to that of organizational consultation. The core clinical modes in psychoanalysis are the *processes* that result in healing and transformation. In the organizational sphere an emphasis on *results* or *outcomes* is the prevailing norm — among practitioners as well as clients. What this means, in effect, is that in organizational work a more pragmatic attitude prevails, with little concern about process or the "purity" of the intervention. Therefore, instead of developing psychoanalytic strategies with the inevitability of technical variations and parameters (for example, Eissler, 1953, 1958) to accommodate special circumstances, as is most often the case in clinical work, even the psychoanalytically oriented organizational practitioner usually feels free to do whatever seems to work, using many sorts of nonpsychoanalytic techniques, strategies, and interventions, as well as invoking many nonpsychoanalytic viewpoints (open-systems theory, family systems theory, communications theory, a variety of sociological and social psychological viewpoints, and so on). The effectiveness of an eclectic approach notwithstanding, the result is that little has been developed in the way of psychoanalytic technique or, more precisely, a theory of psychoanalytic practice in work-group and organizational settings.

Finally, the major obstacles to developing such a theory are the different temporal expectations and the relatively "uncontrolled" nature of the organizational setting, compared to those of clinical practice. Here the issue is not simply one of complexity, but rather the stability and constancy of the environment within which the work is being conducted and the control of the relevant boundaries. In clinical work the patient comes to the psychoanalyst's office and, in accepting treatment, agrees to the conditions the analyst outlines, such as fee, schedule, time frame, technical procedures, and "psychological contract" (the analyst's "neutrality," the sanction to interpret, the use of the couch, and so on). By contrast, the organizational consultant enters the client's setting and system and attempts to negotiate a viable work contract. But "turbulence" in the client system, the necessity for working with groups whose composition may vary and with individuals whose schedules may vary, and the exigencies of the client's coping with the pressure of day-to-day demands all conspire to make the likelihood of setting up and maintaining a regular, predictable, and "protected" work environment extremely small. Even to suggest, then, that there may be organizational analogues to the technical procedures of psychoanalysis that can be utilized for more than the span of one meeting may itself be viewed as a naive fantasy in the work context, where it is often difficult simply to keep one's wits about one and remain "right side up." Such "buffeting" is a far cry indeed from the sheltered, controlled, and relatively enduring character of the psychoanalytic situation. And it is precisely these qualities and characteristics of the psychoanalytic situation that, in fact, define the core of psychoanalytic practice as originally articulated in Freud's "Papers on Technique" ([1911–1915] 1958).

In summary, if "the couch is at sea" (to paraphrase slightly the felicitous title of Kernberg's 1984 paper on organizational psychology) what, in fact, remains of technique? Has it, to continue the metaphor, been swamped or left to languish on a distant shore? It is certainly not much in evidence in psychoanalytic approaches to work-group and organizational consultation.

In what follows, therefore, a necessarily selective overview and appraisal of psychoanalytic theory and practice related to work-group and organizational consultation will be outlined and developed. It should be noted, however, that the intention is not to provide answers to the many obvious questions about the feasibility and utility, if any, of developing organizational analogues to the technical procedures of psychoanalysis. Rather, a conceptual "typing" will be used to locate and assess the current state of work-group and organizational consultation techniques and strategies informed or directly guided by psychoanalytic theory. This will be followed by a brief commentary and discussion, with an emphasis on the advantages of utilizing psychoanalytic perspectives and consultation techniques to work with organizational disturbances and conflicts at the individual, group, and systems level. I hope that this discussion will provide a useful starting point for a more extended and systematic consideration of the issues related to furthering this enterprise that, for reasons suggested earlier, have generally been neglected.

Psychoanalytic Theory and Types of Practice

Two types of work-group and organizational consultation practice can be distinguished within a psychoanalytic context, as shown in Table 1.1. Type 1 practice utilizes the technical procedures and methods of psychoanalysis, while type 2 practice uses psychoanalytic theory to guide an eclectic array of methods and procedures that may include, but are not restricted to, those considered psychoanalytic. This is something of an oversimplification and it should be explicitly noted that these types are distinguished for heuristic purposes only. In practice they most often overlap or shade into each other.

Type 1 (Utilization of the Technical Procedures and Methods of Psychoanalysis)

This type includes, of course, psychoanalysis proper and the variations of psychoanalytic psychotherapy. The major training modality of this type is the group relations conference, which

Table 1.1. Types of Work-Group and Organizational
Consultation Based on Psychoanalytic Theory.

| Type 1
Utilization of the Technical
Procedures and Methods of
Psychoanalysis | Type 2
Utilization of Non-
psychoanalytic Methods and
Techniques |
|---|---|
| Psychoanalysis and psychoanalytic psychotherapy[a] | Psychodynamic psychotherapy[a] |
| Group relations workshops and conferences[b] | Levinson Institute and Menninger seminars[b] |
| In-house group relations conferences[c] | Sociotechnical interventions[c] |
| Psychoanalytic process consultation[c] | Active process consultation[c] |
| Organizational role analysis[c] | Multimodal/multilevel interventions[c] |

[a]Psychotherapeutic interventions
[b]Training and educational methods
[c]Organizational interventions

derives from a tradition developed at the Center for Applied Social Research of the Tavistock Institute of Human Relations in London, under the leadership of the late A. K. Rice (1965) and his colleagues. The primary task of these conferences is to provide members with opportunities to study the nature of leadership and authority, and the interpersonal, group, and intergroup problems encountered in their exercise. To implement this task, participants are involved in a number of group events (the small group, the large group, the intergroup, the institutional event, and so on) that provide opportunities to experience and examine their membership and behavior in varying group configurations and in the conference as a whole. The basic staff role is to provide consultation vis-à-vis taking up a psychoanalytic stance of neutrality and offering interpretations of covert and unconscious group processes, with an emphasis on transference and countertransference manifestations, as these may illuminate the vicissitudes of authority relations. It is hoped

that the ability to exercise leadership and authority effectively
will be enhanced by a heightened awareness and understanding of how these processes and forces operate in group and organizational situations.

One major example of an organizational intervention
strategy based on the above is the in-house group relations conference. While little has been published to date on such events,
several have been held. An example of an abbreviated version
can be found in Gustafson and Hausman (1975), in which the
paradigm of the intergroup event (for example, Astrachan and
Flynn, 1976) is utilized to examine and clarify conflict in a small
psychiatric organization. The basic model for designing such
an intervention is to utilize one event, or a combination of several
events derived from group relations conferences, with a membership composed of individuals who are a natural work group,
or groups, or the totality of an organization. This contrasts with
the typical situation in the group relations conferences offered
as training, in which the participants are, for the most part,
strangers from different organizations.

Another example of the application of the group relations
conference methodology is to be found in Miller's work in Belfast (1977). A group relations conference was designed for interested individuals "representing" major political and/or sentient groupings (see Miller and Rice, 1967) such as Catholics
and Protestants, working and middle-to-upper classes, youths
and adults, and men and women. The hope was that an exploration and understanding of some of the powerful unconscious
individual- and group-level fantasies at work in the relative safety
of the conference setting, and the ways in which these were
projected onto others, would generalize, and thereby enhance,
the leadership potential of the participants in reducing conflict
and fostering community development in the back-home environment.

There are also variants of the group relations conference
approach to be found in the creation of in-house analogues to
the various group events. For instance, a number of psychiatric
institutions have adopted a form of the large group event (Turquet, 1975) by holding regular patient-staff community meet-

ings that are conducted as self-study groups (for example, Edelson, 1970a and 1970b). The purpose of such meetings is to examine the covert forces in the unit of service that may impede (or facilitate) the therapeutic task.

In addition to the above, there is another approach to organizational development that is based on systematically providing group relations training for key staff of an organization. Typically, in this approach, small groups of staff members are selected over a period of time to attend group relations conferences until there is a critical mass who are "trained" (Menninger, 1972, 1985). A variation is to do the training in-house in a series of workshops until the whole staff has been through the experience (Johnson and Fleischer, 1980). The rationale for this approach is that the "training" of a sufficient number of staff in key positions of authority will *naturally* facilitate constructive organizational change and development as a function of increased awareness of destructive covert processes and authority relations, a lowering of anxiety and resistance to change, and an increased capacity for sophisticated leadership and followership.

Another organizational application of psychoanalytic theory and technique is exemplified in what may be termed *psychoanalytic process consultation* — or in Bion's (1959) terms, *therapy of the group* (as distinct from *group therapy*). The general model is for a consultant to join the regular meetings of a natural work group (or an organizational group specifically created for the purpose of fostering organizational change) and to interpret process in much the same way that a consultant would function in taking a small study group in a group relations conference. It is more usual, however, that in consultations with an organizational work group, there is some shift away from interpretations that specifically and systematically focus on the group's relationship with the consultant (although these would be made if necessitated by, for example, manifestations of excessive dependency) to relations between the group members themselves and their approach to the task at hand. This shift in emphasis highlights the fact that the approach is different when the task is consultation, as distinct from training.

Finally, there are a variety of consultations with individuals, focusing specifically on how they take up their work roles, that combine psychoanalytically based theories of individual and group behavior, and psychoanalytic method. One such approach typically takes the form of a time-limited series of consultations with an individual (Reed, 1976). In these consultations (generically called *organizational role analysis* or *ORA,* techniques that derive from projective or semiprojective methods (for example, the production and analysis of "mental maps"), the solicitation and interpretation of dream material and fantasies, and supportive/interpretive interventions are all utilized. This form of consultation can be especially useful in situations where a key executive or manager in the client system either takes up a new role, needs to reassess role performance in light of changing organizational circumstances, or is experiencing chronic difficulties in functioning effectively. With regard to the latter, time-limited consultations may also be useful in helping an individual to recognize more clearly major characterological issues and tendencies that may impinge on role performance (Kernberg, 1979, 1984), if they are not so severe as to be uninfluenced by insight, which can be translated into more adequate self-management.

Type 2 (Utilization of Nonpsychoanalytic
Methods and Techniques)

Therapeutically, the whole gamut of eclectic and/or psychodynamically informed modalities is included in this type. These are (most often) characterized by the selected use of psychoanalytic concepts and explanations either to design more "active intervention strategies" (Wachtel, 1977), or simply to be the backdrop for helping a patient or client focus on or clarify an issue that is the source of emotional distress. In organizational work, many interventions are an analogue of the former—namely, the use of a psychoanalytic understanding of human behavior to design an intervention strategy. It can be said that much, if not most, of the sociotechnical work developed originally at the Tavistock Institute is of this variety. Parenthetically, it should be noted here that, on the psychological side, this work is largely based on the object relations theories of Klein (1948), Bion (1959), and their colleagues, in contrast to the organizational work indigenous to the United States, which has its origins more in classical and ego psychological viewpoints (Levinson, 1972b; Zaleznik, 1967, 1984). In this connection it should also be noted that Kernberg (1976, part 1) has attempted to integrate these perspectives.

An essential element of the Tavistock perspective is to differentiate between behavior and activities geared toward rational task performance (Bion's "Work [W] Group") and those geared to emotional needs and anxieties (Bion's "Basic Assumption [ba] Groups" — Fight/Flight [baF], Dependency [baD], and Pairing [baP], which are viewed as being rooted in early experiences and as having manifestations in unconscious fantasies. Specifically, this view posits the existence of primitive anxieties of a persecutory and depressive nature and the erection of individual and "social defense systems" (Menzies, 1960; Jaques, 1955) against them. Such defenses are conceptualized as either impeding or facilitating task performance, adaptation, and response to change. Bringing this view to bear is at the heart of the Tavistock sociotechnical approach to organizational analysis and development strategies. Interventions based on such strategies typically involve redefining and redesigning some, or all, of the following: tasks, work sequences, administrative procedures, and organizational structure. Major early exemplars of this approach include, for example, Trist and Bamforth (1951) on the psychological consequences of technological changes in a British coal mine; Rice's (1958) efforts to reorganize the work relationship structure in the weaving room of an Indian textile mill; Menzies's (1960) study and action research in a hospital nursing organization; and Jaques's (1950) and Jaques, Rice, and Hill's (1951) attempt to change the method of wage payments in a department of a light engineering factory. In all of the above, organizational change efforts were geared toward providing a better fit between work tasks, work activities, organizational structures, and administrative procedures on the one hand and the social defense system on the other. Typically, as noted, these efforts, while guided by a psychoanalytically

informed appraisal of the situation, involved some form of re-
organizing and redesigning work including, for example, the
creation of new groupings such as autonomous work groups
(Rice, 1958).

In the United States, organizational applications of psychoanalytic perspectives more typically take the form of active
and focused process consultation to work groups, directive and
supportive consultations with key individuals, or a variety of
large-scale, multimodal, multilevel interventions that may overlap with the sociotechnical systems work just outlined.

The most common form of type 2 process consultation
differs from its type 1 counterpart in that it is usually more active, supportive, and directive and rarely makes transference
material explicit, through interpretation. The focus is almost
exclusively on the group itself, and again, compared to the type
1 model, the interpretations are more didactic, developed, and
generally aimed at the manifest level of group process. Awareness of the primitive, covert, or less conscious aspects of the
process are used by the consultant to guide the group and to
facilitate its work more sensitively through an appreciation of
the underlying anxieties, conflicts, and dilemmas.

A well-developed example of the kind of large-scale, multimodal, multisystem intervention, noted earlier, is to be found
in the work of Kets de Vries and Miller (1984). They provide
a case study of a family lingerie business in which powerful unconscious dynamics were creating and intensifying organizational difficulties. The intervention methodology they ultimately
adopted, based on a careful assessment and diagnosis of both
individual and organizational difficulties, included: helping to
rationalize the organization (for example, by providing clearer
definitions of responsibilities and lines of authority), suggesting personnel changes and reassignments, offering supportive
and/or insight-oriented psychotherapy and counseling for key
individuals, giving commonsense business advice, and encouraging appropriate executives to participate in a psychodynamically based management training program with senior executives from other companies.

In effect, then, the psychoanalytically informed consultant uses psychoanalytic theory, conceptualization, and insight

to diagnose and identify emotional "hot spots" at the individual, group, and/or organizational level and designs consultations and/or multimodal intervention strategies based on these assessments. In this approach the consultation strategy takes into account the ways the system is "driven" and distorted by powerful unconscious processes and anxieties and the concomitant defenses raised against them, but it neither attempts to interpret these nor to work them through directly.

Finally, there are several management development and management training programs that are directly based on psychoanalytic theory, but compared, for example, to the group relations conference model outlined under type 1, they use either more conventional educational methods such as lectures and discussion groups or modified experiential learning approaches. Examples of the former include the well-known executive development programs offered by the Menninger Foundation (Rice, 1979), the Levinson Institute, and the European Institute of Business Administration (INSEAD). Examples of the latter (which are usually more structured and focused versions of group relations conference events — particularly the small-group event) are to be found in a wide variety of training programs such as those originally developed for postgraduate social workers and general practitioners (Balint, 1959; Gosling, Miller, Turquet, and Woodhouse, 1967).

Summary

It should be apparent from the foregoing discussion of each of these conceptual types that psychoanalytic theory and procedures applied to work-group and organizational situations can be used separately, or in combination with nonpsychoanalytic methods and techniques, in a wide variety of ways. As I noted earlier, this state of affairs generates a large number of obvious questions and issues regarding the circumstances, conditions, and criteria for making critical decisions when planning and implementing an intervention. In the next section, some general and specific points related to these concerns will be briefly enumerated and discussed, in order to provide a point of departure for considering the issues germane to the practice of a psychoanalytic organizational psychology.

Discussion

As a starting point for discussion, I will use, as an organizing framework, the familiar triadic nature of psychoanalysis: as a theory of human behavior, as a method for the in-depth investigation of mental processes, and as a treatment for mental and emotional illness. In what follows I would like to discuss these three interrelated aspects of psychoanalysis in turn, as they apply to the theory and practice of organizational consultation.

Psychoanalysis As a Theory of Human Behavior

I believe that the richness and diversity of many of the contributions noted previously are more than ample testimony to the generative power of psychoanalytic theory when used as a basis for describing and understanding significant aspects of organizational behavior at many levels, including the dilemmas of an individual manager, the impact of small-group processes on task performance, and the ways the culture and character of the organization as a whole may have a profound influence on the behavior and emotional well-being of its members. Further, I believe that a psychoanalytic perspective can be viewed, in general, as having considerable utility in guiding our interventions, of whatever variety. In this connection two broad considerations may be offered as examples. First, as Levinson (1972a) argues, the failure to diagnose adequately, when planning interventions, may have serious and unintended consequences. These can occur when an intervention does not take sufficient cognizance of the depth and complexity of the psychological forces at work on individuals and groups. A similar point is made by Jaques (1955), who notes that the character of institutions is determined and colored not only by their explicit or consciously agreed-on and accepted functions, but also by their manifold unrecognized functions at the fantasy level. Since such functions include important individual and social defenses against anxiety, interventions that do not take this into account may have little enduring impact, or worse yet, may catalyze considerable anxiety and concomitant decompensation, if these defenses are inadvertently breached. It is my contention, therefore, that the sort of fundamental appreciation and comprehension of the power of unconscious processes that a psychoanalytic perspective affords us is a useful general antidote to all sorts of inadvertencies, even if it does not yet help us to design our organizational interventions with more technical precision.

Psychoanalysis As a Method for the In-Depth Investigation of Mental Processes

While I would argue that the foregoing conclusion is demonstrable, it begs an essential question related to the issues of psychoanalysis as a methodology for investigating the mental life of individuals and collectives, as well as a consideration of what constitutes psychoanalytic data. Kaplan (1984), for example, points out that the empirical concern of psychoanalytic theory is its clinical situation, implying the psychoanalysis of patients. He goes on to note that the major discoveries of psychoanalysis were made in the treatment room, and thereafter applied by analogy to other realms such as art, literature, culture, and so on. While one may disagree with his basic premise, in most instances the same may be said of organizational behavior and character, such as when, for example, one asserts that a manager's difficulties with his supervisor are the result of unresolved Oedipal conflicts. In an organizational situation, what are the data for making such an assertion? Surely not the manager's free associations. How were the data — whatever they are — collected? How were they analyzed and interpreted? By what rules or criteria? The broad issues raised by such questions are fairly obvious. In clinical work we are able to construct a carefully controlled and regulated structure for using our investigative methods like free association, dream analysis, and so forth. Despite the various forms patients' resistances may take — also data, of course — psychoanalytic methods require considerable motivation on their part and their painstaking and continuing cooperation for a long period of time. By contrast, in complex natural settings the situation is entirely different; we generally have neither the psychological contract, structure, or opportunity, nor the level and kind of cooperation necessary to investigate the situation psychoanalytically. We are, therefore, usually stuck with analogizing based, at best, on limited data that may either be erroneous or too general to be of use. Thus, Kaplan (1984) argues, for example, that when one claims Moby Dick is Ahab's mother, one is making too bland a statement to be worth asserting. I suggest that the term *blandness* is equally apposite when one asserts that a manager has Oedipal difficulties with his supervisor.

My purpose in making the foregoing remarks is neither to daunt the reader nor to convey an overly pessimistic view about the possibilities of developing adequate depth-psychological organizational diagnoses and assessments. Rather, these remarks are offered in the spirit of underscoring several caveats. First, our diagnoses must remain fluid. We need to recognize that we run the risk of erroneously or crudely imposing a formulation based on an initial assessment, if we do not fully appreciate the inevitable limitations of our data. Further, we need always to be fully open to the emergence of new or contradictory data. Our assessments are, at all times, simply working hypotheses, rather than fixed, neatly integrated diagnostic formulations. In this connection it may also be observed that, in diagnosing or assessing patients, their responses to treatment (for example, trial interpretations) are an important source of data for understanding the nature of their ailments. The same is true in organizational work. How a client responds to our initial interventions — whatever they may be — is an important source of diagnostic data. That is, *linear* or *a priori* diagnostic models are usually at worst simplistic or misleading, or what, in fact, may amount to the same thing in the end, incomplete at best. Perhaps another way of making this point would be to note that compared to the nature and structure of the clinical inferences we make in the treatment room, those we make in organizational situations are likely to be considerably more tenuous and fragile. An appreciation of the inevitability of this state of affairs will with luck allow us to avoid the worst excesses of "wild" interpretations (Freud, [1910] 1957), and of undertaking clumsy, premature, and counterproductive interventions of other sorts. Finally, following Levinson's (1972b) pioneering lead (see also Chapter Two), much more work is needed to develop diagnostic criteria and assessment methods and strategies, and to test formulations based on them against an evaluation of process and outcome. It is only in this manner that we will begin to define more precise and conceptually coherent links between theory, diagnosis, and practice (see below) than we have at present.

Psychoanalysis As a Treatment for Mental and Emotional Illness

It should be obvious, as Levinson (1984) points out, that we do not psychoanalyze organizations. For the most part, the opportunities for and suitability of type 1 practice are quite limited. On the other hand, the psychoanalytically informed practitioner, as noted in the discussion of type 2 practice, utilizes psychoanalytic theory and a general psychoanalytic perspective to plan and guide organization intervention. Must we be content to settle for such a general derivation of psychoanalysis, or may there not be, for example, more direct and better articulated links between theory and practice, between diagnosis and intervention, and between client characteristics and the nature of our intervention strategy? Put another way, there ought to be something between interventions "driven" by some form of psychoanalytic methodology (for instance, the in-house Tavistock group relations conference), which often fails sufficiently to consider client needs, resources, preparedness, and so forth, on the one hand, and interventions merely informed by psychoanalytic theory, on the other. This is precisely the sort of issue I believe we need to address. Even in clinical psychoanalysis we can observe that such issues are very much in the forefront of current concerns. At a recent panel discussion (Richards, 1984), Wallerstein, for example, noted that running counter to the prevailing view that theory and technique "lock securely together" is the fact that, despite significant theoretical changes and advances in nearly 100 years of psychoanalysis, it is difficult to state with any precision how technique has been correspondingly modified. A similar assertion regarding technique in the organizational realm can easily be made. I would suggest, therefore, that despite the obvious practical difficulties of working with many, if not most, of our organizational clients psychoanalytically, we need to continue our attempts to do so. That is, we need to develop interventions and techniques that are true analogues of our clinical methods, in addition to those simply informed or guided by psychoanalysis. I would argue that even if only an occasional client may be suitable for such an approach, both theory and the theory of practice would be enriched. I believe that we have shrunk all too often from developing a psychoanalytic strategy and taking a psychoanalytic stance in our organizational work because of our own anxieties in the face of client resistance and practical difficulties.

In summary, I would like to note the extent to which the field of psychoanalytic organizational practice has been noncumulative. I do not know what forms a more authentic psychoanalytic approach may take, but I believe that with almost forty years of psychoanalytic organizational psychology already behind us, the time is ripe for attempting to advance our theory of practice more directly, more self-consciously, and more systematically. The hope, of course, is that we may be able to produce the kinds of "structural" change (in the psychoanalytic sense) within organizations that are comparable to the mutative and salutary results of successful psychoanalytic work with patients.

References

Astrachan, B. M., and Flynn, H. R. "The Intergroup Exercise: A Paradigm for Learning About the Development of Organizational Structure." In E. Miller (ed.), *Task and Organization*. London: Wiley, 1976.

Balint, E. "Training Post-Graduate Students in Social Casework." *British Journal of Medical Psychology*, 1959, *32*, 193.

Baum, H. S. *The Invisible Bureaucracy*. New York: Oxford University Press, 1987.

Bion, W. R. *Experiences in Groups, and Other Papers*. London: Tavistock, 1959.

Edelson, M. *The Practice of Sociotherapy.* New Haven, Conn.: Yale University Press, 1970a.

Edelson, M. *Sociology and Psychotherapy.* Chicago: University of Chicago Press, 1970b.

Eissler, K. R. "The Effect of the Structure of the Ego on Psychoanalytic Technique." *Journal of the American Psychoanalytic Association,* 1953, *1,* 104–143.

Eissler, K. R. "Remarks on Some Variations in Psychoanalytical Technique." *International Journal of Psycho-Analysis,* 1958, *39,* 222–229.

Freud, S. "Group Psychology and the Analysis of the Ego." In J. Strachey (ed. and trans.), *The Standard Edition of the Complete Psychological Works of Sigmund Freud.* Vol. 18. London: Hogarth Press, 1955a. (Originally published 1921.)

Freud, S. "Totem and Taboo." In J. Strachey (ed. and trans.), *The Standard Edition of the Complete Psychological Works of Sigmund Freud.* Vol. 13. London: Hogarth Press, 1955b. (Originally published 1939.)

Freud, S. "Wild Analysis." In J. Strachey (ed. and trans.), *The Standard Edition of the Complete Psychological Works of Sigmund Freud.* Vol. 11. London: Hogarth Press, 1957. (Originally published 1910.)

Freud, S. "Papers on Technique." In J. Strachey (ed. and trans.), *The Standard Edition of the Complete Psychological Works of Sigmund Freud.* Vol. 12. London: Hogarth Press, 1958. (Originally published 1911–1915.)

Freud, S. "Civilization and Its Discontents." In J. Strachey (ed. and trans.), *The Standard Edition of the Complete Psychological Works of Sigmund Freud.* Vol. 21. London: Hogarth Press, 1961a. (Originally published 1930.)

Freud, S. "The Future of an Illusion." In J. Strachey (ed. and trans.), *The Standard Edition of the Complete Psychological Works of Sigmund Freud.* Vol. 21. London: Hogarth Press, 1961b. (Originally published 1927.)

Freud, S. "Moses and Monotheism." In J. Strachey (ed. and trans.), *The Standard Edition of the Complete Psychological Works of Sigmund Freud.* Vol. 23. London: Hogarth Press, 1964. (Originally published 1939.)

Gosling, R., Miller, D. H., Turquet, P. M., and Woodhouse, D. *The Use of Small Groups in Training.* Hitchin, England: Codicote Press, 1967.

Gustafson, J., and Hausman, W. "The Phenomenon of Splitting in a Small Psychiatric Organization: A Case Report." *Social Psychiatry,* 1975, *10,* 199–203.

Hirschhorn, L. *The Workplace Within: Psychodynamics of Organizational Life.* Cambridge, Mass.: MIT Press, 1988.

Jaques, E. "Collaborative Group Methods in a Wage Negotiation Situation." *Human Relations,* 1950, *3,* 223–249.

Jaques, E. *The Changing Culture of a Factory.* London: Tavistock, 1951.

Jaques, E. "Social Systems as a Defence Against Persecutory and Depressive Anxiety." In M. Klein, P. Heimann, and R. E. Money-Kyrle (eds.), *New Directions in Psychoanalysis.* London: Tavistock, 1955.

Jaques, E., Rice, A. K., and Hill, J.M.M. "The Social and Psychological Impact of a Change in Method of Wage Payment." *Human Relations,* 1951, *4,* 315–340.

Johnson, J. L., and Fleischer, K. "Reactions of Teachers of Emotionally Disturbed Children to Group Relations Conferences: A New Application of Tavistock Training." *Journal of Personality and Social Systems,* 1980, *2* (2–3), 11–25.

Kaplan, D. Review of E. Kurweil and W. Phillips (eds.), *Literature and Psychoanalysis. Contemporary Psychology,* 1984, *29* (9), 81–82.

Kernberg, O. *Object Relations Theory and Clinical Psychoanalysis.* New York: Aronson, 1976.

Kernberg, O. "Regression in Organizational Leadership." *Psychiatry,* 1979, *42,* 24–39.

Kernberg, O. "The Couch at Sea: The Psychoanalysis of Organizations." *International Journal of Group Psychotherapy,* 1984, *34* (1), 5–23.

Kets de Vries, M.F.R. *The Irrational Executive: Psychoanalytic Studies in Management.* New York: International Universities Press, 1984.

Kets de Vries, M.F.R., and Miller, D. *The Neurotic Organization: Diagnosing and Changing Counterproductive Styles of Management.* San Francisco: Jossey-Bass, 1984.

Klein, M. *Contributions to Psychoanalysis, 1921–1945.* London: Hogarth Press, 1948.

Lawrence, W. G. *Exploring Individual and Organizational Boundaries.* New York: Wiley, 1979.

Levinson, H. "The Clinical Psychologist as Organizational Diagnostician." *Professional Psychologist,* Winter, 1972b, pp. 34–40.

Levinson, H. *Organizational Diagnosis.* Cambridge, Mass.: Harvard University Press, 1972b.

Levinson, H. "Review of R. de Board, *The Psychoanalysis of Organizations.*" *Journal of the American Psychoanalytic Asociation,* 1984, *32,* 3.

Menninger, R. W. "The Impact of Group Relations Conferences on Organizational Growth." *International Journal of Group Psychotherapy,* 1972, *22,* 415–430.

Menninger, R. W. "A Retrospective View of a Hospital-Wide Group Relations Training Program: Costs, Consequences, and Conclusions." In A. D. Coleman and M. H. Geller (eds.), *Group Relations Reader 2.* New York: A. K. Rice Institute, 1985.

Menzies, I. "A Case Study in the Functioning of Social Systems as a Defence Against Anxiety: A Report on a Study of the Nursing Service of a General Hospital." *Human Relations,* 1960, *13,* 95–121.

Menzies Lyth, I. *Containing Anxiety in Institutions: Selected Essays.* Vol. 1. London: Free Association Books, 1988.

Menzies, Lyth, I. *The Dynamics of the Social: Selected Essays.* Vol. 2. London: Free Association Books, 1989.

Miller, E. J. *Task and Organization.* New York: Wiley, 1976.

Miller, E. J., and Gwynne, G. V. *A Life Apart.* London: Tavistock, 1972.

Miller, E. J., and Rice, A. K. *Systems of Organization: The Control of Task and Sentient Boundaries.* London: Tavistock, 1967.

Miller, J. C. "The Psychology of Conflict in Belfast: Conference as Microcosm." *Journal of Personality and Social Systems,* 1977, *1,* 17–38.

Reed, B. "Organizational Role Analysis." In C. L. Cooper (ed.), *Developing Skills in Managers.* London: Macmillan, 1976.

Rice, A. K. *Productivity and Social Organization: The Ahmedabad Experiment.* London: Tavistock, 1958.

Rice, A. K. *Learning for Leadership.* London: Tavistock, 1965.

Rice, B. "Midlife Encounters: The Menninger Seminars for Businessmen." *Psychology Today,* Apr. 1979, pp. 67–70.

Richards, A. "The Relation Between Psychoanalytic Theory and Psychoanalytic Technique" (panel report). *Journal of the American Psychoanalytic Association,* 1984, *32,* 3, 587–602.

Trist, E. L., and Bamforth, K. "Some Social and Psychological Consequences of the Longwall Method of Coal Getting." *Human Relations,* 1951, *4,* 3–38.

Trist, E. L., and Murray, H. *The Social Engagement of Social Science.* Vol. 1: *The Socio-Psychological Perspective.* Philadelphia: University of Pennsylvania Press, 1990.

Turquet, P. "Threats to Identity in the Large Group." In L. Kneeger (ed.), *The Large Group: Dynamics and Therapy.* London: Constable, 1975.

Wachtel, P. L. *Psychoanalysis and Behavior Therapy: Toward an Integration.* New York: Basic Books, 1977.

Zaleznik, A. "Management of Disappointment." *Harvard Business Review,* 1967, *45,* 59–70.

Zaleznik, A. "Power and Politics in Organizational Life." In M.F.R. Kets de Vries (ed.), *The Irrational Executive.* New York: International Universities Press, 1984.

2

Diagnosing
Organizations
Systematically

Harry Levinson

There are two reasons people approach others for help: Either
they have some kind of pain or they are causing others to have
pain, who are in turn compelling them to do something about
that problem. Another kind of relationship is that between a
professional person and others, when the professional approaches
someone else for information, as in research. The same is true
in relationships with organizations. Organizational leaders come
to professionals for help or professionals seek them out for learning. In either case, there is a consultation relationship.

When the consultation is for some form of help, the consultant must assess the nature of the problem to be solved in
its complex context. Despite the assertion by some consultants
that they do not diagnose, every action or intervention by a consultant implies a diagnosis based on some assumptions. The
major purposes of formal organizational diagnosis are to com-
pile sufficient appropriate data to understand the problem and
to clarify one's assumptions by basing inferences on those data.
Together these enable the consultant to act in a scientific way
by constructing hypotheses based on data and being able to revise those diagnostic hypotheses as necessary (see Levinson,
1972).

The Study Procedure

The consultant's initial impressions on entering an organization are critical. He must attune himself to his own subtle feelings because these reflect the impact of various environmental stimuli on him. Others are likely to be affected in the same way, but because the stimuli may be sensed preconsciously, their impact may not be understood. It is helpful for the consultant to ask himself the following questions:

> What did I see on the initial tour?
> What are my initial feelings about the organization?
> What were people's attitudes toward me?
> What occurred on the tour that made me feel good, bad, or indifferent?

It also is important for the consultant to note even vague impressions as soon as they occur. Otherwise, he will lose considerable data.

After having entered the organization, the consultant begins the formal study procedure. Usually this involves several steps (although not necessarily in this order): (1) a breakdown of the organization to be studied into its component parts, (2) the planning of a sample of interviewees to be representative of those parts and of the organization as a whole (paying careful attention to leadership), (3) a supplementary sample of people to be questioned by printed form, (4) observations of people at work, (5) an examination of existing records and relevant data, and (6) interviews with important persons outside the organization. The last may include former employees, others in the community who know the organization, competitors, suppliers, and other similarly informed people. The consultant may not know who the relevant others are until the study is already under way.

General Features of the Procedure and of the Organization

To carry out the preceding steps effectively, the consultant must have a good feel for the kinds of information he needs and for the best ways to elicit it. This means that his relationship to the organization is crucial.

Relating to the Organization. A diagnostic study involves relating to an organization. One does not relate to an organization except as one relates to the people in it and particularly to the leadership.

The consultant will be treated in many different ways. Sometimes he is seen as an evaluator who judges instantaneously the innermost competencies of people. He may be the "unwelcome guest." He may be sought as the hero, the ally who is needed to give "management" or "the workers" the right point of view; or as a punisher; or as someone who rewards. (These prospective relationships often suggest the kinds of relationships people experience with each other in the organization.) His approach must be one of reassurance and support. Yet he may have to move into sensitive areas that are important for his understanding of the feelings and behavior of people.

Factual Data. Every organization has at least some of its policies and procedures and also various kinds of historical information recorded on paper. The consultant should become acquainted with what is on record and develop for himself a perspective on how it all fits together in the form of an organizational history and value system. In some instances he will be the only person who has ever thought of these data as being interrelated. Usually he will be the first to think about their collective significance for the organization.

Outside Information. All organizations have relationships outside themselves — with competitors, suppliers, cooperating organizations, agents, professional associations, and so on. The consultant will find it helpful to understand how the organization appears to these respective publics and should arrange, with the permission of the client organization, interviews with their representatives. These perspectives will enable him to understand how the client organization operates and what impact it has on others.

Pattern of Organization. Almost all organizations have some form of organizational chart that defines responsibilities. The consultant should get a copy from his major contact within the company. However, he should not take the chart to represent the way the organization actually operates, for it may be at variance with what the organizational leadership intends. It is not unusual for working relationships to grow up informally, particularly if the organizational chart has not been published. It is important for the consultant to understand why there are discrepancies and what effect they have.

Settings. The concept of setting has particular application to organizations. One arrives at the observational units, or "settings," by first discerning overall organizational purposes and then analyzing how these purposes are subdivided into specific functions performed by definable groups.

The organizational purposes and subpurposes — service, problem solving, production, and indoctrination — influence the behavioral requirements that a setting imposes on the people who operate within it.

Task Patterns. There are characteristic task patterns in each setting. A task pattern is essentially a group-level variable, referring to the task-required patterns of relationships that exist in any given setting. There are at least four such patterns.

1. *Complementary activities:* the group working toward a shared goal, the contribution of each group member distinguishable from, but connected with, others in the group
2. *Parallel activities:* each group member performing essentially the same task
3. *Sequential activities:* each group member performing some phase of the group task in tandem with co-workers
4. *Individualized activities:* unique functions performed by each member of the group, neither complementary nor sequential

Plan of Study. From the initial mapping of the organization and early impressions, the general plan of study is developed, to be modified on the basis of later observations. If more than one consultant is involved, this will require later coordination of results.

Some settings and subsettings will receive more attention than others, including all settings with large populations having central purposes that are particularly indispensable to the accomplishment of the organization's basic task.

The consultant will then have to arrange his interviewing and questionnaires so that he can be sure of having a representative sample of the organization. He should interview all of the top-management group, the heads of each of the major functional groups he will cover, and randomly selected members of each of those functional groups. The remaining members of each of the groups may be sampled by questionnaire.

Approach to the Setting and Its Incumbents

For administrative reasons and effective functioning, the consultant should move into a setting in steps suggested by persons with formal authority, with successive introductions by top executives through intermediate management and supervisory personnel to the line personnel. Unless this is done, people at each level are uncertain about the legitimacy of their spending time with the consultant.

The general tone of this approach by the consultant is to invite those in the setting to work with him on understanding the problem, even if it is appropriate for him to leave the setting temporarily and come back at a more convenient time. In any case, the consultant should attempt to establish a collaborative relationship rather than an exploitative relationship. Often, resistance is mobilized because the consultant is seen as allied with top management against lower levels. Granted, the consultant has been able to penetrate this far into the organization only because management has allowed him to do so. However, he can demonstrate that it is not his business to obtain information that will be used against people by top management, but to be an independent professional acting, with management consent, to learn and understand as much as possible about the organization for constructive purposes.

The consultant should precede each interview or questionnaire administration by reintroducing himself to the interviewee, restating the purposes of the study or consultation, stressing its confidential nature, and, if it is the case, indicating to the respondent that the interview is not mandatory. Even if a clear description of the study has been given in advance, most people remain unclear about its intent and purposes. Some will have heard rumors that need to be corrected.

When the interview is completed, the consultant should permit the respondent to ask questions to clarify further the consultant's function. Individual interviewees will frequently ask if their answers are like the replies of other respondents. This is usually a question to test the interviewer, who should repeat that inasmuch as the interviews are confidential, he cannot disclose what other individuals have said. However, it is sometimes possible to offer a general response that satisfies the questioner.

The consultant should indicate to the interviewee that the interview will be examined along with others and a summary of the study reported to the group as a whole. He should indicate the same to groups whom he asks to complete questionnaires.

Observation and On-the-Job Contacts

One of the major problems with consultants and researchers is that they depend too much on interview and questionnaire data. Too few spend time observing the actual processes of work, work flow, communications, and work relationships. The on-the-job contact is a way the consultant can ascertain how people feel about their situation while he is in the setting.

I prefer to spend as much time as I can on site, asking people to explain to me what they do, how they do it, and the problems inherent in getting their work done. This may involve sitting in executive offices or keeping notes on the events of the day or walking from machine to machine or attending various kinds of meetings or sitting in on training and orientation programs.

There are no simple rules for initiating contact and conversation on the job. "How long have you worked here?" is an easy start, since the answer is simple and it refers to the past, which is generally less threatening than the present.

Observe the individual's level of comfort in dealing with the investigator. Note how work is initiated and terminated. There may be a rush from the job at break time and heavy sighs of relief. As a supervisor passes, one may see a subordinate make a face or turn to a co-worker and say something that leads to a laugh. The consultant must keep his attention well dispersed to understand interpersonal relations that occur "naturally."

A consultant should also look for obviously stressful experiences. What occurrences disrupt or disorganize people and lead them to seek help? What situations stimulate worry? While one can and should ask about these, there are many opportunities to observe them in everyday life on the job.

There are other questions that will aid a general assessment of characteristic setting experiences:

1. Do people enjoy leaving the job to talk to the consultant because they can get away from it? How do they break off the interview when they are called by their supervisor?
2. Do people go into detail when explaining their job? Do they feel their work is a sufficiently important aspect of what goes on in the organization for the consultant to know it well?
3. What are the difficult, frustrating, or trying aspects of the job? Which are the most gratifying? Can and do people resolve many of these difficulties themselves? From whom do they get support and technical help?
4. What other people are brought in during conversation? Which of them are viewed positively and negatively and why?
5. In the overall context, do people focus primarily on their job, the setting, or the organization as a whole? How much focus is there on the purpose of the job? Do they see themselves as specialists with considerable skill or as doing something that anyone could do?

Work Experience: Rationale

The fact that the consultant interviews an employee at the work site assures the interviewee of the consultant's interest. The consultant demonstrates that he is interested enough in what he can learn not only to come to the organization but also to come "all the way" to the interviewee and that part of the company that the latter knows best.

The on-the-job interview permits the consultant to observe a person reacting to the demands and the uniqueness of the job. The consultant sees what thought and motor skills are demanded by the subject's task, the number and quality of the subject's interpersonal transactions, and sources of gratification and frustration. These observations alone help the consultant to learn a great deal about the experiences that have particular psychological and emotional impact on the person.

The on-the-job interview should be conducted in a more-or-less standard way. This does not mean that exactly the same things should be said and done with each individual. Ideally, each interviewee should be given maximum opportunity to reveal those aspects of the work experience that seem psychologically significant. This requires the consultant to compensate for individual differences in levels and expression of anxiety, talkativeness, clarity of description, and investment in the study process. The consultant may have to keep one person from being too repetitive, while in another instance he may have to prod for more depth in a specific area.

Despite such differences, there are ways in which the form of the interview can be standardized to achieve equal opportunity of expression for each person. One way is to control the duration of the interview. An interview of fifty to sixty minutes provides a balance between the consultant's need to cover large numbers of people and the time it takes to enable a person to reveal major involvements in and reactions to various facets of the work situation.

The general questions to be kept in mind to ensure coverage of key areas during the interview are:

What are this person's sources of involvement and lack of involvement and dissatisfaction?

How does this person's work contribute to personal knowledge and self-evaluation?

How does the subject perceive and respond to others at work?

What personal significance does the interviewee's activity and productivity have?

What are normative stresses for this person, and what techniques are used to cope with them?

After fifteen to thirty minutes, the interviewer should assess for himself what he has and has not learned about the person, separating those areas that he feels he knows well from those in which he wants further information. This assessment should guide the consultant in the remainder of the interview.

At the end of the hour, the consultant should take the time to thank the person and to demonstrate the usefulness of the interview by illustrating something he has learned from it. It is important to leave the interviewee with the feeling of having made a contribution.

The interview should be recorded as soon as possible from the consultant's notes. The form and exhaustiveness of these notes will vary depending on the bent, skills, and memory of the consultant and the particular situation, including the response of the interviewee to note taking. But every effort should be made to record sufficient data during and after the interview to permit a thorough analysis.

The consultant should record, in the order in which they occur throughout the interview, what the interviewee says, does, and feels; the interviewee's reactions to others, including the consultant; and the consultant's reaction to the interviewee. The record of the interview should highlight specific events occurring during the interview, such as interactions with others, specific job activities, the interviewee's emotional reactions, and any personal references. Any topics concerning nonwork tasks, co-workers, or the person's setting should be included, as well as questions the interviewer asked that might have led to these comments, since spontaneous and requested statements often differ in their significance.

Case Study Outline

The outline that follows lists the individual topics to be covered in writing the organizational case study. This case-study method was conceptualized and developed from a psychoanalytic orientation with a view toward consultative intervention. Psychoanalytic understanding, therefore, provides a basis for the recommendations considered here. For consultants trained in this particular discipline, the organizational case study is valid as a tool for understanding, learning, and sharpening professional skills only if it is approached with a view to its ultimate application. For other disciplines with different consultative goals, this need not be the case.

   I.   Genetic data
  II.   Description and analysis of current organization as a whole
       A.   Structural data
       B.   Process data
 III.   Interpretative data
       A.   Current organizational functioning
           1.   Organizational perceptions
               a.   Degree of alertness, accuracy, and vividness
               b.   Direction and span of attention
               c.   Assessment of the discrepancy between reality and perceived reality
           2.   Organizational knowledge
           3.   Organizational language
           4.   Emotional atmosphere
           5.   Organizational action
       B.   Attitudes and relationships
  IV.   Analyses and conclusions
       A.   Organizational integrative patterns
       B.   Summary and recommendations

Genetic Data

Identifying information is used primarily for administrative and classification purposes. This section contains the who, what, when, where, why, and how of the study. Most of the items here should be written up immediately after the initial visit to the organization.

     To be of use in the process of facilitating change, the

description of any organization must cover its historical background. The consultant must know not only how the organization is functioning now but also how those methods evolved and what historical forces continue to influence the organization's activities. However, one must strive for the truly salient points.

All data incorporated here should be verifiable. They provide the factual basis for all subsequent diagnostic hypotheses and for the conclusions that will follow. They form the foundation for explaining (1) how this organization evolved and (2) why it is asking for this particular kind of help now. Like a mystery novel, this section of the case study must contain all the facts needed to substantiate the subsequent inferences.

Description and Analysis of Current Organization As a Whole

Structural Data. Having identified the organization, outlined its history, and defined the purposes and conditions of the study, the consultant now describes the organization as he finds it. This section is largely a factual account of how the organization is put together and how it operates. Much of the data in this section will come from formal reports and records that the organization maintains; some of it will be formulated by the consultant from his observations and interviews.

Process Data. An enormous amount of information is available to all organizations, but most use only a small amount of it. The system for receiving, organizing, and integrating information is usually unclear even to those working in the organization. However, such a process occurs whether the organization recognizes it or not. Observation and interview will quickly disclose that there is a regularity to information acquisition and information handling. The questions for the consultant are: What does the organization "pick up" from its environment? What from inside itself? To what particular kinds of communication is it especially sensitive? How does it transmit internally information it receives? At what point is the communication interpreted, organized, assimilated, or rejected? Having accomplished that process, however inadvertently, how does the organization respond to the data it receives?

Interpretative Data

The data gathered prior to this point in the process will have been almost wholly factual. Those inferences that have had to be made at various points were limited extrapolations from the data and could be made by most people without specialized training.

Now, however, the consultant must begin to exercise his professional judgment. Different consultants may arrive at different interpretations, depending on their training, experience, and theoretical orientation. Regardless of these factors, every consultant should be aware that he is dealing with inference; he must be prepared to offer evidence for the interpretations he makes and the conclusions he reaches. Only by continually presenting evidence to himself or to others can he indicate how well he has tested the hypothesis he advances, specify the sources of his knowledge, and distinguish between speculation and opinion.

Current Organizational Functioning. Current organizational functioning refers to how the organization learns, thinks, feels, and behaves — roughly the equivalent of its physiology and psychology.

Organizational Perceptions

Degree of alertness, accuracy, and vividness: Here the consultant should be concerned with the extent to which the organization recognizes, and the effectiveness with which it uses, that which is available to it. The consultant must make a subjective judgment about the "degree of alertness."

How alert is an organization to what is going on? How accurate and vivid are its reactions to stimuli within the organization — from people and from the physical plant? How accurate and vivid are its reactions to direct stimuli from outside the organization — marketing and purchasing conditions, labor conditions — and indirect stimuli such as government influence, transportation, competition, research developments, and general economic, social, and political trends?

Direction and span of attention: Here the consultant should learn what an organization concentrates its attention on and how wide its focus is. To what stimuli does it give the most attention? In what direction is its organizational radar turned?

All organizations concentrate selectively on some aspects of their environment. In some organizations this is formalized. Other organizations concentrate on those issues that are important to the organization's leadership.

After having interpreted what an organization concentrates on, a consultant must make a judgment about those seemingly relevant matters to which the organization is not attuned. The things that an organization fails to pay attention to — if they are relevant to its survival — will ultimately be the source of its downfall. If an organization fails to recognize relevant stimuli, this suggests some impairment in organizational functioning that must be investigated further.

Assessment of the discrepancy between reality and perceived reality: The consultant must now assess the organizational perceptions he has documented. Is there a difference between reality as the organization perceives it and as the consultant sees it? An organization may be accurate in its perception of some stimuli but incorrect in its interpretation of them. Sometimes an organization believes itself to be inept in a certain area; with new leadership, it may rise to unexpected heights. The converse is also true. Sometimes an organization precipitates its own difficulties and must then live with self-fulfilling prophecies.

Organizational Knowledge

What is the body of information on which the organization acts? Such information is usually transmissible in the form of techniques, history, experience, specialized competence, research data, and project reports. How an organization acquires and uses knowledge is an indication of its adaptability. Here we must

be careful to distinguish "communication," which is a transmission of perceptions, and "internalization," that which is organized, integrated, and anchored within the organization as one
of its strengths. The task of the consultant at this point is to
interpret (from previously noted data) what the organization
has learned and how.

Having observed, described, and interpreted what kinds
of knowledge are acquired by whom, and how, the consultant
must determine whether the information is used as an organizational asset. How is it disseminated and assimilated? Does
the organization benefit from it? Are authority figures consciously used as models in disseminating knowledge? Is new
knowledge stated in memorandum or procedure form with the
assumption that people will then apply it without the need for
models or instruction? Are people formally trained to use new
knowledge?

Organizational Language

Organizational language tells people what is going on *in* the organization. It is, therefore, important to note and interpret the
meaning of the way the organization "speaks." The consultant
should analyze the style, content, syntax, attitudes, and values
that appear in organization communications. He should be particularly interested in feelings that are disguised by the language
used, the degree to which the organizational language is a barrier to discourse within the organization or between the organization and others, and the degree to which it constitutes a cultural or industrial boundary.

Emotional Atmosphere

The consultant needs to find out how it feels to work in the organization. The emotional atmosphere can be hectic but con-
genial, noisy, and joyous, or loud and hostile. It may, in effect,
say to people, "Be on your guard and control yourself," or "Enjoy, enjoy," or "One slip and you're out." In other words, is it
pleasant and supportive? Or is it hostile and threatening?

Organizational Action

Here the consultant is concerned with how the organization acts, its characteristic style of behavior. Sometimes organizations are described as fast moving, lean and hungry, bumbling, and so on. Each of these words or phrases captures a nuance of what we mean by organizational action.

What is the pace of the organization? With what degree of enthusiasm or lethargy does it pursue new products, different markets, and innovative technology? To what extent does the organization confront problems head-on? How aggressive is it in its competitive efforts? In speaking of the degree of vigor of an organization, the consultant will be making a value judgment. Implicitly or overtly he will be comparing this organization to others. It is these subtle distinctions that allow the consultant to feed back to the organization the kind of information about itself that the organization can use.

Attitudes and Relationships. When aspects of an organization's perceptions, knowledge, language, emotional level, and modes of action are integrated, they result in its characteristic attitudes and relationships. Having made inferences from the factual data about the many ways in which the organization is functioning, the consultant must now synthesize his inferences into statements about the organization's psychological stance.

What feelings lie behind the ways in which the organization functions? The focus here is on enduring psychological perspectives that provide unity, cohesion, and consistent direction to organizational behavior or, conversely, that may be detrimental to it. These are reflected in attitudes toward self and others, time, work, and authority. It is imperative to understand attitudes and relationships since they represent methods for coping with continuing problems. Also, any attempt at intervention or change will necessarily involve an alteration in the configuration of the organization's attitudes and relationships. It is the configuration, rather than isolated variables, that must be dealt with in order to effect change.

The consultant's attention should focus on which of the

relations the organization has the strongest connections to and feelings about. In what things and ideas does the organization invest itself psychologically? What differences are there in investment or attachment to objects and ideas within the organization? What psychological purposes do such investments serve? Beyond ideals, what other abstractions have meaning for the organization?

What is the self-concept of the organization? How do members of the organization see themselves collectively? How do they see themselves in relation to other organizations, to their host community, and in their interactions and relationships?

Here it is important to interpret specifically the emotional relationships among key people and different work groups. Who are the key people in the organization? The consultant must write a brief historical character sketch of the key individuals that will summarize a statement of character defenses, transference paradigm, style of handling individuals and conflicts in the organization, preoccupation in the organization, and methods of communication.

Then the consultant should specify what he thinks the most significant groups in the organization are and what the relationships between them are. In specifying these groups, the consultant should look particularly at their points of difference and conflict in an effort to understand why they differ. In assessing their relationships, the consultant will want to look at how the groups and group members communicate with each other, what nonwork activities they undertake together, and what conditions prompt them to mobilize against a common outside threat. The consultant's understanding of the significant groups in the organization will be crucial to his subsequent recommendations.

Analyses and Conclusions

The conclusions the consultant arrives at will establish a basis for his understanding of, and intervention in, the affairs of the organization, and will necessarily be based on subjective interpretations. They will also reflect his professional orientation, and one would expect to find the greatest diversity of interpretation in the conclusions section of the case study. Because of the wide variety of theoretical orientations, the consultant must approach the selection and understanding of data with an open mind, yet with firm conviction about the way he interprets the data, based on his professional orientation.

The distillation and extraction process necessary for a useful body of conclusions is analogous to the making of wine. Just as the vintner selects and processes the grapes, presses them, and filters out the extraneous matter to produce wine, so the consultant, from his accumulated data, must select and condense those that will reveal the essence of the organization's vitality. He must describe comprehensively the dynamic organizational processes, taking into account both internal and external interactions, in order to delineate and clarify the multiple determinants that bring about the organization's current adaptive behavior. The processes that this organizational case study elicits are a reflection of the conflicts with which the organization contends in order to survive. From this study, therefore, the consultant can assess the various strengths and weaknesses influencing the organization's ability to cope with stress.

There are some questions the consultant should always have before him: What is hurting this organization? How do I interpret what the key people cite as their main problem? How do I interpret what other employees say is their main problem? The pain may be literally what the informants say it is or it may be symptomatic of something more deep seated. How does this organization experience its problems? That is, how severe do the problems appear to be to the organization? And how well does the organization relate them to basic causes? This is a vital question because the degree to which the organization acknowledges pain is one measure of how ready it is to accept help.

Organizational Integrative Patterns. The consultant must be particularly careful to indicate where and how, in his judgment, the organization is not integrating effectively. His concern is not to seek out evil or identify the person who is wrong; he must, rather, seek out failure and potential failure for the purpose of helping to remedy those situations. There is a tendency on the part of diagnosticians and consultants to look for culprits—a cause or a person—and to substitute invective for consideration. This will only blind the consultant to the realities with which he and the organization must deal. It cannot be emphasized often enough that the consultant is dealing with inference, that he must be prepared to offer evidence for his interpretations and conclusions, and that he must regard his statements as hypotheses to be tested.

In reviewing organizational integrative efforts, we are talking about the manner in which the organization functions cohesively and effectively as well as where it is disjointed, where it falls, where it errs repetitively, and where it dissipates energy.

Summary and Recommendations. The data the consultant has gathered and interpreted have provided him with the necessary material for viewing the organization and its external and internal environments from both a longitudinal and a cross-sectional point of view. From this dual perspective, the consultant can make a definitive statement of the current status of the organization. Finally, an explanatory formulation will provide him with the dynamic and genetic understanding of the organization's current status. Based on perspective, current status, and explanatory formulation, prognostic conclusions can be stated.

Termination

Whatever the length of his work in the field, the consultant is faced with the task of dealing constructively with the termination of his relationship there.

The general procedure for the consultant to follow includes mentioning his imminent departure to people and, ultimately, a walk through the setting, thanking people and saying goodbye to them individually. He should give people a chance to ask further questions and express any last-minute opinions and ideas they had not taken the opportunity to mention earlier. They should be reassured that they have been helpful in whatever ways are appropriate. The consultant should refer to particular conversations with individuals, conveying that he has come to know them to some degree. He must tell them all that he will be coming back at a later date with a report on the study.

The consultant's last contact is usually with the organizational representative with whom he planned the overall study. Together, they should review where things stand, the general reactions of people to the study, and the consultant's own reactions. The consultant usually picks up whatever loose ends, uncertainties, questions, and future plans need attention at this point.

The feedback report is itself a critical part of the closure process, even if delayed by several months. The various questions posed about what the consultant might do with the information he has gained cannot be resolved until he has returned to the organization and reported back. Only the report can do this. After the feedback and discussion of it with people in the organization, termination can be seen as reasonably complete.

Feedback

Having completed and written up the study, the consultant's next task is to begin the closure process by feeding back the results. This involves two steps: (1) preparing a report to the organization, and (2) presenting the report to the organizational system.

However, these are only the mechanical steps. The closure process is a complex and subtle end-phase negotiating process. The way it is handled will be of significant influence in determining whether the client organization will proceed to work further on the issues discerned.

Preparing the Report

The report to the client should be a summary of those findings abstracted from the analysis-and-conclusions section of the study, together with recommendations for action. It should be no longer than can be read aloud comfortably within one hour. The summary should describe what the consultant did, how he acquired his information, and the period of time covered by the study.

This will enable the client to put the report in perspective and to understand its sources and its limitations.

In the report, the consultant should consider carefully the level of understanding, degree of interest, and opportunities for action of his audience, and, therefore, what they *can* hear. While being sympathetic and factual, the report should avoid the extremes of dishonesty and indictment.

For example, in one situation, the consultant was told a great deal about the aloofness and authoritarian manner of one particular executive. Some of his subordinates resented his authority because of his cold and distant attitude. The consultant recognized that the executive could not significantly change his personality and that his aloofness resulted in part from his not knowing how to get close to people. The consultant reported to the executive that his subordinates looked to him for leadership and support and wanted to see more of him. He recommended regular meetings between the executive and his subordinates to discuss the common problems they faced. Had the consultant merely told the executive he was authoritarian, the executive would have been left with criticism alone, which he could only reject because he saw himself not as authoritarian but as fatherly. Once he had rejected the consultant's findings, there would have been no way for the consultant to help him further. In this particular instance, the consultant was in a position to help him learn to relate more effectively to his people and to mobilize them toward their mutual tasks.

The report should give appropriate emphasis to the strengths of the organization and its ability to cope with its problems. The report should provide a balanced picture of the organization and its problem-solving efforts.

A statement of recommendations should follow the presentation of the findings. The recommendations should offer *specific* avenues for confronting the problems disclosed in the report's findings, and they should be in keeping with the strengths and assets of the organization. There is little point in making recommendations that are beyond the capacity of the organization. Too often, consultants assume that the organization can readily use the strengths it has. However, most will need help in utilizing strengths — help in the form of delineated steps toward more effective functioning, together with support from the consultant or from someone else in taking these steps. Often an organization's leadership will be fully aware of its problems but not know how to go about coping with them. And often the consultant's recommendations are too general to be useful.

Once the report has been prepared, the actual feedback process can begin. The first step in this process is to present the report to the executive who was responsible for the consultant's entering the organization. It is important for the consultant to recognize that the client has the right to be in charge of what is happening. Therefore, I prefer to read the report to the client executive. I ask for a two-hour meeting. I indicate that I would like the client to listen to me read the report, to make notes if desired, and to consider how the report will sound to other people in the organization when they hear it. I want the executive to be particularly alert to my use of words, to be sure that I do not convey meanings I do not intend and to see that I do not inadvertently become trapped in organizational politics. I want the client to be sensitive to the way I present matters so that my phrasing does not create embarrassing or difficult circumstances. I make it clear that I cannot change the substance of my feelings, but I emphasize my need to have the executive's help in stating what I have to say in the most advantageous way.

I then read the report aloud slowly. When I have finished reading it, the client executive is then free to ask questions, to discuss any items or implications, and to advise me on language. I also seek advice on the next steps in presentation.

Ordinarily I prefer to present the report to others in the organization in the same sequence I followed when entering the organization. However, sometimes it is politically wiser to alter course.

After the initial two-hour session, I give the client executive the typewritten report that I have read and that we have discussed. I suggest reading it that evening and meeting with me again for two hours the next morning to review the report and discuss it further. *It is extremely important to follow this arrangement exactly.* Any such report is likely to have some disturbing implications for the executive, no matter how essential the consultant's help is or how desirable constructive diagnosis seemed to be. The client will tend to perceive definitions of problems as personal criticism and brood about it. Unless the discussion is resumed *immediately* the next morning, these feelings will fester and could result in hostile rejection. The client may feel, for example, that the report is no good or that the consultant has been unduly critical, or may decide not to go any further with the project. When such feelings are talked through immediately, the client has the opportunity to reestablish a more accurate perspective and to assist the consultant in planning the next steps in the feedback process. This phase is so critical that the consultant should not undertake feedback to the client executive until an uninterrupted afternoon-evening-morning schedule can be arranged.

For the next steps in the feedback process, the consultant should provide copies of the report for each of the listeners to have as he reads it aloud. (Charts and graphs will complement the presentation.) This sort of concrete reference point can counteract the distortions that are likely to occur in listening to a verbal presentation. It also facilitates questions and discussion. (Each group to whom the consultant reports should have the opportunity to suggest changes in the wording, but not in the substance, and offer suggestions about presentation to those who will next hear the report.)

Usually the feedback process follows a consistent psychological course. At first the listeners tend to be tense and hostile, as if fearing the worst. Then they become more attentive. Once they become more relaxed, they will frequently voice approval during the reading. Finally, the questions that follow, directly or indirectly, say, "Are we really going to do something about it?"

The discussion that follows the reading also tends to take a predictable course. There is usually an initial defensive, hostile phase that includes efforts to escape psychologically; a discussion-of-feelings-and-issues stage; and a stage of consolidation behind the report.

The feedback procedure will be the scene for the mobilization of powerful feelings within the groups to whom the consultant is reporting. Some will feel chagrined that he has discovered organizational secrets; others will gloat in their satisfaction. Some will feel guilty for having "squealed," when they hear something they may take as an indictment of their bosses. Some will feel attacked, some deserted by the consultant from whom they had expected so much. Some will complain that the inferences drawn from their statements are not that important. Some will want to know if top management has heard the report and what they will do about it.

Throughout the presentation, the behavior of the consultant should be a model of how he wants the organization to go about its problem-solving activity: by joint engagement with authoritative leadership around open examination of mutual problems for collective solutions toward more effective organizational functioning. He must demonstrate that he does not fear hostility; that he stands confidently behind his findings despite differences; that he is willing to be cross-examined about what he has learned and how he has learned it, together with the assumptions he has made; and that he is willing to be corrected in an appropriate way and to have his conclusions modified by new data.

Sometimes the chief executive feels too threatened by the report to open up the possibility of discussion at lower levels. The consultant will have to work with this person at length on the more pressing problems — fear, rigidity, anger, helplessness, lack of knowledge about what to do and how to do it. Only when the client is more comfortable and feels supported by the consultant will it be possible to take the necessary steps. Some will need additional support from their boards, who will then also have to hear the report.

Some chief executives who, out of helplessness or fear, want to deny they have problems, do so by avoiding the issues. They assume that the feedback itself should solve their problems. They conclude that people should talk to each other more and everyone will love everyone else. Usually such individuals are afraid to take authoritative action and are uncomfortable with confrontation. They will need greater direction from the consultant about where to begin and support from him when hostility arises from their subordinates.

Conclusion

When the consultant is finished, he should review all his diary notes on the feedback process, together with those of the whole study, and specify on paper for himself what he thinks he has learned, what mistakes he has made, and what he would want to do differently the next time. Unless the consultant himself is always a learner, he will quickly become obsolete.

Of course, there are many more possible psychological issues and problems in the closure and feedback process. Since they all cannot be elaborated here, I can only point out that the closure task is also psychologically an opening task. If the consultant recognizes the critical nature of this process, observes the phenomena of the process carefully, and consciously crystallizes his own experiences, he will find himself increasing his own proficiency in time.

Reference

Levinson, H. *Organizational Diagnosis.* Cambridge, Mass.: Harvard University Press, 1972.

3

----◆•◆•◆----

Exploring
the Dynamics
of Leadership

Laurent Lapierre

Great leaders' lives and achievements are always interesting to those who occupy positions of authority within organizations. As social, political, and economic forces may erode leadership (Zaleznik, 1989, 1990), people responsible for the fate of their organizations look toward those who have succeeded in implementing new visions, daring innovations, or major changes, in order to discover the inspiration for their own leadership. Reading the biographies of well-known leaders and actually meeting them when possible are regular activities for those in positions of authority.

In this chapter, I will first provide a definition of leadership by examining certain aspects of the leadership personality that may help us to understand this complex human phenomenon. I will then discuss the use of case histories as a research method particularly well suited to the study of leadership and will present a few examples.

I will also examine the ways works of fiction may be used to study leadership. Even though they may be considered rather unconventional research material, certain works of fiction permit a deeper understanding of some dynamics of leadership that may otherwise remain inaccessible. Finally, since leadership studies also aim to build a body of knowledge that may benefit practitioners, I will look at some of the conditions that can foster the development of leadership potential in those who hold positions of authority.

Leadership and Personality

Despite the numerous studies of leadership that have appeared in recent years, no real consensus has developed within the research community that has tackled this question (Stodgill, 1974; Burns, 1978; Bass, 1981). This may be due to several factors: the complexity of the phenomenon, the qualitative and interpretive methods that are appropriate to its study, and an understandable ambiguity in the works of researchers — an ambiguity that is a reflection of the phenomenon itself. The study of leadership, like that of art, requires broad definitions that contain the complexity of the phenomenon, qualitative research methods to gather and use a richly complex material, and research reports that are almost works of art in themselves. If one is not something of a leader or an artist oneself, can one claim to understand these phenomena even slightly, or to be able to portray them?

The definition of leadership that I use here follows the lead of those researchers after Freud ([1921] 1955) who have investigated this phenomenon from a psychoanalytic perspective (Erikson, 1958, 1969; Zaleznik and Kets de Vries, 1975, 1991; Zaleznik, 1977, 1989, 1990; Kernberg, 1979; Kets de Vries, 1980, 1984, 1989a, 1989b, 1989c, 1989d, 1990a, 1990b, 1990c; Levinson, 1981; Kets de Vries and Miller, 1984b, 1987a, 1987b). They view leadership as the result of the personal dispositions, qualities, and attributes of the individual occupying a position of authority. Leadership is that part of executive action that may be directly attributed to the inner life of the leader, to her personal vision, her ways of being and acting, her deep-rooted beliefs, her imagination, and her fantasies. The self-confidence that she manifests and her ability to impress and to persuade others rely on a certain theatricality.

The leader presents herself and leads. Thus, as the word itself implies, *leadership* is defined as the part of executive action that may be directly attributed to the person exercising authority, and more specifically, to the projection of the deep-seated elements of her personality. By the term *authority*, I mean more than the mere right to command. Authority also applies to the ascendancy that a person acquires through her qualifications, her professional competence, and her qualities, an ascendancy that elicits respect, confidence, and obedience while not necessarily being linked to any external right to command. This definition of leadership in no way negates the importance of the relationship between the leader and her subordinates, nor of her interactions with existing external forces. However, it does mean that I am principally concerned with the person of the leader, with her personality.

This vision of leadership is in complete contrast to the more conventional definition of *management,* which sees the direction of an organization in more situational terms. In the first instance, we are dealing with executive action that transforms (Burns, 1978) external reality consistently with the personal inner theater of the leader, with the defensive process projection playing a central role; in the second, we are dealing with executive action that is the result of transactions between different external forces, orchestrated by the person in authority. In the latter, analysis of information is the core activity and the art required is that of compromise.

These definitions of leadership and management are inevitably reductionist and simplistic. There are no pure categories in executive practice and there is therefore no clean split between leadership and management; those who hold authority in organizations are in some degree both leaders and professional managers. However, there are executives whose practice may be seen as the product of original vision, of personal qualities that derive their strength from an inner complexity (whether tumultuous, conflicted, or harmonious), while there are others whose practice relies more heavily on their ability to deal with exterior forces. This chapter is concerned with the interior forces that characterize leadership.

Leadership and Unconscious Fantasies

Executives are fascinated by the question of leadership, but they are also deeply troubled by it. It is troubling not only to those who exercise leadership, but also to those who must submit to it and to those who study the phenomenon. It is in its affective elements that the complexity of leadership is most clearly manifested. The exercise of authority, particularly when an individual is in a position to impose her vision on the world, inevitably involves aggression. The more powerful the leader and the greater her authority, the more she will fear going too far in the exercise of that authority (expressing her aggressiveness), and the more susceptible she will become to the internal conflicts related to her success. Our affects strongly influence the cognitive aspects of our personalities (Shapiro, 1965), and executives are no exception (Kets de Vries and Miller, 1984b). The exercise of leadership can activate or reactivate the most primitive and archaic fantasies that lie at the core of intellectual activity and individual behavior.

Understanding the nature of an individual's leadership requires an attempt to understand the core of her inner life. Moments of crisis in an individual's life, when personal defenses are most strongly engaged or weakened, best reveal this core, which constitutes the inner truth of the leader. Without a doubt, understanding organizations assumes understanding by analysis, as thoroughly as we can, the leaders who largely determine what these organizations are like. This type of understanding, as is the case in individual psychoanalysis, includes the discovery of an organization's unconscious dynamic, personalized in the figure of the leader.

Freud was not the first to discover the importance of this "inner truth." Socrates and Plato had already recognized the importance of self-knowledge for enlightened thought and action. Somewhat closer to us, Giambattista Vico, in 1709, was challenging the dominant place of reason in traditional Western philosophy. For Vico, "The first science to be learnt should be mythology or the interpretation of fables," because "truth" exists only in fantasy (*universale fantastico*), which is the first way in which human beings render their world intelligible (Altman, 1991, p. 4). Languages, stories, literature, and fables form the basis of our interpretation of the world. The fantasmal universe, although it appears to be antiscientific, in fact brings us back to the very basis and foundation of science.

Like Vico, modern psychoanalysis maintains that knowledge and science, in fact all human action and behavior, are based in the "universal fantasy" by which human beings find (their) truth and render the world intelligible. Unconscious fantasies are much more than the dreams, daydreams, intuitions, and other mental activities that accompany our actions; they are the profound structures that underlie a person's entire existence (Isaacs, [1952] 1966).

What is true for ordinary human beings is all the more so for those exceptional people, leaders. Apart from case studies, some of which I will be discussing in the next section of this chapter, there have been very few attempts to uncover the unconscious fantasies underlying leadership. Kets de Vries and Miller have established the basis for this type of research by identifying five of these unconscious fantasies that are already well documented in psychoanalytic and psychiatric literature: believing that one is threatened by an external danger and being ready to attack and to defy (the paranoid executive); not wishing to be at anyone's mercy and exerting a tight control over one's surroundings (the obsessive-compulsive executive); needing to be at center stage in order to attract attention or to impress (the dramatic executive); feeling incapable, unworthy, or powerless (the depressive executive); and wishing to maintain distance in relationships with others, in order to avoid pain and conflict (the schizoid executive). (See Chapter Ten of this book for further discussion.)

In another publication, Kets de Vries (1989d) identifies some other unconscious fantasies that underlie the exercise of leadership. Noting that the myth of Narcissus is gradually displacing the myth of Oedipus in people's attempts to understand the unconscious, Kets de Vries describes three types of narcissistic leaders: the reactive narcissist whose unconscious fantasy is, "I was let down and I deserve to be compensated; I have special rights"; the self-deceptive narcissist whose unconscious fantasy is, "I was so favored that I must be (or I am) perfect"; and the constructive narcissist whose unconscious fantasy is, "I have special talents that allow me to make an impression on the world, but I have to deal with my personal limitations and those imposed by external reality." Finally, Kets de Vries (1989a)

uses the term *alexithymia* to characterize "the new version of the
organization man" whose unconscious fantasy is, "By not putting words to feelings, one can live one's life as if they [feelings]
didn't exist." He also identifies the feelings of imposture sometimes experienced by entrepreneurs, leaders, and all successful
individuals, feelings that have little to do with their real worth
(Kets de Vries, 1990a). Their accompanying unconscious fantasy would be, "I don't deserve the success that I have obtained.
If they ever found out where I really come from or who I really
am, it would be a disaster, and would result in the failure I
deserve."

Subjectivity, Personality, and Leadership

People know more than they think about questions dealing with
personality and thus about leadership issues, whether these have
to do with vision, imagination, creation, or exercising authority, and about the determinants of one's success or failure —
Kets de Vries's F-dimension (1989d) or the danger of hubris
(1990c) or the Icarus paradox that Miller (1990) describes. This
knowledge is often neither formal nor explicit. It consists rather
of a felt knowledge that is experiential or intuitive, hidden or
covert, a knowledge that is in part unconscious but that one
can discover throughout one's life. The aim of personal psychoanalysis is precisely this: to uncover what we already know,
to render it explicit, to put words to our knowledge. Analysands
put themselves in a situation where they can overcome their
fears, defenses, and inhibitions in order to regress and rediscover what has been repressed. As far as sensitivity, affects, and
fantasies are concerned, children (candidates for neurosis) experience more than they show and often more than they can
bear. They know too much, and so they are forced to repress
this intolerable awareness. In the course of analysis, analysands
are gradually led to become conscious of, to rediscover, and to
tame their unconscious fantasmal universe of fantasies and the
affects that form its core. They can thus gradually let go of some
of their defenses and acquire an increased capacity for self-
knowledge and understanding of their own behavior.

Of course, not everyone needs to undergo personal analysis in order to discover and to tame their "inner reality." Life provides natural therapy for the majority of human beings. Nonetheless, with or without personal psychoanalysis, any individual, and especially one who is in a leadership position that allows her to project her desires and fantasies onto her world, has a very great responsibility not only to herself but also to those who follow her. She has a moral obligation to be aware of what is going on inside her in order not to become its victim, nor to victimize other people.

Projection is a double-edged sword. Although it fosters the development of a creative imagination, empathy, and understanding, by enabling us to put ourselves in another person's place, it can also be the source of illusions and mirages. This observation also holds true in the therapeutic relationship, in the relationship between researcher and subject, and in the relationship between leader and subordinate. Kernberg (1979) points out the paranoid potential in leadership, since the leader is "utilized" to fulfill the desires of subordinates to place themselves in the hands of an all-powerful omnipotent figure. Kets de Vries (1989c) shows that subordinates sometimes use the leader as a mirror that reflects their own expectations. The leader thus becomes the screen or the container into which they project all their fantasies and demands. We can thus see the need to keep an open mind and nurture the awareness that is indispensable for judgment, in both leader and subordinate.

Case Histories

In this section, I will look at what a clinical case history is as well as at some of the characteristics that underlie the subjective processes that go into its construction. I will then go on to examine the way case studies can contribute to our understanding of leadership.

The Clinical Approach

The clinical approach is a scientific method whose aim is to acquire a thorough understanding of individual cases. It was first used in the study and treatment of individuals, but it has now spread to the study of organizational and social practices. Through a phenomenological approach and exhaustive efforts at description, clinical researchers strive to uncover the subjective experience of their subject and to understand the meaning of this experience (Sillamy, 1980). Whatever information-gathering techniques are used, clinical methods presuppose a direct and relatively extended relationship between the investigator and the object of investigation.

It is a method in which researchers themselves act as information-gathering instruments as well as interpreters of raw material that must be organized and in which meaning must be found. It is only when they are actually writing up a case history that the researchers are transformed into authors, creating a "text," a narrative telling the subject's story. This story is then submitted to the intersubjective interpretations of a scientific community. The case study is not a scientific argument, nor is it an account of causal connections. It is a story that reveals the coherent and complex network of signifiers and signified and that, in psychoanalysis for example, sets out the meaning of the analysand's symptoms, dreams, and parapraxes (slips of the tongue). It translates and decodes rather than explains them (Edelson, 1984, p. 586).

The Clinical Approach and Theory

The clinical method is generally associated with phenomenological processes. Phenomenology is an approach that leaves all theoretical knowledge aside (Sillamy, 1980). Lyotard (1969) states that "subjective certainty" (p. 12) and "a repudiation of science" (p. 7) constitute the essence of phenomenology. However, it seems to me to be impossible to wipe the slate entirely clean of all theory in any research approach, even one that is phenomenological.

Psychoanalysis, which has contributed to the development of the clinical approach as a research method, represents not only a mode of investigation and a form of therapy, but a theoretical corpus as well. It presents the hypothesis that an individual's unconscious holds the latent meaning of all manifest behavior. Thus, in the case studies of leadership that have grown out of this perspective, I use the hypothesis that there is a meaning and a profound structure underlying the actions of those who control the fate of others. There are a number of different subtheories about the unconscious within the psychoanalytic movement. Researchers not only have the obligation to be aware of the theoretical choices made but also the duty to state them as explicitly as possible. A theory, even when it is in a hypothetical state, is the organizing projection behind the research. "Without theory, there is no narrative and without narrative, there is no text to decode or to interpret" (Zaleznik and Kets de Vries, 1991).

Finally, researchers have to make choices. Only some theories can be used; others must be discarded. Investigators must learn to mourn certain possibilities. When we adopt a subjective perspective, when we hypothesize an unconscious that carries the latent meaning of human action, when we use the concept of unconscious fantasy as representing these deep-rooted structures of the personality, we are irremediably turning our back on a certain scientific community, which in turn turns its back on us.

The Subjectivity of Researcher-Authors

When one writes case histories about leaders, one generally does not have access to material that is as direct as the free associations of a patient in the middle of prolonged psychoanalytic treatment. But whether one uses direct interviews with the leader, autobiographies, memoirs, newspaper articles, or other public or historical documents, the spirit and the nature of the process remain the same. Given the impossibility of direct contact with a historical figure, for example, researchers must use an extra measure of caution.

In addition to being on the lookout for all the significant facts, information, or indicators, researchers unable to achieve the state of "free-floating attention" that Freud talks about, or to listen with Reik's "third ear," attempt instead to read between

the lines to gain a thorough understanding of what may constitute the "inner truth" of an individual's existence. Nothing comes
as a surprise; researchers do not judge, and they remain open
to meaning. Although what actually drives a leader may be quite
extraordinary, researchers are not shocked by it. They play the
detective's role (Kets de Vries and Miller, 1987a) and look for
the key or the keys.

A criticism often leveled at leadership studies carried out
from a psychoanalytic perspective is that they are mainly interested in pathological cases. It is true that the clinical approach
was originally developed as a method to treat the sick. The
knowledge gained from it, however, has furthered our understanding of normality, since numerous mental illnesses are
merely an extreme version of what may be found in a more
moderate degree in healthy people. Also, studying exceptional
beings, like leaders or artists, is interesting for several other reasons. Leaders and artists, whose work relies on projection, are
by definition people who propose new visions, who stand outside the norm. They are therefore a-normal, without necessarily being pathological. In addition, studying exceptional beings
holds an interest that goes beyond the boundaries of merely
studying the exercise of authority or power. Those who realize
great things at a given moment in their lives offer us the opportunity to examine openly the elements that often remain hidden potentialities within many other people, and to do so as
if we were using a magnifying glass, because these elements have
been enlarged.

The work of gathering and analyzing data is necessary
but insufficient to provide us with any really profound understanding. The case history must be communicated in a lively,
complete, and detailed manner. A single detail may be extremely
revealing, without bogging the reader down in anecdotal and
commonplace material. The data may be presented in any way
the author chooses (according to behavior patterns, themes, chro-
nology, and so on). Nonetheless, although patterns can emerge
from an analysis of the material, the meaning cannot. The author of a case history has to do the work of an interpreter in
order to touch the "soul" of the leader.

The creation of the text calls not only on the researchers' abilities to gather, analyze, and sort pertinent material but also on their talents as storytellers and writers. It is in the organization of the case material that the true art of case histories is revealed. It is not enough merely to describe, one has to "deeply describe" (Geertz, 1973). The narrative abilities of case history authors depend on the authors' capacity to empathize with their subject, and this in turn depends on their degree of insight. The style, the metaphors, and the images used are all chosen to impart an understanding of the underlying structure of the personality that is being presented, that is, the person's dreams, her inner truth, her drama, or the grand obsession pushing her to act.

The work of interpreting this text, and the work of conceptualizing, explaining, and theorizing still remains to be done; this work is the same as that required by any other undertaking in interpretive science. Nevertheless, I agree completely with Zaleznik and Kets de Vries's statement (1991) that no theory about leadership can serve as a substitute for case histories produced by researchers who have been trained in clinical work. These texts constitute material that is fundamental to any significant study of leadership.

Clinical Case Studies and "Deep Understanding"

We have already seen that it is possible to identify the unconscious fantasies that underlie a number of leadership practices. However, it is by studying leaders case by case that one can best arrive at an understanding of all the distinctive characteristics of these fantasies.

In 1970, Sudhir Kakar published a study of Frederick Winslow Taylor, a leader who has indelibly marked our thinking about management. Kakar draws our attention to the immense degree of suppressed aggression Taylor felt toward his strict, severe, and energetic mother, whom he also idealized, and the manifest aggression he directed toward his gentle, tender, erudite, and distant father, whom Taylor perceived as psychologically weak. The hostility and aggression Taylor felt for his mother, who taught him to repress his emotions and convinced him of the value of hard work, were transformed by reaction into admiration. Disappointed in his expectations from his distant father, who seemed more interested in his hobbies, Taylor transformed his loving feelings for this "weak" or "passive" father into rejection.

By splitting his perception of his two parents (admiration for his "good" mother and contempt for his "bad" father), Taylor blinded himself to the reality that he carried both his (good and bad) father and his (good and bad) mother within himself. He prevented himself from seeing his desire to be loved by both his parents and to love them both as well. In order to become aware of this desire, he would have had to admit his aggression (the repressed emotion that he turned inward against himself during his depressive episodes) and to introject the "feminine gentleness" of his father. One feels that at the end of his life, Taylor attempted to restore the relationship with his father: He returned to Germantown, adopted a family identical to his own, and became a golf-playing man of leisure who devoted himself to defending his system of scientific management. One detects a certain deception and bitterness in Taylor despite all his professional successes. He died at the age of fifty-nine, which corresponded to the age at which his mother suffered a stroke, whereas his father lived to be over eighty years old.

Our understanding of Taylor's affective life allows us to glimpse the inner dynamic that motivated his scientific contribution: his desire to establish external controls in order to control his internal theater and his emotions. His unconscious fantasy could very well have been, "I must set up strict external controls in order not to fall prey to my desires and emotions." The harness of straps and sticks that he built to wake him from a sleep that was often disturbed by nightmares is a typical example of his need to control externally what was happening within.

In another case study, "Gandhi and the Erotic Fantasy," Kakar (1991) goes in search of Gandhi's "inner truth" by revealing the omnipresence of the erotic fantasy throughout Gandhi's life. This eroticism centers on the mouth; its first objects are mother's milk, food in general, and the body (the flesh) of the mother. It is an eroticism filled with ambivalence and Kakar is correct in describing the irony of this struggle, which is an attempt to regain the oral unity with the mother through oral privation. To avoid seeing the aggression that he ascribes to his father within himself, Gandhi identifies with his victim-mother. One can see the manifestation of the feminine aspects of his personality in his "maternal" solicitude for the private lives of his companions.

Kakar has a thorough knowledge of the Hindu religion, Indian culture and history, the state of Gujarat, and psychoanalysis. He is thus very well placed to establish the various connections between the psychic, spiritual, cultural, and political elements of Gandhi's life. His argument goes as follows: In Gandhi's erotic fantasy (his sensual and sexual passion), chastity (the active nonviolent renunciation of sexual relations) and his fasts (the active nonviolent renunciation of food) allow him to transform his libido into psychic power, spiritual strength, physical energy, and political influence (active nonviolent resistance or disobedience).

Kakar's analysis is primarily gleaned from the autobiography that Gandhi wrote in Gujarati during a lengthy depressive period in his midfifties. This depressive period lent itself particularly well to introspection and to a clearsightedness about his inner reality. In this work, Gandhi reveals his internal conflicts and struggles, his torments, his suffering, his self-accusations, his self-reproaches — and his masochism. He needs to atone, to make reparations for the evil that he feels is dwelling inside him (and by extension in all human nature). According to Kakar, the periods of inner crisis provoked by the three depressive periods of Gandhi's life allow us access to his "inner truth."

Kets de Vries (1990b), who has written extensively about narcissism and imposture, paints a modern portrait that lifts the veil on the tragic drama of Roberto Calvi, the Italian banker whose mysterious death in 1982 sparked an international financial and political scandal. This case study is constructed mainly from secondary sources rather than clinical data. We therefore must make inferences, based on fragmented details, about what could have constituted Calvi's psychic reality. We know little about his parents. We know that they were socially withdrawn and emotionally inadequate. We have the impression that Calvi found them cold and weak. His mother (Maria) is described as conservative and not very receptive to others' needs, desires, and emotions. She failed to support her husband in his desire to improve his career. Although her son attended a school for children of the wealthy, she made him wear plain and unfashionable clothing. The result of this double message was that Roberto felt displaced, inferior, and maladapted. His father (Giacomo) is presented as an ambitious but thwarted man, an accountant whose great desire for success was frustrated by his wife's refusal to allow him to accept overseas postings. We can hypothesize that he blamed his wife for the failure of his career. He seems to have transferred his ambition onto his son and to have made him his representative: The son had to succeed where the father failed. Did Roberto want a strong and omnipotent father, a possessor of secret information and magic solutions? In his adult life, the people with whom he chose to associate all had this image, sometimes tarnished, sometimes impeccable.

One can detect a form of reactive narcissism in Calvi (Kets de Vries and Miller, 1984a), marked by the fantasy of omnipotence. He wanted to be above authority and the law (like the church to a certain extent, and the Mafia, both of which he was involved with), to be "the shadowy person who commands and decides." This narcissistic reaction seems to have been a defense against his deep-seated feelings of impotence. This grandiose and excessive dream (one of unrealistic success) gave rise to unconscious feelings of guilt and fears of reprisal. When, in reaction to feeling very small, one makes oneself "larger than life," one experiences oneself as an impostor and becomes prey to fear: "fear of showing his feelings, fear of not having his feet on the ground, fear of revealing his secrets, fear for his physical safety, fear that his financial empire will be taken away . . . " (Kets de Vries, 1990b, p. 11). Calvi's is ostensibly the story of a man with a tragic fate, a man buffeted by implacable external forces, even though it seems clear that it is his own inner forces that make him the victim of these external ones. The fear of success (or a certain unconscious wish for failure) could be at the core of his psychic life. In fact, the steps that he took to ensure his success were also the ideal ways to ensure his failure.

With these case histories, we aim to understand and not to judge. We cannot claim that the understanding of internal reality we arrive at through them explains everything. More "external" qualities or abilities (communication, political savvy, networks of influence, and so on) undeniably play a large role in leadership. These clinical case studies aim instead to discover the meaning, the blueprint, of a leader's inner reality. The less direct and prolonged contact there is with the leader, the more caution must be used in our interpretations of the unconscious fantasy that underlies her existence. Nevertheless, individual cases like these can bring us closer to what may be considered the universal aspects of leadership.

Works of Fiction

Works of fiction not only serve to entertain; above all, they act as outlets for the anxieties and preoccupations of their creators. The sources for these works lie within their imagination, their fantasmal universe; they are the products of their visions and their projections. They could be termed fantasies that have become reality, in the form of novels, films, and plays. But these creations are more than just the products of visions and projections; they grow out of a process that includes play and pleasure, as well as out of the extensive labor of research and composition. We often underestimate the search for accuracy that is so fundamental to works of fiction, and which in no way inhibits the work of projection and creation. For Balzac ([1831] 1981, p. 9), for example, observation and expression are two essential conditions for talent, but it is "a kind of second sight that allows writers to divine the truth in all possible kinds of situations." For Flaubert ([1857] 1983, p. 456), despite the "torments of style" needed to attain beauty, it is also necessary to be an observer of the human soul, with all the impartiality that is used in the physical sciences: "Great art is scientific and im-

personal. . . . Literature is the result of the same kind of precision as an exact science." Finally, Zola ([1867] 1965, p. 8), one
of the "naturalistic" writers, also talks about "the scientific aim
of work that is devoted to the discovery of what is true." Literature, theater, and the cinema are all engaged in a search for
inner truth that can constitute the object of an interpretive
science.

Besides being the products of their creators' projections,
these works of fiction also consciously or unconsciously act as
a screen for the projections of the readers or spectators. They
become "transitional objects" or "potential spaces" for them (Winnicott, 1951, 1971), ways to recognize themselves, to see the
tragic, the comic, the sublime, the petty, the generous, the perverse, the criminal elements of themselves in a relatively safe
way, because it is at a distance. Authors and artists of talent
and genius, while clearly products of their times, are also constantly one step ahead of their audience, seeking new visions
or forms of expression. They may not conduct scientific research,
but their undertaking is nonetheless one of discovery. This is
what prompted Jean Genet (1968, p. 269) to say: "I go to the
theater to see myself, on the stage (restored in one character
or in multiple characters and in the form of a story) as I would
not — or dare not — see or dream, but as I know myself to be."

Unconscious Fantasies and Leadership

Marguerite Yourcenar, in her *Mémoires d'Hadrien* (1951), having retraced the steps of the Roman emperor and having read
everything she could find about him and his times, decided to
get inside the skin of this historical figure at the end of his life
and to write his will in the form of a letter to his adopted grand-
son, Marcus Aurelius — "To rebuild from the inside that which
the archaeologists of the nineteenth century rebuilt from the outside" (p. 327). In devoting several years of her life to this research, Yourcenar had the impression that she was plumbing
the depths of truth about human existence, and was prompted
to write: "Every being who has ever experienced the human adventure is me" (p. 342).

At the end of the novel, Yourcenar incorporates a letter that Arrian, the Greek historian and philosopher, sends to Hadrian on the occasion of the former's voyage to the Black Sea. Arrian tells of his visit to the island of Achilles, where "the shadow of Patrocles appears by Achilles' side" (p. 296). He ends his letter with the following remarks: "Achilles seems at times to me to be the greatest of men, because of his courage, his strength of spirit, the lucidity of his mind coupled with the agility of his body, and his ardent love for his young companion. And nothing in him seems greater to me than the despair that makes him despise life and wish for death when he loses his loved one" (p. 296).

Yourcenar understands that Hadrian, who never recovered from the suicide of Antinous, his young favorite who was said to be "as beautiful as a god," shared Achilles' life drama. Grappling with a depressive state for the rest of his life, Hadrian sought beauty in art and secretly hoped for death. Yourcenar makes him say, "Arrian knows that what is important will never appear in official biographies, nor be inscribed on tombstones. . . . Seen by him, my life's adventure assumes a meaning, takes on the form of a poem" (p. 297). Yourcenar, like Arrian, interpreted the "text" of Hadrian's life and gave us its meaning. It is often the enlightened outside observer who can best grasp and reveal the truth or the meaning that lies behind the life of a leader.

Cinema can clearly demonstrate the way talented creators are able to successfully portray the meaning underlying a person's life drama. In the film *Citizen Kane,* Orson Welles drew inspiration from certain aspects of the life of the American newspaper magnate William Randolph Hearst, as well as projecting some elements of his own personality into the story. The film tells the story of the turbulent career of a rather narcissistic person who is desperate for love; he spends a fortune trying to buy affection and to impress others and attract their attention. At the end of his life, he lives alone in a castle-monument filled with things but empty of love. This film, which for decades has been considered the greatest film ever made, introduces us to a documentary film reporter in search of the "truth" about Charles Foster Kane, who has recently died. With him, we dis-

cover that when Kane was a child, his mother, suddenly becoming unexpectedly rich, decided to entrust her son's upbring-
ing to a banker who was to give him an education that would
guarantee his future success and secure his wealth. Throughout
the rest of his life, he is unknowingly and unsuccessfully attempting to regain this lost childhood, symbolized by the name "Rose-
bud" written on the sled that he had when he was still at home.

In another more recent and very successful work, the film
Mon oncle d'Amérique, the director Alain Renais uses an ingeni-
ous device to illustrate the unconscious fantasies underlying the
existence of each of the main characters. They each have a film
star they consider their hero or heroine. At important moments
of their lives, scenes from the hero's or heroine's films spring
to their minds. For Janine Garnier, who comes from a working-
class background and is looking for a stage from which to shine
and be loved, the hero is Jean Marais; we see him in his famous scenes and in very theatrical poses. René Ragueneau, a
character who comes from a peasant background and who is
looking for raw power, considers Jean Gabin his hero; we see
Gabin in scenes in which he displays his strength and his rage.
Finally, the heroine of Jean Le Gall, who comes from a professional bourgeois background but is looking for tenderness, is
Danielle Darrieux; in her films, she uses her eyes to enchant,
and various Prince Charmings clasp her in their arms. Renais
presents these three characters as "sleepwalkers" (the subtitle of
his film), victims of their unconscious, an internalized sociocul-
ture, all of them expecting success or happiness to arrive by
magic, which is what the expression *mon oncle d'Amérique* ("my
American uncle") signifies in France. The list of works of fiction
that can contribute to our understanding of the inner reality
underlying leadership is quite long. The few examples just discussed can give us an idea of their potential utilization as objects of research.

Leadership Development

Understanding research in leadership does not merely imply a
desire to understand the phenomenon and how it manifests it-

self; it is also intended to help the leaders who are the objects of the research. Like everyone else, leaders can never know themselves completely, nor do they ever stop evolving. As we have seen, through the exercise of her leadership, the leader can come to control her own destiny and that of other people; however, because of the possibility of giving free expression to her desires, her whims, her perverse inclinations, and her inner conflicts, she can also become destructive to herself and to those around her.

How can we encourage the development of an individual's leadership potential? How do we nurture the imagination and the inner life of a leader? How can we encourage each individual to discover her own authentic expressions of leadership? How do we make someone aware of the dangers of paranoid potential in a practice where projection plays a central role, when her basic functioning itself relies on the projection, into the outside world, of the visions arising from her fantasy world? There are no easy answers to these questions. In concluding this chapter, I would like to suggest certain avenues of reflection about the way in which case histories and works of fiction may be used to develop leadership. Earlier, I compared leaders to artists and suggested that the projection of their internal reality is what forms the basis of their practice. Schools of art choose candidates who show evident talent, but who also demonstrate a sensitivity that could be used to advantage in the exercise of a given art. They are taught a number of techniques, are made to practice basic skills, but above all, they are asked to produce, to perform, under the supervision of masters whose task is to make them discover their inner wealth and their own "genuine" talents.

There are many different types of artists, and they require very different approaches on the part of their teachers. There are various ways to devote oneself to creation; this is true also for leadership and management. If one draws an analogy with two different types of performers in the theater, the leader would correspond to the actor who is more inclined to project her own personality into the character she portrays, transforming it and developing it in line with the person she is herself. It is the character who gets under her skin. The manager, on the other hand, would be the actor whose talent lies in internalizing the requirements of his role and allowing himself to be guided by the author's and director's instructions and by analyses of his character, the period, and the play. It is he who gets under the skin of his character. One is not necessarily superior to the other, but it seems clear that the approach of the actor-leader is riskier for the artist as a person, and it can also be more fascinating for the spectator. Because it reposes on her own personality, the training of the actor-leader is a very delicate process.

Even though it is impossible to conceive of schools of leadership modeled after schools of art, they can nonetheless become sources of inspiration for their students. As far as the technical knowledge and basic skills required by the manager are concerned, existing executive training programs are relatively well equipped. As for the discovery of the inner wealth and the genuine talents of the leader, this remains primarily the individual's responsibility, but the case studies and works of fiction that serve as research tools in our attempts to understand the leadership phenomenon could be used as leadership developers in candidates interested in developing their potential.

This can happen in two ways: through identification and through development per se. When discussing these case studies and works of fiction, individuals can identify with the leaders in the case or in the story. They may find certain aspects of themselves in this person (projective identification), or they may attempt to appropriate certain qualities of the leader that they wish to possess (introjective identification). The leadership potential may also be more directly developed. Photographers use a developer, that is, a chemical product that converts the latent image recorded on film into a visible image. In a similar way, leadership candidates may need the influence of a developer to transform the potential that has been lying in a negative state within them into something positive. Clinical case histories and works of fiction could be used as developers of this negative.

Once again, we can establish a parallel with personal analysis, a process of affective development in which the analytical experience acts as a developer whose aim is to transform all that has up until now remained in a latent or negative state within the analysand into something positive. In the same way, guided by clinical teachers who play the role of "tutors," discussions of case histories and works of fiction that present us with leaders (whether pathological or well balanced) provide an increased possibility for the leader-in-training to interpret the "text" of the actions of other leaders. This research material could also be used to raise the individual's awareness of whatever has remained negative within her. The insight thus gained can permit her to mobilize this potential, which has remained hidden, in a creative way and to guard against its destructive aspects. This can represent the work of a lifetime.

References

Altman, E. "Les concepts d'imagination: Une histoire inachevée" [Concepts of the imagination: An incomplete history]. In L. Lapierre (ed.), *Imaginaire et leadership: Fantasmes inconscients et pratiques de leadership* [The imaginary and leadership: Unconscious fantasies and leadership practices]. Quebec: Les Presses de l'Université Laval, 1991.

Balzac, H. de. *La peau de chagrin* [The wild ass's skin]. Paris: Librairie Générale Française, 1981. (Originally published 1831.)

Barnard, C. *The Functions of an Executive*. Cambridge, Mass.: Harvard University Press, 1938.

Bass, B. M. *Stodgill's Handbook of Leadership*. New York: Free Press, 1981.

Boucenne, P., and Pivot, B. *La bibliothèque idéale* [The ideal library]. Paris: Albin Michel, 1988.

Burns, J. M. *Leadership*. New York: Harper & Row, 1978.

Cardinal, M. *Les mots pour le dire* [The words to say it]. Paris: Gasset, 1975.

Cohen, A. *Belle du Seigneur*. Paris: Gallimard, 1968.

Edelson, M. *Hypothesis and Evidence in Psychoanalysis*. Chicago: University of Chicago Press, 1984.

Emerson, R. M. "Observational Field Work." *Annual Review of Sociology*, 1981, *7*, 351–378.

Erikson, E. *Young Man Luther: A Study in Psychoanalysis and History.* New York: Norton, 1958.

Erikson, E. *Gandhi's Truth: On the Origins of Militant Nonviolence.* New York: Norton, 1969.

Flaubert, G. *Madame Bovary.* Paris: Librairie Générale Française, 1983. (Originally published 1857.)

Freud, S. "Group Psychology and the Analysis of the Ego." In J. Strachey (ed. and trans.), *The Standard Edition of the Complete Psychological Works of Sigmund Freud.* Vol. 18. London: Hogarth Press, 1955. (Originally published 1921.)

Freud, S. "The Interpretation of Dreams." In J. Strachey (ed. and trans.), *The Standard Edition of the Complete Psychological Works of Sigmund Freud.* Vol. 5. London: Hogarth Press, 1962. (Originally published 1900.)

Freud, S. "Analysis Terminable and Interminable." In J. Strachey (ed. and trans.), *The Standard Edition of the Complete Psychological Works of Sigmund Freud.* Vol. 23. London: Hogarth Press, 1964. (Originally published 1937.)

Geertz, C. C. *The Interpretation of Cultures.* New York: Basic Books, 1973.

Genet, J. "Comment jouer les bonnes" [How to play the maids]. *Oeuvres complètes.* Vol. 4. Paris: Gallimard, 1968.

Goffman, I. *The Presentation of Self in Everyday Life.* New York: Anchor Books, 1959.

Isaacs, S. "Nature et fonction du phantasme" [The nature and function of fantasy]. In Klein, M., Heimann, P., Isaacs, S., and Rivière, J., *Développements de la psychanalyse* [Developments in psychoanalysis]. Paris: Presses Universitaires de France, 1966. (Originally published 1952.)

Kakar, S. *Frederick Taylor: A Study in Personality and Innovation.* Cambridge: MIT Press, 1970.

Kakar, S. "Gandhi and the Erotic Fantasy." In L. Lapierre (ed.), *Imaginaire et leadership: Fantasmes inconscients et pratiques de leadership* [The imaginary and leadership: Unconscious fantasies and leadership practices]. Quebec: Les Presses de l'Université Laval, 1991.

Kernberg, O. "Regression in Organizational Leadership." *Psychiatry,* 1979, *42,* 24–39.

Kets de Vries, M.F.R. *Organizational Paradoxes: Clinical Approaches to Management.* London: Tavistock, 1980.

Kets de Vries, M.F.R. "Alexithymia in Organizational Life: The Organization Man Revisited." *Human Relations,* 1989a, *42* (12), 1079-1093.

Kets de Vries, M.F.R. *Carlo de Benedetti: The Builder.* Fontainebleau, France: INSEAD, 1989b. (Case study.)

Kets de Vries, M.F.R. "The Leader as Mirror: Clinical Reflections." *Human Relations,* 1989c, *42* (7), 607-628.

Kets de Vries, M.F.R. *Prisoners of Leadership.* New York: Wiley, 1989d.

Kets de Vries, M.F.R. "The Impostor Syndrome: Developmental and Societal Issues." *Human Relations,* 1990a, *43* (7), 667-686.

Kets de Vries, M.F.R. *Leaders on the Couch: The Case of Roberto Calvi.* Fontainebleau, France: INSEAD, 1990b. (Case study.)

Kets de Vries, M.F.R. "The Organizational Fool: Balancing a Leader's Hubris." *Human Relations,* 1990c, *43* (8), 751-770.

Kets de Vries, M.F.R. (ed.). *The Irrational Executive: Psychoanalytic Studies in Management.* New York: International Universities Press, 1984.

Kets de Vries, M.F.R., and Miller, D. "Narcissism and Leadership." *Human Relations,* 1984a, *38* (6), 583-601.

Kets de Vries, M.F.R., and Miller, D. *The Neurotic Organization: Diagnosing and Changing Counterproductive Styles of Management.* San Francisco: Jossey-Bass, 1984b.

Kets de Vries, M.F.R., and Miller, D. "Personality, Culture, and Organization." *Academy of Management Review,* 1986, *11* (2), 266-279.

Kets de Vries, M.F.R., and Miller, D. "Interpreting Organizational Texts." *Journal of Management Studies,* 1987a, *24* (3), 233-248.

Kets de Vries, M.F.R., and Miller, D. *Unstable at the Top: Inside the Troubled Organization.* New York: New American Library, 1987b.

Kohut, H. *The Analysis of the Self.* New York: International Universities Press, 1971.

Kohut, H. *The Restoration of the Self.* New York: International Universities Press, 1977.

Lapierre, L. "Imaginaire, gestion et leadership" [Fantasies, management, and leadership]. In *Gestion: Revue Internationale de Gestion,* 1987, *12* (1), 6–14.

Lapierre, L. "Mourning, Potency, and Power in Management." *Human Relations,* 1989, *28* (2), 177–189.

Lapierre, L. (ed.). *Imaginaire et leadership: Fantasmes inconscients et pratiques de leadership* [The imaginary and leadership: Unconscious fantasies and leadership practices]. Quebec: Les Presses de l'Université Laval, 1991.

Le Guen, C., Flournoy, O., Stengers, I., and Guillaumin, J. *La psychanalyse: Une science?* [Psychoanalysis: A science?] (VIIièmes rencontres psychanalytiques d'Aix-en-Provence, 1988.) Paris: Les Belles Lettres, 1989.

Levinson, H. *Executive: The Guide to Responsive Management.* Cambridge, Mass.: Harvard University Press, 1981.

Lyotard, J. F. *La phénoménologie* [Phenomenology]. In *Collection Que Sais-je?* Paris: Presses Universitaires de France, 1969.

Miller, D. *The Icarus Paradox.* New York: Harper & Row, 1990.

Shapiro, D. *Neurotic Styles.* New York: Basic Books, 1965.

Sillamy, N. *Dictionnaire de psychologie* [Dictionary of psychology]. Vols. 1 and 2. Paris: Bordas, 1980.

Stogdill, R. M. *Handbook of Leadership: A Survey of Theory and Research.* New York: Free Press, 1974.

Winnicott, D. W. *Transitional Objects and Transitional Phenomena.* London: Tavistock, 1951.

Winnicott, D. W. *Playing and Reality.* London: Tavistock, 1971.

Yourcenar, M. *Mémoires d'Hadrien* [Memoirs of Hadrian]. Paris: Gallimard, 1951.

Zaleznik, A. "Managers and Leaders: Are They Different?" *Harvard Business Review,* 1977, *55,* 67–78.

Zaleznik, A. *The Managerial Mystique: Restoring Leadership in Business.* New York: Harper & Row, 1989.

Zaleznik, A. "The Leadership Gap." *The Academy of Management Executive,* 1990, *4* (1), 7–22.

Zaleznik, A., and Kets de Vries, M.F.R. *Power and the Corporate Mind.* Boston: Houghton Mifflin, 1975.

Zaleznik, A., and Kets de Vries, M.F.R. "Le Leadership comme texte: Un essai sur l'interprétation" [Leadership as text: An essay on interpretation]. In L. Lapierre (ed.), *Imaginaire et leadership: Fantasmes inconscients et pratiques de leadership* [The imaginary and leadership: Unconscious fantasies and leadership practices]. Quebec: Les Presses de l'Université Laval, 1991.

Zola, E. *Thérèse Raquin.* (2nd ed.) Paris: Fasquelle, 1965. (Originally published 1867.)

PART TWO

The Leadership Conundrum

4

------◆•◆•◆•◆------

Leading and Managing: Understanding the Difference

Abraham Zaleznik

It appears that many business executives, who used to think of themselves as potential if not actual leaders, became professional managers and absorbed the managerial mystique. While walking blindly along the path of the corporate career, they fell into the trap that Sigmund Freud first identified as "suggestibility," a mental state in which thinking and feeling separate and hence widen the rift between the mind and the heart and between logic and common sense.

The managerial mystique is only tenuously tied to reality. As it evolved in practice, the mystique required managers to dedicate themselves to process, structures, roles, and indirect forms of communication and to ignore ideas, people, emotions, and direct talk. It deflected attention from the realities of business, while it reassured and rewarded those who believed in the mystique.

The extent to which reality becomes distorted in the workings of the managerial mystique is illustrated by a case involving General Motors. A man who had bought a GM luxury car complained to his dealer that the transmission was not working properly. He was told that the problem would clear up after a suitable break-in period. The problem did not clear up and, moreover, the irate customer discovered that he had to replace

97

the transmission at his own expense, because the warranty period
had expired while he waited for the spontaneous cure promised
by the dealer. The mechanic who examined the car pointed out
that he could replace the transmission, but that it would not
last six months because the transmission specified for this large
car belonged to a small car. Evidently, people at GM had specified an inadequate transmission system and neglected product
quality and customer satisfaction, either to rectify their own mistakes in scheduling or to cut additional expenses. The customer
initiated a class action suit, and in February 1989 GM agreed
to settle for $19.2 million.

Within a few days after GM settled the suit, the corporation declared its intention to repurchase up to 20 percent of its
common stock at a cost estimated at over $5 billion. The pur-
pose of the stock buyback was plain: to increase the price of
the stock by dividing the existing earnings among fewer shares.
In the meantime, GM had lost market share not only to foreign competition but also to Ford and Chrysler. Instead of
presenting a program of improved product design, quality, and
value to overcome its competitive weakness, GM chose a financial solution to refurbish its image with the investment community. The solution typifies the thinking inherent in the managerial mystique: act on form and hope substantive solutions will
follow.

Executives, intent on adapting to the world around them
and on making their way up the career ladder, actively seek
to be indoctrinated into modern management. They relinquish
their ability to think. They adopt slogans and formulas instead
of developing the arts of self-examination that stimulate the
imagination as well as toughen analytical thinking. And, unfortunately, the growing impact of business schools, which in
the 1960s began mass-producing M.B.A.'s, drove dissenters
from the managerial mystique underground.

Are Leaders and Managers Synonymous?

In September 1976, *Time* magazine conducted a conference on
leadership in Washington, D.C. *Time* invited 200 young leaders

to consider "that illusive, indefinable, yet recognizable quality" called leadership, which it had become apparent now existed only in a much-diminished state. *Time* also invited four professors to present their analyses of what had gone wrong with leadership in the United States. In the working paper, which subsequently appeared in the *Harvard Business Review* under the title "Managers and Leaders: Are They Different?" (Zaleznik, 1977), I argued that managers and leaders *are* different. They have different personalities and experience different developmental paths from childhood to adulthood. They differ in what they attend to and in how they think, work, and interact.

Interestingly enough, this line of reasoning corresponds with the work of Bernard Bass (1985), one of the foremost scholars on leadership. In his empirical studies he discovered five factors that seem to differentiate leaders from managers: charisma, individual consideration, intellectual stimulation, contingent reward, and management by exception. These factors very much parallel my own clinical observations, as the rest of this chapter will demonstrate.

One of the ideas that generated the most controversy as well as interest at the *Time* conference was that leaders grow through mastering painful conflict during their developmental years, while managers confront few of the experiences that generally cause people to turn inward. Managers perceive life as a steady progression of positive events, resulting in security at home, in school, in the community, and at work. Leaders are "twice-born" individuals who endure major events that lead to a sense of separateness, or perhaps estrangement, from their environments (James, [1902] 1985). As a result, they turn inward in order to reemerge with a created rather than an inherited sense of identity. That sense of separateness may be a necessary condition for the ability to lead.

It is easy to confuse the idea of separateness with narcissism. True narcissism is a pathological state in which the individual unconsciously tries to overcome a fragmented ego by overvaluing personal fantasy and undervaluing the real world, including other people. The historian Christopher Lasch (1979) claims that a whole generation can be infected with the pathology of narcissism and asserts that young people reflect this pathology in valuing their own pleasures at the expense of obligation to others.

The feeling of being separate, which is characteristic of leaders, is different from narcissism. The leader is aware of boundaries and can distinguish the inner and outer worlds, fantasy and reality, self and other people. Career-oriented managers are more likely to exhibit the effects of narcissism than leaders. While busily adapting to their environment, managers are narrowly engaged in maintaining their identity and self-esteem through others, whereas leaders have self-confidence growing out of the awareness of who they are and the visions that drive them to achieve.

On reflection, it is striking to note how rarely leadership is associated with business. That business and leadership are not popularly associated is a result of the anonymity that is cherished in the managerial mystique (Zaleznik, 1989), an antihero ethos that places a premium on the team over the individual. And in its team orientation, the managerial mystique views cooperation as one technical device among many that helps to secure goals while enhancing one's professional image. The tail has come to wag the dog. In our obsession with teamwork, we have collectively failed to recognize that individuals are the only source of ideas and energy.

Why Is U.S. Industry Less Competitive?

The causes of the decline in U.S. industry are complex, but at the forefront is the attitude of American management. After World War II the United States focused primarily on maintaining and exploiting technological developments in the mature industries, such as steelmaking, metal fabrication, and machine tool and electric appliance manufacturing, instead of fostering innovation. In the 1960s and 1970s, managers deemphasized manufacturing and focused instead on superficial product changes and finance, which led to lower-quality products. Essentially, business in America lost its competitive advantage by focusing on profits and stock prices instead of fostering innovation and long-term goals.

Perhaps worst of all, the United States is now a debtor nation and, like any other debtor nation, must deal with the serious consequences of that condition. There will soon be an awakening, when Americans are forced to realize that they must tighten their belts, save instead of spend, and invest instead of consume.

The natural tendency is to look to Washington for leadership in times of economic crisis. Executive and congressional leadership, however, will react slowly and keep the nation asleep until the crisis is full blown. Until that time, business itself will have to assume responsibility for the deterioration in America's competitive position.

It could be argued that the problems of American industry derive from political rather than managerial causes. Labor relations in the automobile industry have always been adversarial. During the prosperous post–World War II years labor leaders exercised enormous political clout and extracted rich wage-and-benefits concessions from management. These agreements, in addition, limited management's ability to control work assignments. The net effect was excessive labor costs compared with competitors in Asia and countries such as West Germany. As less developed countries such as Japan, South Korea, and Malaysia leapfrogged the steps toward modernization, they took advantage of low labor rates to achieve competitive advantage in industries such as shipbuilding, steel, and electronics.

A second political argument that seeks to absolve management from responsibility for the decline in competitiveness lays the blame on the foreign policy of the United States during the post–World War II era. Because of the Cold War a large proportion of resources was spent on the military, in both preparedness and actual warfare. Foreign policy supported the rise of West German and Japanese industrial power, showing a willingness to overlook protectionist policies in order to support the development of friendly economies — to the detriment of the domestic economy.

Although these political arguments contain grains of truth, they overlook the broader aims of society. To maintain the U.S. economy by keeping other economies weak would have been shortsighted and destined to repeat the mistakes of World War I.

The response of business leadership should have been a determined drive to increase productivity through research and development of new products and manufacturing processes. With the exception of the high-technology sectors, their response was just the opposite. Steelmakers, automakers, and other top managers in the traditional industry sectors treated their companies as "cash cows" and left innovation to others.

As for labor relations, scarcely any serious efforts were taken to alter the adversarial relationship between organized labor and management. The shortsightedness of labor representatives was more than equaled by the absence of a long-range perspective by management. Making concessions was easy because increased costs could simply be passed along to consumers who, with ample credit, had become extravagant in their buying habits.

If leadership has a common characteristic in different times and circumstances, it is to face situations actively rather than passively, to overcome and transform conditions, not simply to react and adapt to them. The business failures of the 1980s reflect a lack of this kind of effective leadership and an overconcentration on the false virtues of the managerial mystique.

The Seduction of the Managerial Mystique

Business executives believe erroneously that management and leadership are synonymous, that to manage according to the principles of its mystique is to lead. For too long, business managers have put their faith in numbers, managed by process, and formed elaborate structures to get people to do the predictable thing. The truth is that managing and leading are vastly different activities and that, as a result of confusing the two, corporate enterprise has lost its way.

Managers fail to distinguish between form and creativity, while leadership moves beyond the accepted body of knowledge of how to manage a process. The creative executive strikes out in unexplored directions, perhaps extrapolating from management theory but unencumbered by it. Leadership may manifest itself through an idea so compelling that it forces the formal structure to change either permanently or until the idea has been pursued to its conclusion. Leaders are not bound by a process. Indeed, they overcome it, to establish creative programs, ideas, and actions.

Unfortunately, the managerial mystique seduces business executives and even potential leaders into a false sense of security — believing that running a business is not unlike tending a plant nursery, where one prepares the soil, plants the seeds, applies fertilizer and water, and watches as Mother Nature works her magic with the flowers. The mistake in this analogy is that corporate business caretakers, even if they are kindly and diligent, work with no superior entity — no Mother Nature — on hand to ensure survival and to make creative changes during both stable and unpredictable conditions. As the utopian, yet fallacious, managerial mystique continues to be followed, executive performance and business strategies will continue to stagnate and diminish. A rebirth, indeed a resurgence, of creative leadership is essential to overcome the diminished capacity of executive management in American enterprise.

Harold Geneen, the former chief executive officer of ITT, epitomizes the managerial mystique. He believes (1984) that if you can manage one business, you can manage any business. Geneen's belief reflects the arrogant confidence in the mystique of management that has overpowered the mentality of corporate chief executives. If these executives possessed a modicum of sensitivity, they would soon become aware of the cynicism that their confidence engenders in the subordinates who actually run the business. It is doubtful whether Geneen realized that many ITT people derisively called their employer "International This and That," expressing the confusion generated as the company acted out the tenets of the managerial mystique practiced by its chief executive.

The Leadership Compact

Leadership is based on a compact that binds those who lead and those who follow into the same moral, intellectual, and emotional commitment. There were times when this compact existed widely, and it probably still exists in certain places. But, by and large, the tie that binds men and women in organizations today, particularly at the professional and managerial levels, is narrow self-interest, rather than a sense of mutual obligations and responsibilities.

The leadership compact demands commitment to the organization. In the past this commitment was embodied in strong leaders such as Andrew Carnegie, Henry Ford, Pierre du Pont, and Thomas Watson. In more recent times it has been represented by people such as Edwin Land, Walter Wriston, Kenneth Olsen, Ross Perot, An Wang, and Steven Jobs.

Sam Walton, the founder of the Wal-Mart retail chain, exemplifies the leadership compact. His personal attention to merchandising and customer service expresses what he expects from subordinates in the conduct of business. Failure to maintain these standards is a personal defeat as well as a shortfall in mutual obligation.

The legitimacy of the leadership compact arises either from tradition or from the personal qualities of the leader. Tradition operates in monarchies, the military, and religion. It is not so great a factor in purely secular and modern organizations. For a leader to secure commitment from subordinates in business and political organizations, he or she has to demonstrate extraordinary competence or other qualities that subordinates can admire. If the leader fails to demonstrate these personal qualities and is not maintained in his or her role by tradition, the leadership compact begins to disintegrate.

Ronald Reagan's presidency provides an illuminating case. His repeated conversion of complex problems into apocryphal anecdotes reflected his desire to avoid material issues while fostering management by sentiment. Reagan's style is reminiscent of managers who are long on exhortation to "do your best" and short on helping to solve problems. Under such laissez-faire management, subordinates will either act chaotically or abandon any serious effort to get a job done.

An executive vice president of a manufacturing company complained bitterly about the failure of the CEO to heed warnings about the inadequacy of the company's data-processing methods. The executive vice president tried every device at her command to show what the inadequacies would mean in terms of delayed shipments, poor production and scheduling, and imbalanced as well as bloated inventories. The CEO refused to act, urging all his subordinates to make do with what they had available. When the dire predictions became reality, the CEO had already lost the respect of his key subordinates, and they left him to solve the problems without their active support and intervention. In a sense, his incompetence freed them from their obligations and commitment in the leadership compact.

The claim of the leadership compact is that superiors and subordinates should do their utmost to help the organization succeed. Specifically, everyone should help to make authority effective. The idea is to support superiors, to try to see the world through their eyes, to do everything in one's power to help them do their job, and to make up for their shortcomings by diligently overcompensating for their weaknesses.

Leadership and Followership

The leadership compact tells us that we are all in the enterprise together and we must cooperate with our superiors for the success of it. Therefore, under the leadership compact the central question for each generation to solve is not what is leadership, or where do we find leaders for today and tomorrow, or how are they to be made fit for the responsibility—but how to follow. Followership requires a particular attitude and necessitates certain socialization practices.

Felix Rohatyn, investment banker of Lazard Frères, expressed the emotions that cement the relationship between leader and follower in his eulogy given at the memorial service for André Meyer in New York on October 12, 1979. Meyer was Rohatyn's mentor, teacher, leader, and possibly father figure. In a voice cracked with grief, Rohatyn said that he still instinctively reached for the phone to speak to Meyer: "Sometimes I imagine what the conversations would be like, what he would say, but I can't be sure—it's left a terrible void. . . . " He concluded: "He was an Olympian figure: Zeus hurling thunderbolts.

Then he was my teacher. He taught me not only to achieve perfection, but to do it in style" (Reich, 1983, pp. 355–356).

When the leadership compact is in place and functioning, leadership is a straightforward task. Leadership progresses
from followership. It is legitimate for an individual selected for
formal leadership to expect dedication, support, hard work, and
loyalty from subordinates, so that he or she is not ordinarily
confronting subordinates as rivals and enemies, but is working
in concert with them to further the goals of the organization.

This concept of leadership changes the idea of its being
"lonely at the top" to the idea that the top position involves shared
purposes, mutual trust, and implicit support. But the critical
factor in the leadership compact is the willingness of people in
elevated positions to use their power in the best interest of their
subordinates and their organization. In this sense, a leader is
simultaneously a follower in that he or she serves the interest
of multiple groups such as shareholders, subordinates, and customers in the marketplace. The image of management today
falls far short of the sort of dedicated, sometimes selfless, devo-
tion associated with leadership. Instead of compact, the word
is contract, so that managers prosper whether the enterprise succeeds or fails. This is the era of "golden parachutes," stock options almost guaranteed against market declines, and near-
obscene levels of cash compensation at the top.

The leadership compact in business, government, the military, and education today is more a relic of the past than a vital
idea. Anyone ascending to a position of power has little reason
to believe that his or her job will be simplified because everyone is committed to supporting authority. In business, for example, every newly appointed CEO can expect to find people
within the organization who believe that *they* should have been
named to the job instead and that *they* would have performed
more ably. Instead of finding people who are at least willing
to suspend judgment, if not grant enthusiastic acceptance, new
chief executives find critical observers who are all too often glad
to see them blunder. As one newly appointed CEO put it, "I
didn't necessarily expect to find friends among my vice presidents, but I surely didn't plan on living in a hostile world where
key people see my missteps as a chance to add to their power."

Do Managers Lead?

It often happens that executives who ascend to positions of power have never experienced the leadership compact during their career. They were never really followers during all the years of upward movement. As a result, they come ill-equipped to build mutual responsibility and trust as cornerstones of organizational morale.

Admittedly, the leadership compact worked at its best in a simpler time, when organizations could easily define their competition, when the rate of change was much slower than it is today, when family and community stability provided a buttress of support for authority, and when people's conduct and performance on the job was governed by a work ethic. But it is because of the complexity of the times that business and other organizations need leaders who can revive the leadership compact and make it work for the benefit of everyone.

Instead of being leaders, people who rise to the top of organizations are more often than not managers. To make matters worse, they identify themselves as managers and make what they do and how they think synonymous with leadership. The crucial difference between managers and leaders is in their respective commitments. A manager is concerned with *how* decisions are made and *how* communication flows; a leader is concerned with *what* decisions get made and *what* he or she communicates. In short, for the manager it is *style over substance* and *process over reality.*

One of the reasons for the demise of the leadership compact is the failure of authority figures to do their job. Although the traditional view is that a subordinate should support authority figures and the values represented in the idea of authority, it has become exceedingly difficult to maintain this position. Too many examples of incompetence and selfishness appear at the top to sustain the attachment to authority that is necessary in the leadership compact.

For some, the notion that a manager and a leader are different is wrong, if not offensive. For example, in a letter to the editor of the *Harvard Business Review* (1977, p. 148) about the article "Managers and Leaders: Are They Different?," Fred

Bucy, then president of Texas Instruments, Inc., wrote: "I disagree completely with the premise that distinguishes the manager from the leader and says, in effect, that an individual cannot fulfill both roles. This is nonsense. . . . "

Yet Bucy went on to say that there is a distinction to be drawn between the bureaucrat and the innovator. Bucy said that problems with mature industries in the United States arise when bureaucrats are put in charge as a result of their ability to move up the organization, implying that they have few other abilities. He continued, "However, in high-technology industries, the bureaucratic manager will not succeed. The competition and technology move too fast. A combination of strong leadership and excellent managerial capability is required for success" (p. 149).

Although Fred Bucy and other business executives are correct in believing that management is necessary to the orderly guidance of activity in enterprises, they fail to understand that management alone is not sufficient to maintain the vitality of a business.

The Evans Products Company, with headquarters in Portland, Oregon, was a large conglomerate operating in the housing, rail car, forest products, retail home center, and industrial products business. Its organizational structure was a model of decentralization, with clearly delineated profit centers coordinated by a strong staff sitting in corporate headquarters and reporting to Monford Orloff, the CEO. A McKinsey executive compensation plan assured that bonuses were a direct correlate of earnings, so that financial incentives were directed toward meeting goals. Sophisticated budgets provided the tools for measuring performance even within the divisions of the major groups. From top to bottom the credo governing Evans was order, control, and coordination. Yet the company sought protection under Chapter 11 of the Federal Bankruptcy Code in 1985 and was substantially liquidated in 1987.

Evans failed not because of lack of management, but despite its remarkably efficient management outlook and operation, or perhaps *because* of it. The housing and rail car businesses were in a cyclical downturn common to these industries, particularly in response to rising interest rates. Unwilling to let sales and profits decline as a result of scaling down operations in response to the business cycle, Orloff and two of his group presidents decided to continue operations and encourage sales by providing liberal financing for customers. The company put rail cars out on lease and sold houses to consumers so that sales and profit reports continued to look rosy, while increased borrowings buttressed a negative cash flow for the corporation as a whole. The company continued to borrow short and lend long until it ran out of cash and the ability to borrow.

Evans's troubles, along with those of other well-managed companies, began and ended with bad substantive decisions. The delusion of the managerial mystique is that solid methods will produce good results. Management's overriding fantasy is that an array of organizational devices and techniques of control will overcome all human frailties. Managers find it difficult to believe the reality that good and bad substantive decisions are directly related to the strengths and weaknesses of the individuals involved. Their fantasy ignores the fact that their devices and techniques have little effect on the decision makers at the top of the organizational pyramid.

What's the Difference?

Whereas managers focus on process, leaders focus on imaginative ideas. Leaders not only dream up ideas but stimulate and drive other people to work hard and turn those ideas into reality. One such leader had the opportunity to sell a revolutionary product she had invented to a large, established company. Instead of selling to this formidable competitor, the entrepreneur decided to ignore the advice of business consultants and continue with her own company. The consultants believed that instituting management processes would be too costly, time consuming, and difficult for the entrepreneur. They advised, "Why not sell out? Take a large amount of money now. Avoid the risks of a competitive battle with a world-class corporation that has an infrastructure in place and is ready to do battle rather than give up market share to a newcomer." The consultants overstated the importance of process and underestimated the effects of the driving vision of the leader on key subordinates. The company remained independent and produced enormous wealth for the entrepreneur, her associates, and investors.

In contrast to visionary leaders such as Edwin Land, An Wang, and Sam Walton, managers are essentially practical people. Typically, they are hardworking, intelligent, analytical, and tolerant of others. Because they hold few convictions with passion, except perhaps for the need to extract order out of potential chaos, they exhibit a high degree of fair-mindedness in dealing with people.

Leaders are more dramatic in style and unpredictable in behavior. They seem to overcome the conflict between order and chaos with an authority legitimized by personal magnetism and a commitment to their own undertakings and destinies.

Leaders, like artists, are inconsistent in their ability to function well. They are vulnerable to mood swings and experience periods of depression as well as elation, depending on how events affect their self-esteem. Managers, on the other hand, operate within a narrow range of emotions. This emotional blandness, when combined with the preoccupation with process, leads to the impression that managers are inscrutable, detached, and even manipulative.

Indeed, one writer on management acknowledges that management is manipulation carried to the point that subordinates are not supposed to be aware of the fact that they are being manipulated. As one management scholar has stated, "[A manager's methods] border on manipulation, and the stigma associated with manipulation can be fatal. If the organization ever identifies him as a manipulator, his job becomes more difficult. No one willingly submits to manipulation, and those around him organize to protect themselves" (Wrapp, 1967, p. 93). Those around the manipulator, however, are rarely unaware that they are being manipulated. They recognize it and plan their countermanipulations, simultaneously trying to conceal the manipulative motive behind their moves. The game of politics takes root in organizations run by managers rather than leaders.

A classic example of manipulation was orchestrated in 1923 by Alfred P. Sloan, who was running GM. Sloan was the management genius responsible for developing a balanced program of centralization and decentralization in GM. This organizational innovation became a model for organizing and managing large corporations that remains to this day. Sloan was up against the problem of conflict between his manufacturing people and GM's chief inventor, Charles Kettering. The manufacturing people wanted to standardize design so they could mass-produce automobiles efficiently. Kettering proposed an innovation in engine cooling called the copper-cooled engine. This engine still had bugs, whereas the water-cooled engine operated well. The issue was whether the company should move for a better product in the long run or settle for a good workable product immediately. Sloan sided with the manufacturing people but did not let his views be known. He did not want to oppose Kettering, who had the support and admiration of Pierre du Pont, who held a major block of stock in GM.

The managerial solution that Sloan devised appeared to be a compromise. Instead of exercising his authority to make the practical decision in favor of the manufacturing heads, Sloan maneuvered his way through the problem by creating a new structure, an organization for the copper-cooled engine company, with Kettering in charge. Sloan knew that Kettering was an inventor and not an executive and that the copper-cooled engine probably would not materialize as a practical product because of Kettering's lack of interest in running an organization. His maneuver was superficially brilliant because it ostensibly gave both sides what they wanted. It seemed to be an ideal situation in which everyone won and, presumably, had increased confidence in the process. Years later Sloan (1964, p. 93) wrote: "The copper-cooled car never came up again in a big way. It just died out, I don't know why."

Tactical manipulations are useful to managers, particularly to those who do not know how to confront conflicts that might generate aggression. The stultifying effect they can have on innovation, as happened in the case of GM, is one consequence. Another danger of such manipulations is the politici-

zation of organizations and human relationships. As the French
sociologist Michel Crozier (1964) pointed out in his study of
bureaucracy, what start as logical and objective organizational
practices change into interest politics, and self- and group interests now take precedence over purpose and work. The tendency to encourage the politicization of relationships, although
not intentional on the part of managers, grows from the way
managers use power and their lack of attachment to the substance of the business.

The Politicization of U.S. Business

Politicization occurs in business when substance takes a back
seat to process — when people become preoccupied with power
as an end in itself rather than with what the power is supposed
to accomplish. Perhaps, without realizing what they are doing,
managers shift from working on tasks to working on other people. Under the real conditions of power inequality that are characteristic of organizations, this shift tyrannizes subordinates and
elicits defensive behavior.

   In business, politics is a defensive game. But because of
the superficial effort to adhere to an ideology of cooperation and
teamwork, it is seldom revealed what people are defending themselves against. Politicization is not a malaise of mature industries only. The high-technology industries are also vulnerable,
especially when goals are unclear.

   The structure of American business lends itself to strong
leadership. The benign authority figure who holds no strong
opinions but views the job of running an organization as facilitating instead of directing and as managing instead of leading misunderstands and ultimately misuses the instrument of business.

   The purposes of business are to create products for customers, work for employees, and profit for shareholders. It takes
talent to run a business, and the talent must focus on the content of business. Organizational adroitness is secondary to the
ability to figure out what people want and to create the products
that will succeed in the marketplace.

   In early 1988, IBM announced a major change in its organization. It created broad product groups and eliminated central staffs. IBM's top management intended that this change would push decision making down the hierarchy and flatten the organization. But the really beneficial effect of this decision was the reduction of internal politics by lessening the power of central staffs and strengthening that of line management. IBM's moves came on the heels of less-than-satisfactory results in the personal computer field, flat performance in other sectors of its business, and a general perception that it was being outrun by smaller and more resourceful competitors.

The relative simplicity and unity of authority are the main reasons why business lends itself to strong leadership. Most theories of authority, and for that matter leadership, come from political and social scientists who know more about government than they do about business. Government, with its paradox of political election and bureaucratic continuity, differs from business in the ways in which people obtain and maintain power. Because of these differences, government encourages duplicity, whereas business encourages forthrightness. Often government works toward unclear goals that are subject to conflicting forces within the apparatus and that are obscured by the need for contending groups to preserve their power base. In a business, a person's rise to the position of chief executive should not be an exercise in running for office. However, many people view the process as election politics, misunderstanding both the purpose of business and the flow of authority from top to bottom.

A CEO in a modern corporation has enormous clout. This job is less a problem of persuasion than of deciding what the right thing to do is. Once a course of action has been formed, it is relatively easy to persuade subordinates to work hard to get the job done and easy to appeal to reason, but it is difficult to determine what is rational in a public policy decision.

If chief executives in business follow the example of government and political officeholders in using indirectness and ambiguity to exercise power, one thing is sure: They will generate mischief within the organization and encourage political infighting and backbiting. Why create aberrations in business by distorting the essence of authority relations? Business thrives on the principle of unity of command. To give up this principle destroys the ability of business to perform.

The rationale for the uncommitted position in politics is that the chief executive can maintain control over all the options until it is timely to reach a decision. If the chief executive commits too early, before all the agencies are persuaded, the decision may be undermined by opponents within the government apparatus who know too well how to use their independent power bases to fight for their position. But, even in government, a chief executive who remains uncommitted too long soon discovers that desirable policies may be buried among the ruins of the power conflicts that ensue.

That there are no power bases independent of the CEO is the reality of power in corporate business. Authority flows from the shareholder to the board of directors to the CEO and from there to other executives. Any subordinate who seeks to create a power base independent of the chief executive, who so to speak creates a barony within a princely state, can do so only because the CEO is weak or misunderstands authority and executive responsibility.

Some types of business do breed politics, family business being a notorious example. These situations, in which people tend to spend excessive time building and maintaining coalitions, resemble elective politics. Control of the organization depends on the ability to create alignments of power. The net result, however, is to arrive at innocuous decisions that create the least divisiveness within the ruling alliance. Divisive decisions put the alliance at risk. One of the reasons for the high mortality rate of family businesses is that coalition politics allows incompetence to gain the upper hand. The exception, of course, is where one family member dominates, either through ownership or force of personality. During the time of that person's dominance the situation is one of command, but if power later passes to people involved in fostering alliances and coalition politics, the business will be in danger. One way to address the problem is to institute integrity of command and marry competence with power.

Sidney Rabb, the late chairman and CEO of the Stop &

Shop companies, was the undisputed head of this public company, which remained under family control from its inception before World War I until 1988, when Kohlberg Kravis executed a leveraged buyout. The oldest child in his family, Rabb gained the early respect of his siblings as the family leader. They deferred to him not only because of the force of his personality, but also because the business prospered, enabling the whole family to accumulate wealth. His outstanding reputation as a community leader augmented his personal power in the family and the corporation, enabling him to direct the company in its diversification from food retailing to discount merchandising. While neither corporation nor family was entirely free from political sensitivities, Rabb himself proved an attractive focus for his siblings' and professional managers' desires and ambitions, so that he in turn controlled the way power was distributed in the business.

Some will argue that as a business grows larger and becomes organizationally complex, it inevitably becomes political because of the increased possibility of independent power bases and the differences in perception that arise from different positions. Although it is true that these differences do arise, they can be exacerbated or minimized by leadership. If a forewoman, for example, sees her major responsibility as meeting production deadlines, efficiency will be more important to her than quality. But if she views the enterprise as a whole, she will recognize the value of extra time for quality control. Executives who leave people's perceptions of their position unchallenged permit them to develop into the politics of self-interest and ultimately into organizational paralysis. Although such phenomena may be inherent in elective politics, in business — where logic necessitates unity of command — they are distortions. One of the goals of leadership is to keep politics out of human relationships.

It is precisely the job of leadership to create commitments that override the immediacy of personal interests. Perceptions based on position can affect thinking, but perceptions can be focused and challenged by desire, reason, and necessity. One of the critical jobs of leadership is to overcome political inclinations and to encourage the expression of talent and the performance of useful work.

What interests people in business is substance. When they lose sight of their work, when they become insecure as a result of poor leadership, or when they are asked to do what they are incapable of doing and therefore have to endure the humiliations of poor performance, they turn to process, which is equivalent to politics. As a result of these distortions, people learn how to be devious. Whether it is in the form of nondirective counseling, management-by-objective, participation, or quality circles, the end result is the same: Work becomes detached from authority relations and irrationality is encouraged.

So What's Wrong with the Managerial Mystique?

One of the tasks of business leaders is to keep politics out and substance in. The managerial orientation, with its emphasis on form over substance, on structure over people, and on power relationships over work, is at the heart of the disability of modern business in the United States and probably in other countries as well.

What started out as a rational attempt to organize, motivate, and control the actions of large numbers of people in business organizations has been transformed into a managerial mystique that subordinates the work of organizations to the forms in which people relate to each other. These forms, in turn, are dominated by conceptions of authority that discourage assertiveness, individual responsibility, and creativity.

While attending an advanced management course, a group of senior executives holding responsible jobs in marketing in a number of Fortune 500 corporations met with a group of business professors to discuss new trends and problems in marketing. It was surprising that the executives had little to say about the substance of marketing and what lay ahead in this field. Instead, they spoke about organizations and politics, claiming that one cannot separate the substance of marketing from process in large organizations. They appeared to have given up their attachment to the concepts and techniques involved in moving products from the designer's workbench and the factory floor to customers. After the meeting the academics met to review the material presented and to speculate on possible interpretations.

Were these executives confirming a view that business school academics frequently espouse, the view that the substance of large-scale business is the process of getting things done in organizations? Or was this meeting an example of how insecure people may try to protect themselves by deflecting attention from substance to process? Or was this meeting an example of the executives' technique of telling others what they think the others want to hear? Any one of these explanations reflected the pathology of organizations in which the medium has become the message and people give little thought to what they are supposed to be doing.

Whatever the true explanation, the material revealed at the meeting suggested a fundamental weakness in decision making in organizations. When senior executives feel disengaged from the content of their work and instead focus exclusively on process, they cannot lead their organizations. They are reduced to being conveners and leaving to others, usually subordinates, the important work of generating ideas. There are several results: The rational uses of power become obscure and reduce the confidence people feel in their leaders; a model of style over knowledge is established for those who aspire to leadership; and communication goes out of focus, so that people try to concentrate on the hidden instead of the manifest messages. The net effect is that people feel as though they are dealing with a monumental structure, immovable and insensitive to the pressure of reality.

The managerial mystique is inherently optimistic but also misguided. It believes in progress through the perfection of structures in order to control behavior. It believes in process as the performance of roles assigned to people in the various structures. It believes in politics, the art of manipulating people to get things done.

Finally, it believes in personal advancement through single-mindedly holding and practicing these beliefs.

The managerial mystique has dominated the consciousness of American business executives for the past twenty-five years. But as with any set of ideas, it has a history. Starting at the end of the nineteenth century and continuing through World War II, a change occurred in authority relations. The heroic, often autocratic personalities at the head of corporations became dinosaurs, doomed to extinction.

Managers imposed a new order on corporations. They brought what they learned from the business schools, namely, principles of bargaining, emotional control, human relations skills, and the technology of quantitative control. They left behind commitment, creativity, concern for others, and experimentation. They had learned to be managers instead of leaders. In exercising their craft, professional managers revealed no less a penchant for power than the autocrats they succeeded. But the achievement of power shifted from control through ownership to control through manipulation in the guise of eliciting participation and cooperation.

American business lost its way while the professional manager ascended the corporate hierarchy, empowered with the tools of organizational control and the mystique of a new elite. Professional management was born out of necessity. The newly emerging corporation could not sustain the irrationality of autocratic leaders. But the antidote of the managerial mystique overlooked the need for personal influence as the driving force for economic growth and human satisfaction.

References

Bass, B. M. *Leadership and Performance Beyond Expectations*. New York: Free Press, 1985.

Bucy, F. Letter to the editor. *Harvard Business Review*, 1977, *56*, 148–149.

Crozier, M. *The Bureaucratic Phenomenon*. Chicago: University of Chicago Press, 1964.

Geneen, H., with Moscow, A. *Managing*. Garden City, N.Y.: Doubleday, 1984.

James, W. *The Varieties of Religious Experience*. Cambridge, Mass.: Harvard University Press, 1985. (Originally published 1902.)

Lasch, C. *The Culture of Narcissism*. New York: Norton, 1979.

Reich, C. *Financier: The Biography of André Meyer*. New York: Morrow, 1983.

Sloan, A. P., Jr. *My Years with General Motors.* Garden City, N.Y.: Doubleday, 1964.

Wrapp, H. E. "Good Managers Don't Make Policy Decisions." *Harvard Business Review,* 1967, *45,* 91–99.

Zaleznik, A. "Managers and Leaders: Are They Different?" *Harvard Business Review,* 1977, *55,* 67–78.

Zaleznik, A. *The Managerial Mystique: Restoring Leadership in Business.* New York: Harper & Row, 1989.

5

---•••---

On Becoming a CEO: Transference and the Addictiveness of Power

Manfred F. R. Kets de Vries

So you're a CEO. You've finally made it. Your persistence has paid off and you've landed the plum job you've been striving for all these years. The chief executive's office is now yours. At times you may still find it hard to believe. But there's no question about it, you are finally in a position to make yourself heard and to implement your ideas about where the company should be going.

Some years later, this overwhelming sense of exhilaration has quite likely undergone a subtle transformation. Whether we like it or not, imperceptible changes quickly begin to take place in the way CEOs work. Being in the top position influences the way others relate to them, and this in turn may affect their behavior. Although the phenomenon can be observed with any executives in senior positions, the role CEOs occupy is so special that these processes tend to become magnified. How can CEOs cope with the specific pressures that come with the job? What does the new role in the company do to them?

In this chapter, I will discuss some of the psychological pressures CEOs are subjected to and how some manage to deal with them while others fail. Central to a person's vital sense of inner balance is the question of dealing with power: Power can be used for good but it also has a darker side. Given the great amount of power CEOs wield, this sense of balance is crucial.

To illustrate the dynamics of leadership, let me give two examples of what may happen when someone has been in the position of CEO for some time.

Don Vail was CEO of Rodex, a company specialized in data-processing equipment. He was feeling very good about the way he had just handled his weekly executive committee meeting. Things were much better now that he had fired his executive vice president. How tiresome it had been to have a person around who always needed to challenge him. Now everybody fell into line. To the best of his knowledge everyone shared his views of where the company should be going. The only major headache he had left were two of his external board members who had recently raised questions about the danger of overexpansion and the possibility of financial losses. They were not convinced that the recent strategic alliance he had made with a company in another product group had been a wise move. But he would deal with those two in due course.

Meanwhile, some of Vail's subordinates, who had known him for a long time, felt that he had undergone quite a metamorphosis since becoming CEO. Although he had never exactly been an extrovert and had always had a reputation for being a little standoffish, his behavior had made it increasingly difficult for people in the organization to communicate with him. He seemed to be more interested in getting his name in the newspapers than in discussing the reasons behind some of his decisions with his people. Real dialogue was no longer tolerated. And if people knew what was good for them, they took care to bring him only news that made him look good.

Moreover, the two board members were not alone in their concern that Vail might be steering the company in a dangerous direction. For some time market share and profitability had been slipping. Worse yet, Vail refused to recognize that this was happening.

The problem in this case seems to be the CEO's loss of grip on reality, worsened by his increasing isolation from dissenting voices and dependence on sycophants within the organization.

To take a second example, Mary Sands felt herself becoming less and less attached to her work. She found it increasingly difficult to deal with all the pressures surrounding her. What a contrast with the years immediately after she had been asked to take over the cosmetics firm that she had now been running for longer than she cared to remember! What had the passing of time done to the enthusiasm she had had when new at the job? Her spirit of adventure seemed very remote. Her physical condition, particularly her stomach problems, added to her low spirits. Business trips or meetings with clients were now nothing but chores. She had tried to fight these negative feelings, but to no effect. Recently, one of her closest friends had hurt her deeply by implying that she was turning into an old grouch, lashing out at anyone who did not behave according to her wishes. But if she were really honest with herself, she had to admit that she had indeed become more irritable. When was the last time she had laughed?

Sands knew that she had been blamed for the departure of several good executives who had left for the competition, departures that had certainly affected the bottom line of the company. Instead of welcoming new ideas, she found herself defending her earlier decisions. Her private life was nothing to be proud of, either. Her relationship with her daughters could barely be called civil. However, in spite of her present ambivalence about her job, for some reason she was very reluctant to consider resigning. What would she do with herself if she did? The idea of sitting at home was a singularly unattractive proposition.

What is happening to Don Vail and Mary Sands and why can they no longer tolerate people whose opinions differ from their own? What is the reason for their increasing sense of detachment from those around them and their jobs? What makes them so irritable that they lose their sense of humor? What is making them feel so low? Most important, how are their states of mind affecting their organizations?

The Two Faces of Power

A major contributing factor to the changes we frequently see in the behavior of CEOs is the way the power that comes with the job affects their thinking. However, CEOs must accept the fact that power is an essential dimension of human reality; indeed, it is the lifeblood of organizational life. To deny its importance for day-to-day functioning is nonsensical. Furthermore, we must bear in mind that power itself is not necessarily evil: It is the darker side, the abuse of power, that gives power its bad reputation. Power can be used for both good and evil.

To become a CEO, one inevitably needs a healthy interest in power. And there is nothing wrong with that — there is no reason to apologize for it. The need to influence others is the enabling factor in creating a shared vision of the direction in which an organization should be going. Power helps in implementing change. It is the catalyst for making things happen. It can be used to attain performances beyond expectations both for oneself and for others.

For some people, however, power takes on a different quality and becomes like a drug. No wonder some CEOs find it difficult to disentangle themselves from its grip. Even when they are no longer effective in their jobs, they keep hanging on to power at all costs — they cannot let go. For some CEOs, the power that comes with the position may affect their state of mind. Some may be consumed by it. Others become depressed. Still others may slide down the slippery slope leading to the abuse of power. Conversely, there are many executives who recognize what the position of CEO entails and know how to handle the attendant pressures. They are also the ones who give up power gracefully when their time has come and thus are remembered with appreciation.

Power is rooted in the heart of human nature and behavior, involving fundamental feelings about superiority and inferiority, autonomy and dependence, even love and hate. Its principal psychological lever is a phenomenon called *transference*.

Transference

As figures of authority, leaders become prime targets for certain reactions. This is what transference is all about. Basically, it is the process by which one person displaces onto another thoughts, feelings, ideas, or fantasies that originate with figures of authority encountered very early in an individual's life.

The concept of transference is grounded in observations of how human beings develop and mature. It is a revival or reliving of the situations and conflicts of infantile life now directed toward persons in the present. Transference is a natural process; it is part and parcel of everyday life, albeit unrecognized most of the time. On occasion, however, it can become problematic when individuals are unable to see those ties from the past in perspective and, without realizing it, become stuck in inappropriate, repetitive, and sometimes even bizarre behavior.

As a practicing therapist, Freud came across what he called a "false connection," a confusion on the part of his patients between himself and past figures in their lives (Breuer and Freud, [1893–1895] 1965). Feelings, emotions, and reactions from the past were projected onto the therapist in the present just as if he had been the original source. Freud was struck by the consistency of these patterns over time. He came to realize that transference represents the general human tendency to repeat certain types of behavior. Transference is an organizing activity, demonstrating the continuing influence of our early formative experiences (Kets de Vries and Miller, 1984; Kets de Vries, 1989). Through interactions with parents, other family members, teachers, doctors, and other authority figures we encounter, we develop repetitive, well-rehearsed behavior patterns that become the basis of specific cognitive and affective "maps." These "maps" are decisive in creating a certain amount of consistency in our dealings with others; the various "scripts" that can be drawn from them are activated by particular cues and become operative, usually without our being aware of it, when we meet other people.

Freud recognized that transference can be a powerful therapeutic tool in that it enables therapists to observe in the "here and now" the patterns of behavior that are unique to their patients. Bringing specific thoughts, feelings, and actions to the attention of patients as they occur will give the latter insight into the nature of their preoccupations, conflicts, style, and behavior. Given the way the therapeutic setting is devised, transferential processes become artificially intensified for the purpose of demonstration and interpretation, an essential element in the process of change. Thus, transference reactions of one form or another are at work in any kind of relationship.

The psychiatrist and psychoanalyst Heinz Kohut (1971, 1977) postulated two universally applicable kinds of narcissistically invested transference reactions: mirroring and the idealizing transference.

Mirroring originates in the parent's recognition of the emerging capabilities of the developing child and the need for appropriate responses to them. Kohut refers to mirroring as "the gleam in the mother's eye," the degree of approval perceived by the child in her face as she actively and positively reacts to the child's exhibitionistic displays. When the parent is sensitive to the child's need for recognition and confirmation, phase-appropriate responses occur so that the needs, capacities, and vulnerabilities of the child are duly appreciated. And when frustration is given in tolerable doses to the narcissism of the developing child, the boundless demands of the child's "grandiose self" are gradually transformed into the healthy ambitions of the adult. In instances of empathic failure—when there is a lack of phase-appropriate responses and consequent damage to a child's self-esteem—this process of transformation may not occur. Archaic, unsatisfied wishes and configurations may linger on and the adult may retain a lifelong hunger for recognition.

At the other end of the scale is the idealizing transference reaction. The basis for this particular process is the illusory wish (as a way of coping with childlike feelings of helplessness) to "merge" with someone who is perceived as an omnipotent and perfect other person (originally the parent) and thus acquire some of his or her power. To realize the intensity of this wish we need only to attempt to recall what it was like being a small child living in a world of grown-ups—a world of giants and confusion.

It may be difficult to remember to what extent we were looking for supporting figures at that time in order to decrease our sense of insignificance.

In normal development, the idealized parent image is eventually internalized and becomes the matrix for one's own ideas and guidelines. The followers of powerful organizational leaders may be inclined to reactivate their suppressed dependency needs and reinstate the childhood illusion of all-powerfulness using their leaders as a screen on which to project their wishes and fantasies, as they originally used their parents or other early authority figures. In this manner, followers extend their own sense of grandiosity through identification with their leader. And some leaders like that kind of admiration, especially if it feeds an unfulfilled hunger for recognition. The end result is a mutually reinforced pattern of interaction whereby idealizing and mirror transference reactions become complementary.

To give an illustration: John Rodale, president of Ablis, a financial services company, was surprised during a planning meeting when Rose Johnson, one of his subordinates, accused him of being prejudiced against women. He was disturbed by the remark, particularly in light of the fact that he had made a major effort not only to bring more women into the company, but also to see to it that they held senior positions.

Later on that day, Johnson came to his office, quite apologetic. She had thought about her behavior, trying to understand what had caused the sudden, intense feelings that led to her blowup. Her reaction had reminded her of her painful feelings growing up in a family where her brother had always been favored. In spite of her being brighter than her brother, she had always felt held back — unlike him, she had not been encouraged to go on to college.

As it turned out, her parents had had a rather traditional outlook toward the role of women: They believed women should get married and have children. At most, a secretarial job was good enough for their daughter. Getting a college degree had been an uphill struggle for Johnson. She had had to make her own way, which she had always perceived as being blatantly unfair. Thus, it did not come as a surprise that she was very quick to see unfairness in any situation. An innocuous remark made by Rodale about who should be assigned to a certain task had triggered her unwarranted outburst.

As CEO, Rodale was the unwitting catalyst of a hostile reaction due to the phenomenon of transference. As a figure of authority he had been held momentarily "responsible" for the difficulties Johnson had suffered with her parents. Without dwelling further on this specific example, we can remark that it speaks highly for Rodale that he had created the kind of atmosphere that allowed for contrarian thinking (even if expressed inappropriately). It must also be said that Johnson demonstrated unusual self-knowledge in understanding her behavior, as well as sufficient maturity to admit her mistake and apologize.

This incident clearly illustrates how CEOs are likely to revive unresolved conflicts about authority. Under certain conditions (usually encouraged by subtle signals from the CEO), subordinates may endow executives with the same magic powers and omniscience that they once attributed to their parents or other significant persons early in their lives. Because of this general human tendency to look for someone to admire, subordinates will frequently do anything to applaud, please, or charm the leader. The trappings of office, with all its attendant pomp and circumstance, and the corollary of the awe it inspires, worsen the situation. Some subordinates start to behave as if they were under the spell of the Pied Piper.

Sir John Harvey-Jones recognized this human foible all too well when he was chairman of ICI, the giant chemical concern. Reflecting on his career in the company, he said (1988, p. 227) that "There are also the added hazards which go with any top job. I have referred many times to the dangers of sycophancy, and my fears of the effects of power. It is almost impossible to avoid contact with one, or more likely both, of these hazards to one's ability to see oneself and one's motives clearly."

Wise CEOs should distrust subordinates who never find fault with them. They should constantly be on their guard against the perils and temptations of sycophancy. Unfortunately, not all CEOs possess a sufficiently high degree of self-awareness to realize that in fact they are not as wonderful as others may say they are. Some may even start to think that they really are that special and do indeed deserve that kind of attention. They may get stuck in a vicious circle of self-delusion about their own importance and capabilities. A suspension of their critical faculties may then occur.

The need for self-confirmation can turn into what resembles an addiction, so that CEOs thus afflicted can never get enough attention. They want to be in the limelight all the time. Some even begin to think they are infallible. As leaders, they may come to believe that they have the license to do anything, that the normal rules of conduct do not apply to them. They have lost all touch with reality and have moved into the sphere of eventual abuse of power.

It could be said that CEOs in this sort of situation have become "high" on power. Letting go of it, and losing their "fix," becomes a very unattractive proposition. It becomes extremely difficult to remove people like this from their top position.

Additional Psychological Pressures

Transference is not the only pressure that affects the way CEOs handle their job. A number of others can be mentioned.

The Job As Sole Identity

Some CEOs suffer from the very real fear that loneliness and depression will follow if they relinquish power. Having had the experience of living in a hall of mirrors, that is, of having continuous, admiring attention, what they dread most of all is the sudden silence — a situation where from one day to the next nobody has any real interest in them any longer. The fear of turning into a nonentity on stepping down from the job causes an enormous amount of anxiety. And there is certainly some reality to this fear. The late President Harry S. Truman was quite candid about it when he said shortly after his term was over, "Two hours ago I could have said five words and been quoted in every capital in the world. Now, I could talk for two hours and nobody would give a damn" (Graff, 1988, p. 5).

Moreover, because of the sense of isolation that comes with their position, some CEOs may have lost the only genuine friends or contacts they ever had. The overused phrase about the loneliness of command contains an element of truth. CEOs may never have had, nor have been able to maintain, a good relationship with their spouse, nor have had friendships with people other than those within their circle of influence. In fact, their behavior may have estranged them from others. If they step down, they may have no one to turn to for emotional support. This intensifies the fear of the loss of office. Dreading a feeling of "nothingness" once they are deprived of their power base, some CEOs may prefer to cling to their position, notwithstanding their lack of enjoyment in the job and the realization that they are no longer effective. Instead, they delude themselves into preferring any kind of contact, regardless of how devoid of meaning it may be, to no contact at all.

Another factor is that, in their drive to get to the top, some CEOs have sacrificed interest in all other things, if they had any interests beyond work in the first place. Although in some instances such a narrow outlook on life may have contributed to their original success, there can be a high price to pay for it. Such individuals become ill at ease when they have no job to go to, when their structured environment is no longer there. Losing one's position turns into a catastrophe; it becomes a total loss of identity.

The fear of nothingness and accompanying depression are accentuated by the basic human need to leave behind a legacy. A common preoccupation of CEOs is the question of whether their successors can be relied on to respect their legacy, the tangibles or intangibles that distinguished their regime. The looming suspicion is that few can be trusted. There are too many examples of CEOs witnessing the destruction of everything they had built up so carefully after their departure.

For some CEOs the fear of not having their legacy respected becomes a very strong force motivating them to hold onto their position for as long as possible. Leaving behind a reminder of one's accomplishments can be equated symbolically with defeating death. If we really delve deeply, each of us has a carefully guarded wish to believe in our own immortality. The ultimate narcissistic injury seems to be the realization of the inevitability of death. Thus, everything possible is done to hang onto something tangible in order to postpone this painful encounter with the self. CEOs are anything but immune to this predicament.

The Assault on the Self

The most powerful reminder of the temporary nature of one's existence is the aging of the body. Most CEOs fall within the age range where physical changes become quite noticeable. Studies of the human life cycle concur in showing an increased preoccupation with physical defects in middle age, and there is certainly an element of reality to these concerns. Body monitoring becomes more intense and this is a time when hypochondria may come to the fore. It is a critical point in marriage, and in relationships with teenage children and aging parents, all of which necessitate the playing of new and different roles. These factors combined, added to the strain of physical aging, can cause a lot of stress. In trying to deal with these tensions, some CEOs find stimuli outside their work; some men may even look for a new wife as a way of refueling their emotional life.

Self-consciousness about physical deterioration and the consequent personal stresses often make the search for substitute outlets a necessity. In such cases the exertion of power becomes an important substitute activity. CEOs are prime candidates for this. Henry Kissinger hinted at power's compensatory relationship to sexuality, for example, when he said in a half-joking manner that "power is the greatest aphrodisiac!" This statement translates symbolically into something like, "If I can no longer be a Don Juan and find favor in the eyes of the opposite sex, I at least have power and can affect people that way."

With all the losses that are corollary to aging, letting go of power becomes a singularly unattractive idea for many people. Frequently, they hang on to power for as long as possible, with extraordinary intentness, single-mindedness, and persistence. We can hypothesize that this is one way of compensating for the effects of the narcissistic injury inflicted by the physical decline of the body.

Maintaining the Balance

Many CEOs have no difficulty in overcoming the pressures of leadership. They are aware of what can happen to them and keep their strengths and weaknesses in perspective. They have a sense of humor and, more important, retain the ability to laugh at themselves, sure signs of mental health. They do not take themselves completely seriously, a quality that can otherwise be suffocating for others.

These CEOs possess the inner resources to fight the regressive pulls of leadership and can differentiate between reality and fantasy. They know how to cope with the dangers of excessive grandiosity or depression, and they are capable of creating the internal challenges that prevent them from becoming stale. Thus, they retain their creative potential and the ability to get the best out of others. Moreover, they are sensitive to the business environment: They are able to identify new opportunities, new markets, innovative products, and other challenges.

These executives also know how to balance their private and public lives. They have spouses who keep them firmly in touch with reality. Their relationships with their children may help. They also recognize the warning signs when they are under too much pressure or are beginning to go stale.

Francine Gomez is one such example. The flamboyant former CEO of Waterman, a French company manufacturing high-quality pens, commented in a recent private interview: "A few years ago I noticed I was always doing the same thing at the same time in the same place. I wasn't bored but I thought it was ridiculous the way my life was going. I was like a rabbit caught in a trap. I was sitting in my chair at the office the same way every day at the same time. I thought, no, you can't do that. That is the reason why I got into politics." Gomez's attempt to enter French politics was not totally successful, although she won a seat on a regional council. But her feeling of being in a rut clearly contributed to her decision to resign from her Waterman position soon after this interview took place and find challenges elsewhere.

Not all CEOs are as decisive as Gomez. Not all of them recognize their predicament — that they may be trapped in a golden cage—and act on it. Not all have the same facility to deal with the human dilemmas of leadership. Some cannot do without the trappings of power. This brings us to the question of why some CEOs are more successful than others in dealing with these phenomena. Are there certain career strategies that make a person less susceptible to them? What can a CEO do to avoid them?

"The Gauguin Way"

"Do you want to spend the rest of your life selling sugared water or do you want a chance to change the world?" This question, asked by Steven Jobs, then chairman of Apple Computers, became the ultimate challenge for John Sculley, then CEO of Pepsi Cola (Sculley, 1987, p. 40). Sculley had become increasingly aware of his restlessness in running Pepsi. The excitement he had felt when new to the job was rapidly fading. Instead, he was stuck more and more in an administrative role, always doing the same thing and no longer playing the role of a creative marketer. What else could he do at Pepsi after having made the cover of *Business Week* at the age of thirty-four? Sculley (1987, p. 104) stated: "I had been president for five and a half years, and I was getting tired, physically tired, of doing what I was doing year after year. No one at Pepsi Cola had been measured by Nielsen share points for so long. No longer did I wake up in the morning excited about the job as I used to years ago."

The wearing routine of Sculley's life turned a headhunter's call into an opportunity. After some initial wavering, Sculley decided to meet the challenge head on and switch from Pepsi to Apple as its new CEO.

A more dramatic change of corporate culture was hard to imagine. To use Sculley's own description, he went from a second- to a third-wave company, that is, from an organization where the source of strength was stability to one that depended on continuous transformation. The magnitude of this change made Sculley's personal decision a major news event.

For Sculley himself, the change became a way to revitalize his life and break the chains of power that were binding him at Pepsi. It is interesting to note that he had had a long love affair with electronics when younger. It seems the time had come to pick up the broken thread. By joining a high-tech, high-risk, more participative environment, Sculley embarked on a new life adventure of continued learning.

Like the painter Paul Gauguin, who made a complete break with his past by ending his career as a stockbroker's clerk and devoting the remainder of his life to painting the people and landscapes of Tahiti, Sculley decided to take his life in hand once he realized he was stuck in a rut. Although he appreciated the power that came with his job, he was not addicted to it and knew when to change. He realized that staying on in his job at Pepsi would only lead to more of the same thing—that the added value to him personally would be limited. Sculley had the courage to search for new inspiration and a chance to learn and thus find a new beginning somewhere else.

Taking the Role of Mentor

Vicarious gratification—the pleasure that comes from guiding and directing the next generation—is another very constructive way of forestalling addiction to power and the CEO "blues." Losing oneself in others—helping others to deal successfully with the same challenges one once had to manage oneself—is an excellent way of avoiding the perils of excessive narcissism. The natural wish to have one's offspring become individuals in their own right can easily be transferred to an organizational setting.

George Foster, CEO of a fast-growing multinational firm in the communications industry, is a good case in point. He took great pleasure in grooming the high potentials in his company for senior positions and made them his envoys in fighting battles in the marketplace. His talent in developing and training younger executives was a major contributing factor to the success of his company.

Foster asked many of his protégés to set up new ventures abroad. They were his "alumni," spreading the good word about how to run an international company successfully. He kept in close contact with them, proudly sharing in their successes and counseling them when the going got tough. Eventually, when he felt that he had been in his position long enough and had groomed the right successor, he handed over the reins, causing a minimum amount of strain to the organization.

Shaping the occupational identity of others is a very adaptive way of dealing with what otherwise could deteriorate into a conflict between generations. It diminishes the risk of a person's abusing power through envy, spite, and vindictiveness about his or her own lost opportunities. It transcends narrow concerns about status and position. At the same time it creates a sense of legacy. However, the ability to act in such a way requires a certain amount and kind of wisdom — the wisdom to recognize the necessity of encouraging others and helping them to generate ideas. But it is that attitude, as demonstrated by George Foster, that facilitates both interdependence and continuity in organizational life.

The Public Service Interchange

There is a kind of person who makes an easy shift between life in the private sector and life in public service. These people distinguish themselves by the need to make a lasting imprint on the world.

A preoccupation with broader issues is common to many CEOs. Granted, one sometimes has to make an effort to get these concerns out into the open. But something that often reveals them is the public role executives have to assume when reaching the top of the organization. CEOs come into contact with other constituencies, which can be the basis for a very healthy use of their power base. Building up relationships with very different people and organizations and going beyond narrow, self-defined company interests can be a very effective antidote to certain aspects of the CEO blues. Moreover, a concern for broader public interests does not necessarily have to create conflict — on the contrary, it often benefits the company's reputation, even when the CEO eventually decides to leave to spend all his or her time in some public service capacity.

Peter Doren, CEO of a company making highly specialized machine tools, went through a dramatic transformation.

It all started when he began to suffer from severe migraine headaches. A general medical checkup found nothing physically wrong with him. That led Doren to wonder if perhaps his body were trying to tell him something he did not really want to hear. Maybe it had something to do with his unrelenting pace at work. Or perhaps it was related to his perfectionism. Whatever the reasons, his physician made some vague reference to stress and referred him to a psychotherapist.

Visiting a psychotherapist was not an easy decision for Doren, who had always thought therapists were for crazy people, not for him. But eventually, spurred on by his continuous migraines, he took the step. From his visits to the therapist he gradually learned that much of his feeling of being under pressure was self-inflicted — that he had fallen into the habit of setting himself unnecessary deadlines. He also began to question his way of managing people. He had an intense need to control and had the tendency to go into the smallest details of affairs at the office. Reflecting on his behavior during therapy made him realize that being a CEO did not mean that he had to take over the jobs of others who were not as quick as he was. It also gave him insight into how overpowering he could be at times. The bottom line was that he had to learn how to listen and how to delegate. He had to spend more time thinking about priorities and long-term goals.

Doren was surprised to discover that this gradual change in work habits gave him time for other things. He rediscovered his family, who had received short shrift due to his pace of work. Through this process of personal reassessment of priorities, he renewed his childhood interest in music. One thing led to another and he found himself quite involved in the local opera company. He took great pleasure in working to make the opera company more professional and even initiated a number of fund-raising performances to provide housing for the many homeless in his city.

All these activities gave Doren visibility in the local press. It led to his being asked to sit on a task force for the homeless, where he became a champion for housing rights. Quite remarkably, in spite of all these new activities he felt much less harassed than before — physically, he felt better than ever and his migraines

disappeared. He deeply enjoyed his improved relations with
members of his family. Moreover, he liked coming to the office,
where he increasingly saw himself as a conductor leading an
orchestra and deriving great pleasure in getting the best out of
his "artists." In the end he decided to run for public office.

In Doren's case, the public service aspect of his new activity was combined with an interest in aesthetic matters. Because of the pressures in the early stages of the career life cycle,
many executives may have neglected or suppressed their cultural and recreational interests. The point at which CEOs feel
they are stagnating may be the time to pick up the broken thread.
A more balanced life-style, implying a variety of interests, may
lead to a turnaround in orientation. In many instances, including the example of Peter Doren, the catalyst for change is some
kind of physical problem.

Breaking the Routine

There are a number of other ways of defeating the CEO blues.
Activities such as participation in seminars, conferences, and
workshops break up the routine and offer CEOs the chance to
talk about work preoccupations with their peers in a relatively
neutral atmosphere. Such exchanges can have a liberating effect
and lead to the discovery of new options.

Consultants can also play an important role as confidants.
Because they are not part of the political system of the organization and are often in a neutral position vis-à-vis the company, they
can be used to bounce back ideas. Given the sense of isolation
that often comes with the position, quite a few CEOs are really
lonely people, superficial appearances notwithstanding. As confidants, consultants can play a supportive role in emotional refueling. They can be used to help sort out priorities, an essential
factor in maintaining personal and organizational health.

A more unconventional way of breaking the addiction to
power, overcoming the CEO blues, and revitalizing one's mental
state is to take some kind of sabbatical. Although the sabbatical
is common practice in academic life, business organizations have
only occasionally experimented with a similar form of emotional
refueling, usually too short a break to really fulfill its function.

The sabbatical poses problems for both individual and organization. The individual fears that there might not be a job waiting for him or her on returning. As for the organization, its concern is whether the individual will come back at all. But these are risks well worth taking given the potential benefits of the sabbatical.

A noteworthy example is that of Olivier Lecerf, who was chairman and CEO of Lafarge Coppée, one of the world's largest cement producers. After nine years in the top job, Lecerf decided to take a one-year leave of absence. He felt it was time to break up his routine. One of the vice-chairmen, who was going to retire the following year, was made the new chairman and CEO.

Lecerf's sabbatical was very well thought through. He had set himself a number of goals for his year's leave. For example, he wanted to understand the international environment better, get to know all the activities of his group, consider what strategic guidelines were needed for the future, and plan a reorganization. His sabbatical gave him the time to rediscover and reflect on the values underlying business and society and look at the possibilities for synergy of these values across cultures—a major issue if Lafarge Coppée was really serious about being a global company.

Olivier Lecerf's bold initiative deserves emulation. It is a creative approach to dealing with the dangers that come with the job of CEO. Sabbaticals do not necessarily have to be as long as a year—shorter variants can bring similar benefits. Whatever the length, a diminution of specifically structured activities will refresh the mind and lead to a new perspective on things, which in turn is a way of helping the individual reach his or her full potential. Organizations should be sufficiently imaginative to create the conditions that make such sabbaticals possible. In spite of the difficulties involved, resolving them is well worth the effort given the sabbatical's potential to unleash creative energy.

The Art of Letting Go

We have seen that to let go and find new challenges is not an easy task. But it is imperative to do so, particularly if our minds and bodies are telling us that our habitual way of operating is no longer satisfactory, that we are becoming ineffective on the job. For a CEO, being able to face up to an addiction to power and prevent the perils of grandiosity or the destructiveness of the CEO blues requires a lot of courage. As with other forms of addiction, we should not underestimate the withdrawal symptoms that come with letting go.

If an executive is caught between the Scylla of an addiction to power and the Charybdis of feeling in a rut and suffering from decreased effectiveness, the price in the form of blocked creativity, frustration, and even symptoms of stress will be high. When this happens—if what were once feelings of exhilaration turn into a sense of exhaustion—it is high time for a reminder that life is not a rehearsal: We must make the most of it and take advantage of our gifts and talents. A change is essential.

Since physical decline comes with age, it becomes more important than ever for older CEOs to spread their gradually diminishing energy and resources over fewer but more key activities in order to conserve their strength and escape less important demands. And eventually they should have the courage to realize that their added value to the organization is limited and that it is time to move on. It is essential to be able to look back at life with a sense of satisfaction, not as a series of missed opportunities. This requires not only acceptance, but also a creative congruence between inner mental state and external circumstances.

In all cases, this sort of outlook requires a balanced lifestyle, the desire to combine business interests with family interests, and the ability to maintain both business acquaintances and personal friendships. Research on the human life cycle has shown that, in the long run, those people who have good marriages and good friendships are the healthiest (Vaillant, 1977).

The CEOs who are able to combine action with reflection and passion with reason, who have sufficient self-knowledge to recognize the vicissitudes of power, and who will not be swept away when the psychological forces that affect power are beckoning are, in the final analysis, the most powerful. They will be remembered with respect and affection. They will also be able to have truly creative and productive lives.

Perhaps it is appropriate to end with an anecdote about

the composer Johannes Brahms. Late in life Brahms surprised his friends with the announcement that he was going to stop composing music entirely. His argument was that he wanted to enjoy his old age and was therefore not going to write another note. Brahms kept his promise for a short while. Several months later, however, a new masterpiece of his was played in public. One of his friends who heard it confronted the composer and reminded him that he had said he was going to stop working. Brahms is alleged to have answered that he had indeed stopped, but that after some days of leisure he had been so happy at the thought of not having to write that the music just came by itself.

References

Breuer, J., and Freud, S. "Studies on Hysteria." In J. Strachey (ed. and trans.), *The Standard Edition of the Complete Psychological Works of Sigmund Freud*. Vol. 2. London: Hogarth Press, 1965. (Originally published 1893–1895.)

Graff, H. F. "When the Term's Up, It's Better to Go Gracefully." *International Herald Tribune*, Jan. 26, 1988, p. 5.

Harvey-Jones, J. *Making It Happen*. London: Collins, 1988.

Kets de Vries, M.F.R. *Prisoners of Leadership*. New York: Wiley, 1989.

Kets de Vries, M.F.R., and Miller, D. *The Neurotic Organization: Diagnosing and Changing Counterproductive Styles of Management*. San Francisco: Jossey-Bass, 1984.

Kohut, H. *The Analysis of the Self*. New York: International Universities Press, 1971.

Kohut, H. *The Restoration of the Self*. New York: International Universities Press, 1977.

Sculley, J., with Byrne, J. A. *Odyssey*. New York: Harper & Row, 1987.

Vaillant, G. E. *Adaptation to Life*. Boston: Little, Brown, 1977.

6

---•◆•◆•●---

Magnificent Obsession:
The Impact of
Unconscious Processes
on Strategy Formation

Alain Noël

Strategic management literature has been dominated for over the last decade by deterministic resource dependence or population ecology models, which are very popular among economists. Although the roots of this approach are found in the works of authors like Pfeffer and Salancik (1978), who have proposed that organizations depend on the availability of critical resources to survive, or Hannan and Freeman (1977), or Aldrich (1979), who go as far as proposing a process of natural selection of species for organizations, it was really made popular by models "à la Porter" (1980, 1985, 1990). According to these models, an environmental iron law determines who will and will not survive, and executives themselves have a minimal impact on corporate development.

These models have been attractive to many management scholars. They reduce the complexity of environmental dynamics to four or five forces exerting pressure on strategy. Because managerial work is so complicated, managers like simple models. In my consulting practice over the last few years, most managers have wanted to use these models until they have discovered that they are ill-suited to their situation. To put it bluntly, although many would like to be one of the "big five" in their particular industry in terms of volume and cost leadership, most of the companies who consult my practice fall short of that status. Worse still, most of them cannot even collect, or afford to collect, the data needed to conduct Porter-type analyses. For all these companies, who are not industry leaders and probably never will be, I prefer to stick to a more classic, freewill perspective.

This approach, popularized by more traditional business policy scholars (Chandler, 1962; Ansoff, 1965; Ackoff, 1970; Andrews, 1971) and experienced practitioners, may be termed "the art of the general." It results in more or less implicitly formulated resource allocation choices implemented by their organization to secure victory, which means attaining the objectives selected by the dominant coalition in the company, if not by the CEOs themselves. Hofer and Schendel (1978, p. 11) define this strategy as "a match between an organization's resources and skills and the environmental opportunities and risks it faces, and the purposes it wishes to accomplish."

It is popularly suggested that strategies do not always result from choices made by the CEO. Graham Allison (1971) has argued that organizational inertia and politics may themselves determine the actions taken by organizations. But this is forgetting the time-lag factor, and CEOs can influence decision making in the long run through structures that they themselves were responsible for establishing. The influential work of the historian Alfred Chandler (1962) neatly demonstrates how managers react to environmental changes, try to find better solutions to problems, and change structures to implement their strategies. But the proposition that an executive can have the power to make changes in corporations seems to run counter to the democratic ideal. The academic community, if not North American society as a whole, is not prepared to accept such a state of affairs. It prefers to believe in the checks and balances of day-to-day reality in order to maintain an ideal of a democratic world where no one has the power to impose his or her will on others.

A similar amount of controversy exists about the strategy-making process. Several authors have stated that strategies are not sequentially formulated and implemented but simply formed over time. According to Mintzberg (1978, p. 935), "A strategy may *form* gradually, perhaps without intention, as [the CEO] makes his decisions one by one." Such a supposition ignores the planning process and other forms of managerial work that are concerned with defining coherent future action. Of course I would be the last person to suggest that CEOs always stick to their intentions. I also disagree with the idea that strategies simply emerge by themselves, without planning. This runs contrary to the things I observe in my consulting practice.

My research and consulting experience has strongly supported my belief that CEOs do influence the strategy formation process in companies. I think that this is the most important contribution they can be expected to make to their firms. CEOs do not spend their time arbitrarily but concentrate on activities they feel are crucial to the survival or growth of their firm. These activities constitute what I call the strategic core: Enacted by CEOs, the strategic core is central to the existence of the organization, to its mission (Steiner and Miner, 1977), and to its purpose (Andrews, 1971). It varies greatly from one organization to another, depending on the organization's state of development and the major problems it has to face.

Looking for Strategic Clues

If management problems are universal, every management situation one encounters is unique and the executives who call consultants for help will expect it to be treated in this way. The same thing applies to strategies. Strategy very much reflects the CEO's personality (Kets de Vries and Miller, 1984a, 1984b). Because the actions of CEOs have such a great impact on organizations, I believe they warrant a careful analysis if we want to understand the strategy formation process. In their daily activities, CEOs deal with a large set of ill-structured environmental, organizational, and personal issues. Their particular values stand central to their action (Guth and Tagiuri, 1965; Andrews, 1971; Miles, Snow, and Pfeffer, 1974; Steiner and Miner, 1977; Wissema, Van der Pol, and Messer, 1980). Therefore, both actions and values (Noël, 1984; Bowman, 1986) need to be studied if we want to understand strategy formation in corporations.

Management consulting, given the role of personal interaction, is very much a clinical process (Schein, 1987). Fieldwork is very important in such situations because it aims at producing descriptive data, that is, written or spoken expressions and the observable behavior of the subjects under study. Many important contributions have been made, based on fieldwork in management: the Hawthorne Studies (Roethlisberger and Dickson, 1939), the Glacier project (Jaques, 1951), Melville Dalton's *Men Who Manage* (1959), studies of bureaucracies (Blau, 1963; Crozier, 1964), and studies of managers (Carlson, 1951; Stewart, 1967; Mintzberg, 1973).

Field research demands both flexibility and rigor in gathering, analyzing, and interpreting data. To conduct good fieldwork with CEOs, a consultant must be careful to stay close to them, be factual, remain descriptive, and rely as much as possible on quotations to analyze people in their own terms. Glaser and Strauss (1967) put forward the notions of *accurate description* and *saturation* in abstracting theory from data and developing grounded theories. Clifford Geertz (1973) talks of *thick description* and states that the researcher must read the data and look for interpretations that satisfy the subjects under observation. He elaborates (1973, p. 452) that "the culture of people is an ensemble of texts, themselves ensembles, which the anthropologist strains to read over the shoulders of those to whom they properly belong. . . . But to regard such forms as 'saying something of something,' and saying it to somebody, is at least to open up the possibility of an analysis which attends to their substance rather than to reductive formulas professing to account for them." Taking a clinical perspective is like playing detective: To study strategies, a consultant has to proceed rigorously in interpreting data. Kets de Vries (1978) proposes four rules: *thematic unity* (shaping the data into an interconnected, cohesive unit), *pattern matching* (searching for structural parallels over time and events), *psychological urgency* (identifying the most pressing problems in any situation), and *multiple function* (analyzing from many different points of view, since all data can have more than one meaning).

"Playing detective" is a powerful means to understanding the impact of CEOs on strategy. Some time ago I played detective for one full month with each of three company presidents: John Palmer, president of a private nonprofit institution; André Beaulieu, president of a medium-size advertising agency; and Tim Wiseman, owner of a printing company (all names and companies disguised). In each instance I was trying to go beyond the more traditional observational management studies by tying in manifest with latent concerns. I took note of all their activities and of what they said during a day's work. Through interviews, I tried to discover their values, their strategic concerns, and their preoccupations; I also gathered complementary data on the company and its environment. As my observation went on, I conducted interviews, as necessary, to clarify what they did or said; finally, I engaged in exit interviews to test my interpretations and get as much data as possible on the CEO's personal history, which I needed to complete my analyses. All my observations were made from a point physically close to my subjects: a desk just outside John's office, André's secretary's desk, and a table in a corner facing Tim.

Data of this type have to be analyzed several times. Every time we go back over them, we try to go further and further in our interpretations, moving back and forth from the manifest to the latent clues, getting more and more specific and proceeding, as if in concentric circles, from observable behavior to the hidden intentions behind these activities. By the time our analysis is completed, we usually have a thorough understanding of the strategic capabilities of CEOs and their companies.

John Palmer and Insertion Inc.

John Palmer was a brilliant graduate student in psychology. At the age of twenty-three he lost his sight after a swimming trip during which he contracted an eye infection: After unsuccessful eye surgery, he remained permanently blind. He often thought of committing suicide, especially during the first year after the incident, but twelve years later he is still alive. Fighting against the idea of living on welfare and unable to find a regular job, he had started Insertion Inc. to help handicapped people live a normal life. After ten years of existence, Insertion Inc. had grown to a yearly budget of $1 million. Insertion Inc. is a modest operation: There are only thirty full-time employees on site, working on different projects. However, there are also some 250 listed volunteers who work on a part-time basis.

The observer has the strange feeling that nobody is working in this company. Financed by government employment creation grants, designed for unemployed, less-specialized workers, only a minority of permanent employees stays for more than twenty weeks: The turnover rate averages 250 percent a year. Insertion Inc. is an organization permanently made up of unskilled temporary personnel, either physically or socially handicapped.

Every work day begins with a more than hour-long coffee break in the meeting room where all employees sit, reading their horoscope and spending a great deal of time talking together. John usually joins in after most of his people have arrived. After listening for half an hour, he starts questioning some of them, a sign that they should get to work. He usually is the last one to leave and goes back to his office with the controller. Once John is at his desk, his time is spent as it would be in any other organization: The phone rings, people come and go, his office door is always open. Since he lives only three blocks away from the office, John normally goes home for lunch and comes back for the afternoon. Days at the office seldom end later than 5:00 P.M. but he always brings home work he considers important, like budgets, instruction manuals, or methods and procedures guidelines. He works on these every morning between 4:00 and 7:00 A.M. Back at the office, he spends his time controlling the budgets, the employees, and the programs, which have, on average, a three-month life expectancy. To everyone's surprise (John's included), Insertion Inc., permanently temporary, manages to keep growing year after year.

André Beaulieu and Communiplus

The seventies were booming years for advertising agencies operating in Quebec, the French-language province of Canada. In line with political evolution in Quebec, customers expected more and more material in French. André Beaulieu was one of the French-speaking entrepreneurs who had, by 1984, started twenty of the thirty-six established advertising agencies in Quebec.

Work in this industry is generally tough but can be very exciting. Although the work days are long, there is compensation in drinking good wines at first-rate restaurants with important customers, stars, and artists. Advertising attracts an aura of glamour. There are minimal barriers to entry, suppliers are very easy to get hold of, and clients like to invite many agencies to pitch (compete) for an account. Competitive pressures are high and costs often prove hard to control. The advertising industry is usually a good indicator of economic conditions, often entering a growth or recession phase as much as six months ahead of other sectors. In the severe recession of the early eighties many agencies, both small and very large, went bankrupt and the originally exciting race for growth turned into a fight for survival.

André Beaulieu, president of Communiplus, lives only for advertising and has sacrificed everything to the agency he created some fifteen years ago. He has lost most of his friends, alienated employees whose performance did not meet his expectations, seldom takes holidays or days off, and has recently been divorced. He likes to describe himself as a "coach," and, in keeping with this image, he arrives at the office at 8:00 A.M. and normally stays past 10:00 P.M. The fight for survival is so tough that André feels his people cannot go into battle without their coach. He is a born fighter. As a child he had to hold his own against older twin brothers. In college he played football, a tough fighting game. In the advertising world, he lost battles in his first job when he discovered that his M.B.A. degree was not the asset he had assumed it would be in dealing with the creative people he had to supervise as an account executive. It was then he decided to start his own company.

He likes to say that clients pay for ideas, not for the flashy reception desks, decor, carpets, and expensive furniture they find when they visit his competitors. In an industry where revenues are unpredictable, he focuses on expenses and keeps them to a minimum. André believes advertising must be a team effort and he tries to coach his employees to behave like team-mates. At Communiplus people work in meeting rooms, around a central table, because André sees no need for large personal offices. This makes it simpler for him to go from one meeting to another throughout the day and to follow the progress of each project, making sure there is a "Communiplus trademark" on all of them. In the meantime, visitors come and go through his open office door, presentations are made to clients, the phone keeps ringing, and messages pile up on his desk, while lunches and dinners are scheduled in such a way to get the most out of each work day.

Tim Wiseman and Wiseman Printing

At the end of the last century Tim Wiseman's grandfather opened a general store in a village near Saint-Joseph, a small town 150 kilometers from Montreal. Four sons made a good living out of the family store until the dark days of the Depression. Only Tim's father stayed in the village and kept the business working. As the years went by, a small printing operation in the back of the store became the central business concern of Mr. Wiseman.

In the sixties, Tim completed a business education at a prominent business school in Montreal before going to work as general manager of a large Board of Trade. Two years after graduation, his father called him to say that he was ready to sell the business to four employees who had offered to buy it, unless Tim was interested in running the family business himself. Two days later Tim decided to move back to Saint-Joseph. When he took over Wiseman Printing it was barely profitable; father and son could not earn a decent living out of it, and the four most experienced employees had, not surprisingly, left. Using his accounting training, Tim discovered that most product lines were unprofitable. He decided to close them down and bought new sophisticated machinery to specialize in a printing niche that would be more difficult for the competition to enter. His decision proved to be a success and he soon had to expand. Within five years, he moved into larger, modern premises in

Saint-Joseph. Wiseman Printing kept growing 25 to 30 percent a year. Tim kept on buying more and more modern printing equipment and built a reputation for excellence in the trade.

When the firm grew to over 100 employees five years ago, Tim decided that he could no longer manage Wiseman Printing alone. He started to recruit better-trained managers and bought two computer systems: one for the production operation and another for management. Tim likes to keep to a very regular working schedule at the office. He tries to bring home trade magazines only. He walks around the production area once or twice daily and spends most of the time in his office with the door closed. Since people nevertheless come and go, he focuses his attention on brief, face-to-face conversations or talks to important customers on the phone. Since Tim also owns two newspapers, he holds weekly meetings with the editor to discuss the editorials. He lunches every day at the same table in a Saint-Joseph restaurant called Le Pornic, where all the influential people of the region meet daily. This way, he keeps informed about political issues as well as the general state of the regional economy. Looking at the future, Tim hopes to find more and more time to live, rather than living for work.

From the Manifest to the Latent

To get a handle on what the CEOs did at work, I started by using basic frequency measures (Table 6.1). This deceptively simple form of data gathering provided the proverbial tip of the iceberg from which many inferences could be drawn. To this I added a minutes-of-contact index in which I evaluated the minutes spent in an activity multiplied by the number of people directly involved, to measure the impact of CEOs on different parts of their organization. Analysis of this data revealed that the CEOs worked at different paces. The number of daily activities averaged 44 for John, 58 for André, and 103 for Tim. The average length of a working day varied from 402 minutes for John to 742 for André and 562 for Tim.

The minutes-of-contact measure shows that André gets 2.03 minutes of contact with people out of every minute at work

Table 6.1. The Activity Patterns.

	John Palmer	André Beaulieu	Tim Wiseman
Organization	Insertion Inc.	Communiplus	Wiseman
Length of work day	402 minutes	742 minutes	562 minutes
Lunch use	Solitary rest	Work oriented	Socialization
Door attitude	Open door	Open door	Closed door
Number of daily activities	44	58	103
Dominating types of activities	Encounters/ meetings	Meetings/ encounters	Encounters/ solitary work
Importance of communications	327 minutes (81%)	670 minutes (90%)	433 minutes (77%)
People met	11	22	22
Names dropped	13	5	11
Minutes-of-contact ratio	1.39	2.03	1.11
Importance of the telephone	23 minutes (6%)	87 minutes (12%)	95 minutes (17%)
Proactive calls	64%	73%	64%
Telephone focus	Network	Merger target	Customers
Activity Pattern	Controller	Coordinator	Operator

while John and Tim respectively get only 1.39 and 1.11. Tim spends more time in person-to-person encounters, whereas the reverse is true for John and André. Finally, Tim, the only CEO to work behind closed doors, spends more time doing solitary work even if he is the most interrupted CEO of the three. With this rough sketch in mind, we can now start going deeper into interpretation, moving from the most specific, objective, measurable, manifest dimensions to the latent ones. This method of analysis will help us understand how CEOs influence strategy formation.

First Interpretation Level: Patterns in Activities

Taking into account the most frequent activities and the nature and importance of communications, I looked for emerging gestalts in the data.

A *controller* pattern best describes John: blind, he works with his door open in order to hear everything happening at the reception desk beside his office. People walk freely into his office to report on their work. John prefers encounters and small meetings to large ones. He does not make or receive many phone calls but constantly drops names for his employees to contact. Work on all the important files (for example, financing) is done at home. He does allow others a share in decision making. Even at the level of the dozen ongoing projects, John keeps control over all the important issues, although he seems to leave a great deal of autonomy to the project teams.

André's whole life is devoted to Communiplus: lunches become meetings, interviews, or public relations affairs. His activity pattern is that of a *coordinator*. He gets to the office before anyone else; he goes to every meeting (with a ratio of 2.03 persons contacted per minute, his day is mostly spent in meetings) and leaves last. He works with the door open: His subordinates know they can always enter for a suggestion, an opinion, guidelines, or for approval. He says that a good coach always has to be as near to his team as possible. André initiates 73 percent of the time he spends on the phone. As the CEO, he touches on everything from recruiting new creatives to negotiating a merger, still overseeing the preparation of "pitches" and coordinating the production of the total agency's output.

Tim does not work much longer at the office than his employees. He rarely works at home, believing that after a day at work one becomes less efficient and needs rest. Every morning, on arriving at the office, he carefully runs over his agenda in order to tackle as many problems as possible during the day, striving, as he says, for both efficiency and effectiveness. He has an *operator* pattern, spending equal time on solitary work and encounters. Tim does not believe that large meetings are very productive and he favors short work sessions. Although he closes his door to work, it does not stop subordinates from coming in: He is interrupted twice as often as John or André. Tim has a lower contact-per-minute ratio than André or John in spite of the fact that he meets a greater number of different people in a day. He makes greater use of the telephone (17 percent of his time), mostly with customers to solve pricing or production issues. Owning two newspapers in the region, he uses his lunches to socialize with influential people from Saint-Joseph; he therefore feels better prepared to manage the editorial policies. Wiseman Printing is growing into a mature organization with functional directors, efficient methods and procedures, and sophisticated EDP systems. But although more and more decisions are taken by the managers, Tim remains an important part of operations, keeping his hands on the quotation process.

Second Interpretation Level: The Nature of Contacts

John, André, and Tim, who spend 81 percent, 90 percent, and 77 percent of their time communicating, respectively, confirmed the studies of managers done by such researchers as Mintzberg (1973) and Kotter (1982), who have stressed the importance of networking. In light of this previous research, I was interested in finding out the motives for these contacts, to be able to classify them under personal, environmental, or organizational issues. By listing the names daily, as observation went on, I discovered fewer and fewer new names, indicating that executives worked within smaller networks than originally expected. Tracing names to activities or occupations, I noticed much "name-dropping": Real person-to-person contact was never undertaken with many of the people mentioned by the CEOs. I thus understood that real contacts and dropped names had to be analyzed differently (Table 6.2).

The word *grandiose* probably best describes the nature of John's contacts. A good personal illustration of this is that he introduced me to other people as a "psychiatrist studying his megalomania." Although he had the longest list of contacts, 63 percent of them turned out to be simple name-dropping to impress his subordinates. Most of these names (97 percent) belonged to the environment category: The list was made of influential people in business or politics, including the prime ministers of Quebec and Canada. On the other hand, 72 percent of his real contacts were organizational, the controller being

Table 6.2. The Nature of Contacts.

Activity Pattern	John Palmer Controller	André Beaulieu Coordinator	Tim Wiseman Operator
Total number of contacts/month	183	157	166
Names dropped	63%	8%	24%
Real contacts	68	144	126
Personal	12%	10%	11%
Organizational	72%	52%	60%
Environmental	16%	38%	29%
Leading environmental contacts	Lobbyists	Related to ongoing issues	Customers
Leading organizational contacts	Finance and accounting people	Creatives	Marketing and production people
Purpose of most contacts	Nebulous: protection against uncertainty	Utilitarian: decision making	Informative: evaluation of industry trends
Nature of Contacts	Grandiose	Proactive-Directive	Scanning

the single most important one. Lobbyists were most prominent among the 16 percent of environmental contacts. Finally, 12 percent of his contacts were personal. Analyzing the data and discussing them with John, I concluded that his main preoccupation was to feel grandiose and powerful. Insertion Inc.'s strategy can probably be divided into two parts: the first generating short-term funds in order to survive, and the second building community support as a type of long-term life insurance. John splits his time daily between "name-dropping," in the hope of building a strong lobby to protect the organization against the ever-present threat of bankruptcy, and managing a series of short-term projects that generate funds for Insertion Inc. The controller in his company gets most of his attention: Other people keep generating new projects—which are seldom profitable or long-term oriented—and dropping names that will, they hope, impress John.

André is totally different from John in his contacts: 92 percent of his names were contacted with a clear purpose in mind. Coaching his employees accounted for 52 percent of his contacts, 38 percent dealt with environmental issues with people external to Communiplus, and only 10 percent were devoted to personal matters. André lost no time with unproductive contacts; proactive and directive as he was, he initiated most contacts in order to solve pressing issues like a merger, recruitment, or handling major clients. At Communiplus the strategy could probably be described as aiming to be the lowest-cost advertising agency on the market with products unavailable elsewhere.

Tim looked more like a scanner in managing his contacts. The purpose of many was the evaluation of industry trends. He was successful in obtaining the needed information. Although he engaged in 24 percent name-dropping, 83 percent of these names were external references given to his directors looking for information. Customers dominated the real environmental contacts (29 percent), whereas people from marketing and production led the organizational ones (60 percent). Strategy at Wiseman Printing seems to be related to the desire to deliver a high level of high-quality service with high profitability. In an industry where entry is easy, Wiseman Printing differentiates itself by its professionalism: Everything is much more sophisticated at Wiseman Printing than elsewhere in the industry.

Third Interpretation Level: The Essence of Activities

Managing strategically rests on a delicate balance of personal, organizational, and environmental issues. By establishing a complete list of activities recorded minute by minute, day by day, I was able to sort the issues into several preoccupations (Table 6.3).

John spent 6,980 minutes on 31 distinct activities. Thirteen percent of his activities, like walking to the bathroom, saying hello to someone in the hall, getting no answer to a phone call, and so on, were left unclassified. Of the activities, 64 percent were directly related to environmental issues (mostly stakeholders to whom John devoted over 30 percent of his total working time). For example, he wrote a speech for a deputy minister and organized a dinner for his lobbyists. Suppliers and competitors

Table 6.3. The Essence of Activities.

	John Palmer	André Beaulieu	Tim Wiseman
Activity Pattern	Controller	Coordinator	Operator
Nature of Contacts	Grandiose	Proactive-Directive	Scanning
Total categories	31	27	48
Personal	10%	10%	9%
Organizational	26%	56%	46%
Environmental	64%	34%	45%
Personal activities	Private 93%	Partners 46%	Reflection 26%
	Agenda 4%	Consultants 37%	Mother 24%
	Reflection 3%	Private 9%	Private 24%
	Reflection 5%	Agenda 15%	City merger 11%
		Agenda 3%	
Organizational activities	Project management 31%	Creatives 62%	Operations management 28%
	Coffee 15%	Operations management 17%	New projects 26%
	Fund-raising campaign 14%	Human resources management 15%	Sales management 18%
	Operations management 13%	General management 4%	General management 11%
	Financial management 13%	Annual party 2%	Financial management 8%
	Methods and procedures 12%		Human resources management 5%
	Corporate image 2%		Newspapers 4%
Environmental activities	Stakeholders 48%	Competitors 74%	Customers 63%
	Suppliers 25%	Customers 12%	Lunches at Le Pornic 25%
	Competitors 14%	Visitors 8%	Competitors 6%
	Customers 9%	Public relations 6%	Suppliers 4%
	Members 4%		Government 1%
			Neighbor 1%
Essence of Activities	Eclecticism	Execution	Innovation

came next in importance. Organizational issues came way behind, involving only 26 percent of John's activities under seven headings. Management of projects represented the largest category of this group, followed by the morning coffee sessions! Finally, phoning friends, buying furniture, or discussing personal issues with the researcher accounted for the remaining 10 percent of his activities. John divided his time among so many activities and people who were not necessarily important for Insertion Inc. that *eclecticism* seems to be the only word to characterize the nature of his preoccupations.

André worked at least twice as long as John during the month I spent with him. His 15,311 minutes of work uncovered 27 activities: *Execution* best describes their nature, with 56 percent of his time going to organizational issues, mostly concerning the creatives who can make or break an agency. André was not trained as a creative but as a manager; yet despite or perhaps because of that, he spent a great deal of his time directing creative work. He gave his attention to managing the production operations; the pricing, accounting, and collecting processes; recruiting; and the management of human resources. Environmental issues came second, taking 34 percent of André's total time: Assessing a competitor for a merger also took much of his attention, leaving less for actual or potential clients. Questioning his partners or consultants on his merger intentions accounted for the largest part of his personal activities. Managing his agenda came last in importance and nobody but himself — neither secretaries, receptionist, nor subordinates — had any control over his activities.

An analysis of Tim's working time revealed 48 different activities. Given his well-structured organization his managers took most of the routine decisions. This gave Tim time to deal with many more issues than John or André. The organizational (46 percent) and environmental (45 percent) issues were equally important. The remaining 9 percent of the observed 8,555 minutes of work was devoted to personal matters. It is interesting to note that Tim spent 26 percent of his personal time on reflection. During these periods Tim often told me what he was thinking about. His other personal activities were concerned with his mother, his private affairs, and managing his agenda. Of his organizational preoccupations (which took up 46 percent of his working time), production management took 28 percent. He made sure that the production group followed market needs and stayed ahead of the competition. This explains the importance he gave to special projects: Six were currently being studied by his employees, each launched to maintain Wiseman Printing's technological edge. Tim also devoted time to various management functions: sales (18 percent), general management (11 percent), finance (8 percent), personnel (5 percent), and the newspapers, a separate strategic business unit (4 percent). Of the environmental preoccupations (45 percent), customers got 63 percent of his attention, spread between negotiations, visits, golf, discussions, exchange of information, and so on. Daily lunches at Le Pornic came second, while competitors, suppliers, the government, and a neighbor accounted for the balance. Of the three CEOs, Tim spread his time over the largest number of issues in order to keep things in balance. But everything he did was directed toward the same goal: to maintain Wiseman Printing's competitive edge through product, service, management, and manufacturing innovation in order to give the best service to the customers and to maintain the highest profitability ratios in the industry.

As we can see from these analyses, CEOs define for their subordinates (through their evident preoccupations) the issues on which they should concentrate: This is how they enact a context for the development of strategy. People at Insertion Inc. played the "name-dropping" game initiated by John. At Communiplus, where André monitors the competitors, tries to recruit the necessary resources, and has a hands-on approach to the products, the employees do not spend much time looking for clients: They concentrate on the projects that André brings back. Finally, Tim clearly enacts a context where people strive to serve the customer better through profitable innovations in product design, manufacturing processes, and service. Balancing all these issues at Wiseman Printing makes for a tightly knit set of strategic components.

Fourth Interpretation Level: The Nature of Preoccupations

The easiest way to study preoccupations is to keep asking CEOs what is on their mind and to note their answers. We can see from Table 6.4 that John's preoccupations focused on himself, that Communiplus stood central for André, while Tim had a more balanced response. Once again, patterns begin to emerge. John's preoccupations were characterized by *ambivalence:* He rarely made up his mind about an issue and kept all avenues open. He may have had no other choice with Insertion Inc.'s very uncertain future. *Efficiency* best describes André's preoccupations. Tim showed *vigilance:* He kept hesitating and "pushing ideas a little further."

But how can we make sense out of these data? It is of course irrelevant to measure preoccupations in the same way as activities. What we can do is to use the widely accepted psychoanalytic concepts of latent and manifest content developed by Freud in his theory of dreams ([1900] 1962) and consider the preoccupations as latent material and the activities as the manifest content to be interpreted with the help of general concepts derived from object relations theory (see Greenberg and Mitchell, 1983).

Using the style typology developed by Kets de Vries and Miller (1984a, 1984b), I found that John showed a narcissistic behavior pattern characteristic of *dramatic* styles. Driven by grandiosity, ambivalence, and eclecticism, he did all he could to get attention. Sometimes easy to influence, he would go one way or another according to his latest inspiration. Many of his decisions were very risky and did not always show much coherence. André clearly showed a *compulsive* style: He did all he could to make sure his subordinates would follow his instructions, looking at every possible detail. He never took any rest; he kept phoning partners or friends for opinions, thus delaying important decisions; he saw the world as a battlefield where you either won or lost. He tried to control everything and managed a very efficient and profitable operation. Tim, finally, had a somewhat *schizoid* style. He tried to stay at a distance from people, minimiz-

Table 6.4. The Nature of Preoccupations.

	John Palmer	*André Beaulieu*	*Tim Wiseman*
Pattern	Controller	Coordinator	Operator
Contacts	Grandiose	Proactive-Directive	Scanning
Occupations	Eclecticism	Execution	Innovation

Personal preoccupations	Salary inequities
	Help weak people
	Be less a
	  figurehead
	Board composition
	Understand
	  everything
	Produce changes
	Fear of security
	Have an impact
	Create jobs
	Get close to
	  powerful people
	Get into power
	  circles
	Have a probabilist
	  vision
	Remain
	  independent
		Slow down
		Become no. 1
		Profitability
		Merger or
		  acquisition
		Communiplus style
		Buy an English-
		  speaking agency
		Find a creative
		Build synergy
		  between creatives
		  and ABC merger
		Better structure
		Get ABC for free
		Creative team
		Profit centers
		Preserve his
		  market share
			Quality of life
			Balance his needs
			Find a "guru"
			Wiseman Printing
			  or newspapers?
			Share ownership
			How to use his
			  free time?

Organizational preoccupations	Long-term
	  planning
	Structure
	The SRL project
	The MTL branch
	New equipments
	Increase revenues
		Fewer freelance
		  employees
		Controlled growth
		Financial health
		Have aggressive
		  employees
			Growth rate
			Replacing the
			  operations VP
			Space needs
			Joint venture
			Product lines
			Profitability
			Number of
			  employees
			Human resources
			Better
			  communications

Environmental preoccupations	Private funding
	Government
	  funding
	Fund-raising
	  campaign
	Evolution of
	  politics
	Ottawa branch
		Get on U.S.
		  market
		Find a merger
		  opportunity
		Win pitch XYZ
			Industry war
			New technologies
			Customer no. 5
			Impact on Bill 17
			Get on U.S.
			  market
			Competitors'
			  offensive
			Relative
			  performance

Table 6.4. The Nature of Preoccupations, Cont'd.

	John Palmer	André Beaulieu	Tim Wiseman
Focus	Himself	Communiplus	None: Balance
Pattern	Ambivalence	Efficiency	Vigilance
Style	Dramatic	Compulsive	Schizoid
Myth	Handicap	Fighting	Technology
Magnificent Obsession	Autonomy	Money	Quality

ing the problems human beings created in management by buying advanced technological equipment. He also wished to distance himself from Wiseman Printing, did not want to see it grow too much, but still could not envision the future without it.

Given the unique style of each CEO, their preoccupations influenced their subordinates mainly through the use of organizational myths. Trice (1985, p. 228) defines myths as "imaginative, taken-for-granted explanations of how collective behavior should go forward." At Insertion Inc., handicaps provided a collective explanation for all actions: Everybody, everything, *even the organization itself* was seen as handicapped. Communiplus's myth was to be locked in battle: In an advertising agency, one has to fight to survive and to work long hours to "make it"; like a battle or a football game, the troops keep close together when facing the enemy. Finally, at Wiseman Printing, technology was the powerful myth spread through the company. It had once saved it by creating a niche; now everybody believed that products, production facilities, and management systems needed to be state-of-the-art for the company to succeed.

But why were these myths generated? Why did these styles emerge? Why did the managers concentrate on the preoccupations I have identified? What was behind these preoccupations? What was it that gave them meaning and pulled everything together? With all these observations in mind, and looking for final interpretations according to the rule of multiple function, I discovered an underlying central theme in each CEO's inner theater; I termed it the Magnificent Obsession.

Behind John's grandiose preoccupations, I found a deep fear of dependency. I would describe his Magnificent Obsession as a strong need for *autonomy*. He wanted as much autonomy as possible for himself through Insertion Inc. John had no ownership in the company but he did all he could, by developing systems and procedures manuals, to be in total control of Insertion Inc. His strategic activities were in line with his dramatic style and by dropping names he maintained an image of himself as a powerful man. He maintained Insertion Inc., seemingly unconsciously, in a state of vulnerability that confirmed his personal strength. By recruiting mainly socially handicapped people, and by continually working on short-term projects, he played strongly on the myth of the handicap to maintain cohesion between the people around him.

André's preoccupations were detail oriented and everything was a dollars-and-cents issue, uncovering his Magnificent Obsession to make money and to get rich. Owner of the largest share in Communiplus, he wanted to see and hear as little as possible of his other minority partners. He also managed to get the highest return out of each one of his employees, who had little hope of becoming partners. André strongly resisted extending partnership to his key employees, as many of his competitors do, because in these firms, partners "have a lot of fun, spend a lot of money, but do not get rich." In return, Communiplus is not attractive to the brighest talents or the more experienced people on the market, who look for more money and autonomy. In crisis situations André does not have easy access to the best freelancers in the industry. The company has to rely mostly on itself to realize its bids and contracts. Communiplus attracts young people looking for a first job who run to competitors as soon as they can get a better deal. André's obsession with efficiency and money precludes him from keeping or even finding the single most important ingredient for growth and long-term survival in the advertising industry, that is, loyal, dedicated, and talented creative people.

Finally, Tim's Magnificent Obsession is for *quality*, in products, machines, facilities, management, and above all, in life in general. Tim Wiseman studied in Montreal, where he made friends and met his wife. He never really intended to come back to Saint-Joseph to run a small manufacturing company in an environment where employees would rather go hunting and fishing than show up for work. He wanted all the things a large city has to offer. To some extent he developed Wiseman Printing to compensate for coming back to a small country town: He buys sophisticated machinery not only to reduce his dependence on human beings but also to prove to himself and to others that he could have stayed and run a sophisticated company in the city. He built the most modern house in Saint-Joseph, drives an expensive German car, drinks expensive French wines, and travels to exotic countries during his holidays. He insists on quality in everything that surrounds him, at home as well as at Wiseman Printing. He does not behave like his competitors, who simply cut costs in order to survive in a highly competitive industry. As most of them rapidly go bankrupt and are replaced by newcomers who do the same, Tim is now thinking of sharing ownership with his best managers, another "quality" type of innovation to differentiate Wiseman Printing from its competition.

From Obsessions to Strategies

I have gone as far as I can in my interpretations with the data available. Strategies are unique patterns of decisions in a company. The uniqueness of the strategies of Insertion Inc., Communiplus, and Wiseman Printing are now clear. Long-term clinical observation of CEOs brings their individual preoccupations to the surface. By carefully interpreting the data, going systematically from their manifest to their latent content, as in Figure 6.1, we can uncover the Magnificent Obsessions central to all their activities.

I believe that Magnificent Obsessions are the roots of the enactment processes (Weick, 1970) that can be observed during consultation. I am not referring to a restricted definition of obsessive-compulsiveness, but to what Shapiro (1975, p. 29) calls "a capacity for volitional direction of attention." My three CEOs showed a rigidity in their visions that gave a strategic direction to their activities. They could simplify complex situations and look only at the important details. They were also

Figure 6.1. Uncovering Strategies.

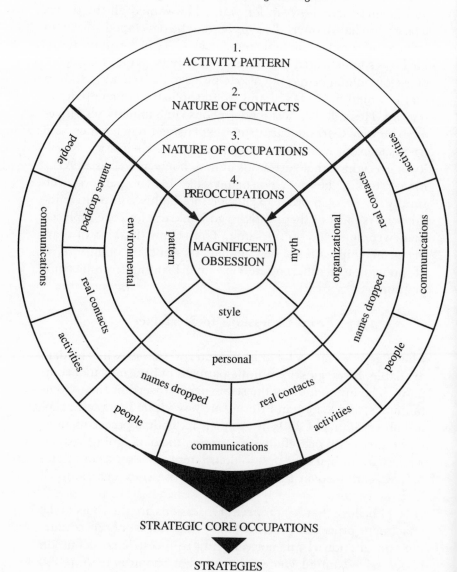

capable of maintaining their concentration despite frequent interruptions. To be able to manage daily despite a high level of uncertainty, CEOs focus their activities on strategic core preoccupations. They also use rituals, metaphors, and organizational myths (Hedberg and Jonsson, 1977; Jonsson and Lundin, 1977) to disseminate their obsession.

In this chapter I have indicated that the systematic search for Magnificent Obsessions in activities and preoccupations of CEOs is a powerful tool for understanding the strategy and thus the uniqueness of an organization. Discovering the daily strategic core activities of CEOs enables us to understand how they influence the strategy formation process. These preoccupations can help a consultant or a subordinate to understand how CEOs make decisions and can also help them to predict how the strategy may evolve, given several hypothetical problems or foreseeable changes. For example, five years later on, at Insertion Inc., more effort is still being concentrated on building contacts and developing systems and procedures than on being efficient or serving the customer appropriately: The systems are not yet implemented and Insertion Inc. is, as always, very near bankruptcy. In the case of Communiplus, it is no surprise to hear that André never completed a merger operation or signed a partnership, that employees still come and go, that Communiplus has not grown—but that André has made a lot of money. As for Wiseman Printing, they have expanded successfully to Toronto: Sales and profits have more than doubled while the workforce increased by only 50 percent. Of course they still have plans for further expansion, to the United States.

Were these strategies industry specific? The decisions made by John, André, and Tim were naturally specifically related to the methods and needs of their different industries. On the other hand, analysis of their Magnificent Obsessions revealed how and why they behaved differently from their competitors. Since strategies need to be company specific, I believe this clinical approach is a good way for consultants to bring them to the surface, to understand them and to help their clients.

References

Ackoff, R. L. *A Concept of Corporate Planning.* New York: Wiley, 1970.

Aldrich, H. E. *Organizations and Environments.* Englewood Cliffs, N.J.: Prentice-Hall, 1979.

Allison, G. T. *The Essence of Decision: Explaining the Cuban Missile Crisis.* Boston: Little, Brown, 1971.

Andrews, K. R. *The Concept of Corporate Strategy.* Homewood, Ill.: Irwin, 1971.

Ansoff, H. I. *Corporate Strategy.* New York: McGraw-Hill, 1965.

Blau, P. M. *The Dynamics of Bureaucracy: A Study of Interpersonal Relations in Two Government Agencies.* Chicago: University of Chicago Press, 1963.

Bowman, E. H. "Concerns of the CEO." *Human Resource Management,* 1986, *25* (2), 267–285.

Carlson, S. *Executive Behavior: A Study of the Workload and the Working Methods of Managing Directors.* Stockholm: Strömberg, 1951.

Chandler, A. D., Jr. *Strategy and Structure: Chapters in the History of the American Enterprise.* Cambridge, Mass.: MIT Press, 1962.

Crozier, M. *The Bureaucratic Phenomenon.* Chicago: University of Chicago Press, 1964.

Dalton, M. *Men Who Manage.* New York: Wiley, 1959.

Freud, S. "The Interpretation of Dreams." In J. Strachey (ed. and trans.), *The Standard Edition of the Complete Psychological Works of Sigmund Freud.* Vol. 5. London: Hogarth Press, 1962. (Originally published 1900.)

Geertz, C. *The Interpretation of Cultures.* New York: Basic Books, 1973.

Glaser, B., and Strauss, A. *Discovery of Grounded Theory: Strategies for Qualitative Research.* Chicago: Aldine, 1967.

Greenberg, J. R., and Mitchell, S. A. *Object Relations in Psychoanalytic Theory.* Cambridge, Mass.: Harvard University Press, 1983.

Guth, W., and Tagiuri, R. "Personal Values and Corporate Strategy." *Harvard Business Review,* 1965, *43,* 123–132.

Hannan, M. T., and Freeman, J. "The Population Ecology of Organizations." *American Journal of Sociology,* 1977, *82,* 929–964.

Hedberg, B. L. T., and Jonsson, S. A. "Strategy Formulation as a Discontinuous Process." *International Studies of Management and Organization,* 1977, *3,* 88–109.

Hofer, C. W., and Schendel, D. E. *Strategy Formulation: Analytical Concepts.* St. Paul, Minn.: West, 1978.

Jaques, E. *The Changing Culture of a Factory.* London: Tavistock, 1951.

Jonsson, S. A., and Lundin, R. A. "Myths and Wishful Thinking as Management Tools." *TIMS Studies in the Management Sciences,* 1977, *5,* 157–170.

Kets de Vries, M.F.R. *Solving Mysteries: Playing Organizational Detective.* Working paper. Cambridge, Mass.: Division of Research, Graduate School of Business Administration, Harvard University, 1978.

Kets de Vries, M.F.R., and Miller, D. *The Neurotic Organization: Diagnosing and Changing Counterproductive Styles of Management.* San Francisco: Jossey-Bass, 1984a.

Kets de Vries, M.F.R., and Miller, D. "Neurotic Style and Organizational Pathology." *Strategic Management Journal,* 1984b, *5,* 35–55.

Kotter, J. P. *The General Managers.* New York: Free Press, 1982.

Miles, R. E., Snow, C. C., and Pfeffer, J. "Organization-Environment: Concepts and Issues." *Industrial Relations,* 1974, *13,* 244–264.

Mintzberg, H. *The Nature of Managerial Work.* New York: Harper & Row, 1973.

Mintzberg, H. "Patterns in Strategy Formation." *Management Science,* 1978, *29* (4), 934–948.

Noël, A. "Un mois dans la vie de trois présidents: Préoccupations et occupations stratégiques" [One month in the life of three CEOs: Strategic preoccupations and occupations]. Unpublished doctoral dissertation, Faculty of Management, McGill University, 1984.

Pfeffer, J., and Salancik, G. R. *The External Control of Organizations: A Resource Dependence Perspective.* New York: Harper & Row, 1978.

Porter, M. E. *Competitive Strategy: Techniques for Analyzing Industries and Competitors.* New York: Free Press, 1980.

Porter, M. E. *Competitive Advantage.* New York: Free Press, 1985.

Porter, M. E. *The Competitive Advantage of Nations*. New York: Free Press, 1990.

Roethlisberger, F., and Dickson, W. *Management and the Worker*. Cambridge, Mass.: Harvard University Press, 1939.

Schein, E. H. *The Clinical Perspective in Fieldwork*. Newbury Park, Calif.: Sage, 1987.

Shapiro, D. *Neurotic Styles*. New York: Basic Books, 1965.

Steiner, G. A., and Miner, J. B. *Management Policy and Strategy*. New York: Free Press, 1977.

Stewart, R. *Managers and Their Jobs*. London: Collier Macmillan, 1967.

Trice, H. M. "Rites and Ceremonials in Organizational Cultures." *Research in the Sociology of Organizations*, 1985, *4*, 221–270.

Weick, K. E. *The Social Psychology of Organizing*. Reading, Mass.: Addison-Wesley, 1970.

Wissema, J. G., Van der Pol, H. W., and Messer, H. M. "Strategic Management Archetypes." *Strategic Management Journal*, 1980, *1* (1), 37–47.

PART THREE

Change Processes in Work Groups

7

Managing Boundaries in Organizations

Susan C. Schneider

The notion of boundaries is a key concept in the psychology of individuals, families, and groups. In organizational literature, boundaries are discussed more implicitly, for example, in terms of boundary spanners and boundary spanning activities and the importance of managing boundaries effectively (Aldrich and Herker, 1977; Adams, 1976). The questions of how boundaries are managed and how this relates to the levels of differentiation and integration necessary for effective functioning within organizations, however, have not been addressed sufficiently.

Boundaries separate a system from its environment and delineate the parts and processes within that system. Boundaries also determine relatedness and relationships within and between systems. Thus boundaries need to be defined yet flexible. As systems develop, they become increasingly differentiated, requiring greater integration for internal coherence and coordination and external responsiveness (Lawrence and Lorsch, 1967; Katz and Kahn, 1978; Galbraith, 1974). This chapter explores how boundaries are managed, that is, established and negotiated, at multiple levels of analysis. Several common themes emerge. The case of a partial hospital program will then be discussed to illustrate the application of these themes. Finally, implications will be drawn regarding organizational analysis and intervention.

169

Levels of Analysis

Establishing and negotiating boundaries occurs both at the intrapersonal (intrapsychic) and interpersonal levels.

Individual Level

At the intrapsychic level, boundary management reflects the process whereby the psyche becomes better differentiated and integrated. In Freud's ([1932] 1961) tripartite system of id, ego, and superego, boundaries evolve to a point at which ego functioning achieves autonomy from id and superego demands. "Where id was, there ego shall be" means that the ego will control rather than be controlled by the id. This strengthens the boundary between fantasy and reality so that perceptions are less distorted by desires or wishful thinking (id-derived) (Hartmann, 1950). The differentiation of ego and superego reduces the inhibition and restriction of ego functioning (Freud, [1932] 1961). The increased ego autonomy, in turn, strengthens the boundary between the individual and the external world (Shapiro and Zinner, 1979). Yet in mediating between the id, the superego, and the environment, the ego negotiates these boundaries to achieve integration.

The process of establishing and negotiating interpersonal boundaries has also been described by Mahler, Pine, and Bergman (1975). Infants initially are unable to differentiate self from other. In this stage of autism, there is no awareness of other or self. A gradual awareness of self emerges but not as separate from other (symbiosis). At around eighteen months the process of separating and individuating begins, which establishes a sense of self as separate from mother. This stage, *rapprochement* (often referred to as the "terrible two's"), is marked by the child's incredible bossiness and willfulness. The ability to say no and efforts to control self and exert control over others are crucial for developing a separate and autonomous self, that is, for establishing boundaries. Yet these boundaries must be negotiated to meet the child's need for relatedness.

Subsequent stages of development—mastery of the environment, establishing identity, and developing intimacy—

are dependent on the successful resolution of these early stages (Mahler, Pine, and Bergman, 1975; Erikson, 1963; Freud, [1932] 1961). For example, identity requires establishing boundaries that delineate self from external other as well as differentiating internalized objects and self representations (Klein, [1932] 1975). Yet integration is necessary to create a coherent identity. Intimacy is possible only when the boundaries are secure enough to allow closeness. Otherwise intimacy raises fears of loss of self and engulfment by the other. Psychological health requires establishing boundaries, while maintaining the necessary relatedness. These boundary issues are revived and become increasingly salient when individuals negotiate their roles in families, groups, and organizations.

Family Level

In family systems, managing the boundaries between members is an important process. Role and generational boundaries need to be established. Family dysfunction often reflects difficulties in establishing boundaries, because they are either overly diffuse at one extreme or overly rigid at the other. Problems negotiating boundaries result in a failure of mutuality (relatedness) (Minuchin, 1974; Bowen, 1976). Pseudomutuality refers to a condition in which families appear to be well integrated or well related but, in fact, lack sufficient differentiation since the boundaries within the family are blurred (Wynne, Ryckof, Day, and Hirsch, 1958). In these families, individual and generational boundaries are poorly defined and the roles and functions are confused (who is mothering or parenting whom?).

For example, the identified patient, who through symptom formation requires being taken care of, is actually taking care of the system by preserving its interdependence (Bateson, 1972; Haley, 1987). The family is brought together to address what to do about the patient, thereby forcing relatedness. An underfunctioning family member establishes a role boundary to complement the role boundary established by an overfunctioning member, thereby negotiating the type of relatedness needed to keep the family together. Furthermore, family fighting is often seen as a symptom that redefines the boundary when

individual autonomy is threatened. However, fighting may also
be seen as a substitute for intimacy since it maintains relatedness. The task of treatment is viewed as redrawing the generational and role boundaries; for example, father and mother are
united in parenting the child. Family therapy assists in negotiating boundaries and allowing for individual identity and autonomy while preserving the relatedness of the family system.

Hirschhorn and Gilmore (1980) suggest that family therapy
models may be useful in intervention in organizations, particularly since they stress the need to clarify boundaries (differentiate) and to increase relevant communication (improve integration). They warn, however, that boundaries in organizations
are far more complex than in families. There is greater differentiation — for example, greater role complexity in organizations —
and integration is not as easily threatened by the loss of one
individual. However, dynamics at the family level are often
played out at the work-group level as family roles are replayed
and conflicts (for example, with authority) are reexperienced
(Levinson, 1976).

Thus, at the family level, boundaries are managed so that
both individual identity and family relatedness are maintained
while the boundary around the family is reinforced. The way
in which these boundaries are managed influences the roles that
family members establish in the outside world.

Group Level

Boundaries in groups need to be managed for the individual
vis-à-vis the group and for the group vis-à-vis other groups. The
development and ongoing dynamics of groups reveal how boundaries are established and negotiated (Tuckman, 1965; Bion,
1959; Miller and Rice, 1967; Slater, 1966). In the early stages
of group development, individual boundary and control issues
become most salient. Dependency needs are revived as the group
serves some function (the reason for joining) for the individual. Group membership requires negotiating individual boundaries, seeing oneself as part of a group and accepting being controlled by the group norms. At this point, members often reassert

individual boundaries and reassert autonomy by testing the group's rules or norms. Leadership is often challenged and power struggles are frequent until a new balance of power is established. As group cohesiveness evolves, the boundaries between members are lessened and the boundary between group and other groups becomes better defined.

Group boundaries are established and continually negotiated when new members join and when old members leave. These events are often marked by induction ceremonies (such as hazing) and retirement rituals (Trice and Beyer, 1984). Boundaries are also strengthened and internal integration facilitated by identifying internal scapegoats or external enemies (Janis, 1972). Conflicts between groups often reflect efforts to reassert group boundaries while enhancing internal integration. Renegotiating roles within or between groups is required, however, to clarify the necessary differentiation while strengthening integration.

At the group level, another boundary exists between fantasy and reality. Groups often operate according to basic assumptions (fantasies) regarding the purpose of the group that may not pertain to task performance (Bion, 1959). These shared fantasies of being taken care of (dependency), of persecution (fight-flight), or of salvation (pairing) reduce the boundary between the individual and the group. Group boundaries are strengthened by creating an all-powerful leader whom everyone will follow, an enemy whom everyone will fight, or a messiah for whom everyone will wait. To the extent to which these fantasies interfere with task performance, the boundary between reality and fantasy needs to be strengthened. Sometimes these fantasies facilitate task performance—for example, when unquestioning loyalty to the leader is required.

The basic assumption operating may also relate to the stage of group development and reflect the boundary and control issues relevant to that stage. Early in development, as dependency needs are revived, the fantasy of being taken care of may be more relevant. This allows the group to coalesce around a strong leader, blurring individual boundaries. Later on, between-group boundaries may be reinforced by persecution fantasies that coalesce the group by identifying an enemy. Concerns with task performance may elicit "pairing" fantasies, in that the coming together of group members will magically (without effort) produce what is hoped for.

Organization Level

The boundary issues present at the group level exist between groups within organizations and between the organization and its environment (Miller and Rice, 1967). Organizations can establish their boundaries by buffering or isolating their operations (Thompson, 1967), by creating "niches" in developing distinctive competence (Kotter, 1977), and by controlling the flow of inputs and outputs (Katz and Kahn, 1978). How the boundary between organizations and their environments is negotiated relates to the extent to which organizations control or are controlled by their environments (Aldrich and Pfeffer, 1976; Pfeffer and Salancik, 1978; Child, 1972). This determines the degree to which organizations respond proactively or reactively to environmental change (Miles and Snow, 1978), or in fact select the aspects of that environment to which to respond (Weick, 1979). Public sector organizations and professional bureaucracies, such as hospitals and universities, are often unable to define and negotiate external boundaries since environmental stakeholders (for example, regulatory agencies) may dictate goals, methods, or strategies.

Strategies for managing the boundaries within the organization and between the organization and its environment may differ in terms of increasing differentiation or enhancing integration. Often innovations or new ventures within the organization need to be isolated, allowed to develop separately, become better differentiated, before integration (Zaltman, Duncan, and Holbek, 1973). The IBM personal computer had to be developed in this manner, "protected" from the organization's bureaucratic system, which would have strangled it. Other strategies such as co-opting, building coalitions, developing networks, and takeover reflect efforts at increasing integration (Kotter, 1977). These strategies emphasize relatedness by demonstrating the need for interdependence.

Problems within the organization may reflect excessive or insufficient boundaries. Insufficient boundaries create symptoms of overlap and redundancy. Tasks, roles, or functions are duplicated, creating wasted resources. On the other hand, boundaries may be overly defined or rigid so that tasks are not performed — the "it's not my job" syndrome. Excessive differentiation or boundary formation can result in fragmentation. Attempts to create interdisciplinary study groups, task forces, or projects are often thwarted because maintaining the professional group boundary is seen as more important than the task.

During reorganizations, boundaries are redrawn and redefined. The individual and group dynamics previously described combine with the organizational context to determine how boundaries are established. The individual's personal boundaries are negotiated with others, within groups, and through the organizational structure in terms of roles and hierarchical position. The renegotiation of boundaries is often marked by a scramble for power and by pervasive anxiety among the individuals and throughout the groups affected. The resolution of boundaries rests on the required interdependence or the amount of interaction. But the resolution is dynamic in that it is continuously changing. The role of leadership is to manage the boundary between what is inside and what is outside in order to preserve the integrity and the internal coherence of the system (Shapiro and Zinner, 1979).

From this discussion, we can see the process of managing (establishing and negotiating) boundaries across levels of analysis. Several common themes emerge: First, boundary management at each level is apparent and important; second, boundary management determines the levels of differentiation and integration within and between systems; third, boundary management is a dynamic process that changes over the stages of development; and, finally, boundary management is closely related to issues of autonomy and control. In what follows, the case of the design and implementation of a partial hospital program is described and discussed to demonstrate how boundaries were managed in this particular situation and the implications for the program's effectiveness.

The Partial Hospital Program: A Case Example

In 1980 I was hired to design and implement a partial hospital program (PHP). The purpose of this program was to provide mental health care to patients at risk of hospitalization and to patients reentering the community following hospitalization. Programs of this nature were developed as part of the deinstitutionalization effort to decentralize mental health care services from the state to the community level. The PHP was a service required by federal mandate as part of a community mental health center (CMHC). The CMHC in turn reported to the department of psychiatry of the municipal hospital in which it was housed. As shown in Figure 7.1, the reporting lines were further complicated given the multiple stakeholders—federal, state, municipal, and private agencies—on which the CMHC was dependent for resources. My task was to create a program that would address the needs of the patient group targeted (primarily chronic psychiatric patients) and to manage the relationships with the numerous stakeholders.

Chronic psychiatric patients suffer primarily from schizophrenic or affective disorders as well as from the effects of long-term institutionalization, for example, learning to be patients (Goffman, 1961). The deinstitutionalization effort meant not only moving the locus of care to the community level but also unlearning the role of patient and learning the role of community member (Schneider, 1984). Therefore, one of the goals of the program was to teach the skills, roles, and behavior necessary to stay out of hospital. Group and family therapy were the predominant treatment modes since the primary task of treatment was to develop and strengthen both intrapsychic and interpersonal boundaries while managing dependency needs, exacerbated for some by the "custodial care" approach of the state hospitals. Activity therapy was critical to developing both social and daily living skills. Patients were assigned "primary therapists" who would coordinate treatment plans with the other staff. Patients were actively involved in developing their treatment plans, because every effort was made to unlearn the role of patient as incompetent, helpless, and passive.

Figure 7.1. Partial Hospital Program Boundaries.

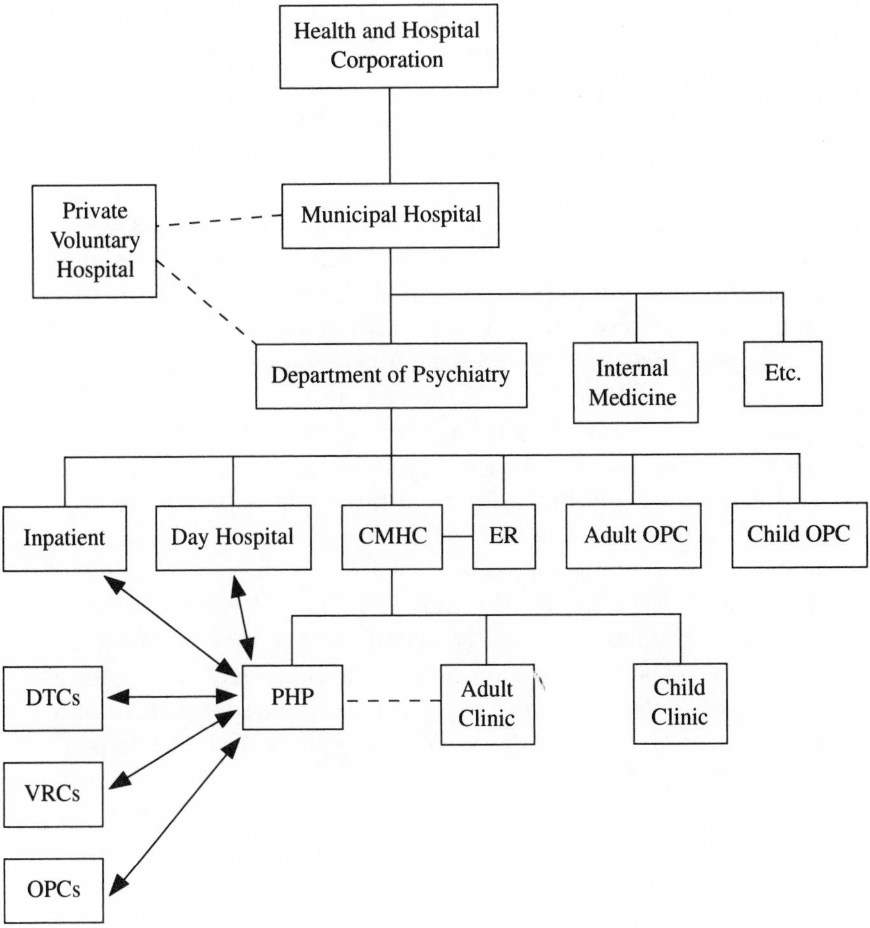

The program staff consisted of a program coordinator (myself, a clinical psychologist), a part-time psychiatrist, a nurse, two social workers, occupational and recreational therapists, and therapy aides. With the exception of the psychiatrist, all performed as primary therapists (generalists) responsible for coordinating treatment plans of their assigned patients as well as providing specialized services to the unit (nursing, social work,

and so on). All staff members reported to their functional departments. The staff were hired from within the municipal hospital
as well as from the outside and were selected on the basis of
their interest in a more generalist approach and a willingness
to take on more program and patient responsibility. They were
expected to participate in the program design, in the development of policies and procedures, and in administrative functions, and to pursue individual interests and ideas that related
to group goals. It was felt that if the staff were involved in developing the program and themselves within the context of that
program, they would then provide the model for the participation of the patients in program and personal development.

This participative approach was in keeping with the grass
roots ideology of the CMHC but ran counter to the prevailing
medical ideology of the municipal hospital (Schneider, 1987).
Because many had been recruited from the latter, this created
an internal role conflict — for example, in how they were supposed to behave as social workers. Role generalization also meant
that some less-than-appealing tasks were shared rather than
dumped on the aides. Furthermore, the participative approach,
while appealing in principle, is difficult in practice since it means
assuming responsibilities for which one may feel ill-prepared
or ill-paid. Over time, as the program's demands on the staff's
energy, creativity, and resourcefulness increased, the dependency assumption became apparent. The greater autonomy and
broader roles created stress, which in turn increased the desire
to be taken care of by a strong leader, in this case for the M.D.
to make all the decisions and to take care of the staff. Thus,
like the tug of departmental reporting lines, passivity on the part
of the staff had to be counteracted. Staff meetings often involved
reiterating roles and relationships in keeping with the overall
purpose of the program in order to help the team differentiate
as well as integrate.

Boundary problems between professional roles and tasks
within the larger system created potential problems within the
program. For example, an investigation was conducted regarding
tensions between psychiatrists and psychologists that concluded
that the psychologists were "overstepping their boundaries" and

needed "to be brought in line." This rigidified the boundary between professional groups, impairing the needed integration, which posed a potential problem in the PHP. For example, in our first meeting, the psychiatrist assigned part time to the unit demanded to know who was responsible for the program. Boundaries were drawn by stating that the program responsibility was mine (a psychologist) while the patient responsibility belonged to him. The negotiation of this boundary was begun by stating that interdependence was desired. This boundary flexibility evolved over time as a function of the quality of interpersonal relatedness, that is, with the experience of mutual respect for one another's expertise and autonomy. The psychiatrist, who had long tenure in the municipal hospital, did not react strongly to the pull of departmental reporting lines and in fact reacted strongly against them, perhaps part of his own personal boundaries issue. He was, however, consistently late in arriving for staff rounds wherein patients' treatment plans were discussed.

With other disciplines (nursing and social work), boundaries were not as well negotiated. Here the pull of reporting lines to disciplines was stronger, particularly for those assigned from within the hospital. For example, when I wanted to conduct a seminar for the staff (all disciplines) on family therapy, the social work staff protested that family therapy was their domain, not that of the other disciplines, and furthermore, the social work department ruled that they did not have to attend a seminar given by a non–social worker. The interpersonal boundaries here were more problematic, perhaps out of personal rivalries and jealousies. We were more similar in terms of being young and female than was the case for the psychiatrist, an older man. The clear age and gender boundaries may have facilitated role-boundary differentiation.

Despite these struggles, a united front was presented outwardly. The innovativeness of the program fostered a utopian assumption — that the group together would create an "ideal" program (Miller, 1979). The "newness" furthered the sense of a "special" identity and group cohesiveness. These shared fantasies helped to establish the group's boundary in the initial phase of development. Furthermore, the program was housed in a building on the other side of campus from the CMHC and the department of psychiatry. We were also helped by the fact that it took several weeks for the telephones to function. Few guidelines existed as to how the program should be developed. This provided autonomy and encouraged the development of a separate identity and group cohesiveness, creating, however, an us-and-them attitude vis-à-vis the CMHC and the department of psychiatry. The fight-flight assumption served to resist appeals for better integration and reinforced the group's boundary.

However, this period of splendid isolation did not last forever. Eventually our presence began to be known. The inpatient programs moved in across the hall. At administrative meetings of the department of psychiatry that I was required to attend, I was repeatedly asked, "What's the difference between the partial hospital and the day hospital programs?" The day hospital was part of the municipal hospital and was predominantly staffed by psychiatrists and psychologists. Psychiatric residents and medical students rotated through this service as well. This unit operated within a "medical-model" ideology in that roles and tasks were specialized and decision making was rather centralized, that is, the doctors made the decisions. According to the PHP staff that had previously worked there, "They did therapy with a capital T." Given the difference in staffing patterns — the day hospital being heavily M.D. and Ph.D. dominated — the boundaries were drawn according to the psychosocial and rehabilitative purpose of the partial hospital. Care was taken to emphasize the complementary nature of the program and thereby address concerns that there would be competition for patients. Thus the boundaries were drawn and the relationship negotiated so that the day hospital became a source of patient referrals to the PHP. The boundary flexibility was enhanced by the physical proximity of the day hospital and inpatient services, which moved to the same building as the PHP. In many ways, the PHP was better linked to the department of psychiatry than to the CMHC. Because the former had more power, establishing good relations and providing a necessary function could aid the long-term viability of the PHP.

The CMHC administration was also calling for more accountability and better links with their services. Links between the other CMHC services were weak and there was strong pressure for better integration. However, other CMHC services were under threat of merger or absorption by the municipal hospital, because the continued existence of the CMHC was in question (due to funding uncertainties). Therefore, the preservation of a strong boundary between the PHP and CMHC may have been important to ensure the PHP's survival.

The department of psychiatry was at best unenthusiastic about and at worst hostile to the existence of the CMHC, due in part to the excessive overlap of services, which created competition. However, the emergency room, which was a shared service (blurred boundaries), required much negotiation regarding staffing, responsibility, and accountability. Part of this hostility was also created by ideological boundaries of a community-oriented versus medical-model approach that was also in line with that of the private/voluntary teaching hospital, which was a major source of resources (money and residents). These ideological differences were, in part, the cause of the role-boundary conflict mentioned earlier. These conflicts demonstrate that excessive differentiation and/or boundary rigidity can interfere with task performance such as patient care. Trying to establish a program based on a generalist model in a specialist context becomes difficult. Trying to create multidisciplinary teams, particularly when professional discipline boundaries are long-standing and rigidified, is also problematic.

Finally, boundaries had to be established and negotiated with various stakeholders in the community, such as agencies that were responsible for funding, and had to be satisfied with regard to their specific criteria. For example, for insurance companies, reimbursement for clinical visits meant medical consultation. Discussions with several local agencies that had similar, potentially competing programs helped to define the program boundaries in such a way as to complement other existing services and to fill identified gaps in the broader community network of mental health care service.

In summary, the program's boundaries were established by virtue of its mandate, its uniqueness in its therapeutic approach and nonprofessional staffing pattern, its initial separate physical location, and its initial autonomy. Roles and tasks were negotiated and decision making was participative. The group cohesiveness that develped within the PHP reinforced its boundaries. This helped the program subsequently to negotiate its boundaries within the organization and with the environment. By stressing how the PHP differed from other services, this boundary was reinforced; the fact that the PHP provided a needed function enhanced integration. The boundary between the program and the external environment was established by defining a "niche," by providing a necessary service, and by controlling the flow of customers (patients). Boundary negotiations involved developing a network of services that emphasized interdependence. In this way, boundary flexibility evolved, instead of the rigidity that would have been established by "competing camps." This was done to encourage longer-term viability. In this manner external differentiation and integration were established. The program began six weeks after my arrival on a trial, part-time basis and was fully implemented six weeks later. I left after a further fifteen months to do postdoctoral work in organizational analysis. Five years later, the program was still running.

Taking Stock

Working with chronic psychiatric patients and within the systems created for them highlights individual boundary issues. First of all, the treatment approach must explicitly address the patients' boundaries through individual, group, family, and activity therapies. Chronic patients are primarily psychotic if not organically (sometimes due to the iatrogenic effects of long-term psychotropic medication) and developmentally impaired as well. Often they have been cared for at home or in institutions where their dependency and helplessness are reinforced. Within their families, their illness may become an integrating force, since it unites the family in deciding (or arguing) what to do about them. Their illness also serves as a differentiating force in that roles are often defined by "who's crazy and who isn't." However, the role of "being crazy" often serves as a repository of the other family members' fears and anxieties. Family therapy with schizophrenics involves redefining the boundaries and finding other mechanisms for relating, for being interdependent, as discussed earlier. Group or milieu therapy approaches provide a more neutral, supportive environment in which the patients can develop ego functions, such as reality testing. Activity therapy further assists in the development of skills and therefore the "autonomous ego." Individual treatment most often involves supportive psychotherapy to help strengthen boundaries between fantasy and reality as well as to help reinforce the boundaries between self and other. Thus individual, group, family, and activity therapy were all considered to be important and interlinked modes of treatment that became the rationale for services provided by the partial hospital.

Working with psychotic patients, however, creates strains on the individual boundaries of staff members. Providing individual therapy normally requires establishing empathy, a regression in the service of the ego. The psychotic material brought to the sessions can stimulate associations on the part of staff members and thereby threaten their own (more-or-less well-established) boundary between fantasy and reality. Furthermore, the intense dependency needs of these patients threatens the interpersonal boundaries of staff members. "Helping" professionals frequently choose their careers in reaction to personal and family issues. For example, interests in psychotic processes may reflect concerns for their own normalcy. In locked units, the symbolic value of the key should not be underestimated; the key is often jokingly referred to as that which distinguishes staff from patients. Addressing the extreme dependency needs of the chronic patients may represent a way of working through their own needs. Caretaking and being taken care of can be opposite sides of the same coin. Many have also served in the caretaking role or as the overfunctioning member in their family and seek careers that will continue this role.

Working within systems created to treat chronic psychotic patients can also threaten individual boundaries. Public hospitals are often bureaucratic, clearly differentiated, and hierarchically organized along professional lines. Doctors are medically trained and responsible for patient care. Other disciplines, including "doctors" qua "psychologists," generally have little decision-making responsibility with regard to patients or programs and perform specialized tasks in keeping with their training. Professional boundaries are jealously guarded since the hierarchy determines who has status, if not power, over whom. The patient, of course, is at the bottom of the hierarchy and often has the least say about the course of treatment. These systems create an overly centralized and specialized approach to providing health care services that can encourage a passive dependent reaction on the part of the staff—for example, "It's not my job," or "Sorry, I can't do anything about it, the doctor says. . . ." Bureaucracies can thus encourage and reinforce dependency needs. Personal and professional conflicts often erupt due to the regressive tendencies stimulated by these systems and out of frustration with the limits imposed by them.

Conclusions and Implications

This chapter has discussed issues of managing boundaries at several levels of analysis. The way in which boundaries are established and negotiated determines the appropriate levels of differentiation and integration assumed necessary for effective functioning. Common themes emerge regarding how differentiation and integration are achieved through boundary management and how establishing and negotiating boundaries evolve throughout development. The study of the innovation of a partial hospital program demonstrated how the manner in which the program's boundaries were established and negotiated affected its long-term viability. What can be learned by drawing the parallels across levels of analysis? What are the implications for organization analysis and intervention? Several issues and some paradoxes emerge and need to be addressed.

    1. Boundaries are necessary and need to be established and negotiated in order to ensure appropriate levels of differentiation and integration. This is a critical task of development across levels. In organizations, the process of managing boundaries is most readily apparent and necessary during birth, innovation, creation of new departments and internally developed new businesses, mergers and acquisitions, and internal reorganization, and under threat of forces in the external environment

(for example, government regulation, competition). More explicit attention needs to be paid to how this is done.

2. Boundaries cannot be managed without autonomy. A certain amount of autonomy is necessary to be able to separate and develop. This is the underlying rationale for "skunkworks," that is, letting projects develop outside established organizational structures and policies. This has also been the criticism in the management of mergers and acquisitions wherein organizations impose their policies on the newly acquired businesses far too quickly. Therefore, how is the autonomy necessary for boundary setting achieved and preserved by these units?

Establishing and negotiating boundaries both requires and provides autonomy and control. The less autonomy, the more difficult it is to manage boundaries. Establishing boundaries results in greater control, which in turn reinforces boundaries. Therefore, what are the dynamics of boundaries and autonomy and control over time within an organization?

3. Stronger boundaries incur the risk of reduced integration, while strong pressures for integration threaten boundaries. When autonomy and control are threatened, boundaries are reinforced and rigidified, resulting in the loss of necessary interdependence. During periods of external threat, change, or reorganizations, turf battles and fragmentation of effort may be evident. How can flexibility be maintained to ensure the required integration, particularly in situations of crisis and change?

4. A crucial dilemma faced by organizations is how to maximize a sense of identity and autonomy in individuals and groups, yet maintain the necessary interdependence and integration as well as efficiency. Participative management and power sharing ("empowerment") are frequently preached, but how feasible are they? How is it possible to maximize autonomy and coordination simultaneously?

5. Interventions at other levels (such as individual, family, and group therapy) suggest that the primary task of intervention at the organizational level should be to:

- Help differentiate: clarify boundaries through identifying and defining roles, structures, functions, and units; determine "niche" or distinctive competence in relation with the larger

system; develop understanding of where, when, and how
to separate or reduce interdependence and how to gain and
preserve autonomy.

- Help integrate: clarify key links; determine necessary inter-
dependencies; develop the understanding of the distribution
of power within an organization; promote the ability to
negotiate boundaries in order to achieve the required level
of integration without loss of capability.

- Help design structures and processes that facilitate rather
than interfere with the pursuit of organizational goals; enable
interdisciplinary teams to perform required tasks without
unnecessary adherence to ideology or professional/functional
loyalties.

To function effectively, organizations need appropriate
levels of differentiation and integration. This requires boundaries that are firm yet flexible and the management of the paradoxes and dilemmas just mentioned. Firm but flexible boundaries enable interpersonal intimacy, group cooperation, and
organizational interdependence without fear of loss of identity
and autonomy. An effective leader must define and redefine
boundaries, particularly in the face of undue external or internal
pressures that can interfere with performing tasks and maintaining distinctive competence. This requires the autonomy
necessary to preserve the system's integrity and internal coherence while achieving the integration necessary for the effective
functioning of the larger system.

Boundary and control issues are becoming increasingly
relevant given the recent upsurge of activity involving hostile
takeovers, acquisitions, mergers, and joint ventures. Organizational integrity, identity, and autonomy are being threatened.
The notion of organizations as hierarchies is being challenged
as the emphasis is being placed more and more on horizontal
versus vertical differentiation. Organizations are now viewed
as networks, as linked points of distinctive competences or areas
of specialized expertise on a global scale, which require greater
and greater efforts at integration without losing differentiation
(Ghoshal and Bartlett, 1990). Differences between internal and

external stakeholders are becoming less clear—for example, when customers become organizational members and vice versa.

Boundaries within and between organizations must be considered subjective and not objective (Fiol, 1990). All boundaries are *perceived;* they cannot be taken as given. Therefore, in order to study boundaries within and between organizations, an interpretive approach is required. Fiol (1989), using semiotic analysis of letters to shareholders, has demonstrated that the strength of boundaries within the organization, as opposed to those between the organization and its environment as expressed in these letters, related to the propensity to engage in joint venture activity. Fiol (1990) has also demonstrated that internal versus external boundaries are stressed at different stages of development. According to her analysis of management newsletters at TWA, boundaries at the business-unit level were first stressed, followed by external and then internal boundaries.

Walsh's (1990) discussion of cycles of internal versus external control in the case of the hostile takeover of TWA by Carl Icahn raises the question of how the boundaries between internal and external are established. This also raises an interesting question for research: In what ways do the cycles of internal and external control mechanisms relate to the focus on internal versus external boundaries? To what extent is the vulnerability to external control a function of the nature of organizational boundaries? Investigating the relationship between organizational boundaries and control is an exciting area of future research at a time when the very nature of organization is being challenged.

References

Adams, J. S. "The Structure and Dynamics of Behavior in Organization Boundary Roles." In M. D. Dunnette (ed.), *The Handbook of Industrial and Organizational Psychology.* Chicago: Rand McNally, 1976.

Aldrich, H., and Herker, D. "Boundary Spanning Roles and Organization Structure." *Academy of Management Review,* 1977, *1,* 217–230.

Aldrich, H. E., and Pfeffer, J. "Environment of Organization."

Annual Review of Sociology. Vol. 2. Palo Alto, Calif.: Annual Review, Inc., 1976.

Bateson, G. *Steps to an Ecology of Mind.* New York: Ballantine Books, 1972.

Bion, W. R. *Experiences in Groups, and Other Papers.* London: Tavistock, 1959.

Bowen, M. "Theory in the Practice of Psychotherapy." In P. Guerin, Jr. (ed.), *Family Therapy: Theory and Practice.* New York: Garden Press, 1976.

Child, J. "Organization Structure, Environment, and Performance: The Role of Strategic Choice." *Sociology,* 1972, *6,* 1–22.

Erikson, E. *Childhood and Society.* (2nd ed.) New York: Norton, 1963.

Fiol, C. M. "A Semiotic Analysis of Corporate Language: Organizational Boundaries and Joint Venturing." *Administrative Science Quarterly,* 1989, *34,* 277–303.

Fiol, C. M. "Who's 'In' and Who's 'Out' in the Battle to Control TWA? A Semiotic Perspective." Paper presented at 50th annual meeting of the Academy of Management, San Francisco, Aug. 1990.

Freud, S. "The Ego and the Id." In J. Strachey (ed. and trans.), *The Standard Edition of the Complete Psychological Works of Sigmund Freud.* Vol. 19. London: Hogarth Press, 1961. (Originally published 1932.)

Galbraith, J. R. "Organization Design: An Information Processing View." *Interfaces,* 1974, *4,* 28–36.

Ghoshal, S., and Bartlett, C. A. "The Multinational Corporation as an Interorganizational Network." *Academy of Management Review,* 1990, *15* (4), 603–625.

Goffman, E. *Asylums.* New York: Doubleday, 1961.

Haley, J. *Problem-Solving Therapy.* (2nd ed.) San Francisco: Jossey-Bass, 1987.

Hartmann, H. "Comments on the Psychoanalytic Theory of the Ego." *Psychoanalytic Study of the Child.* Vol. 5. New York: International Universities Press, 1950.

Hirschhorn, L., and Gilmore, T. "The Application of Family Therapy Concepts to Influencing Organizational Behavior." *Administrative Quarterly,* 1980, *25,* 18–37.

Janis, I. L. *Victims of Groupthink.* Boston: Houghton Mifflin, 1972.

Jones, M. *The Therapeutic Community.* New York: Basic Books, 1953.

Katz, H., and Kahn, R. L. *The Social Psychology of Organizations.* New York: Wiley, 1978.

Klein, M. *The Psychoanalysis of Children.* New York: Delacorte, 1975. (Originally published 1932.)

Kotter, J. P. "Power, Dependence, and Effective Management." *Harvard Business Review,* 1977, *55,* 125–136.

Lawrence, P. R., and Lorsch, J. W. *Organization and Environment: Managing Differentiation and Integration.* Homewood, Ill.: Irwin, 1967.

Levinson, H. *Psychological Man.* Cambridge, Mass.: Levinson Institute, 1976.

Mahler, M. S., Pine, F., and Bergman, A. *The Psychological Birth of the Human Infant.* New York: Basic Books, 1975.

Miles, R. H., and Snow, C. C. *Organizational Strategy, Structure, and Process.* New York: McGraw-Hill, 1978.

Miller, E. J., and Rice, A. K. *Systems of Organizations: The Control of Task and Sentient Boundaries.* London: Tavistock, 1967.

Miller, J. C. "The Psychology of Innovation in an Industrial Setting." In W. G. Lawrence (ed.), *Exploring Individual and Organizational Boundaries: A Tavistock Open Systems Approach.* Chichester, England: Wiley, 1979.

Minuchin, S. *Families and Family Therapy.* Cambridge, Mass.: Harvard University Press, 1974.

Pfeffer, J., and Salancik, G. R. *The External Control of Organizations: A Resource Dependence Perspective.* New York: Harper & Row, 1978.

Schneider, S. C. "Whose Patient Is This Anyway? Policy and Planning Issues in the Care of the Chronic Psychiatric Patient." Paper presented at 44th annual meeting of the Academy of Management, Boston, Aug. 1984.

Schneider, S. C. "Conflicting Ideologies: Consequences for Structure and Motivation." Working paper, INSEAD #87/22. Fontainebleau, France: INSEAD, 1987.

Shapiro, R. L., and Zinner, J. "The Adolescent, the Family,

and the Group: Boundary Considerations." In W. G. Lawrence (ed.), *Exploring Individual and Organizational Boundaries: A Tavistock Open Systems Approach.* Chichester, England: Wiley, 1979.

Slater, P. E. *Microcosm.* New York: Wiley, 1966.

Thompson, J. D. *Organizations in Action.* New York: McGraw-Hill, 1967.

Trice, H. M., and Beyer, J. M. "Studying Organizational Culture Through Rites and Ceremonials." *Academy of Management Review,* 1984, *9* (4), 653–669.

Tuckman, B. W. "Developmental Sequence in Small Groups." *Psychological Bulletin,* 1965, *64,* 384–399.

Walsh, J. P. "The Battle to Save TWA: Internal and External Corporate Control Mechanisms at Work." Paper presented at 50th annual meeting of the Academy of Management, San Francisco, Aug. 1990.

Weick, K. E. *The Social Psychology of Organizing.* (2nd ed.) Reading, Mass.: Addison-Wesley, 1979.

Wynne, L. C., Ryckof, I. M., Day, J., and Hirsch, S. I. "Pseudomutuality in the Family Relations of Schizophrenics." *Psychiatry,* 1958, *21,* 205–227.

Zaltman, G., Duncan, R., and Holbek, J. *Innovations and Organizations.* New York: Wiley, 1973.

8

Stresses of Group Membership: Balancing the Needs for Independence and Belonging

Michael A. Diamond

Two or three times a decade, there is a population explosion among Norwegian lemmings, and food shortages force the animals to move. Huge groups of them set out in search of food. Some reach the sea and drown—giving rise to the popular myth that lemmings commit mass suicide.

The *lemming syndrome* is a metaphor for the work group under organizational and environmental stress. Forced to change, work groups—like lemmings—may take destructive and counterproductive actions. These collective actions are often regressive and defensive in nature, more infantile than adultlike. Lemmings respond to food shortages and increased population as a group; once they take action, however, there is no likelihood of correcting the response if it should prove to be destructive and ineffective. Their reaction is impulsive and unconscious, and they are incapable of learning. Regardless of whether hundreds of lemmings drown in the sea, hundreds more will follow. But people—*unlike* lemmings—are capable of examining their own behavior, and learning, if they are encouraged to do so.

Given a framework in which they can understand their actions and examine their own motivations, individuals in work groups can avoid the lemming syndrome.

In this chapter I will address the following questions: Why do people in groups behave like lemmings? What factors are at work that cause an apparent reduction of intelligence and foresight among group participants? What form do these regressive tendencies take in work groups? And what is the nature of the alternative, nonregressive, work group?

The Dilemma and Value of Group Membership

The central dilemma for the individual in the work group rests in his or her ability to maintain a balance of relative independence (personal identity and self-esteem) and group membership (a sense of belonging and affiliation) without becoming overly distressed. Establishing a separate identity in a group is essential to ego integrity and emotional well-being. That requirement of independence and autonomy is what distinguishes us from each other as well as from lemmings. However, group affiliation draws on narcissism — both healthy and pathological. Individual requirements for self-esteem and reassurance differ. Some need more reinforcement than others, and some require finding others that make them feel more powerful and safe. Regardless, all of us need others and therefore require some degree of affiliation. In the case of the lemming syndrome, we are talking about an extraordinary demand for affiliation — a merger with the other and the loss of self-other boundaries. What we can observe is an excessive yearning to belong and to be a part of something. Group membership can give many a feeling of omnipotence — being part of a group gives individuals a sense of being larger, greater, and better than they really are. Group membership is a way of fulfilling their ego ideal — that is, the sense of oneself at one's future best. Therefore, some affiliation with others is important in that it provides them not only with a defense, but also with a sense of being greater than themselves.

Consequently, people often go to great lengths to maintain their affiliation with the group, doing things that they would not consider doing outside the group. Thus, the lemming syndrome arises out of a fear of rejection by the members of the group, which for many means self-annihilation.

So while independence may be important to individuals in work groups, membership and affiliation are predominant drives for many. In fact, regressive and defensive actions in groups arise to ward off the fear of annihilation. Critical organizational events often ignite anxiety and aggression that, in turn, trigger regressive and defensive group responses. Regression, for our purposes, is defined as an immature and counterproductive reaction against environmental and organizational incidents that are perceived as threatening to the self. In order to understand these group dynamics more fully, we must begin with a discussion of individual regression in groups.

Individual Regression in Groups

Freud ([1921] 1955), Klein (1959), Jaques (1955), Bion (1959), Menzies (1960), and Kernberg (1980) all observe that regressive and primitive defensive actions are critical psychodynamic components in interpreting the meaning of group and organizational behavior.

What is individual regression? Rycroft (1968, p. 139) writes that "the theory of regression presupposes that, except in ideal cases, infantile stages of development are not entirely outgrown, so that the earlier patterns of behavior remain available as alternative modes of functioning. It is, however, not maintained that regression is often a viable or efficient defensive process; on the contrary, it is usually a question of out of the frying-pan into the fire, since regression compels the individual to re-experience anxiety appropriate to the stage to which he had regressed."

The group cultures discussed in this chapter not only describe regressive and psychologically defensive work groups but, consistent with Rycroft's conceptualization, they may be viewed in a developmental sequence as well (see Table 8.1).

Regressive behavior in the individual is the result of anxiety provoked by an unstable, inconsistent, insecure, or hostile external world (fantasied or actual) — what Winnicott (1965) calls the *holding environment*. A metaphor originally meant to represent the mother-infant relationship as the first and most critical object relationship, the holding environment can also symbolize the family, work group, or organization. Each of these may or may not facilitate personal identity, self-esteem, and ego integrity and may or may not provide adequate freedom and psychological space within its social structure to reinforce individuation as well as affiliation. Nevertheless, some individuals bring to the work group or organization excessive demands for association that represent a compensatory need for a sense of self and identity that is otherwise lacking. Unconsciously, they expect the group or organization to provide them with the stable, all-loving holding environment absent from their past. Whatever the degree of individual need for membership, organizational and environmental stress triggers some level of annihilation anxiety in all of us.

Kernberg (1980, p. 217) puts it this way: "Group processes pose a basic threat to personal identity, linked to a proclivity in group situations for activation of primitive object relations, primitive defensive operations, and primitive aggression with predominantly pregenital features. These processes, particularly the activation of primitive aggression, are dangerous to the survival of the individual in the group as well as to any task the group needs to perform." Individual regression, therefore, is likely to occur when uncertainty is experienced regarding self, others, and environment, and, concomitantly, where weak ego defenses fail to protect the self from the onslaught of anxiety, anxiety that arises from threatened personal identity.

Within organizations, the balance between personal identity and group affiliation is threatened by the stress of change and uncertainty. A few of the most common conditions causing stress are retrenchment, decline, management cutbacks, leadership transitions, suspicious publics, unclear or ambiguous objectives, ambiguity of authority and leadership, and the unwillingness to delegate authority.

What prompts regressive group action? It is essentially a protective reaction, preserving the self from annihilation by withdrawal into a safe and secure inner space. Melanie Klein refers to this state of regressed withdrawal as the need to save the ego by internal object relations, to withdraw "inside" and out of the external world (Guntrip, 1969, p. 82). For example, some people's experiences may lead them to withdraw and isolate themselves as much as possible from society in order to avoid persecution and disappointment. Persecuted work groups, ethnic groups, and even nations have been known to withdraw and isolate themselves from an external world they perceive as hostile and dangerous. Alternatively, an individual or group may withdraw psychically by denying or taking flight from reality, in which case distorted perceptions and fantasies are substituted for reality testing. Like lemmings, the work group reacts in order to preserve itself—but in doing so is rendered ineffective and may die.

In the final analysis, individual regression in groups is due to the annihilation anxiety that arises from each individual's fear of rejection from the group and the loss of affiliation that threatens his or her self-identity. Group membership and affiliation are based on the fear of self-disintegration. Consequently, one resorts to regression in order to protect the self from the anxiety associated with uncertain object relations brought on by external stress and change. Work-group cultures are often characterized by unconscious actions and shared fantasies stemming from the sum of individual regressed and primitive coping defenses (self- and object-splitting and denial) associated with the presence of individual regression.

Individual regression and other primitive defenses are observable at the group level of analysis and lend themselves to description as a group culture. These defenses belong to specific stages of human development: projection, denial, and splitting belonging to the oral stage; and reaction-formation, isolation, and undoing to the anal stage of development. Thereafter, "identification with the aggressor" is a common defense associated with superego development and object love in the Oedipal and puberty stages (Anna Freud, 1966).

The comprehension of the psychodynamics of individual and group regression can be more readily understood when placed in an operational context. The development of the following group cultures illuminates the full impact of regressive and primitive defensive actions on work groups.

Regressive and Defensive Group Cultures

Table 8.1 shows an assortment of regressive and defensive group cultures based on participant observations from organizational consultations and psychoanalytic object relations frameworks. It is not my intention to refute previous psychoanalytic frameworks for interpreting group dynamics (for example, Freud, Bion, and others). However, the study of group processes in complex organizations enhances our comprehension of collective human behavior (for instance, Fairbairn, Winnicott, Guntrip, Kohut, Mahler, Kernberg, and so on).

The group categories in Table 8.1 are based on the assumption that groups exist in organizational settings and that the meaning of their behavior can be interpreted separately from, but not independently of, the individual behavior of group members (Freud, [1921] 1955; Bion, 1959; Rice, 1969; Kernberg, 1980). The categories are an attempt to relate various levels of group-member response to annihilation anxiety. Each group culture represents a predominant coping pattern adopted by group members as they attempt to contain their anxious feelings of potential rejection and loss of affiliation. Three regressive and defensive groups are proffered: the *homogenized* culture, the *institutionalized* culture, and the *autocratic* culture. A fourth nonregressive and nondefensive group, the *intentional* group culture, is also presented.

The Homogenized Work Group

The homogenized group represents the most primitive and regressive collective flight from annihilation anxiety. It is characterized by an absence of self-other differentiation. Developmentally, it is a forerunner to the separation-individuation phase of infancy (Mahler, Pine, and Bergman, 1975; Kernberg, 1980; Frosch, 1983). That is, individuation is absent. In the same way that the

Table 8.1. Work-Group Cultures.

	Group Types			
	Homogenized	*Institutionalized*	*Autocratic*	*Intentional*
Authority	Leaderless	Hierarchical	Charismatic leader	Collaborative and participative leadership
Structure	Fragmented/polarized	Bureaucratic	Autocratic and patriarchal	Sophisticated work group
Transference	Persecutory	Idealizing and/or mirroring	Idealizing and/or mirroring	Nonneurotic
Psychic structure	Id	Primitive ego	Superego dominance/ideal	Ego strength and self-cohesion
Psychosexual character	Oral	Anal	Phallic and Oedipal	Post-Oedipal
Self-object relation	Schizoid (dedifferentiated)	Paranoid (differentiated)	Depressive (differentiated)	Individuated (differentiated)
Psychosocial dilemma	Trust vs. mistrust	Autonomy vs. shame/doubt	Initiative vs. guilt	Industry vs. inferiority through integrity vs. despair
Political model	Isolationist laissez-faire	Totalitarian and state bureaucratic	Dictatorial and authoritarian	Democratic and pluralistic
Work relationship	Incapable of performing work; no learning	Capable of work; emphasis on quantity, routinization, and control; little delegation; single-loop learning	Capable of work; emphasis on quality; stable leadership; supports work capacity; single-loop learning	Work is of high quality and is collaborative, significant, and purposeful; reflective practice, double-loop learning capability

PSYCHODYNAMICS FEATURES

newborn merges with its love object, the mother, homogenized group members are as one. They do not distinguish between self and other and find interactions meaningless.

Homogenized group members are cut off from external object relationships and become detached and withdrawn. An unconscious, collective wish to return to the safety of the womb produces a welcome avenue of flight from a hostile environment of bad relations (Guntrip, 1969). In this way, group members gain psychic safety, if only momentarily, within their delusional subculture, a subculture of sameness in which members experience similar feelings and act uniformly. But this psychic safety is short-lived; withdrawal from an external world of perceived persecution and self-annihilation results in a *schizoid* group culture capable of unusual social denial and, therefore, incapable of reality testing. Primitively regressed group members (similar to the schizoid personality) unconsciously operate in an internalized world of introjected bad objects (internalized bad mother) that threaten to devour the group self.

Differentiation of one's self from others in the group is feared because of the latent (if not actual) threat of primitive group violence directed toward any deviant individual. Panic about the possible loss of control over group aggression exaggerates annihilation anxieties among group members. Consequently, group members fear both differentiation by other group members and potential group hostility if others openly express their individuality. Under these circumstances the individual member defends himself or herself against self-disintegration by a psychic splitting of self and others into "all-good" (accepting) and "all-bad" (rejecting) part images. Group members typically introject "all-good" self-object representations into themselves and project "all-bad" self-object representations onto others, typically those outside the group.

The homogenized group culture is indicative of the *schizoid problem* described by object relations theorists (Klein, Fairbairn, Guntrip). Individual members of the homogenized group experience primitive aggression, which Guntrip (1969, p. 30) describes as "an oral sadistic and incorporative hunger for objects [that] sets up intolerable anxiety about their safety." This "hunger for objects" is believed to take the form of a fantasy in which the subject has the desire to devour others whom he or she perceives as threatening and hostile. Eventually, individual members withdraw and deny their violent thoughts and feelings. They may also deny their terror of fellow group members, wishing, conversely, to devour them.

Freud ([1921] 1955) argues that "libidinal ties" join group members to one another by means of identification with a common ego ideal represented by their collective leader, who ultimately gives the group an identity and its members a sense of belonging and commonality. In the homogenized group, libidinal needs for others are present but viewed as dangerous and potentially destructive. Love itself is preceived as destructive (Guntrip, 1969). Group members fear the thing they need most, the good lost object — the "all-protecting," "all-loving," and "perfect" mother-infant relationship. In their search for this "good lost object," group members are confronted by annihilation anxiety — a sense of depersonalization and fear of total destruction of the self.

Anxiety results in the schizoid problem for homogenized group members who identify with each other's feelings of self-annihilation and persecution. Homogenized group members may then resort to persecutory transference as a schizoid defense. The subjects of the persecutory transference feel that others, like their abusive and hurtful parents, are out to destroy them. This displaced and distorted interpersonal relationship is distinguished from the idealizing and mirroring transference combination implicit in Freud's description of the mob ([1921] 1955). While persecutory transference may become the particular pattern of individual coping and defense against perceived anxiety, cognitive and emotional splitting is characteristic of the frame of mind of homogenized group members in which relations between oneself and others are defined in either-or terms. Group members perceive themselves as ideal and all-good, and others as persecutory and all-bad.

A critical attribute of the homogenized group is that it is leaderless. In fact, the homogenized group culture emerges as a response to the loss of group and organizational leadership.

It is, as I mentioned earlier, most common under conditions of either very weak, ambiguous leadership or simply the absence of a leader. Moreover, the probability of an individual who aspires to lead surviving annihilation (because of self-differentiation) by the group is very low. Homogenized group members refuse to acknowledge individual differences, such as race, gender, class, perceptions and emotions, talents and skills. Group members create a fantasy image of themselves by rationalizing their actions, often claiming to promote a state of equality and social justice. In fact, members of homogenized groups exist in an infantile schizoid position of regression that is "pre-moral" (Guntrip, 1969).

Under these primitive circumstances group members are incapable of accomplishing work. The primary unacknowledged task is individual and group survival. But the severely suppressed and redesigned quality of the homogenized group culture produces a form of group paralysis in which group members find themselves on the horns of a dilemma. They experience themselves as neither in nor out, neither willing to commit themselves to group participation nor willing to commit themselves to a separateness apart from the group identity. Guntrip's (1969) description of the schizoid retreat from objects, which he calls the in and out program, illustrates the paradox of the homogenized group. Guntrip (1969, p. 36) writes: "This 'in and out' programme, always breaking away from what one is at the same time holding on to, is perhaps the most characteristic behavioral expression of the schizoid conflict."

The homogenized work group emerges as a response to the lack of organizational commitment to group-member objectives. The absence of commitment, for example, may take the form of diminishing allocations and temporary authority structure in which leaders are discouraged from leading. This type of situation results in uncertainty, distress, poor morale, low self-esteem among group members, and feelings of persecution.

This schizoid withdrawal into a homogenized group culture was exhibited by a university department that found itself operating in a hostile environment. In response to very poor understanding and lack of financial support from the dean of the school, department members retreated, psychologically, into a schizoid space. The dean had been obliged to appoint a non-tenured, assistant professor to the chair of that department. It was deemed impossible to recruit a tenured professor because of the department's poor financial situation. Department members viewed the dean's decision as further evidence of the school's lack of support and recognition, and the individual appointed was both ineffective and unacceptable. In response, members felt leaderless and persecuted. Psychic splitting occurred. Members expressed ambivalence, feeling neither in nor out of the department. Good and bad feelings could no longer be tolerated in the same individuals. Faculty members needed a relatively safe externalized target for their anger. Instead of targeting the dean, they aimed their bad feelings both at the weak assistant professor and, ultimately, at one another. That is, projections of aggression produced a bifurcation of the department into two antagonistic subgroups of M.D.'s and Ph.D.'s as a mechanism for coping with primitive feelings of hostility and rage. Each camp viewed the other as "all-bad" and, together with the impotent assistant professor, entirely to blame for the current predicament. Two homogenized subcultures had emerged within the department.

The Institutionalized Work Group

The threat to group membership and affiliation in the homogenized group produces primitive defenses such as splitting and schizoid withdrawal. Participants obliterate individuality, project aggression and hostility onto others, and withdraw into a suppressed state. In contrast, institutionalized group members respond to annihilation anxiety by producing an externalized social defense system that encourages submission to a formal hierarchical structure and impersonal authority. Rather than withdrawing into an internal world, institutionalized group members attempt to contain anxiety by constructing an impersonal controlling social structure in the external reality (Diamond, 1984; Kernberg, 1980; Menzies, 1960).

Underlying paranoid feelings in the group produce primitive infantile aggression and hostility among members. These feelings are in turn contained by defensive social structuring of interpersonal relations in the group. For example, Kernberg (1980, p. 218) writes: "The study of large-group processes highlights the threat to individual identity under social conditions in which ordinary role functions are suspended and various projective mechanisms are no longer effective (because of the loss of face-to-face contact and personal feedback). Obviously, large-group processes can be obscured or controlled by rigid social structuring. Bureaucratization, ritualization, and well-organized task performance are different methods with similar immediate effects."

One underlying reason for constructing rigid social structures like bureaucracies is the reaction-formation against the "overwhelming nature of human aggression in unstructured group situations" (Kernberg, 1980, p. 218). Whereas homogenization is a very primitive response to unstructured group situations that perpetuate the threat to group membership, institutionalization represents another response that calls for a predominance of "anal" defenses, such as reaction-formation, isolation, and undoing. I have written elsewhere: "Ritualistic behavior in bureaucracy arises from unconsciously motivated obsessional thinking and compulsive behavior aimed at defending one's self from anxiety, which is the unpleasant experience of a momentary loss of self/object boundaries and identity. This occurs in the organizational recruit at the moment of entry into the bureaucracy where he acts to deny reality by 'undoing' the self-alienation that has occurred (signal anxiety) and 'isolating' its affects" (Diamond, 1985b).

Bureaucratization and ritualization are institutionalized forms of control that promote dependency on rigid and routine impersonal structures. Group membership dominates personal identity and independence. Discussing the role of anality in one individual's behavior, Frosch (1983, p. 72) comments: "The analysis, as is often the case with obsessional patients, highlighted the issue of maintaining control. This issue was reflected in the way he brought up material, in the transference, in his work, and in his relations with others. Like most obsessionals, he couldn't really delegate work, as people were seen as extensions of himself, whom he had to control." A special instance of projective identification is operating in the institutionalized group. Members react defensively by splitting the self and other into "good" and "bad" parts, where a persecuting sadistic (bad) object is identified in the group self. Due to its sadistic potential, the persecutory self-object must be contained by group members. Group members' obsessive-compulsive preoccupation with control of sadistic aggression fosters a paranoid position with respect to the actions of group members. This phenomenon, in turn, reinforces submission to oligarchical and hierarchical authority. Anxiety and aggression are contained by institutionalized repression. Kernberg (1980, p. 218) elaborates further: "An important part of nonintegrated and unsublimated aggression is expressed in various ways throughout group and organizational processes. When relatively well-structured group processes evolve in a task-oriented organization, aggression is channelled toward the decision-making process, particularly by evoking primitive-leadership characteristics in people in positions of authority. Similarly, the exercise of power in organizational and institutional life constitutes an important channel for the expression of aggression in group processes that would ordinarily be under control in dyadic or triadic reactions. Aggression emerges more directly and much more intensely when group processes are relatively unstructured."

In summary, institutionalized group members rely on structure to control aggression and annihilation anxiety. Rigid routines and impersonal office authority perpetuate an illusion of stability, equality, and dependability—a form of externalized (organizational) defense system (Diamond, 1984). Dependence on rules, regulations, and procedures, and reliance on hierarchical impersonal authority, evoke "disclaimed action" (Schafer, 1976, 1983) and lack of personal responsibility (Diamond and Allcorn, 1984; Diamond, 1985a). Institutionalization also results in rigid structuring of boundaries, insistence on loyalty and role conformity, and a general obsession for control of subordinate behavior—all of which is indicative of a paranoid regressive trend underlying the group's actions and structuring of itself.

The institutionalized work group accomplishes work in a routine and rational fashion. Procedure, rules, and regulations may take priority over quality of work, substance of product and service, and overall meaning and purpose of task accomplishment. Intra- and interorganizational boundaries are often rigid and inflexible. Bureaucratic administration replaces leadership. An emphasis on the control of subordinate behavior renders delegation of authority unlikely. The underlying closed system of institutionalized group culture, on the one hand, generates unconscious, perpetual insecurity and paranoia among group members, while, on the other hand, promoting overdependency on the part of group members for overprotection from aggression and anxiety. Many politically unpopular public agencies often operate under these regressive and defensive arrangements due to the politics of overzealous subcommittee or overambitious political appointees in positions of authority.

For example, a public agency had defensively overstructured itself into a professional bureaucracy, to such an extent that it could no longer effectively coordinate its specialized staff and units to accomplish primary tasks. In response to persistent legislative criticisms and investigations, the division's leadership had produced an institutionalized group to control its product in an effort to avoid criticism, and the resulting culture made the coordination of tasks and communications across interdisciplinary organizational boundaries exceedingly difficult. Secrecy and withholding of information were characteristic defensive responses to fear of both public and organizational leadership. Excessively layered and complex hierarchical channels of communication had to be negotiated for minor authorizations and approvals. This virtually paralyzed otherwise competent members of the system, who consequently felt powerless, angry, and fearful of the leadership. These feelings further reinforced the need for defensive strategies and rigid structures in order to achieve control. In confidential discussions with consultants, members consistently expressed a desire for greater autonomy and independence (or greater delegation of authority).

The Autocratic Work Group

In the autocratic work group, participants also find themselves forfeiting their independence and separate identity for group membership. In contrast to members of homogenized and institutionalized groups, members of autocratic work groups identify with an all-powerful charismatic leader from whom they derive control of their aggression and anxiety. Guilt, arising from feelings of ambivalence and hostility toward the idealized object-person, also develops. In contrast to the institutionalized group, which is characterized by too much organization and impersonal leadership, the autocratic group is characterized by the personal authority of one leader. Group members exchange their own personal ego ideal and internal authority for that of their group leader, who then, wittingly or unwittingly, begins to dominate the group conscience.

The autocratic group is, therefore, built on a so-called "mirroring" transference. Members begin to experience guilt about their vacillation between affectionate and aggressive feelings toward their idealized leader, whom they both love and fear. The autocratic group is similar to Freud's classic portrayal of the primal horde. He states ([1921] 1955, p. 54): "Human groups exhibit once again the familiar picture of an individual of superior strength among a troop of equal companions, a picture which is also contained in our idea of the primal horde. The psychology of such a group, as we know it for the descriptions to which we have so often referred—the dwindling of the conscious individual personality, the focusing of thoughts and feelings into a common direction, the predominance of the affective side by the mind and of unconscious psychical life, the tendency to the immediate carrying out of intentions as they emerge—all corresponds to a state of regression to a primitive mental activity, of just such a sort as we should be inclined to ascribe to the primal horde."

Autocratic group members endow their leader with primitive, sadistic, and omnipotent qualities. Group members are guilt-ridden and submissive. They either turn their anger and aggression back on themselves, evoking a depressive and ambivalent

quality in the group climate, or project their aggression outside the group boundaries. The autocratic group offers members a prototype of infantile feelings of guilt, atonement, and
forgiveness. As Frosch (1983, p. 184) writes: "Guilt derives from
the ambivalence and hostility toward the object, with its possible
destruction. Atonement is achieved by the ego taking itself as
a weak, hateful object and placing the superego in the role for
parents whose forgiveness has to be sought by abject behavior.
We find here a double identification: the ego as bad parent and
the superego as the good one. Ultimately forgiveness may be
achieved through fusion with the superego."

Inevitably, group members are disappointed with their
"godlike" leader, who cannot possibly meet their fantastic expectations nor control their feelings of hatred, aggression, and
basic anxiety. The primitive crime of the primal horde's symbolic murder of the father-leader is reenacted. The leader is
replaced from time to time. Each reenactment is followed by
a period of remorse and mourning. Members who sense their
capacity to love and hate the same object must work through
their ambivalent feelings in order for the group to progress and
develop toward what I call the intentional group.

In contrast to the oral sadistic defenses of the homogenized
group and the anal sadistic defenses of the institutionalized
group, the autocratic group relies on an "identification with the
aggressor" (Anna Freud, 1966). Identification with the aggressor is a common Oedipal defense against the anxiety of an external threatening object associated with superego development
during puberty. In further contrast, the institutionalized group
represents a manner of containing the anxious, violent, and explicitly sadistic social organization of the primal horde, and the
homogenized group offers a solution to annihilation anxiety and
aggression by schizoid withdrawal, where thoughts and feelings
are severed indefinitely.

Finally, the autocratic group is capable of carrying out
work. The presence of a stable identifiable leader serves to direct
and coordinate the work capacity of the group. A utopian climate is created when group members identify with the leader.
However, their feelings of fear and disappointment toward their

idealized leader, and the group's unconscious wish to replace the leader, produce a sense of guilt. As a result, the group's work is affected by shifts in climate from a utopian elation to a depressed position filled with mourning and guilt.

Although most common to family-owned businesses characterized by the norms and authority of a patriarchal system ruled by the "law of the father," the autocratic group also appears in the traditionally conservative and partriarchal culture of many public agencies under the domination of career bureau chiefs in government. Typically, units or offices within a complex public organization may operate as semiautonomous kingdoms where subordinates come to idealize their autocratic boss, and in which intergroup (interoffice) boundary disputes over jurisdictional authority and the relative status and prestige of each unit are commonplace, while loyalty and deference to authority are strongly encouraged among members *within* these units.

For example, agencies within a government department were managed by bureau chiefs who had fifteen to twenty years' experience in the department. Subordinates often publicly espoused their loyalty and admiration for the chiefs, while obedience to authority and societal cohesion were characteristic traits of the units. However, in private consultation with staff when bureau chiefs were absent, negative feelings and otherwise unvoiced problems were acknowledged. In the presence of bureau chiefs, on the other hand, staff members consistently deferred to the chiefs' authority and suppressed personal ideas, feelings, and thoughts. Identification with the aggressor (the bureau chief) was a predominant regressive and defensive group strategy. This case illustrates a common theme among regressive work groups in organizations under pressure: Group membership and affiliation take precedence over the autonomy and independence necessary for self-identity.

The Intentional Work Group

In contrast to the previous groups, where unconscious actions and covert goals predominate, the intentional group is first and foremost a *work* group, or what Bion (1959) calls a "sophisticated" group. The *intentional* group is distinguished from the previous three groups by a reflective process that promotes awareness of fantasies and covert actions among the membership. Participants realize the necessity of reflective practice as a learning skill that, in turn, supports the emotional well-being and competence of all group members. However, the intentional group is not a utopia. It comprises all the potentially regressive and defensive characteristics of the other three groups, and its members may resort to regression and primitive defenses in response to perceived danger and annihilation anxiety. Intentional group members recognize that progress and change are impossible without periodic regression into the defensive patterns characteristic of the other three groups. Its members acknowledge that change is unlikely without individual and group resistance to that change. It is, therefore, sensitive to acts of resistance and defense as opportunities for learning and developmental change. Intentional group members endeavor to learn from experience and are capable of recognizing and publicly testing fantasies and defensive actions. Intra- and interpersonal conflicts, contradictions, and inconsistencies in espoused theory (what people say) and theory-in-use (what people do) (Argyris and Schön, 1978) are confronted and publicly tested by group members.

It should be noted that the intentional group differs from traditional humanistic organization theories of sophisticated, collaborative work relations by emphasizing the need to attend to regressive and defensive actions. These actions underlie all group and organization dynamics. The intentional group represents a qualitative difference from more traditional prescriptions for collaborative work groups, in that it stresses the necessity for understanding and explaining cognitive and affective work dynamics in order to achieve effectiveness and intentionality in the work group.

Intentional work groups may emerge from organizational change efforts that stress learning from experience by attending to unconscious group process, particularly leader-follower transference relations, regressive and defensive group actions, and basic assumptions of fight-flight, dependency, and pairing. The social construction of intentional work groups is possible within organizational settings that value collaboration and participation, and where sociotechnical and political factors do not function as serious constraints on change and development.

What are the psychodynamic processes at work that promote such a progressive shift in work-group culture? Let's explore that question in the next section.

The Psychodynamics of Group Transition

Striking a balance between personal identity and group affiliation is the central dilemma. Each of the four group types described here represents one possible solution to the problem of anxiety and aggression that this dilemma produces within a group. The three regressive work groups solve the problem of annihilation anxiety by overemphasizing group membership and underplaying — in some instances destroying — personal identity and autonomy. Any of the four groups can, momentarily, resolve anxiety and control aggression. However, these groups are not static, nor do they fit into rigid categories that exclude the potential for change. A group's change from one of these types to another is always, however unwittingly, a collective (or collusive) option. In order for these transitions to occur, the leader-follower relations that are critical to shifts in group culture must change.

For example, the homogenized group appears leaderless due to a group culture antagonistic toward the individuation necessary for any leader to emerge within the group. A sufficient combination of power, authority, personality, and risk taking on the part of one member is necessary to move the group from schizoid withdrawal and repression into a state of object relatedness (paranoid or depressed). This is not to say that the leader is pursuing an intentional process of assuming leadership and leading. While this may be true to some degree, it must be acknowledged that the leader may be identified, wittingly or unwittingly, by the group as displaying the social characteristics "best suited" to the role of leadership. In this instance, the "best-suited" person may be the most schizoid in character and most capable of facilitating fight-flight by developing powerful images of an external group threat. The nascent leader first influences his or her followers by gaining their attention and, second, by manufacturing an alternative defensive and seductively attractive fantasy. In other words, the leader mobilizes, wittingly or unwittingly, a shift in the group's culture to the basic assumption of fight-flight (Bion, 1959).

The basic assumptions under which groups operate proposed by Bion partially capture the underlying psychodynamics of group transition from one group culture to another. These basic assumptions help the participant-observer to illuminate the subtle shifts in leader-follower interactions that foster transformation of group culture. The actual transition itself involves resorting to a new *compromise formation* in the group's search for a collective defense against annihilation anxiety (see Figure 8.1). The categories of group cultures (see Table 8.1) help to identify different levels of maturity in object relationships and defensive routines.

The key dynamic behind any such transformation resides in the transference relationship between leader and followers.

Figure 8.1. Group Transition.

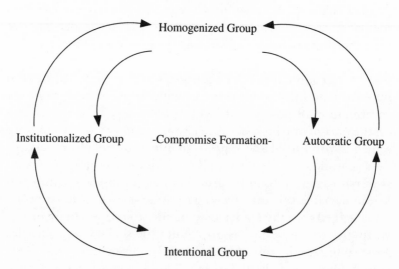

The persecutory transference felt by members of the homogenized group must give way to a mirroring and/or idealizing transference between a leader and his or her followers. The leaderless, withdrawn group must be persuaded by rationally perceived, impersonal leadership, on the one hand, or emotional, charismatic leadership on the other. In any case, members of the mistrustful homogenized group culture must foster dependency and project the wish to be taken care of (or to be led in fight or flight from their anxiety and aggressive feelings), so that pairing with a leader can result. A more mature work-group culture may be established by either of these compromise formations.

The dependency group indicates a willingness by group members to be taken care of, to be led, regardless of the regressive quality of their present group culture. Members wish to be taken care of and the concomitant emergence of a leader heightens their expectations, enhancing projective identification of a positive transferential nature. Once a leader who has the necessary agenda is identified (an unconscious leader-follower fit), whether impersonal or charismatic in nature, group members pair and then either follow in flight from their current predicament or in fight against a common enemy. The emergence of a shift in transference and basic assumption (dependency or pairing), therefore, signals a readiness to accept a new structure for group process and leadership. Consequently, a new group culture arises (either *institutionalized* or *autocratic*) in a compromise formation stimulated by altered transference relationships and basic assumption dynamics. The collective escape from the most primitively regressive homogenized group culture begins with the often-unconscious establishment of leader-follower relations. The homogenized group, it should be stressed, represents the ultimate unconscious fear of group rejection and loss of group membership and affiliation. Its hostility toward independence and autonomy demonstrates its likelihood of falling vulnerable to the lemming syndrome.

Both institutionalized and autocratic groups are capable of regressive action in the direction of homogenization, on the one hand, and progressive action in the direction of intentionality, on the other. In actuality, group and organizational action is in constant motion and, at any time, may be found somewhere along a continuum from regressive homogenization to progressive intentionality. The institutionalized and autocratic groups represent a middle point on the continuum from regressive to progressive actions.

Conclusion

The secret to emotionally healthy and organizationally effective work groups may be uncovered in individuals' attempts to strike a balance between needs for independence and belonging. Regressive work groups are characterized by an imbalance that favors group membership and affiliation over and above personal identity and autonomy. In fact, critical organizational incidents trigger regressive group responses, which suppress and, in some cases, nearly destroy the self-identity and independence of members. When autonomy is forfeited for group membership, the lemming syndrome becomes a dangerous probability. In this chapter, I have outlined three primary defensive responses to annihilation anxiety provoked by organizational and environmental stressors, and a fourth nondefensive response.

An understanding of and explanation for regression in work groups, I submit, improves the probability of group analysis and, therefore, the group's opportunity for learning and effectiveness should increase as well. More important, the "sophisticated" (Bion, 1959) or intentional work group that values analysis of group process is capable of intervening in and turning around regressive and often destructive group actions.

Finally, the intentional work group does not perceive itself as superior but as human and psychodynamic. Its commitment to analysis of the group self does not obliterate regressive action but, rather, produces group awareness through a reflective process that creates the opportunity for change and development. Its members remain aware that it is not only lemmings that are vulnerable to the lemming syndrome — we all are.

References

Argyris, C., and Schön, D. A. *Organizational Learning: A Theory of Action Perspective.* Reading, Mass.: Addison-Wesley, 1978.

Bion, W. R. *Experiences in Groups, and Other Papers.* London: Tavistock, 1959.

Diamond, M. A. "Bureaucracy as Externalized Self-System." *Administration and Society,* 1984, *16* (2), 195–214.

Diamond, M. A. "Psychological Dimensions of Personal Responsibility for Public Management: An Object Relations Approach." *Journal of Management Studies,* 1985a, *22* (6), 649–667.

Diamond, M. A. "The Social Character of Bureaucracy: Anxiety and Ritualistic Defense." *Political Psychology,* 1985b, *6* (4), 663–679.

Diamond, M. A., and Allcorn, S. "Psychological Barriers to Personal Responsibility." *Organizational Dynamics,* 1984, *12* (4), 66–77.

Freud, A. *The Ego and the Mechanisms of Defense.* New York: International Universities Press, 1966.

Freud, S. "Group Psychology and the Analysis of the Ego." In J. Strachey (ed. and trans.), *The Standard Edition of the Complete Psychological Works of Sigmund Freud.* Vol. 18. London: Hogarth Press, 1955. (Originally published 1921.)

Frosch, J. *The Psychotic Process.* New York: International Universities Press, 1983.

Guntrip, H. *Schizoid Phenomena, Object Relations, and the Self.* New York: International Universities Press, 1969.

Jaques, E. "Social Systems as a Defence Against Persecutory and Depressive Anxiety." In M. Klein, P. Heimann, and R. E. Money-Kyrle (eds.), *New Directions for Psychoanalysis.* London: Tavistock, 1955.

Kernberg, O. *Internal World and External Reality.* New York: Aronson, 1980.

Klein, M. "Our Adult World and Its Roots in Infancy." *Human Relations,* 1959, *12,* 291–301.

Mahler, M. S., Pine, F., and Bergman, A. *The Psychological Birth of the Human Infant.* New York: Basic Books, 1975.

Menzies, I. "A Case Study in the Functioning of Social Systems as a Defence Against Anxiety: A Report on a Study of the Nursing Service of a General Hospital." *Human Relations,* 1960, *13,* 95–121.

Rice, A. K. *Learning for Leadership.* London: Tavistock, 1965.

Rice, A. K. "Individual, Group, and Intergroup Processes." *Human Relations,* 1969, *22* (6), 565–584.

Rycroft, C. *A Critical Dictionary of Psychoanalysis.* New York: Penguin Books, 1968.

Schafer, R. *A New Language for Psychoanalysis.* New Haven, Conn.: Yale University Press, 1976.

Schafer, R. *The Analytic Attitude.* New York: Basic Books, 1983.

Winnicott, D. W. *The Maturational Processes and the Facilitating Environment.* New York: International Universities Press, 1965.

9

---•••---

Dealing with the Anxiety of Working: Social Defenses As Coping Strategy

Larry Hirschhorn
Donald R. Young

Computers and automation create increasingly integrated production systems that, while efficient and flexible, can fail "catastrophically" (Hirschhorn, 1984; Perrow, 1972). For example, downtime in an automated assembly factory can cost hundreds of thousands of dollars. More serious examples: The failure of controls in a nuclear reactor can cause a meltdown, and the rapid flow of gases and fluids in a chemical factory creates an ever-present danger of fires and explosions. How do people manage the anxiety of working in groups in a dangerous setting? How do they work productively yet carefully? How do they remain vigilant without becoming excessively preoccupied by the dangers they face? In other words, how do they cope? While cognitive psychologists focus on how individuals deploy their attention, this chapter suggests that powerful psychosocial dynamics shape people's capacity to work safely in groups.

Based on a case study of a consultation to an oil refinery, this chapter illustrates how groups in organizations may develop particular "social defenses" (Hirschhorn, 1988) that help people contain the anxiety of working while actually reducing their ability to work safely. Social defenses, expressed in relationships, procedures, and organizational rituals, help people cope with the anxiety they feel while working at difficult or risky tasks. Thus, for example, hospital procedures that depersonalize a nurse's relationship with very sick patients, or rituals of decision making that diffuse responsibility, help people limit the anxiety they experience. Working in dangerous industrial settings, people in groups may also develop procedures, relationships, and rituals to help them feel safe. Paradoxically, these may create new dangers as well.

This chapter, divided into four sections, unpacks the structure and dynamics of a social defense system in an oil refinery. Describing two fires that prompted the refinery manager to seek consulting help, the first section of the chapter examines a core social system "split" between two production units in the refinery. The second section links this split as a social defense to the psychodynamics of safety, to the dilemmas of acting vigilantly but not fearfully in dangerous settings. The third shows how this social split supported a culture of the "good" invulnerable hero who acts alone, while stereotyping "bad" heroes whose isolation reaffirms the plant's goodness. Summarizing the argument of the chapter, the fourth and last section suggests that we need a new way to investigate accidents, based on community self-study, if we are to transcend such social defense systems.

The Presenting Situation

The Smalltown oil refinery, employing about 200 people and producing 50,000 barrels of gasoline a day, was the main employer in a Western city in the United States. Situated on a plain with lakes in the background, the refinery dominated part of the cityscape. The city's culture was modern frontier. Blue-collar workers came from families long native to the area, while the financial and commercial managerial elites often came from elsewhere, the product of corporate transfers.

The refinery appeared orderly, with the large tanks and

pipes laid out over acres of land. Two control room structures, each a cross between an office building and a shack, stood at different parts of the refinery. "Indoor" workers sat in these buildings monitoring the flow and refining of oil into gasoline, while "outdoor" workers toured the wide expanse of the yard, checking meters and valves while looking for danger signs such as leaks and pockets of gas. Standing at one end of the refinery, the main office building was unpretentious, its corridors narrow and paneled; senior managers' offices were sensibly carpeted and furnished. The refinery manager's office held a recently installed computer console, which gave him up-to-the-minute information on refinery operations in all the significant parts of the yard. The refinery manager was beginning to wonder what role his mid-level managers would have now that he could get information about refinery operations without going through them.

Two Fires

The previous year, the refinery had had two severe fires, one in the summer and the other in the fall. No one had been killed, but in the second several workers narrowly escaped severe injury. After the second fire, the refinery manager contacted Donald Young, the company psychologist at the corporate office, to assess how stress might be affecting safety. Young then contacted Larry Hirschhorn to help him.

Studies of both fires carried out by a company audit team showed that each fire had several causes. Indeed, accident audits typically highlight the system of relationships that both sustain production and lead to production failures. Like slips of the tongue, the accident provides a window into the system's dynamics. For example, before the first fire, operators shutting down the refinery were unaware of piping changes that led distillate to be pushed through an open valve and into the yard. As a result, the area around the pipe smelled gassy. Some operators noticed the distillate leaking around a pump but did not connect it to any evident safety problem. Others assumed the gassy smell was normal for a shutdown. As distillate accumulated on the ground, a flame from a nearby furnace ignited the liquid, creating a fire. Hence, the stress of a shutdown, a valve left open, operator ignorance of changes to the piping, and inattention to danger signs all conspired to create the fire.

Similarly, in the second fire, one operator tried to control seepage of oil and water through a leaky gasket. He linked the valve to an open bleeder and cleared away asphalt that was blocking the flow of liquid. Later, when other operators prepared to start up the refinery, they failed to isolate the valve from the bleeder, so that propane gas flowed through the bleeder and a plug. The gas, pushing the plug outward, rushed out into the air and created a dangerous propane fire. Later investigation showed that an improperly sized gasket had been installed in the valve. Thus, a combination of circumstances—an ill-fitting gasket, a plugged line, a start-up, and an operator's failure to isolate a valve from a bleeder—all contributed to the fire. In integrated production systems like refineries, chemical plants, and power stations, accidents highlight the systemic nature of the production system itself. Everyone and no one is to blame.

The Consultation Process

After talking with the refinery manager, George, we agreed to visit the refinery for two days to help workers and managers assess some of the issues that affected safety and organizational functioning. After conducting interviews with individual managers and workers, we met with three groups. The first group, the refinery's health and safety committee, was composed of two managers and five union members. The second group, composed of different categories of workers, was brought together during the consultation to discuss the relationships between operators and their assistants called *controlmen*. The third group, of workers and supervisors from the "back end" and "front end" of the refinery, was assembled to focus on the development and staffing of the soon-to-be-completed centralized control room.

At each meeting we and George sat around a conference table and talked with between six and eight other people. We presented some general propositions about safety to the first group, stimulating them to examine when and why refinery workers behaved in an unsafe manner. The second group examined the refinery's chain of command, assessing whether its many levels made it difficult for people to feel accountable. The third group talked about the design of the centralized control room, focusing on the links between control room and yard workers and between the back end and front end of the refinery. These conversations led to no immediate decisions. Instead, they were intended to help raise awareness about safety and bring people from different units and levels together.

A Social Split

Our interviews prior to these meetings helped us understand more about the history and structure of the refinery. It was a profitable forty-year-old refinery going through a slow process of modernization and development. Responding to a company-sponsored early retirement program three years prior to our visit, 25 percent of the workforce had left the refinery. Consequently, the refinery hired skilled operators from other company refineries as well as well-educated young people from the Smalltown region to fill these jobs, so that the overall educational level of the workforce rose. In addition, at the time of our visit, management was building a centralized control room using up-to-date computer graphics and electronic control systems to improve workers' ability to monitor and control plant conditions. Finally, George, who came to the plant in 1985, was working to improve a once-contentious labor-management relationship. The previous refinery manager, who once noted proudly that "boss" spells "double-S.O.B. backward," had little interest in working with the union to improve safety and working conditions. By contrast, George actively consulted the union president and instituted a labor-management safety committee.

But despite these important changes, the refinery was still bedeviled by tensions and accidents. Most striking was the history of a key split within the social system of the refinery itself. The refinery was divided into two units, the cracking unit or front-end unit, and the refining or back-end unit. The first unit took up the crude and divided it into fractions of different weights, while the second refined the resulting fractions. All those interviewed described the second unit, which we will call unit two, as fractious, divided, conflict-ridden, the "black-sheep group," while the first unit, or unit one, was described as peaceable, a real team, and fun to work in.

Thus, for example, people noted that the members of unit two had to deal with a difficult operator, Gerry, who constantly got into fights with her workmates, while the first unit had a nurturing woman, called "Princess," who held weekend barbecues at her house for her team. Similarly, several people, highlighting the fractious character of unit two, told us how, just before we came to the refinery, two members of that unit got into a fistfight on second shift — further evidence of the tensions besetting the group. By contrast, when management reprimanded one member of unit one for his role in the second accident, the unit's members wrote a letter of support and protest to management.

Why was unit two so fractious and divided? Its work, several people told us, was no more difficult, dangerous, or dirty than unit one's. One technician suggested that unit one simply received more attention and resources: "They were the first to get computers in their control room, and there may be a feeling that the refining unit [unit two] just gets less attention." Indeed, when touring the two units we were struck by the difference in the quality of their monitoring equipment. Unit one had numerous computer terminals arrayed along a tabletop, each capable of displaying, in the brightest colors, the status of temperatures, pressures, flow rates, and composition of the different fractions of oil. In comparison, unit two's controls room looked like a boiler room. A large control panel dominated the cramped space, with its meters, resembling the instrumentation in the engine room of a locomotive, seeming to fill it to confusion.

Other people, however, suggested that unit two's dilemmas were linked to its history. Unit two was not weak because it had been neglected, but neglected because it was weak. Several people thought the unit functioned poorly because it had suffered the leadership of an unsupportive and heavy-handed general foreman. John, who had led the unit for ten years from the mid seventies, had controlled all the details of the work and would not let unit members think for themselves. When he retired, the unit just seemed to fall apart. As one person noted, "The group, at that time, looked up to John very strongly. More or less they wouldn't make a move unless he said so. I used to fill in for him, and the men would question me to make sure that John would want to do this or that. . . . He had a real upper hand on his people." His successor, Frank, lacked John's strength and experience. Instead, as several people noted, he was a likable engineer, who, since he had not come up through the ranks, was too eager to please. But he could not command respect. As one manager noted, "Frank had a lot of experience to go through and his people did not have a lot of confidence in him. They called him the 'short little boss that didn't know much.'"

At first we were convinced by the explanation. The data we gathered from our interviews suggested the following story. Unit two had grown far too dependent on John, and consequently its members could not function effectively after his departure. John had monopolized authority and therefore undermined his operators' self-esteem, but they could still function effectively by identifying with him. They were powerful because he was. After his departure, however, their own self-contempt could not be contained and so they began to hate each other. In other words, their self-contempt was projected into the unit. This interpretation suggests, moreover, that the operators had contempt for Frank's likability, not because he was simply weak or inadequate, but because they could only respect brute power. Indeed their reference to Frank's size (he was their "*short* little boss") points to the depth of their contempt and the irrationality of their response. By hating another person's physical appearance people turn him into a cripple, a freak, and can then use the person as a projective screen for their own feelings of self-hate or disregard. Frank, we thought, had been a victim of the group's dynamics as well as his own limitations.

This explanation satisfied us initially, but other facts continued to tug at our sleeves. Most important, the theme of splitting and division characterized many of the ways in which the refinery presented itself as a whole during the consultation. The split between the two units, while fundamental to the operations of the refinery, was one instance of the tendency of refinery members to create and sustain splits across many levels and divisions. Thus, people discussed the tensions and divisions between operators and their subordinates (the *controlmen* mentioned earlier), between union and management, and between refinery workers and the engineering staff. They also talked about the split between the bad woman Gerry and the good woman Princess and the split between Gerry and the rest of unit two's members. Beginning with the key split between the two units, it appeared as if the refinery's social system was built on its social divisions — *it was its divisions* — so that people experienced the whole system as the endless interplay between "good" and "bad."

Indeed, when touring the still-unfinished centralized control room, we found that the split between the two refining units had been reproduced in the control room's design. The control room was arranged so that chairs, fixed to the ground, were placed alongside a long and narrow tabletop, much like the long countertop of a 1950s-style cafeteria. Each chair was placed up against a terminal sitting on the table. Because the new control room would convey information to the operators from all parts of the refinery, and since each terminal could display data from any part of the refinery, refinery managers and the control room designers had many choices in designing the room's configuration. Most important, there was no longer any compelling rationale to separate the two units. Indeed, using centralized control technology, managers and operators would be able to monitor some of the important flows and changes in the oil as it went between the two ends of the refinery. Yet the tabletop was semicircular in shape, so that unit one operators, sitting on the left of the semicircle, *would have their backs to unit two operators sitting on the right-hand side.* The design assured that members of the two units would not work face to face.

Finally, and most strikingly, we learned during the course of our interviews that over a decade before the two fires, the social relationships between the two units had been reversed! Unit two had been the peaceable and functioning unit, and unit one, fractious and unmanageable. As one person noted, "We saw many of the same things that we see now in the refining unit [unit two] in the cracking unit [unit one]. It was a hotbed of troublemakers then, but many left to get into the mechanical/ maintenance group."

These observations — the existence of splits at many levels of the refinery, the reproduction of the split between the two refining units in the new control room's physical design, and the reversal in the position of the two units ten years before the fires — led us to the following hypothesis: The split between the two units was built into the fabric of the refinery's sociotechnical system. It was part and parcel of its psychosocial arrangement. At any particular moment in its history one or another unit, level, or person might be bad, or weak, or the source of conflict, but there always had to be such "bad" or problematic units.

The Psychodynamics of Safety

Splitting As a Social Defense

Psychodynamic theory provides a rationale for this process in organizations as well as among individuals (Hirschhorn, 1988). It suggests that a work group will divide internally in response to difficult or risky conditions and tasks. This division then becomes a *social defense,* a system of relationships that helps people control and contain feelings of anxiety when facing their difficult work.

Thus, for example, in many companies people describe the controller's office as "rigid," "cold," and "nit-picking," even though the controller's formal role is to account meticulously for how the company's money is spent. Uncomfortable with mobilizing the discipline and aggression they need to control their own spending, people outside the controller's office project these feelings and their associated images onto the controller's office. "We are easy, we make exceptions," so the stereotyping goes, "while *they,* the controller's office, are rigid and unforgiving." People's internalized image of the controller, shaped partly in response to their own anxieties about money and spending, thus creates a split in the social system itself. The controller's office becomes "bad" and "rigid" because everyone else wants to be good and easy.

Looked at psychodynamically, such splitting is closely linked to the processes of projection and scapegoating. When people feel vulnerable, inadequate, guilty, or inferior, they project these feelings onto some outsider, who is then experienced in just these ways. For example, men unwilling to acknowledge their sense of vulnerability may imagine that women are the vulnerable ones; poor whites unable to acknowledge their feelings of inferiority may decide that blacks are truly inferior, and, as we have suggested, unit two members had only contempt for Frank, "the short little boss," as a defense against their own self-contempt. Splitting is therefore a defensive operation that helps members of one group control their experience by stereotyping or scapegoating another group.

We experienced this defensive character of splitting throughout the consultation. Two examples from the meetings we conducted during the consultation are telling. When meeting with the refinery manager and a cross section of refinery personnel to discuss some of the problems and conflicts facing operators and controlmen, Princess, the "good" woman in the "good" unit, expressed surprise and puzzlement at unit two's problems, for after all, her unit "had no such problems." In response to her expressions of surprise, we stated that it was important to acknowledge that people in the two units did experience their work very differently.

Later, reflecting on this encounter, we were puzzled by Princess's comment. Surely she was not really surprised that the second unit was divided, that people were unhappy in it, and that Gerry, the "bad" woman and an operator, symbolized the problems people were having with the operator role. Everybody talked about these issues. Rather, we suggest she was puzzled by the implicit acknowledgment that people in the second unit were really suffering, were truly in pain. It was not that the two units differed but that these differences were important. That is why we responded intuitively, insisting that she acknowledge the other group's experience.

Projection and scapegoating culminate in just such a denial.

The scapegoat becomes the repository of feelings that cause pain, and then others deny that these feelings are indeed painful.

Similarly, we experienced the defensive character of such splitting when discussing how the new centralized control room might bring the two units together. As we noted, at the time of our visit, each unit controlled its portion of the refining process from its own control room or shack. To modernize the refinery, management was building a new centralized control room with up-to-date computer console equipment. Why, we asked, should there be a distinction between the units any longer? They would, after all, share the same physical space, and the "outside" workers who repaired or adjusted equipment in the yard could then be shared by both groups.

People at first said nothing and seemed tense and anxious. The refinery manager, speaking slowly, noted that they had to proceed very cautiously, and he was not prepared to consider this issue now. We did not push the point. However, reflecting on this encounter later, it seemed to me that we had attacked the refinery's defensive system. While, as we have seen, the new technology made the division between the two units increasingly unnecessary, the unconscious system of defense required it.

Safety and Splitting

But what were people defending themselves against? If people were using the bad unit as a repository for unwanted feelings, what feelings were they projecting into it? Let us return to the challenges of running a refinery. In the aftermath of two dangerous fires we were asked to help refinery workers and managers develop a safer refinery. If the refinery presented itself to us in a manner and through a process linked to the stated purposes of our visit, then its splits were linked directly to the problem of safety.

Consider the psychodynamics of managing and contributing to a safe industrial setting. If you are to act safely and prevent accidents you must be vigilant. This means that you must imagine that you are vulnerable to being hurt. By previewing the possible consequences of a dangerous situation in your mind, you then take appropriate preventive action. *You prevent accidents by imagining that you have already had them.* Indeed, people working in industrial settings are hurt most frequently because they ignore the ways in which seemingly minor hazards are nonetheless dangerous. Experienced operators working near welding operations stop wearing goggles and then suffer eye burns due to flashing, when they fail to turn their heads in time. A worker on a scaffold successfully avoids a weak plank but then falls through it when, under the pressure of a schedule, he steps on it rather than around it. A worker uses a ladder without rubber stops on its legs and then falls when the ladder slips along a grease spot on the floor.

Clearly, vigilance is a complex activity because if you become excessively preoccupied with potential accidents you will be unable to work. Moreover, your excessive anxiety is likely to infect others, disabling them as well. For example, workers who put up skyscrapers and walk the steel girders hundreds of feet above the ground shun novices who cannot keep their worries to themselves. Thus, in acting safely, workers in a dangerous setting must be vigilant without disabling their ability to focus on their work.

The refinery manager thought his workers found it hard to strike this balance. He believed that workers failed to notice dangers when they made their rounds because they "got into ruts." Similarly, he noted that when production pressure was low, backbiting and fighting among workers increased, leading to carelessness and more danger. Just as people get jumpy on weekends when they should be relaxing, feelings of danger become more prominent and disabling when people cannot contain their anxiety by working at their accustomed pace.

We suggest that the social splits at the refinery helped people manage the anxiety of working in a dangerous setting. The bad unit, we suggest, represented all that was bad and dangerous in the refinery. Projecting their feelings of being vulnerable, weak, and potentially helpless into the bad unit, people in unit one could feel safe and good. But since, to feel safe, they were acting irrationally, this splitting also prevented them from acting safely. Thus, the second fire, the more serious of the two, *happened in unit one's part of the yard.*

The Problem with Procedures

The safety director at the plant acknowledged that he felt ineffective both in enforcing safety procedures and in educating people to behave safely. Yet procedures play a critical role in helping people strike the balance between work and worry. They reduce the burdens of vigilance by helping people act safely without thinking excessively about the potential dangers that shape these procedures. Enacting the procedures without a great deal of conscious thought, people protect themselves without obsessively previewing the accidents that may hurt them. Free of excessive worry, they can focus on their work.

Reflecting on his ineffectiveness, the safety director highlighted two seemingly contradictory processes. On the one side, he noted, men often play the "hero" role by taking shortcuts, refusing, for example, to wear safety belts when working over a pit. But on the other hand, he noted, men would often employ some laborious and apparently useless procedure, arguing that "it's written that you have to do it this way." Examining old records the safety director would find no evidence for such a procedure. Thus, the procedural system was itself split between dangerous shortcuts and senseless protocols. By using shortcuts, workers could pretend that they were invulnerable. By following senseless protocols unconnected to actual dangers, workers did not have to preview potential accidents. In each case they denied the dangerous world confronting them. The workers could not apply procedures *intelligently,* and with just enough conscious thinking to assess why they were acting in a particular way. As the safety director noted, "Procedures are like a checklist, but you can't execute them if you have no understanding of them." Similarly, the refinery manager noted that "people feel snowed under by the rules, and I am not sure they can see the forest for the trees." Tied up and defended by a more irrational system of social splits, the workers could not apply procedures rationally.

To summarize, the social system of the refinery was defined by its psychosocial divisions. Units one and two were split between good and bad, and procedural behavior was cut off from thinking and planning. These splits, we suggest, were part and parcel of the refinery's social defense system, helping workers to contain the anxiety of working in a dangerous setting. But because these defenses blocked rational behavior they also increased the chances of accidents.

Social Defenses and the Hero System

The safety director's allusion to the term *hero* provides more insight into the plant's social defense system.

The Hero As the Ego Ideal

Heroes are invulnerable and independent, and they do not need other people. Indeed, the refinery was located in a part of the country where heroes as loners were celebrated in local lore, and frontier practices, such as owning a gun and valuing physical prowess, shaped men's conversation and behavior. Facing a complex technology that poses dangers to life and limb, people who imagine themselves to be heroes contain their anxiety in two ways. They believe that they are invulnerable, and as "loners" they need not feel dependent on others. But by denying their dependence, they also deny the dangerous features of the technology itself. In a refinery people depend deeply on each other because each person monitors and controls an operation that affects all other operations. This is the hallmark of any continuous-process production system. Thus just as the split between the good and bad units helped people *project* their anxiety onto the bad unit, the culture and image of the lone hero helped them *deny* their anxiety.

Our experience in the consultation suggested that the plant's social defense system — the split between good and bad — was reinforced by the culture of the hero. There were two particularly revealing examples.

The Pair As Hero

Meeting to discuss safety, the refinery manager George, the members of the health and safety committee, and a few other high-level supervisors examined obstacles to improving safety at the refinery. Describing the process of bringing suggestions from workers to management, Mike, a union representative on the committee, noted that he took workers' ideas to managers without involving or informing the foremen. Hirschhorn suggested that this could really backfire because foremen might feel that health and safety programs were designed to undermine their authority, and they might not cooperate. This statement seemed to create discomfort. People were silent, and then George noted, "Well, I don't know if people agree with that." Feeling the anxiety, Hirschhorn said, "People are not saying all that they are thinking." Then Jim, the assistant manager, got up and with an audible "Whew" said, "I guess it's time to take a break." Later, Jim noted that this had been his most important learning of the day.

Thinking back, we suggest that the dynamics of the health and safety committee itself had helped create a fantasy that George, with a few cooperative union people like Mike, could circumvent the institutional matrix of the refinery — the historically complex union-management relationship and the refinery's complex chain of command — and create a safe, happy, and productive place to work. Indeed, throughout the morning we were struck by the way Mike, a young and intense man and the most active union member on the committee, seemed eager to defend the plant and speak well of it, even though he was a union man. He sat directly opposite George and as the morning discussion progressed, it appeared that this pair, George and Mike, represented what Bion (1959) calls the *pairing fantasy,* the wish that two special people together can help a group overcome obstacles without involving everyone in the difficult work of development. Like heroes, the pair saves the group.

Seen in this context, Hirschhorn's statement threatened to undermine this fantasy. By pointing them back to the messy world of disgruntled foremen, he suggested that this committee, despite the fantasy it enacted and contained, could not magically and heroically transform the refinery. Other people could undermine it.

Manager As Hero

Our relationship with the refinery manager, George, also highlighted this culture of the hero. While he sponsored the consultation and worked with us over the course of the two days, incidentally making himself vulnerable to us, he would at times communicate that he did not really need us, that he could go it alone. For example, sitting at the conference table, arms folded, with the three different groups, he did not lift his pencil to take notes or jot things down, as if to communicate that he either knew everything or could remember it anyway. Similarly, after the first day of work, reflecting on its value, he said to one of us, "It's useful to have the other people here learn about these issues," as if to suggest that he had personally learned nothing new. Hirschhorn replied by reminding him that he too had been surprised by the discussion of the foreman's role in assuring safety, and he agreed. In other words, he did learn something, but like a hero, he was reluctant to acknowledge that he could profit from being with or working with others.

Yet while projecting invulnerability—his ability to avoid being influenced by us—he periodically expressed enormous frustration. He could not imagine how, despite any insights he might obtain during the meetings, he could actually improve safety. In a moment of frustration he said, "I guess all I can do is go out there and really start to walk around, take people on tours with me, show them what is dangerous, why this ladder can't be left in the middle of the yard when it snows." In other words, he could not imagine working *through* his organization, of leveraging his efforts through others. Instead he would be the hero, sweeping workers into his yard tours and showing them, by example, what it meant to be safe.

This idea per se was not wrong, but spoken in frustration it reflected George's sense of isolation and his compensatory fantasy that he could act heroically. As the hero, he had nothing to learn, but as a loner, as someone who could not collaborate, he could not act effectively.

The Negative Side of Heroism

The hero is a complex mythical figure, and we develop a many-leveled response to him. Most obviously we appreciate the hero because he saves us. More subtly, we admire the hero for his

courage; more primitively, we envy the hero for his independence; and most unconsciously, we hate the hero because we
cannot control him. Because he does not need us he may hurt
us as well as help us. Acting out of this cultural and mythical
ambivalence, assassins, while crazy in their own right, kill presidents and movie stars. Others, less disturbed but prone to wor-
ship heroes nonetheless, use the cult of a particular hero to gain
access to them, and in their fantasy lives get their power and
control their behavior.

While the refinery promoted a culture of heroism, it also
created two scapegoats who represented the *negative* side of heroism. These scapegoats were punished because they were too independent. Just as the refinery's social defense system split the
two units, it split the image of the hero in half. Some people
could enact the hero role, because others represented the dangers
that heroes pose.

The "Bad" Woman As Scapegoat

Consider the case of the "bad" woman, Gerry, in unit two. Everyone described her as obstinate, difficult to work with, and "someone who always thinks she's right." Indeed, toward the end of
our consultation one member of unit two asked to see Don
Young privately to discuss the trouble he and others were having with Gerry. People were wary of her and seemed to resent
the ways in which she was different. She lived alone, could fix
cars, knew the martial arts, and was separated from a man who
had abused her.

Half expecting to meet an ogre, our experience of her was
quite different. She had a boyish and tough look, but in an interview with Hirschhorn she appeared lively, feisty, demand-
ing, committed to productive work, and unhappy with the lazi-
ness and inattention she observed around her. Describing the
first fire in unit two, which occurred on her shift, she felt that
the workers and managers knew they were using "dirty charge"
but decided to forget about it and "pretend that they didn't have
a problem." At the second of the three group discussions, she
took the role of the fighter to be sure, arguing that the controlmen

had to be more accountable for their work. But her affect was vital, and we felt strongly that she wanted to connect to us, to the group, and to contribute to the discussion.

We suggest that people were scapegoating Gerry. An obvious reason is that — unlike Princess — she engaged in behavior that violated the gender norms that prevailed in their male-dominated work environment. But we could look at it somewhat differently. On the one hand, by noting that she lived independently and was a master of the martial arts, her co-workers were in effect describing the characteristics of a hero. On the other hand, by describing her as aggressive and obstinate, they reframed her heroic characteristics as signs of excessive willfulness and an inability to get along and cooperate with people. We suggest that people were using Gerry as a symbolic repository for the negative images of the hero. If the image of the hero evokes both positive and negative feelings, then refinery members could retain the positives for themselves — they could take heroic shortcuts — while projecting the negative traits of heroes — their uncontrollability and independence — onto Gerry.

Gerry's role as the negative hero may have contributed to the accident in unit two. On the night of the fire a controlman who officially worked under Gerry's direction openly defied an instruction she gave him. The audit did not identify this fight as the cause of the accident. But our hypothesis points to a plausible indirect connection between the two. By defying Gerry in public, the controlman created a "psychodrama," or group ritual, in which the group, satisfied that they had "destroyed" the bad and unreliable person Gerry, was now safe. Consequently, they became less vigilant and created the conditions for a fire.

Finally, Gerry suffered significantly because she was isolated and distrusted. Reflecting on the social process of the refinery, she noted, "Paybacks are a bitch here and they last forever. A person can make life absolutely hell out here. If you ever let any one see that anything bothered you they would pick at that." In short, to be safe, not from the technology but from attacks by other people, you had to appear invulnerable. Thus Gerry was saying that the negative parts of the hero role had been thrust on her. She could not risk showing her vulnerability since people, discovering her weak points, would attack her.

The Would-Be Hero As Scapegoat

Bill, a controlman's helper who had recently joined the refinery as a member of the "good" unit, was also the victim of this hero system. When the propane gas blew up in the second fire, Bill, risking his life, rushed toward the blaze to shut off a valve.

But his experience as hero was to be short-lived. The day before the fire, Bill was walking by two operators who were working to start up the refinery and volunteered to climb up a steel structure to open a valve. However, he and they failed to close a bleeder that had to be lined up with the valve. While officially being supervised by the operator standing below, it was his responsibility to look down the line to check if the bleeder and the valve were lined up. This open bleeder was the proximate cause of the fire, and after a careful investigation, management sent Bill a letter of reprimand. A hero one day, he became a villain the next.

Toward the end of the second day of our consultation, Bill's supervisor, Tom, approached Don Young and asked if Don, as company psychologist, would see Bill. Tom noted that after receiving the letter Bill "was really hurting." His teammates on the unit wrote a counterletter to management asking that the letter of reprimand be withdrawn. Management did not back down, but as Tom reflected, the letter of support from the unit did little to lift Bill's spirits. We decided to interview Bill together.

Several hours later Tom brought Bill to an office in the main suite. We were struck then by the image of Bill's helplessness as Tom, escorting Bill, gently pushed him by his elbow into the office, suggesting that this man had to be guided like a child or invalid. Bill sat down and began recounting the accident and its aftermath.

After describing the accident in some detail he noted how hard it was to be a hero one day and a villain the next. He said how bad he felt the next day when people, unaware of his role in the accident, congratulated him for his courageous behavior. He mentioned how horrible he felt when passing a particular teammate in the yard who had almost been killed in the fire. He then said that he had held a job as a pipe fitter in another

factory, and there, "when you screwed up, they beat you up
and sent you down the road."

At first glance this creates the impression of a depressed
and guilty man who has been punished by his superiors and
is punishing himself. But four other parts of the conversation
point to a more complex picture. First, in recounting the fire
and accident itself, his face and voice were animated, as if he
were describing an exciting sports event or movie. Highlighting the initiative he took to open the valve the day before and
then describing his courageous behavior during the accident,
it appeared as if he were telling us "you had to be there."

Second, he spoke contemptuously of his teammates' letter
of support. He termed it "that little letter," saying that he did
not care about it, and he criticized the first draft for being in-
sufficiently diplomatic.

Third, testing for depression, we asked if he was having
trouble sleeping or was waking up early and he said no. "How
about eating?" we inquired. "I have to lose some weight," he
suggested.

Fourth, try as we might, we were unable to say anything
helpful to him. "Would it help talking to the man you almost
killed?" we asked. "No," he answered. Perhaps he did not like
all the care he was getting and would rather be beaten up, as
he was when employed as a pipe fitter, we suggested. No, he
didn't think that was it. "Why did he think he was solely responsible?" we asked. "Well, I opened the valve," he replied. Unable
to say anything useful to him, we began to feel increasingly helpless. Indeed, as the conversation wound down Bill said somewhat
sardonically, "Well you guys are giving me all these theoretical
ideas. I thought you were going to help me."

What was going on here? We suggest that far from being depressed and guilty, Bill was both ashamed and enraged:
ashamed for his failure and enraged at his subsequent humilia-
tion. To get back at the plant community, which was sophisticated enough to try to help him after it had punished him, he
refused to be helped. In this way his own feelings of helplessness, of impotence, were transferred back onto the plant community and of course onto us. In other words, he did not want
us to help him, he wanted us to feel helpless.

The Dance of Projection

We suggest that Bill and the plant were engaged in a complex dance of projection. The plant community, anxious to control its own sense of vulnerability, of helplessness, after the accident, scapegoated Bill by reprimanding him. To be sure, he was partly responsible and had been careless. But one operator, after all, was supervising him, and the other was participating in the work. More important, management was pushing the workers to work quickly so that the refinery could be started up without delay. Indeed, Bill's supervisor, Tom, who brought him to his appointment with us, told us that he worried that he had pushed the men too hard prior to the accident.

But because Bill was easily humiliated — a reflection of the omnipotence that led him to act heroically, if sometimes carelessly — he refused to be scapegoated. Instead, by refusing to be helped he put his own sense of helplessness *back into the system.* Anxious to protect themselves from feeling vulnerable, the plant community now felt helpless to help Bill. Just as social splits distributed feelings of helplessness between the good and bad unit, Bill had turned feelings of helplessness into a "hot potato," as these feelings passed from him to the refinery and back.

Clients often transfer feelings stimulated by a work system onto consultants. This is the analogue of the transference in psychotherapy. We suggest this happened to us as we worked with Bill. In making us helpless, Bill brought us to the edge of such feelings as despair, anger, and contempt. We disliked him for having made us helpless and disliked ourselves for failing. We suggest that these feelings shaped the unconscious experiences of refinery members. Feeling vulnerable in a dangerous situation and unable or unwilling to trust the "heroes" around them, people developed feelings of contempt and anger for social scapegoats such as Gerry, unit two, or the troublemakers that once populated unit one, to control their own feelings of vulnerability.

Finally, we suggest that Bill was singled out in part because of his capacity to act heroically. He was a young controlman's helper who had acted eagerly in opening the valve and had acted truly heroically during the accident. Looked at rationally, he both needed discipline and to be disciplined. But looked at irrationally, as a newcomer he was an easy projective target for people's ambivalent feelings about heroes, for their anxiety that heroes were uncontrollable, too independent, and therefore dangerous. The hero in him had to be tamed so that it could be manifested in subtler ways, in ways acceptable to the plant's culture—like violating a procedure or keeping to himself. Thus, we suggest that he was reprimanded, not because he had caused an accident, indeed much evidence suggests that he was not solely to blame, *but because he was a hero.* This explains why, despite the evidence that the fire was linked to the pace of work during the start-up, Bill was singled out.

Summary

The problems just discussed point up the inadequacies of traditional methods of auditing accidents. This final section touches on the kind of broader developmental response that is needed if society is going to create safer work environments.

The Problem of Vigilance

People working in dangerous settings need to be vigilant without being fearful. This requires sophistication. They need to follow procedures but to do so with intelligence. They need to focus on their work but also to see the pattern of relationships, the links between pipes, valves, pumps, and controls that create unexpected pathways for the evolution of accidents.

Looked at psychodynamically, people behave safely when they care about a setting, and in integrated production environments they must care about the whole setting. This means that they must project feelings of their own self-worth onto the workplace, so that just as they care for themselves they protect their environment. But if the experienced dangers are too great, or the organizational climate promotes feelings of inadequacy, or finally, management does not develop procedures and techniques for working safely, people will split up their internalized image of the workplace—they will project their sense of danger onto one part and their feelings of safety and security onto another.

This is the genesis of dangerous social splits. Thus at the Smalltown refinery, its members had developed a complex social defense in which one unit was bad and the other good, a bad, obstinate woman was compared to a nurturing princess, procedures were split off from thinking, and bad heroes who created accidents allowed good heroes to take shortcuts.

As workers project their feelings of vulnerability onto scapegoats, they feel safe without paying sufficient attention to signs of danger. More important, they do not simply become less vigilant. Rather, *they turn their vigilance inward,* away from the technology and the artifacts of production and toward the social system itself. People pay undue attention to the defensive relationships they have constructed with one another, ensuring, for example, that the bad unit would not contaminate the good unit in a centralized control room, ignoring the bad unit's dilemmas and pain, isolating negative heroes such as Gerry, and constraining their own expression of vulnerability for fear of "paybacks." The social defense system itself becomes the focus of attention. As people pay too much attention to their relationships and too little attention to the technology, the sociotechnical system is split apart.

Auditing Accidents

How can managers and operators working in dangerous settings help shape and develop a climate in which scapegoating and splitting are minimized and people at all levels can rely on each other? Accident audits provide an occasion for change and development. Typically, as was the case at the Smalltown refinery, the auditors try to pinpoint the accident's proximate causes and the people who were responsible. The audit is conducted as if it were a legal inquiry, interviews are conducted in confidence, evidence is assembled, and a report is issued that purports to be the truth.

But such a tradition denies the multicausal and sociotechnical nature of most accidents. Most serious studies of accidents show how inadequate maintenance, pressures of production, a failed control system, as well as an operator's error all combine to create the accident. Indeed, in any complicated industrial system — such as a chemical plant, nuclear reactor, or oil refinery — accidents are "always about to happen," but operator vigilance combined with good safety, effective maintenance practices, and control systems prevent them. An accident "breaks through" this system of defense when a series of failures converge at a particular moment to upset the system. There is always a proximate cause for the accident — the broken valve, the leaky pipe, the failed sensor — but invariably accident audits show that these proximate causes create accidents because other defenses, such as a maintenance protocol, or a sensor, had already failed or been violated. By highlighting proximate causes, and then pinpointing blame, accident audits become ritualized expressions of the same social defense system that helps create the accident in the first place.

New Approaches to Investigating Accidents

To break through this defense system, to create a new and less distorting social system, we need to change this tradition of accident investigation. Two recent examples of responses to accidents in the U.S. Navy are suggestive here.

In April 1989, forty-seven seamen died aboard the USS *Iowa* when a gun exploded during an exercise. The Navy's auditors blamed a single seaman, Clayton Hartwig, suggesting that he was a homosexual distraught over a failed love affair and committed suicide by blowing himself and the other seamen up. Arguing that they recovered traces of a detonator that Hartwig had presumably built, they nevertheless could never duplicate it and acknowledged that Hartwig could not have had time to build it — he did not know he would be the gun captain until the day before the exercise. While blaming Hartwig, the Navy also acknowledged that it had uncovered — but discounted — such factors as serious safety problems in a turret, poor supervision of seamen, and poorly trained gunmen. It appears as if the Navy, eager to put the accident behind itself and exonerate its systems, chose to scapegoat Hartwig, by painting him as a deviant seaman. Ironically, there was no firm evidence that he was in fact a homosexual.

Consider by contrast the Navy's response to a series of accidents and fires aboard Naval ships in November 1989, about six months after the explosion of the USS *Iowa*. Arguing that no single thread "tied the accidents together" (indeed the USS *Iowa's* explosion may have been just the beginning of this series of accidents), that there was no single cause, the chief of naval operations ordered a forty-eight-hour "safety standdown" in which seamen were to stop all normal operations and instead review all safety procedures. In other words, recognizing that there was no single cause or reason for the series of accidents, the admiral suggested that the *system* for ensuring safety was weakening. Thus he wanted people to stop acting and by reviewing safety procedures raise their awareness.

The admiral's order highlights four features of a developmental response to accidents. First, no single person or system is blamed. Second, unlike the case of the USS *Iowa,* people cannot use the audit and its findings simply to put the accident behind them. Third, safety is more readily assured when everyone takes responsibility by reviewing their own personal experience and responsibility for behaving safely. Fourth, people can undertake such a review if, as a *community,* they suspend action and focus their attention on the system and its safeguards.

Indeed, there is a hidden psychodynamic logic to these principles. As psychoanalysis suggests, we can start to overcome our defenses when we stop acting and start thinking, when instead of working to sustain normality we let go to extend and deepen our awareness. Similarly, instead of using the accident audit as an excuse to continue normal operations, instead of using normal operations as defense against awareness, a work community must create a place, a time, where normal operations are suspended and community members, aware of how they must depend on each other to operate safely, can deepen their understanding of their interdependence.

This suggests that the plant community, rather than simply relying on independent auditors, should study the accident; while looking for causes, such a self-study report should eschew blame. Indeed, at the time of our visit the Smalltown refinery stood uneasily between these two approaches. Conducting a traditional audit, they identified proximate causes and disciplined one worker. Yet concerned that wider cultural and social forces could shape the refinery's capacity to produce oil without incurring accidents, they invited us to help them assess how as a community they could work more safely.

To develop safe work practices in our increasingly automated plants, managers and workers need to rely increasingly on community self-study to complement the findings of a technical audit. As our consultation suggests, the struggles a community would face in managing the anxieties and conflicts associated with such a self-study would then provide it with the very experiences it needs to prevent future accidents.

References

Bion, W. R. *Experiences in Groups, and Other Papers.* London: Tavistock, 1959.

Hirschhorn, L. *Beyond Mechanization.* Cambridge, Mass.: MIT Press, 1984.

Hirschhorn, L. *The Workplace Within: Psychodynamics of Organizational Life.* Cambridge, Mass.: MIT Press, 1988.

Perrow, C. *Complex Organizations: A Critical Essay.* New York: Scott, Foresman, 1972.

PART FOUR

The Question of Organizational Character

10

Leadership Styles and Organizational Cultures: The Shaping of Neurotic Organizations

Manfred F. R. Kets de Vries
Danny Miller

All of us in dealing with the vicissitudes of life have specific styles, "ways of thinking and perceiving, ways of experiencing emotion, modes of subjective experience in general, and modes of activity that are associated with various pathologies" (Shapiro, 1965, p. 1). We all possess certain ways of dealing with the environment, patterns that are deeply embedded, pervasive, and likely to endure. The "fantasies" that make up a person's interior world — the stereotyped, well-rehearsed, constantly repeated ways of behaving and acting that determine an individual's particular cognitive and affective map — are essential to understanding that person. Human functioning is generally characterized by a mixture of styles derived from these "fantasies." The same person may possess elements of many different styles, each of which is triggered by different circumstances. Among a group of individuals, however, one specific style will dominate and consistently come to the fore in stressful situations. Extreme manifestations of any one style can signal significant psychopathology that seriously impairs functioning. In our observation of top

243

executives and organizations we discovered that parallels could be drawn between individual pathology—the excessive use of one neurotic style—and organizational pathology, the latter resulting in various forms of problems and particularly poor performance.

The person-organization interface is much more apparent in firms where the decision-making power is centralized in the hands of either a top executive or a small, homogeneous, dominant coalition. Where power is broadly distributed throughout a firm, its culture and strategies will be determined by many executives and the relationship between style and organizational pathology becomes more tenuous. Consequently, although neurotic styles can have an impact at all levels of the organization, in this chapter we will limit our scope to top management.

Neurotic Styles and Organizations

Strategy, and even structure, can be influenced strongly by the personality of the top manager (Miller, Kets de Vries, and Toulouse, 1982). So can organizational culture (Jaques, 1951, 1970; Kernberg, 1979; Kets de Vries, 1980, 1984, 1989, 1991; Maccoby, 1976; Payne and Pugh, 1976; Zaleznik and Kets de Vries, 1980). Management literature is filled with evidence to support this contention. Much of the research, however, has examined simple aspects of personality and related them to one or two organizational variables (Tosi, 1970; Vroom, 1960). Such studies have led to the oversimplification of often very complex phenomena.

In an attempt to broaden the treatment of personality in management, psychoanalytic and psychiatric literature has frequently been drawn on, in particular, the works of Fenichel (1945), Freedman, Kaplan, and Sadock (1975), Laplanche and Pontalis (1973), Nicholi (1988), and Shapiro (1965). These studies provide a far more integrated view of intrapsychic functioning and behavior than is found in traditional psychological literature. Thus, we will focus on clusters of behavior patterns, personality styles that remain relatively stable over the years, as opposed to simple dimensions of behavior. These may enable us to better link what happens in the inner world of the executive with his or her actual behavior.

The central thesis of this chapter is that the stable and global psychological orientations of key organization members are major determinants of the "neurotic styles" of their organizations (Jacobson, 1964; Klein, 1948; Laplanche and Pontalis, 1973; Mahler, Pine, and Bergman, 1975; Sandler and Rosenblatt, 1962). This has many consequences. Top executives may create shared fantasies that permeate all levels, influence organizational culture, and underlie a dominant organizational adaptive style (Kernberg, 1976). This style greatly influences decisions about strategy and structure (Kets de Vries and Miller, 1984a, 1984b, 1984c, 1987).

The original idea behind this framework is that parallels can be drawn between common neurotic styles of behavior and common modes of organizational failure, particularly those delineated by the empirical taxonomy of Miller and Friesen (1978, 1984). Pathological organizational types seemed in many ways to mirror the types of dysfunctions common to the most widely discussed neurotic styles among individuals (American Psychiatric Association, 1987; Shapiro, 1965). For example, Miller and Friesen's "stagnant bureaucracies" had no clear goals, lacked initiative, reacted very sluggishly to external changes, and were pervaded by managerial apathy, frustration, and inaction. The depressive personality style exhibits very similar features. A quantity of anecdotal literature, as well as our own experiences with organizations, led us to the conclusion that firms that fit Miller and Friesen's stagnant bureaucracy types are run by depressive CEOs.

One more example may help to illustrate this theme. Miller and Friesen's "impulsive" firms are characterized by centralized power, bold and risk-taking decisions, and a tremendous urge for growth and expansion, often satisfied by the acquisition of other firms. The dramatic personality reflects many of these traits — the need to dominate others, the need to display prowess through major projects, and the need to impress others with dramatic action. Again, there seemed to be a link between a common mode of organizational failure and a very prevalent neurotic style (Kets de Vries, 1989).

However, it is important to note that we do not believe that organizational pathology necessarily requires the CEO involved to exhibit the neurotic styles we discuss here. Clearly, some organizations might manifest such styles for completely different reasons. For example, a depressive firm might be found in a declining industry that has dwindling markets or too much foreign competition. Depressive pathology might also be seen in a firm that has been acquired and dominated by a conglomerate, or in a firm that has too few resources to be able to initiate a significant turnaround.

In this chapter we identify a number of very common, well-established fantasies and neurotic styles (Fenichel, 1945; Millon, 1981; Nicholi, 1988; Shapiro, 1965), and personality disorders as defined in the latest *Diagnostic and Statistical Manual of Mental Disorders (DSM-III-R)* published by the American Psychiatric Association (1987). The chapter is based on the common pathological organizational strategies and structures isolated by the empirical work of Miller and Friesen (1984). Conjectures about the relationship between each style, each style's predominant motivating fantasy, the emerging organizational culture, and the strategy and structure of the overall organization are developed (see Table 10.1 and Exhibit 10.1). It is worthwhile to bear in mind that common gestalts found in many failing firms, and discussed here, are by no means the only sort of dysfunctional types, and mixed types are quite common.

Table 10.1. Summary of the Five Constellations.

Fantasy	Style	Culture	Organization
Persecution	Suspicious	Paranoid	Paranoid
Helplessness	Depressive	Avoidant	Depressive
	Dependent		
Grandiosity	Dramatic	Charismatic	Dramatic
	Histrionic/ narcissistic		
Control	Compulsive	Bureaucratic	Compulsive
Detachment	Detached	Politicized	Schizoid
	(Schizoid/ avoidant)		

Exhibit 10.1. General Hypotheses.

1. The more centralized the organizations are and the more power the CEOs have, the greater the impact of their personality (that is, fantasy and neurotic style) on culture, strategy, and structure.

2. The more similar the personalities of the top executives, the purer the cultural and organizational types — that is, the more closely they will adhere to the five types discussed.

3. The purer and more pronounced the personality type of the CEO — as measured by the DSM-III-R (American Psychiatric Association, 1987) or the Millon Inventory (1981) — the more it will be reflected in the culture, structure, and strategy of the firm. This will be especially true in smaller, centralized organizations.

4. Healthy firms will have a mixture of personality types.

The Persecutory Preoccupation

The predominant concern associated with the suspicious style is the fantasy that nobody can be trusted, that there is a menacing, superior force that is "out to get" one. Thus a major preoccupation is to be on guard, to be ready for any attack — real or imagined. This suspicious style is characterized by mistrust of others, hypersensitivity, and hyperalertness. Guardedness and secretiveness are pervasive (Nicholi, 1988). Suspicious executives are constantly prepared to counter perceived threats. They may take offense easily and respond in anger. Envy and hostility are ever present. Those executives are overly preoccupied with hidden motives and special meanings. The actions of others are easily misread and distorted; minor slights become magnified. Suspicious executives expect to find trickery and deception and look for facts to confirm their worst expectations. They possess an intense, narrowly focused attention span and may come across as cold, rational, and unemotional (American Psychiatric Association, 1987). Our experience indicates that top executives with this style often give rise to paranoid organizational disfunctioning.

Paranoid Cultures, Paranoid Firms

In paranoid organizations, interpersonal relationships between leaders and subordinates are often characterized by a persecutory theme. Leaders may feel hostile toward subordinates. They may want to harm or attack others as a defensive reaction to their own feelings of persecution and mistrust. Clearly, this is one of the most destructive of leadership attitudes. Suspicious leaders see subordinates as malingerers and incompetents, or as people who are deliberately out to provoke their anger. As a consequence, these leaders are likely to gravitate toward two extremes. They might try to exert a tremendous amount of control through intensive personal supervision, formal rules and restraints, and harsh punishment. This removes all initiative from managers, lowers their self-esteem, and may cause them to engage in a contest of wills with the leaders. The absence of opportunity for growth or development can induce the most promising managers to leave.

The second, less common, reaction of hostile leaders toward subordinates is one of overt aggression. Leaders may be reluctant to give subordinates emotional or material rewards, striving always to come out on the winning side of any "trades." Morale can suffer a good deal under these conditions, as subordinates hold back their contributions and concentrate on protecting themselves from exploitation.

Suspicious top executives generate organizational cultures that are pervaded by distrust, suspicion, and the identification of enemies. Bion (1959) has called these *fight-flight cultures*. In these cultures the members come to fear the same things as the top executive. There is a constant atmosphere of fear of attack, while energy is expended on identifying the enemy on whom to blame everything. The world and the people inhabiting it are split into simple good and bad parts, those that act in accordance with the group members' needs or against them. Group members deny responsibility for their own actions. They lack insight into their weaknesses. Again, fear and suspicion are the predominant emotions (Kets de Vries and Miller, 1984a).

It is important to note that Bion (1959) believes that all groups have these fight-flight phases, and various others, as part of their normal evolution. But paranoid cultures become arrested at this level, so that the fight-flight fantasy endures and begins to dominate perceptions.

The paranoid culture tends to be a uniform one. Leaders are careful to hire, reward, and promote only those who share their views. People who differ or dissent from the leaders' opinions are mistrusted. They are ignored or refused promotion. Thus the dominant coalition will generally see things the same way — sharing the same fears and enemies.

In fact, the search for the enemy calls for a great mobilization of energy and a strong sense of conviction among organizational members about the correctness of their actions. Unfortunately, too much stereotyping can lead to rigidity in decision making. "Enemies" are vigorously analyzed and explicitly countered with a competitive strategy. Employees suspected of disloyalty are fired. Power is centralized in the hands of leaders since "no one can be trusted."

The suspicious atmosphere in these organizations will often carry over to interpersonal and even interdepartmental functioning. A premium is placed on information as a power resource; therefore, departmental personnel may be reluctant to discuss common problems. An adversarial relationship can develop, making coordination difficult as secrets abound and a "protect yourself" ethic prevails.

In this type of company, managerial suspicions translate into a primary emphasis on organizational intelligence and controls. Managers develop sophisticated information systems to identify threats from government, competitors, and customers. They develop budgets, cost centers, profit centers, cost-accounting procedures, and similar methods to control internal activities. The elaborate information-processing apparatus reflects their desire for perpetual vigilance and preparedness for emergencies.

This paranoia also influences decision making. Frequently, key executives decide that it may be safer to direct their distrust externally rather than withhold information from one another. They share information and make concerted efforts to discover organizational problems and to select alternative solutions for dealing with them. Unfortunately, this type of decision making can become overly cautious, with different people being asked for similar information. This "institutionalization of suspicion" sometimes ensures that accurate information gets to the top of the firm, but it may also reduce morale and trust as well as waste valuable time and energy.

Paranoid firms tend to react rather than anticipate. If competitors lower prices, the firm may study the challenge and eventually react to it. If other firms introduce a product successfully, the paranoid firm will probably imitate them. But strategic paranoia carries with it a sizable element of conservatism. Fear often entails being afraid to innovate, to overextend resources, or to take risks. This reactive orientation impedes the development of a concerted and consistent strategy. The paranoid firm's direction has too much to do with external forces and not enough to do with consistent goals, plans, or unifying themes and traditions.

Paranoid firms frequently try product diversification to reduce the risk of reliance on any one product. But because diversification requires more elaborate control and information-processing mechanisms, it actually reinforces the firm's paranoia.

Corporate paranoia often stems from a period of traumatic challenge: A strong market dries up, a powerful new competitor enters the market, or damaging legislation is passed. The harm done by these forces may cause managers to become very distrustful and fearful, to lose their nerve, or to recognize the need for better intelligence.

Helplessness and Hopelessness

The fantasy that it is hopeless to try to change the course of life, and that one is just not good enough, dominates this particular style. Depressive-style managers lack self-confidence and initiative. According to DSM-III-R, depressive-style managers often have dependent personalities. Psychiatrists claim that these dependent personalities have a strong need for affection and nurture, and possess very little self-esteem (Jacobson, 1971; Nicholi, 1988).

In this depressive style, feelings of guilt, worthlessness, and inadequacy are pervasive. Individuals downgrade themselves; they are self-deprecating and feel inferior to others, claiming a lack of ability and talent. They abdicate responsibility. A sense of helplessness and hopelessness prevails. External sources of sustenance are needed to combat insecurity. Depressives submerge their individuality and look for protectors. They try to be ingratiating, adapting their behavior to please those they depend on and allowing others to assume responsibility for major areas of life.

Depressive-style leaders are subject to feelings of powerlessness as a result of unpleasant past relationships. Anger about their powerlessness may give rise to feelings of guilt and wariness toward others. They turn their hostility inward in a phenomenon known as *moral masochism*. They may seek psychic pain as a redemptive act, as a means of assuaging their guilt about wishes that are perceived as unacceptable. Defeat is seen as a just reward (Jacobson, 1971).

At the same time such leaders seem to be looking for a messiah, someone to protect them from the dangers around them (Bion, 1959). They experience a need to idealize others — consultants, important people such as bankers or directors, or other figures with whom they are in regular contact.

Those in charge thus display incompetence and fail to show any imagination. They wait for others to take initiative, often fearing success because they think it will make people envious and hostile. This sometimes prompts them to snatch mediocrity from the jaws of victory. Executives adopt a passive orientation, shying away from action and becoming reclusive (Kernberg, 1979).

Avoidance Cultures, Depressive Organizations

The culture of a firm with this sort of leader can be characterized as "avoidant." The executives view the organization as a machine that simply has to be fed routine input. There is a pervasive sense of futility; executives reduce their contributions to the minimum that is required of them. The CEO sets a climate of negativity and lethargy and the second-tier executives take their cues from this. In some cases the leader's personality alone causes the depressive atmosphere. In others, an external force, such as the loss of the founder or a takeover by a conglomerate, causes healthy executives to lose their sense of control, their authority, their self-esteem, and consequently their initiative. In either event, an avoidant culture is permeated by unmotivated, absentee executives, buck-passing, delays, and an absence of meaningful interaction and communication among managers. Things continue along the same path, even when the firm begins to run into trouble.

Depressive firms are characterized by inactivity, lack of confidence, extreme conservatism, and insularity. They have an atmosphere of passivity and purposelessness. The only things that are achieved are those that are programmed, routinized, and require no special initiative.

Most depressive firms are well established and serve a mature market, one that has had the same technology and competitive patterns for many years, with trade agreements, restrictive trade practices, and substantial tariffs. Depressive firms are most commonly found in the primary steel industry and agricultural or industrial chemical businesses. The low level of change, the absence of serious competition, and the homogeneity of the customers make the administrative task fairly simple.

Although formal authority is centralized and based on position rather than expertise, the issue of power is not very important. Control is really exercised by formalized programs and policies rather than by managerial initiative. Suggestions for change are resisted and action is inhibited. It is almost as if the top executives share a sense of impotence and incapacity. They do not feel they can control events or that they have what it takes to revitalize the firm.

Content with the status quo, these organizations do little to discover the key threats and weaknesses in markets. It is difficult to say whether stagnation causes inattention to information gathering, or vice versa. In either event, the two aspects go hand in hand in the depressive firm.

The sense of aimlessness and apathy among top managers precludes any attempt to give the firm clear direction or goals. Strategy is never explicitly considered, so no significant change occurs. Yesterday's products and markets become today's, not because of any policy of conservatism, but because of lethargy. Managers spend most of their time working out routine details while procrastinating about major decisions.

The Need for Grandiosity

Central to the dramatic style are the need to draw attention to oneself and a fantasy that revolves around grandiosity. This style seems to mix characteristics of two personality types: the histrionic and the narcissistic. Although the genesis of these two personality types is quite different, there are many behavioral similarities that make it difficult to differentiate between the two types in action. Consequently, for purposes of expediency, they are frequently lumped together. Dramatic individuals experience a great need to impress and get attention from others. They often exaggerate their achievements and talents and display excessive emotion. Their behavior has an exhibitionistic quality (Kets de Vries, 1981). Dramatic people seem to be driven by a need for excitement and stimulation that is often without substance. They lack self-discipline; they have a poor capacity for concentration and a tendency to overreact. Many of these individuals possess a sense of entitlement. They may be superficially warm and charming, but in fact they often lack sincerity and are inconsiderate of others. Exploitativeness is not uncommon and empathy is usually lacking (Kernberg, 1979). Often unwittingly, these CEOs take others for granted. Relationships thus tend to be unstable. In many instances they alternate between extremes of overidealization and devaluation. When fantasies of unlimited power, success, and brilliance are cut short, dramatic CEOs may experience marked feelings of rage and anger, and act vindictively.

The dramatic-style leader may give rise to a specific role constellation in the firm. Dramatic leaders often attract subordinates with dependent personality structures. Their action-oriented, grandiose style suits the dependency needs of insecure subordinates, allowing the latter to take responsibility for major areas of functioning while subordinating their own needs to those of the dramatic leader. The results are frequently as follows.

Charismatic Cultures, Dramatic Firms

Subordinates tend to idealize charismatic leaders, to ignore their faults, and to accentuate their strengths (idealization is often motivated by feelings of insecurity and unworthiness in the absence of a figure who can be admired). They become highly dependent on the idealized executives, feeling a need to support, appeal to, and ingratiate themselves with these individuals. They are prone to feel very flattered by a few words of praise and devastated by the mildest of reprimands. They thus become extremely dependent on the leaders and very easy to control and manipulate. This is generally the exact situation that dramatic leaders want to encourage. Dramatic leaders want to be "nourished" by subordinates' confirming and admiring ("mirroring") responses. In fact, mirroring superiors seek out idealizing subordinates — they demand not only confirming behavior but also praise and adulation (Kohut, 1971).

In the charismatic culture, everything seems to revolve around the leader. The hopes and ambitions of the other executives and managers center around this idealized person. Charismatic leaders are people of action who strive aggressively and single-mindedly to implement a central goal that becomes a focal concern for the followers. A tremendous uniformity derives from the leader's "charisma" — there is only one leader and many followers. There is thus an unquestioning, trustful climate of subordination among group members. Zealous followers help create an atmosphere in which the leader is seen as infallible. There is little reflection or analysis, since managers rely on the inspired judgment of the boss. The leader's power, both formal and informal, is so vast that it translates into a great deal of latitude to make very bold and unilateral decisions. Typically, the leader does not permit any resistance or dissent from subordinates. Independent-minded managers cannot last very long in this culture.

Dramatic firms are hyperactive, impulsive, dramatically venturesome, and dangerously uninhibited. Impulsive decision makers live in a world of hunches and impressions rather than facts, as they haphazardly address an array of disparate markets. Their dramatic flair encourages the top people to centralize power, reserving their prerogative to initiate bold ventures.

Audacity, risk taking, and diversification are the corporate themes. Instead of reacting to the business environment, the top decision maker attempts to create an idiosyncratic environment, entering some markets and leaving others, constantly switching to new products while abandoning older ones, and placing a sizable proportion of the firm's capital at risk. The goal is unbridled growth, reflecting the top manager's considerable narcissistic needs and desire for attention and visibility. This leader wants to be at center stage.

The structure of the dramatic organization is usually far too primitive for its broad markets. First, too much power is concentrated in the chief executive, who meddles even in routine operating patterns in order to put a personal stamp on (and take credit for) everything. A second problem follows from this overcentralization: namely, the absence of an effective information system. The top executive does little scanning of the business environment, preferring to act on intuition rather than on facts. Finally, the leader's dominance obstructs effective internal communication, which is mostly from the top down.

The Need for Control

Compulsive-style executives feel a need to counteract their fear of being at the mercy of events. Their overwhelming preoccupation is to master and control anything that may affect their lives. These people see relationships in terms of dominance and submission; they insist that others submit to their ways of doing things. They can be deferential and ingratiating to superiors while at the same time behaving in a markedly autocratic way toward subordinates. Their sense of perfectionism interferes with their ability to see the whole picture. Compulsives are preoccupied with trivial details, rules, and regulations. They are attracted by routines and find it difficult to deviate from planned activity. The unfamiliar is upsetting and form takes precedence over substance. Meticulousness, dogmatism, and obstinacy are common traits. Compulsives demonstrate an excessive concern about order, organization, and efficiency. They lack spontaneity and are unable to relax. Although they may come across as industrious, their behavior is rigid, showing a lack of imagination and much repetition. Compulsives are excessively devoted

to work, to the exclusion of pleasure and productive relationships. Other elements of their style are indecisiveness and pro-
crastination, growing from the fear of making mistakes (Fenichel,
1945; Shapiro, 1965). What sorts of organizations do these managers create?

Bureaucratic Cultures, Compulsive Organizations

In the compulsive firm, there is a degree of mistrust between
leader and subordinates. The leader would rather rely on formal controls and direct supervision to effect coordination than
on the goodwill, shared objectives, or talent of a management
team. As a result, there are overtones of suspicion and manipulation and a constant preoccupation with losing control. Controls, however, can rob subordinates of their sense of discretion, involvement, and personal responsibility. The prescription
of work and an atmosphere of suspicion sap executives' enthusiasm and robs them of initiative.

Above all, the bureaucratic group culture is depersonal-
ized and rigid. It is permeated by top management's preoccupation with control over people, operations, and the external
environment. The rules may be legacies of the past, codifying
the original founders' notions about how to run a successful company. There are established, formal policies, standard operating procedures, and detailed specifications for the accomplishment of tasks and the management of personnel. All these are
vehicles used by top managers to control the firm. They manage
by rules rather than through personal guidance or directives.
They want to avoid surprises and to determine what is to happen throughout the firm. The only managers that can survive
happily in this setting are bureaucrats who love to follow rules
and who fear taking initiative. Independent managers will find
that they do not have enough latitude to act on their own and
will leave. The controlling top executive is not willing to relinquish sufficient control over operations to allow for a participative mode of decision making. Instead, company policies are
the manifestation of compulsive features rather than objective,
adaptive requirements. As such, they are not subject to discus-

sion. The term *bureaucracy* is not used here in a strictly Weberian way. The notions discussed do not so much conform to a sociological construct describing an ideal form of formal organization, as to a mode of operating that is highly ritualistic and inwardly focused.

The compulsive firm is wed to ritual. Every operative detail is planned carefully in advance and carried out in routine fashion. Thoroughness, completeness, and conformity to established procedures are emphasized (see Mintzberg's "machine bureaucracies," 1979).

Like the paranoid firm, the compulsive firm emphasizes formal controls and information systems, but there is a crucial difference. In compulsive organizations, controls are designed to monitor internal operations, production efficiency, costs, and the scheduling and performance of projects, while in paranoid firms controls chiefly monitor external conditions. Operations are standardized and an elaborate set of formal policies and procedures evolves. These policies include not only production and marketing procedures but also dress codes, frequent sales meetings, and even suggested employee attitudes.

The compulsive firm has a particular orientation and distinctive competence and its plans reflect them. This orientation, rather than what is going on in the outside world, provides the major guide for the firm's strategy. For example, some organizations take pride in being the leader in the marketplace; they try to be the first with new products, whether or not these are called for by customers. Innovation may be inappropriate in the light of new market conditions, but the firm's strong inward focus prevents any realization of this. Change is difficult.

The Need for Detachment

Some individuals are guided by a detached style and fantasize that the outside world does not offer them any satisfaction. They sense that interactions with others will eventually fail and cause harm, that it is safer to remain distant. Psychiatrists have identified avoidant and schizoid personalities who are often beset by such preoccupations. Both personality types elicit a pattern of social detachment. Avoidant personalities have experienced interpersonal rejection and deprecation that have caused them to be mistrustful and to avoid close relationships; however, they long for closer attachments and greater social acceptance. In contrast, schizoid personalities often have cognitive and emotional deficits that render them unconcerned about their social isolation (Kernberg, 1975; Kets de Vries, 1980, 1989). Given the similarity in the behavioral manifestations of the two types, it is difficult to differentiate between them since both tend to be socially hesitant and unresponsive (American Psychiatric Association, 1987).

A pattern of noninvolvement and withdrawal characterizes this detached style. Detached individuals are most unwilling to enter into emotional relationships. They prefer to be alone and feel no need to communicate. Although on the surface, there may be great indifference to praise, criticism, or the feelings of others, this behavior is often a defense against being hurt. Whatever the underlying reasons, these individuals appear cold and aloof. They display emotional blandness and an inability to express enthusiasm or pleasure. Detached managers are unable to engage in the give-and-take of reciprocal relationships, appearing to possess minimal human interest. To protect themselves, they refuse to enter into relationships and they minimize involvements for fear of social derogation. The following type of organization may result. Another form of detached behavior typifies the senior executive who has become bored with the daily work routine: Activities not directly work-related, whether politics or social concerns, come to seem more attractive. This shift in interests means that the executive is less available than before at the office. Such behavior may resemble that which characterizes the person with problems of a schizoid/avoidant nature.

Politicized Cultures, Schizoid Organizations

Politicized corporate cultures are a product of withdrawing executives who abdicate their responsibilities as leaders. These leaders' detached style causes them to avoid contact with others; therefore, the management of their firms is left to second-tier managers, none of whom are very clear about their responsibilities. The members of the second tier are "gamesmen" (Lasch, 1978; Maccoby, 1976) who spend their time jockeying for position and power against "rivals" in other departments. They fill the leadership vacuum by lobbying for their own parochial interests with the detached leader. In this, they see opportunities for enhancing their spheres and resource bases. Problems of coordination, cooperation, interdepartmental rivalry, and vacillating strategy are quite common.

Strategy making in the schizoid organization resides in a shifting coalition of careerist second-tier managers who try to influence the indecisive leader and simultaneously advance their own pet projects and minor empires. The firm muddles through and drifts about, making incremental changes in one area and then reversing them whenever a new group of managers gains favor. The initiatives of one group of managers are often either neutralized or severely blunted by those of an opposing group.

The divided nature of the organization thwarts effective coordination and communication. Information is used more as a power resource than as a vehicle for effective adaptation; in fact, managers erect barriers to prevent the free flow of information. But this is not the only shortcoming of the information system; another is the absence of information about the outside business environment. The company's focus is internal, on personal ambitions; it caters to the top manager's desires. Second-tier managers find it more useful to ignore real-world events that might either reflect poorly on their own behavior or conflict with the wishes of the detached leader.

Conclusion

In describing these five dysfunctional types, we have, for purposes of simplification, focused on the characteristics of "pure" constellations. In reality, however, the clinical picture is usually much more complicated. Combinations or mixtures of types often occur. The pages of *Fortune, Forbes, Business Week,* and the *Wall Street Journal* portray hybrids such as the paranoid-compul-

sive type, the depressive-compulsive type, or the detached-
depressive type. To make matters more complex, movement
across organizational types is found, depending on who is in
power and the stage of the organization's life cycle. A certain
style may be very effective at one point in the company's history. It is excess that leads to pathology, and the equilibrium
between normality and pathology is easily breached. Holding
on to a particular style when the circumstances have changed
can lead to corporate disaster. It can be said, however, that
the style of the leader or of the dominant coalition may become
modified through interactions with the evolving organization.

Also, it must be stressed that although the personality of
the top manager can vitally influence an organization, a reverse
relationship also exists. A failing organization, rife with disappointment, can cause a leader to become depressed. A series
of vicious threats from the competition can awaken dormant
paranoia. Clearly, then, the influence between organizational
orientations and managerial disposition is reciprocal. Mutual
causation is the rule.

It may be useful to highlight several advantages of the
typology used here. First, it is holistic. It avoids the complexity
of the "one-variable-at-a-time" approach by searching for common types and the psychological and cultural factors that underlie these types. Second, it treats personality in a global way,
looking for major adaptive styles that motivate and characterize much of behavior, while eschewing narrow dimensions of
affect or cognition. Third, the framework gets at the roots of
some strategic, structural, and cultural problems in organizations. Fourth, the assignment of firms to a particular type can
alert the organizational analyst to a range of unobserved but
frequently related manifestations (thus helping in the selection
of the appropriate intervention strategy). Instead of dwelling
on specific symptoms about the distribution of authority or the
design of information systems, one can search for the underlying cause of the conjunction of various symptoms. In doing so,
we should become more effective as organizational diagnosticians (or at least more attuned to the limits of change).

One of the more pessimistic aspects of this research is that it seems to point to great areas of resistance to change. Styles of behavior are deeply rooted; CEOs are very hard to change, especially when they hold all of the power. In many cases, significant turnaround in the organization would be expected to occur only after dramatic failure has eroded the power base of the CEO, or after a new CEO takes over. Therefore, much of the normative literature on policy, structure, and culture might do well to recognize that many managerial prescriptions will run counter to the personality of the CEO and will therefore be resisted, or, if they are implemented, they will not fit into the overall configuration of the organization and will therefore be lacking in appropriateness and impact.

References

American Psychiatric Association. *Diagnostic and Statistical Manual of Mental Disorders (DSM-III-R)*. (Rev. ed.) Washington, D.C.: American Psychiatric Association, 1987.

Bion, W. R. *Experiences in Groups, and Other Papers*. London: Tavistock, 1959.

Fenichel, O. *The Psychoanalytic Theory of Neurosis*. New York: Norton, 1945.

Freedman, A. M., Kaplan, H. J., and Sadock, B. J. (eds.). *Comprehensive Textbook of Psychiatry*. Vols. 1 and 2. Baltimore: Williams & Wilkins, 1975.

Jacobson, E. *The Self and the Object World*. New York: International Universities Press, 1964.

Jacobson, E. *Depression*. New York: International Universities Press, 1971.

Jaques, E. *The Changing Culture of a Factory*. London: Tavistock, 1951.

Jaques, E. *Work, Creativity, and Social Justice*. New York: International Universities Press, 1970.

Kernberg, O. *Borderline Conditions and Pathological Narcissism*. New York: Aronson, 1975.

Kernberg, O. *Object Relations Theory and Clinical Psychoanalysis*. New York: Aronson, 1976.

Kernberg, O. "Regression in Organizational Leadership." *Psychiatry*, 1979, *42*, 24–39.

262   Organizations on the Couch

Kets de Vries, M.F.R. *Organizational Paradoxes: Clinical Approaches to Management*. London: Tavistock, 1980.

Kets de Vries, M.F.R. "Leiderschap in een narcistisch tijdperk" [Leadership in a narcissistic age]. *Management Totaal*, 1981, 5, 20-25.

Kets de Vries, M.F.R. *The Irrational Executive: Psychoanalytic Studies in Management*. New York: International Universities Press, 1984.

Kets de Vries, M.F.R. *Prisoners of Leadership*. New York: Wiley, 1989.

Kets de Vries, M.F.R. "Leaders, Fools, and Impostors." Unpublished manuscript, INSEAD, 1991.

Kets de Vries, M.F.R., and Miller, D. "Group Fantasies and Organizational Functioning." *Human Relations*, 1984a, 37, 111-134.

Kets de Vries, M.F.R., and Miller, D. *The Neurotic Organization: Diagnosing and Changing Counterproductive Styles of Management*. San Francisco: Jossey-Bass, 1984b.

Kets de Vries, M.F.R., and Miller, D. "Neurotic Style and Organizational Pathology." *Strategic Management Journal*, 1984c, 5, 35-55.

Kets de Vries, M.F.R., and Miller, D. *Unstable at the Top: Inside the Troubled Organization*. New York: New American Library, 1987.

Klein, M. *Contributions to Psychoanalysis, 1921-1945*. London: Hogarth Press, 1948.

Kohut, H. *The Analysis of the Self*. New York: International Universities Press, 1971.

Laplanche, J., and Pontalis, J. B. *The Language of Psychoanalysis*. London: Hogarth Press, 1973.

Lasch, C. *The Culture of Narcissism*. New York: Simon & Schuster, 1978.

Maccoby, M. *The Gamesman*. New York: Simon & Schuster, 1976.

Mahler, M. S., Pine, F., and Bergman, A. *The Psychological Birth of the Human Infant*. New York: Basic Books, 1975.

Miller, D., and Friesen, P. H. "Archetypes of Strategy Formulation." *Management Science*, 1978, 24, 921-933.

Miller, D., and Friesen, P. H. *Organizations: A Quantum View.* Englewood Cliffs, N.J.: Prentice-Hall, 1984.

Miller, D., Kets de Vries, M.F.R., and Toulouse, J. M. "Top Executive Locus of Control and Its Relationship to Strategy-Making, Structure, and Environment." *Academy of Management Journal*, 1982, *25*, 237–253.

Millon, T. *Disorders of Personality: DSM-III: Axis II.* New York: Wiley-Interscience Books, 1981.

Mintzberg, H. *The Structuring of Organizations.* Englewood Cliffs, N.J.: Prentice-Hall, 1979.

Nicholi, A.M. (ed.). *The New Harvard Guide to Modern Psychiatry.* Cambridge, Mass.: Harvard University Press, 1988.

Payne, R., and Pugh, D. S. "Organization Structure and Climate." In M. D. Dunnette (ed.), *Handbook of Industrial and Organizational Psychology.* Chicago: Rand McNally, 1976.

Sandler, J., and Rosenblatt, B. "The Concept of the Representational World." *Psychoanalytic Study of the Child*, 1962, *17*, 128–145.

Shapiro, D. *Neurotic Styles.* New York: Basic Books, 1965.

Tosi, H. "A Re-Examination of Personality as a Determinant of the Effects of Participation." *Personnel Psychology*, 1970, *23*, 91–99.

Vroom, V. H. *Some Personality Determinants of the Effects of Participation.* Englewood Cliffs, N.J.: Prentice-Hall, 1960.

Zaleznik, A., and Kets de Vries, M.F.R. *Power and the Corporate Mind.* (Rev. ed.) Chicago: Bonus Books, 1980.

11

How Bureaucracy Discourages Responsibility

Howell S. Baum

Work means a great deal to people. It enables them to be competent, allows them to identify with a powerful enterprise, offers them responsibility and the authority to produce something, and holds out recognition for their efforts. People expect that work will bind them to communities by allowing them to develop social relationships that offer them rewards such as these.

These expectations form people's "demands" in negotiating psychological contracts when they enter an organization (Levinson and others, 1962). Depending on the course of these negotiations, workers may feel like members of the organization and identify with it, work hard but not feel part of the organization, or simply feel like employees using the organization for a paycheck. These negotiations are partly conscious and partly unconscious, and they may extend over years. Their eventual success depends on a new worker's expectations, developmental concerns, veterans' offerings, and organizational resources and culture (Erikson, 1963, 1968; Baum, 1990).

This chapter looks at how the character of bureaucratic organizations limits workers' possibilities of negotiating satisfying psychological contracts. The first section describes organizational character in terms of psychological structure. The second presents a case example of someone who reacts to an unsatisfactory contract by creating compensatory activities inside the organization. The third presents an example of someone who responds by escaping the organization. The final section draws conclusions about bureaucratic character from these two cases.

Organizational Character and Psychological Structure

One common way people talk about organizational character is in terms of organizational "culture" (Deal and Kennedy, 1982; Frost and others, 1985; Kilmann, Saxton, Serpa, and Associates, 1985; Naisbitt and Aburdene, 1985; Peters and Waterman, 1982; Schein, 1985; Smircich, 1983). In doing so, they recognize that workers' beliefs about their organizations influence their actions. Still, many of those who talk about "organizational culture" often overlook three common anthropological observations about culture (Bettelheim, 1954; Geertz, 1973).

First, culture does not consist simply of stories or ideas about what people should do but is inherent in people's activities. Interpretations of day-to-day practices may or may not be congruent with articulated lore. Second, culture and social structure are reciprocally related. People's beliefs about social structures shape their actions, and they create social structures to enable actions that fit their beliefs (Schneider and Shrivastava, 1989). Third, the meanings of stories, practices, and structures are both conscious and unconscious. People may pursue actions on the basis of unconscious meanings that have little to do with, or even conflict with, their conscious avowals (Schwartz, 1985, 1990).

A familiar example of unconscious desires in the workplace is the wish for a paternalistic boss. The possibilities for a manager to act paternalistically would be an indication of the unconscious content of an organization's culture—or, more broadly, its character (as well as, clearly, the manager's personality). The unconscious character of an organization can be described in terms of its *psychological structure*.

The social structure of an organization sets certain patterns for relatively enduring modes of interaction. Members of a management team may consult frequently, and supervisors and subordinates may talk according to prescribed rules. An organization, however, also has a *psychological structure*, consisting of a relatively enduring pattern of feelings and emotional relationships (Baum, 1987). For example, staff members may not only respect a director but unconsciously concentrate on making that person feel loved and perfect (Kets de Vries and Miller, 1984). Or people in one division may think of themselves as perfectly conscientious workers and attribute only sloth and carelessness to another division (see Chapter Nine). Such unconscious beliefs are powerful regulators of workers' actions.

An organization's psychological structure is an interactive product of its social structure and workers' personalities analogous to what has been called a *group mentality* (Bion, 1959). There can be no psychological structure in the absence of workers, because their needs shape their interpretations of the social structure and their actions. Moreover, some personalities, especially those of people in authority, weigh particularly heavily. Nevertheless, in the context of general human aims and wishes, we can talk about general tendencies encouraged by certain social structures. This is the sense in which I shall examine typical elements in the psychological structure of bureaucratic organizations. The discussion focuses on two predicaments confronting workers when they try to solve problems (see Baum, 1987, for a more complete analysis of the vicissitudes of bureaucracy).

Two Bureaucratic Predicaments

Bureaucratic situations have both conscious and unconscious meanings. The overt meanings of hierarchical subordination, for example, in which workers may have insufficient authority to carry out their responsibilities, may make action difficult. However, when subordinates unconsciously see similarities between bureaucratic authority figures and earlier authority figures from their infancy and childhood, they may transfer assumptions from those earlier relations to contemporary relations in ways that make situations and action much more complicated (Brenner, 1976; Greenson, 1967; Hodgson, Levinson, and Zaleznik, 1965; Kets de Vries and Miller, 1984; Orr, 1954;

Racker, 1968). Both the "invisibility" of unconscious meanings and their incongruity with conscious meanings add to the ambiguity of situations. In addition, insofar as conscious and unconscious meanings point to different actions, workers may feel ambivalent about particular courses of action. These unconscious processes transform common bureaucratic situations into anxiety-ridden predicaments.

One common predicament involves *combined ambiguity and inequality of responsibility and authority.* Consciously, this situation may lead someone to fear that responsibility becomes ambiguously large while authority becomes ambiguously small, with the result that efforts go wasted. Still, workers with normal faith in their competence and interest in recognition for it may want a lot of responsibility. If they do not have commensurate authority, at best they may be disappointed. However, others with more authority may use their authority not only to take credit (responsibility) for successes, but also to assign blame (responsibility) for problems. Thus responsibility can be perilous.

These real conflicts about taking responsibility are often unconsciously compounded by transference of assumptions about parents onto people with organizational authority. On the one hand, a wish for "parental" recognition may lead to efforts to take on more responsibility. On the other hand, if achieving results seems competitive with the "parent," or if the "parent" seems punitive, then recognition is dangerous. Unconsciously, fear of retribution, particularly if a supervisor seems to speak with the voice of parental conscience, may give rise to anger, fortification against anticipated punishment, and reassertion of now apparently justified aggression toward the supervisor (Klein, 1948; Rivière, 1964).

In short, typical unconscious patterns make a situation seem increasingly ambiguous and make the worker feel increasingly ambivalent about what to do—whether, for example, to take responsibility or not. In defense, workers often resort to counterambiguity—further clouding their role so that others cannot find them out—even if doing so eliminates opportunities for their competence to be recognized.

A second common predicament particularly encourages

transference of negative assumptions about supervisors. A subordinate may perceive the supervisor as relatively anonymous and self-sufficient, able to satisfy his or her own needs without any assistance from the subordinate. In such work the supervisor is seen as possessing *autonomous authority*. Overtly, supervisors are defined as people who know so much about their subordinates' tasks that they can direct and evaluate their performance. The real consequences of evaluation can make this an unpleasant process. What aggravates the situation, however, is that a supervisor's judgmental role contributes to unconscious confusion with a parent.

In a pyramidal organization, managers exercise considerable authority over many individuals with whom they have little contact. Subordinates want to understand the motives of those who control so much, but, because they are distant, the subordinates must resort to guesswork. If they do so unconsciously, they may think they really "know" about those in authority. Commonly, subordinates experience this situation as if they were again children confronting parents whose accessibility they cannot control. Supervisors' autonomy may remind them of apparently perfect parents who seemed to need nothing from them and only judged them (Sennett, 1980).

Under these conditions, administrators often appear to be powerful and authoritative, but also ambiguous, unknowable, and arbitrary. Workers come to believe that their performances will inevitably be found inadequate in unpredictable ways—that shame is a certain result of any effort. Shame anxiety interferes with a realistic assessment of organizational authority and keeps subordinates from learning how to assume sufficient authority to define and execute their own responsibilities (Lewis, 1974; Lynd, 1958; Piers, 1971). The likelihood of being scapegoated for problems created by others only seems greater (Baum, 1987).

This second predicament, like the first, not only discourages workers from taking responsibility, but, by raising the costs of responsibility, creates an incapacitating ambivalence in people about what they should do.

Reactions to Disappointment

These predicaments make it difficult for workers to clarify, present, and satisfy "demands" for responsibility and authority. Yet, whatever the character of an organization, if it disappoints expectations, workers do not give up. When the organization injures them by frustrating them, they turn right around and insist on making it the perfect workplace. They do this unconsciously, following a pattern that infants develop for treating their injuries: They play.

Play is repetition: When people passively suffer an injury, they try to repeat it in a symbolic way that allows them actively to master it (Freud, [1920] 1955; Klein, 1976; Peller, 1954; Waelder, 1933). By "making passive into active," someone can contain and compensate the anxiety evoked by the injury. The *intention* is to control an injurious situation. When this intention succeeds in offering relief, it has the joyful quality conventionally associated with play.

Playful Compensation: Creating Responsibility in the Organization

The following cases illustrate workers' play in response to their disappointments with organizational conditions. Both construct a set of activities to replace an initial injury — the denial of satisfying responsibility or authority — with an alternative situation where they can take and enjoy as much responsibility or authority as they want. Their play both presents a critique of organizational reality and enacts an ideal organizational situation to displace or replace it.

These two workers' playful activities are typical of what all workers do until they can satisfy their conditions for a psychological contract (Baum, 1987, 1990). These activities are quite significant and often of an unconscious nature. If they are a diversion from formal tasks and relations, the reason is that the latter do not satisfy the worker's expectations of the organization. Much of what is commonly called "informal organizational behavior" consists of these efforts to enact ideal organizational conditions. In this way, workers reject the prevailing organizational psychological structure and try to create an alternative.

Reversal As Indictment

Phyllis Jones's play involves creating and acting in the literal sense of the words. She describes herself in this way: "Because of the way I come off and the way I dress . . . I can deal effectively with men. When I was in the Director's Office, I was a brunette. I am now a blonde. Men are attracted to me as a blonde. I have undergone a personality change. There I was perceived as an overbearing bitch. I don't see myself as that. Now I am fun to be with."

Her metaphor and language for understanding bureaucracy are sexual. Some of her concerns probably reflect her troubled childhood, but she does not obviously describe sexual content where none exists. Rather, she seems to be an especially interested and faithful reporter on this realm. Among other things, she uses sexual imagery to talk about responsibility. She is concerned about how people respond to others. She wants to know whether people can perform significantly and whether others respond realistically and appreciatively—in organizational language, whether responsibility is fairly allocated. Her playacting arises from her conclusion that the organization is "dishonest" about assigning responsibility.

Jones started work as a secretary with a federal housing agency sixteen years ago. She needed an income to support her children and wanted a job that offered her a challenge. Relatively quickly she found she could do some of the work assigned to others, and she gradually gained some technical responsibilities. She eventually became the agency director's secretary. And yet she observed a number of discrepancies in the organization. Some of the technical staff, most of them men, really could not do their work well. Some of the clerical people, mostly women, could have learned those jobs, but management would not give clerical staff technical training. The result was that responsibilities did not match abilities.

Jones did some technical work, but when a new director came in, he moved her to a lower, mainly clerical position. The barrier between clerical and analytical work injured her by denying her the responsibilities that fitted her abilities. The centrality of this disappointment is evident in her response to a question about what she does on the job: "I am in a situation where I was raised to be an honest person. What I have learned is that in a bureaucracy you can't operate that way."

Her organization is full of dishonesties. She works "in a section that is called Documentation; we do no documentation." She works for managers and administrators who "know nothing about managing and administration." As a result of outdated job descriptions, "A lot of employees were in jobs that no longer existed."

From cumulative experiences of organizational dishonesty, Jones "learned to question everything, even the obvious. Never assume, because it makes an ass of you and me" (assume = ass + u + me). Because responsibility in the organization is unstable and arbitrary, or a subordinate with little authority to assume responsibility (or anything else) carries the risk of being made an ass, a term which in both its animal and anal references connotes shame.

Jones reacts to her shameful inability to get high-level responsibilities and recognition for success by reversing the terms of her relationship with her superiors. First, she sets standards for their work and then finds their performance inadequate and, therefore, shameful. She does this with the managers-who-are-not-managers: "I am clearly responsible to my section chief. I can get assignments from my division director, and I can say that I am working on this for him or her. Much of what I do is signed off perfunctorily. They know nothing about managing and administration." She asserts that her supervisors do not know how to do their job, and, because she does know, she sets standards for them. But she does not tell them what they should be doing or how to do it, nor does she show them up. Instead, she does their job for them, covertly. This secret performance is sublimely satisfying. Not only does she shame them, but they are so stupid that they do not even understand they are being shamed.

The principle of a second reversal is indicated by her comments that bureaucracy does not permit her to act honestly. She recasts her relationship with the organization in moral terms (rather than those of performance, which can shame her) and then indicts the organization for dishonesty: She is quick to find her supervisors guilty. As with the determination of shame, the assessment of guilt is private.

These reversals become the principles of an active effort to create a domain that provides the satisfactions withheld by the organization. The theme of her play, as her indictment of the organization for dishonesty proclaims, is *disclaimed responsibility*. Her implicit accusation that "the organization made me do it" is her basic disclaimer of responsibility for her actions. She arranges a series of incidents, comprising a loosely structured play or side game, with two aims: to show the organization that she recognizes the dishonesty with which responsibility has been allocated and to create conditions where she may take responsibility and get others to respond to her honestly.

Jones's play, where responsibility is ambiguous, is a reaction to the unreliability of responsibility in the bureaucracy. Her play, like everyone's, is motivated by earlier personal injuries as well as contemporary organizational problems. Perhaps that is why she seems to want to avoid responsibility to such a degree that she may be unable to satisfy her interest in "honest" responsibility by what she does. Still, even with all the disavowals and even with the recurrent sexual references, her flirtatious activities are, among other things, experimental efforts to exercise authority denied by the organization. Her manner is idiosyncratic, but her concerns and efforts are commonplace.

Reversal As Enactment

In the series of encounters that constitute Jones's play, she alternately tries to show others that they cannot control responsibilities themselves and to create situations where she has significant responsibility. To serve the first aim, she begins by declaring that she is not responsible for her actions: "As a woman, I can get things done that men can't get done. Men basically

want to help women. There are women in my section who can't
get things. I have no problem with that. I do have problems
with some women who have gotten into higher positions simply through physical use. I wouldn't do that. I have no problems using my God-given abilities, because men want that. Men
don't get that same feeling helping fellow men."

These comments characterize relations in bureaucratic organizations in terms of gender, but they also deny her
responsibility—or liability—for these relations. "As a woman"
she can get things done; it is her gender, not she personally,
that affects others. "Men basically want to help women"; because of their sex they respond spontaneously and predictably
to women. She has problems with women who have advanced
"simply through physical use"; still, whatever these women get
comes from what others do to them. Although she would not
involve herself sexually with co-workers, she has no problems
using her "God-given abilities, because men want that." She is
only a vehicle for others; God called her to do what she does
because men want it. "Men don't get that same feeling helping
fellow men"; even the passions aroused belong to others.

In part, Jones means her discussion of the sexual content
of her relations with men frankly and literally. In addition, she
is speaking generally of responsibility for the consequences of
relationships. Implicitly, she is giving others notice that, although
they may react to her, she will not be responsible for what happens to them.

One prominent incident in her career involves a recent
office move and her efforts to have the new space set up like
the old one. When she describes her efforts to influence the move,
she continues to deny her responsibility, but she also indicates
the importance of relations with others and expresses satisfaction that she has successfully taken some responsibility. In influencing others, she says: "I am only limited by the people I
know, unless I maintain a growing span of friends that includes
the newcomers. I recognize that. I make a point of meeting people, getting them to know and like me. When the office next
to us moved, they took one of the women's partitions. It happened that I am friends with the branch chief. I said, do me

a favor, and so forth. We need the partition. We need to separate
smokers from nonsmokers. He said, by Monday you will have
a partition. He is a new friend. I have new friends in the Director's Office. There is something in the human psyche that denotes
authority. People assume that I have authority that I didn't
know. There is something about my demeanor that denotes authority." She concludes: "Right now I have influence because
of who I know. I know people in high positions, and I can say,
Hank, I have a problem, because they know and like me. My
organization has had problems, and they know management
will not support them, and they tell me to go up and mention
it to so-and-so, and I have done it. I have influence because . . .
for example, we are moving. We have different kinds of partitions. I am not in charge of the move, but we want partitions
that can be anchored to the floor. The guy in charge told us
we couldn't get them. And they told me, see what you can do.
And because of my influence we are getting screw-into-the-floor
partitions. I have no real authority, but I know everybody, many
on a first-name basis. I have powers that I don't know." On the
one hand, she continues to disclaim responsibility. She "didn't
know" about her authority; it is her "demeanor that denotes authority," not she personally, that makes things happen. She has
"no real authority" and innocently benefits from "powers that
I don't know."

On the other hand, she twice notes that men "know and
like" her, and she repeatedly characterizes people as her "friends."
Friendship is a reciprocal relationship bound by respect and
affection. These relations stand apart from the formal bureaucracy. She values them for their honesty and mutuality, including such instrumental help as getting partitions. She seems
pleased with herself.

Phyllis Jones responds to bureaucratic predicaments in
two ways. Defensively, by trying to influence others but denying responsibility, she creates counterambiguity to cloud her position. Along the way, she may strike a couple of blows at her
tormentors under cover of obscurity. Developmentally, she attempts to repair and compensate for the injury of being denied
real responsibility by creating her own responsibility. Both

courses are typical responses to the bureaucratic psychological structure. Which one ends up dominating her interpretation of the organization depends largely on her.

Playful Escape: Creating Authority on the Outside

David Smith, assistant director of a state agency, also feels that bureaucracy is too ambiguous to respond appropriately to him, but his complaint differs from Jones's. In contrast with her, he has the authority to stake out considerable authority, he wants credit for what he does, and he claims his actions. And yet, unlike Jones, who complains about ambiguous responsibility, he rails against ambiguities in authority. He does not mean that it is unclear what he may ask others to do or what others can ask of him. Rather, there is no real relationship between his actions and their consequences.

One escape from frustrating situations is daydreaming. It is a form of play: Instead of passively suffering certain deprivations, one actively imagines the reverse, where life would be satisfying. Sometimes this fantasy involves planning for a new job. Smith has not only made such plans, but he is ready to carry them out. He recently purchased a hunting lodge in northern Canada and intends to go and run it soon.

He is entrepreneurial. A high school vocational interest test suggested he become a real estate broker or a forester. Middle management in a public bureaucracy fails to satisfy either interest. He uses the languages of business and nature to contrast bureaucratic employment and entrepreneurship in a hunting lodge. He complains that bureaucracy is "ambiguous," and he portrays his lodge as "more real."

"Ambiguous" Bureaucratic Authority

On the surface, authority where Smith works is not ambiguous. He, like Jones, is a subordinate, and his subordinate position limits his influence, but the constraints are not all ambiguous. He observes: "Influence, in my judgment, is the degree to which one makes use of his independence. Here, the exercise of influence is so contaminated with so many factors, like your status or your network of friends. Generally, there are three major components. Status in the organization, formal titles are important. For example, if the Secretary demands something, 99 out of 100 times something will happen. Secondarily, when you cross operational lines but you are talking with people who are perceived to be in a higher level, theoretically you in no way can influence my day-to-day activities, but *de facto* it has an effect. Another thing—the informal network. It could be anywhere from outside the agency, the community, a politician: 'This is the position I am taking; by the way, Senator Meathead said this.' These are the major things."

In an important way, authority in the hierarchy is unambiguous. If the secretary can get what he wants 99 percent of the time, predictability is high. Similarly, if hierarchical superiors are normally able to influence hierarchical subordinates even when they do not have direct line relationships, authority is not altogether arbitrary. In addition, patterns of informal influence have regularities. One might say that Smith's authority is limited but unambiguous.

But Smith regards authority as more than simply the ability to cause predictable outcomes. Outcomes, he insists, should be reasonably related to preceding actions. It is the certainty of limits to his authority that he feels makes it ambiguous. Because bureaucracy regulates workers' actions, beyond some point, no matter what intentions or how much effort a worker invests in a project, the results are likely to be more or less the same. Smith complains that the relationship between actions and their consequences has diminishing meaning.

As the epitome of ambiguities in bureaucratic authority, Smith describes an important current project. He was assigned to implement new federal legislation in his agency's programs. He has to maintain services with declining federal support. He worked long days and weekends for more than a year on both complicated technical analyses and intense political negotiations. In the end, he says, his primary organizational reward is compensatory time. Only he is given further assignments that make it impossible to take time off, and regulations specify that if he does not take the time soon, he loses it. This is not a reward for success.

At the same time, some constituents of his programs, angry about what he has done, have threatened litigation. However, he notes, just as he is buffered from reward for success, his risks, too, are limited: "The consequences are less severe on this job than they would be on that one [in the hunting lodge]. For example, if you want to sue me, you can sue the department, but you can never get me. But in that case [the hunting lodge], it is pretty clear that you can nail the corporate structure. To me it is more real."

Not only will he never be called to account for his actions, but also he is deprived of the chance to confront his accusers and defeat them.

A Reversal: The "More Real" World of Business and Nature

Smith plays with these injuries by measuring the "ambiguous" bureaucracy against a model of a "more real" world. These standards both indict the organization and guide his plans for an escape to the lodge. His expectations combine two themes.

The first is that of the entrepreneur in the free market. The entrepreneur formulates an idea, saves and invests the necessary money, awaits the interplay of opportunity and risk, and then confronts the outcome. With prudent investments and a modicum of luck, he or she prospers. If the project is ill-conceived or misfortune occurs, the entrepreneur fails. The outcome is the measure of the person.

The second theme is that of the solitary pioneer, who strives against the forces of nature to establish civilization. Nature may be worked and wooed to provide sustenance, but it is unforgiving. Crops must be planted with care and attention to seasonal vicissitudes. Animals may be hunted but must not be killed in such numbers that the balance of species is disturbed. Intelligence, caring, and fortune separate those who survive from those who do not. Survival is the measure of a person's fitness.

In these terms, Smith indicts the bureaucracy for "ambiguity" while sketching out what he expects to find "more real" in the lodge: "Here I have autonomy, but [the hunting lodge] is the epitome of autonomy. This is important. Secondarily, working outdoors. You are working indoors in the bureaucracy. There you are out in the rain, the cold. Here you are in an office, overheated, overcooled. Thirdly, I enjoy working with my hands a lot. Another thing, the incentive system. I think the results are much more quickly realized [in private business]. I will know when I have made a mistake on the job. But secondary is the insulation from the economic realities of profit. In the lodge operations, I will not be. If you buy the wrong motor, you are down eight grand. Bureaucracies are a little slow to recognize or develop and instill an incentive system that rules financially or otherwise."

Bureaucratic "ambiguity" alienates people from their nature in several ways. First, Smith says, he exercises at best only pseudoautonomy in the bureaucracy. No matter how definite he makes responsibilities, and no matter how authoritatively he acts, bureaucratic structures limit the range of consequences that may follow. Unlike Jones, who is wary of being scapegoated for problems she cannot control, Smith complains that the bureaucracy offers no real risks equal to his abilities. Bureaucracy mediates between effort and outcome.

Second, bureaucracy intervenes between people and nature. Offices are artificial environments over which an individual has no control. One reason Smith is moving to northern Canada is "geography — I am tired of the East Coast, the rotten weather." The weather is "ambiguous" — never definitely hot, cold, wet, or dry. Northern Canadian weather, however, will never be uncertain, and he will be free to decide how to respond.

Third, he charges, bureaucracy mediates between mind and body. Bureaucratic work is mental, extremely intellectualized. By discouraging physical activity, bureaucracy further alienates people from their nature.

Finally, the faulty bureaucratic incentive system blocks people from their potential. Results do not follow quickly from actions. There are no commensurate financial rewards for success. The bureaucracy does not even offer recognition. Moreover, despite pervasive anxiety about being shamed, mistakes are identified haphazardly. As a result, people do not confront their potential, along with attendant risks and opportunities.

The hunting lodge is the positive antithesis of all this: Outcomes and survival will be immediately measurable. If he has not invested thoughtfully and if nature is not favorable, he can expect his customer to complain: "I was here three days, the food was rotten, it rained, and I didn't catch any fish." And he can expect that the customer may demand at least a partial refund, may not return, and may advise friends not to patronize the lodge. However, if Smith works hard and wisely, the rewards can be substantial: "There, I will be working during the season seven days a week, from five in the morning to nine at night. But I will see the results. People put $10,000 on the desk: 'We have five people; we will stay here five days.'"

Indeed, with boldness and good fortune, within a few years Smith might amass both wealth and influence: "It will really be dictated by the level of involvement that I want to pursue. Two to three years along, I will want to influence the planning of roads, airways, and so on. That will be because I will own one of the biggest lodges up there. 'I am bringing in a half million dollars, you jokers; listen to me!' That turns heads."

The Shame of Bureaucratic Ambiguities

Jones fears that, because she cannot control what she is responsible for, she will eventually be shamed for doing something wrong. Smith can manage responsibility, but working with ambiguous authority, where he can never be certain he will produce something significant, leaves him vulnerable to shame. Summing up his situation, he expresses doubts about himself and a sense of isolation that contrast with his boasts about running things and ordering people about: "I believe in hard work, because I am not a brilliant thinker. As the famed American sociologist Lily Tomlin said, 'We're all in this alone.'"

He also talks about isolation, drawing a contrast between the bureaucracy and the hunting lodge: "The physical environment is important. I don't like a lot of people sharing with me what I want to do. This is not going to happen where we are."

The first remark, ambiguously self-depreciating and self-respecting, depicts solitude as an existential condition. He is not as bright as he would like to be, but he works hard. He might like others' recognition, but he is forced to accept whatever esteem he can give himself. The second comment similarly asserts that being alone is natural. In addition, it expresses his satisfaction that he may, finally, escape other people in the wilderness. His relief is not just that others will no longer interfere with his ambitions by opposing him or getting in his way. More than that, others who "share" what he does are an audience. He can imagine they share his doubts about his brilliance. How can they think much of him, when all he can get for his hard work is compensatory time he cannot take?

Smith's planned journey to the deserted north responds to the shame of exercising ambiguous authority in two ways that are similar to Jones's play. It is a defensive move in two respects. Most simply, he is fleeing all bureaucratic responsibilities where he cannot exercise authority with meaningful results. More generally, he wants to escape as many observers as possible, so that, whatever his performance, few will be able to judge him. He recognizes, as psychoanalysts emphasize, that shame is a social experience, in which one disappoints another as well as oneself (Chasseguet-Smirgel, 1985). At the same time, developmentally, he envisages a place where, because there are few people, there will be few impediments to his efforts and, indeed, he will satisfy his ambitions better. He will be able to exercise authority with results commensurate with whatever responsibilities he chooses. As with Jones, it remains to be seen which aim dominates.

Conclusions

Any action is a product of both environmental conditions and personal interpretations of them. This chapter has emphasized the influence of organizational structures on personal actions. Specifically, it has examined how two predicaments in the psychological structure of bureaucracy frustrate interests in responsibility and recognition and how workers react by playing with these injuries to create compensatory domains or paths of escape.

This discussion has said little about individual personalities. Jones's pseudosexuality, her continual disclaimers of action, the sadistic overtones of her seductiveness, as well as her dramatic orientation suggest a hysterical character, but it would be necessary to know more about her to make any diagnosis (Fenichel, 1945; Freud, [1905] 1953). Smith simultaneously expresses a grandiose view of his potential and feels insecure. He believes he can do great things — challenging people and nature — but he dislikes having others around. He conjures up a majestic environment to mirror his grandiose self and expects everything from forests to government agents to give in to him. In that world he is central and self-sufficient. His plans suggest a narcissistic personality, but, again, it would be necessary to know more about him to be certain (Kernberg, 1975; Kohut, 1971).

Everyone's personality makes him or her particularly sensitive to certain social situations. Jones feels especially hurt when people in authority do not respond appreciatively. Her story shows, sometimes in exaggerated ways, how a wide range of people react to not getting what they consider proper recognition and responsibilities for their abilities. They try to find or create other activities that will satisfy these needs. Smith feels especially hurt when he does not have the power to get others to help him achieve great things. His story shows, geographically, how many people react to being unable to do what they think they are capable of. They try to find or create an arena where they can build what reflects properly on them. Smith may be particularly sensitive about the adequacy of his accomplishments, but he and Jones both react to working under autonomous authority, where subordinates feel constantly questioned about whether they have done well enough.

Although Jones looks for compensation and Smith seeks an escape, the distinction between compensation and escape is complex. In an important sense, any departure from formal responsibilities, even for purposes of compensation, is escape. Investing in activities outside the workplace, with or without resigning, is simply a more extreme form of escape. What distinguishes compensatory play from escapist play is that the former makes up for injuries sufficiently to allow someone to stay in an organization and maintain some investment in work, even

while not identifying with the workplace. Escapist play, in contrast, follows a failure to do this and is a withdrawal from the
organization, where someone keeps minimal connection with it.
Escapist play thus takes place outside the organization, whereas
compensatory play may occur inside (Baum, 1990).

Jones and Smith work in public bureaucracies, but what
they describe is not unique to public organizations. Such organizations may, as some argue (Zaleznik, 1989), be more continually subject to political activities that manipulate responsibility and authority to serve personal interests rather than task
requirements. But ambiguity is inherent in organizational work,
and overtly self-interested politics is only one variant of a wide
range of efforts to use discretion and control opportunities.
Jones's organization, in fact, has been the object of repeated
changes in top management as a result of new presidential ad-
ministrations, but she recounts what subordinates (especially
women) experience in many organizations. Central to Smith's
complaints is that he cannot be an entrepreneur in the bureaucracy, that he cannot earn equity in it. Very few workers in
the private sector can share in organizational profits, and few
have opportunities for unlimited entrepreneurship.

There are three lessons in these stories. One is that workers want psychological contracts that give them what they need
to develop. Often what they want — such as responsibility and
authority — is quite consistent with organizational aims. Second,
workers will persist in trying to get what they want, even to the
neglect of their formal assignments. In other words, much "informal organizational behavior" involves determined, purposive
activities to make the organization a satisfying place. Together,
these two lessons suggest a third: Managers may do more to
get workers' loyalty if they try to recognize what people want
from psychological contracts and, more explicitly, try to negotiate these "demands." There may not be easy solutions, but just
the act of taking these expectations seriously begins to reshape
the psychological structure of the workplace.

References

Baum, H. S. *The Invisible Bureaucracy.* New York: Oxford University Press, 1987.

Baum, H. S. *Organizational Membership: Personal Development in the Workplace.* Albany: State University of New York Press, 1990.

Bettelheim, B. *Symbolic Wounds: Puberty Rites and the Envious Male.* New York: Free Press, 1954.

Bion, W. R. *Experiences in Groups, and Other Papers.* London: Tavistock, 1959.

Brenner, C. *Psychoanalytic Technique and Psychic Conflict.* New York: International Universities Press, 1976.

Chasseguet-Smirgel, J. *The Ego Ideal: A Psychoanalytic Essay on the Malady of the Ideal.* (P. Burrows, trans.) New York: Norton, 1985.

Deal, T. E., and Kennedy, A. A. *Corporate Cultures: The Rites and Rituals of Corporate Life.* Reading, Mass.: Addison-Wesley, 1982.

Erikson, E. *Childhood and Society.* (2nd ed.) New York: Norton, 1963.

Erikson, E. *Identity: Youth, and Crisis.* New York: Norton, 1968.

Fenichel, O. *The Psychoanalytic Theory of Neurosis.* New York: Norton, 1945.

Freud, S. "Fragment of an Analysis of a Case of Hysteria." In J. Strachey (ed. and trans.), *The Standard Edition of the Complete Psychological Works of Sigmund Freud.* Vol. 7. London: Hogarth Press, 1953. (Originally published 1905.)

Freud, S. "Beyond the Pleasure Principle." In J. Strachey (ed. and trans.), *The Standard Edition of the Complete Psychological Works of Sigmund Freud.* Vol. 18. London: Hogarth Press and Institute of Psychoanalysis, 1955. (Originally published 1920.)

Frost, P. J., and others (eds.). *Organizational Culture.* Newbury Park, Calif.: Sage, 1985.

Geertz, C. *The Interpretation of Cultures.* New York: Basic Books, 1973.

Greenson, R. R. *The Technique and Practice of Psychoanalysis.* Vol. 1. New York: International Universities Press, 1967.

Hodgson, R. C., Levinson, D. J., and Zaleznik, A. *The Executive Role Constellation.* Boston: Graduate School of Business Administration, Harvard University, 1965.

Kernberg, O. *Borderline Conditions and Pathological Narcissism.* New York: Aronson, 1975.

Kets de Vries, M.F.R., and Miller, D. *The Neurotic Organiza-tion: Diagnosing and Changing Counterproductive Styles of Manage-ment.* San Francisco: Jossey-Bass, 1984.

Kilmann, R. H., Saxton, M. J., Serpa, R., and Associates. *Gaining Control of the Corporate Culture.* San Francisco: Jossey-Bass, 1985.

Klein, G. S. *Psychoanalytic Theory: An Exploration of Essentials.* New York: International Universities Press, 1976.

Klein, M. "A Contribution to the Theory of Anxiety and Guilt." *International Journal of Psycho-Analysis,* 1948, *29,* 114–123.

Kohut, H. *The Analysis of the Self.* New York: International Universities Press, 1971.

Levinson, H., and others. *Men, Management, and Mental Health.* Cambridge, Mass.: Harvard University Press, 1962.

Lewis, H. B. *Shame and Guilt in Neurosis.* New York: International Universities Press, 1974.

Lynd, H. M. *On Shame and the Search for Identity.* New York: Harcourt Brace Jovanovich, 1958.

Naisbitt, J., and Aburdene, P. *Reinventing the Corporation.* New York: Warner Books, 1985.

Orr, D. W. "Transference and Countertransference: A Historical Survey." *Journal of the American Psychoanalytic Association,* 1954, *11,* 621–670.

Peller, L. E. "Libidinal Phases, Ego Development, and Play." *Psychoanalytic Study of the Child,* 1954, *9,* 178–198.

Peters, T. J., and Waterman, R. H., Jr. *In Search of Excellence: Lessons from America's Best-Run Companies.* New York: Harper & Row, 1982.

Piers, G. "Shame and Guilt: A Psychoanalytic Study." In G. Piers and M. B. Singer, *Shame and Guilt.* New York: Norton, 1971.

Racker, H. *Transference and Countertransference.* New York: International Universities Press, 1968.

Rivière, J. "Hate, Greed, and Aggression." In M. Klein and J. Rivière, *Love, Hate, and Reparation.* New York: Norton, 1964.

Schein, E. H. *Organizational Culture and Leadership: A Dynamic View.* San Francisco: Jossey-Bass, 1985.

Schneider, S. C., and Shrivastava, P. *Interpreting Strategic Behavior:*

The Royal Road to Basic Assumptions. Working paper no. 28. New York: Lubin Schools of Business, Pace University, 1989.

Schwartz, H. S. "The Usefulness of Myth and the Myth of Usefulness: A Dilemma for the Applied Organizational Scientist." *Journal of Management,* 1985, *11,* 31–42.

Schwartz, H. S. *Narcissistic Process and Organizational Decay: The Theory of the Organizational Ideal.* New York: New York University Press, 1990.

Sennett, R. *Authority.* New York: Knopf, 1980.

Smircich, L. "Concepts of Culture and Organizational Analysis." *Administrative Science Quarterly,* 1983, *38,* 339–358.

Waelder, R. "The Psychoanalytic Theory of Play." *Psychoanalytic Quarterly,* 1933, *2,* 208–224.

Zaleznik, A. *The Managerial Mystique: Restoring Leadership in Business.* New York: Harper & Row, 1989.

12

---•◆•◆•◆---

Organizational
Decay and
Loss of Reality:
Life at NASA

Howard S. Schwartz

The summer of 1990 was not a good season for the National
Aeronautics and Space Administration. On May 30, a serious
fuel leak was discovered during the countdown for a launch of
the space shuttle Columbia, leading to a postponement of the
launch. On June 27, NASA engineers announced that the Hubble Space Telescope, a $1.5 billion device widely ballyhooed as
the greatest astronomical advance since Galileo developed the
telescope, failed to work. Two days later, a fuel leak similar
to that on the *Columbia* was discovered on the *Atlantis,* leading
NASA to ground the shuttle fleet.

    These problems led William J. Broad (1990c, p. 16), writ-
ing in the *New York Times* on July 1, to ask: "How could the
agency that repeatedly put men on the Moon suddenly find its
$25 billion space shuttle fleet grounded by a fuel leak? How could
the agency that sent unmanned spacecraft throughout the solar
system find that its greatest scientific instrument, the Hubble
Space Telescope, has a serious flaw that severely cripples the
$1.5 billion instrument and that escaped notice by numerous
experts and inspectors?"

    To be sure, the string of failures that afflicted NASA could have been the result of a run of bad luck and the difficulty of predicting an uncertain environment. That view was held by some observers of the space program (Broad, 1990c, p. 16).

But consider this explanation in the light of a study carried out by a panel of space experts and reported in the *New York Times* of July 11 (Broad, 1990a, pp. A1, B6). That study found that NASA's planned $37 billion space station would require 3,800 hours of outside maintenance per year, as against the 130 hours NASA had estimated for the job. Moreover, it was learned that the space station would require 6,000 to 7,000 hours of maintenance *even before becoming permanently manned.* "The significance is that there's no one up there to do this," said panel chairman William Fisher (Broad, 1990b, p. 1). Under the circumstances, one can easily understand why a number of engineers, typically speaking to the *Times* anonymously, maintained that the space station, as designed, could not be built.

What this study suggests is that luck and the difficulty of working in uncertainty are only partial explanations of NASA's failure. For gross flaws in the design process do not come about through bad luck or limited ability to predict. Gross flaws in design, discoverable on the basis merely of reexamination of the plans themselves, can point to nothing but a failure of management.

We begin to gain insight into the exact nature of the failure of NASA management by considering the views of observers who are less willing to exonerate NASA. Thus, Alex Roland, a former NASA historian, said: "What's wrong is that they seek quantum leaps to new operational technology instead of building up to it incrementally. . . . They want revolution instead of evolution" (Broad, 1990c, p. 16).

To which the *New York Times* added: "This attitude, he said, grew out of the agency's thirst for triumphs to surpass the Apollo success," and quoted Bruce Murray, a former director of NASA's Jet Propulsion Laboratory, whose analysis was similar, as saying, "We're paying for the fantasies of the 1970s" (p. 16).

But the sort of grandiosity that would lead NASA to attempt goals that are beyond its capabilities is only part of the picture. Looking more closely, we see a seamier and even more troubling side of life at NASA: "A different engineer, who also spoke on the condition of anonymity . . . also said political pressures were mounting for technical personnel to fabricate solutions. 'A lot of people are concerned about the integrity of this process,' he said. 'There's a lot of pressure to make this problem not a problem'" (p. 16). An example, he said, is a proposed solution in which a thermal blanket meant to protect the station from the temperature extremes of outer space would be designated as having a thirty-year lifetime instead of one year. "'But just because you can say you can do it doesn't mean you can,' he said. 'There's no design or study to back up the solution. That's what we are seeing here'" (p. 16).

Thus, the problem with NASA's management is not simply a matter of grandiosity. In addition, there appears to be a commitment to that grandiosity that corrupts the system and forces it to lose touch with reality. We see here not simply the presence of fantasy, but the choice of fantasy over reality and the suppression of reality when it interferes with the fantasy—a suppression that is evidenced again by the fact that engineers would only talk about NASA's problems if their anonymity was assured.

In a series of articles (Schwartz, 1987b, 1988, 1989; also see Schwartz, 1990), I have discussed the failure of NASA from the standpoint of a psychoanalytic theory of organizational pathology that I call the *theory of the organization ideal*. The theory explains how NASA changed into an organization that had abandoned reality and come to live in fantasy. It shows further how an organization that has lost contact with reality in this way cannot manage its affairs in the real world, and especially not in a technological environment that demands fine attention to detail. In this chapter I review the theory of the organization ideal and give an idea of how it applies to the loss of reality at NASA.

Theory of the Organization Ideal

Early in life, the positive response of the mother to whatever the child does leads the child to experience the world as being an extension of itself, as lovingly structured around itself. Freud refers to this experience as *primary narcissism* (Freud, [1914] 1957; Chasseguet-Smirgel, 1985, 1986).

Alas, sooner or later, the fact that the world is not lovingly structured around itself is borne in on the child. The basic discontinuity between the child's needs and impulses and the alien structure of the world, existing in-and-for-itself, to use Sartre's expression (1953), results in separation anxiety. Far from being the center of a loving world, the child feels as if it has no place in the world, does not belong in the world at all.

Later on in life, we may begin to understand that this existential isolation is part of the human condition and we may be able to find kinship with each other, basing that kinship on a recognition of and identification with the isolation of the other. For the child, however, and indeed for many adults, this identification has not yet taken place and the isolation feels absolute.

One can easily understand how, under these phenomenological conditions, the unconscious fantasy of a return to the state of narcissistic omnipotence would develop and gain power over psychological life. Indeed, one can see that psychological life would come to be structured around it. Freud ([1921] 1955, [1914] 1957; Chasseguet-Smirgel, 1985, 1986) calls this fantasy the *ego ideal*. The unconscious fantasy of the ego ideal, then, has the return to the infant-mother matrix as its unconscious root. But on the conscious level, other ideas gain significance from this same primordial appeal.

In American society, the dominant symbol that gains its meaning from the ego ideal is the idea of success. Success for us is being able to do what we want and be loved for it. It represents an end of the isolation and limitation that accompany our individual existence, but at the same time it is very much a notion that has us as its focus. Success means the preservation of our individuality without the anxiety of the separation of that individuality from the rest of the world. It is an image of ourselves as the center of a world that is intrinsically loving toward us, a world that has us as its meaning.

But this only specifies the ego ideal in the abstract. More concretely, the ego ideal is given form by our ideas of valued social interaction — indeed, valuing a form of social interaction largely means projecting the ego ideal onto it. Thus, for example, married life (for the single), single life (for the married), and being "rich" for those who have only a finite amount of money come to take on an aura of perfection, of a flawless concordance of desire and necessity, spontaneity and order. More generally, our mythologies of the nation, the team, the race all represent this longing.

Similarly, our ideas of organizational life can also represent the ego ideal for us. Within this image, members of the organization are imagined to have desires that are perfectly in concordance with their roles in an organization that is, itself, perfectly adapted to its environment. There is no anxiety in this picture because there is no separation of self and world. The organization, indeed, is conceived as mediating between the individual and the environment, as permitting the opportunity of a perfect fusion. I call this image of an organization the *organization ideal* (Schwartz, 1987a, 1987b, 1987c). Theorists of organizations will understand the organization ideal as the idea underlying a good deal of normative organization theory.

The trouble with the organization ideal, as with any ego ideal, is that it never happens. The existential reality of human life is that the individual is, as a unique individual, separate and distinct from the rest of the world — a reality that is revealed most vividly in the fact of each individual's eventual mortality. We may attain intimations of immortality, moments in which we feel that everything has come together, that we are indeed the center of a loving world, but these are only fleeting. Inevitably we return to the business-as-usual of our limited, imperfect lives.

Nevertheless, given the appeal of the ego ideal, an appeal that draws its potency from the pain of separation anxiety, it is not surprising that organizations attempt to maintain the idea of the organization ideal even in the face of their failure to manifest it.

In one way or another, organizations attempt to portray a picture of themselves and their participants as perfect and perfectly matched to the organization. Organizational actions are explained in such a way that the organization is seen to act correctly while failure is attributed to outside forces. Organizations require the presentation of self to adhere to a norm of a perfect concordance between individual motivation and organizational necessity. Thus, a well-trained executive never speaks of herself as having problems. Rather, she says that she faces "challenges," adding immediately, "and I love challenges!"

Perhaps most important, organizations enact a gradient of being within the organization, in which some are seen as being more identical with the organization than others, and therefore more the ego ideal. This gradient, which I call *ontological differentiation*, typically takes the form of hierarchy. Thus, the organization can still be the organization ideal even if one is not the center of a loving world because one is not yet truly one with the organization. Others, who are higher in the organization, may be believed to have attained the organization ideal (Schwartz, 1987a, 1987c).

Thus, as Klein and Ritti (1984, p. 185) put it: "Information is both given and withheld in order to create mythical explanations of events that then provide the framework for the subsequent consensual interpretations of such events. That framework is constructed to increase the probability that people will see the organization as effective and higher management as heroic."

One can easily understand the attraction of this way of managing an organization. It ties individuals into the organization on the basis of their most deeply loved image of themselves. Indeed, experience suggests that individuals often demand that organizations portray themselves in this way.

The trouble with this way of managing is that it only works at the expense of an accurate perception of reality. For the organization ideal does not and cannot exist, and when the organization organizes itself through the generation of a fantasy of its perfection, it necessarily requires its participants to subordinate their perception to the fantasy. This process of subordinating the perception of reality to the fantasy of the organization ideal gives rise to a process of increasing organizational ineffectiveness that I call *organizational decay* (Schwartz, 1989, 1990).

Organizational decay, like alcoholism, and for much the same reason, is a progressive illness (Schwartz, 1990). In choosing an image of its own perfection in the face of a reality that contradicts it, the organization abandons realistic engagement with part of its environment. This makes it impossible to cope well with that part of its environment. It therefore copes ineffectively and inefficiently with it. This makes it more difficult to maintain a realistic idea of the organization's perfection. Thus, more abandonment of reality and increasingly radical immersion in the fantasy become necessary, with the consequences of further degradation.

This degradation is typically given added impetus through the impact of ontological differentiation. As we have seen, high officials in the organization start to play the role of the organization ideal. In the decaying organization, they not only play the role, but start to believe in it as their identity. This brings them a great degree of narcissistic satisfaction. They begin to see themselves as perfect and use their power to ensure that subordinates play out this fantasy of their perfection.

This phenomenon ties the organization's power into the maintenance of the fantasies of its high officials and into the denial of the experience of lower participants when that experience contradicts the official fantasies. Moreover, it turns the capacity to be able to see things in terms of the superior's fantasy, and to deny discrepant reality, into an important and promotion-worthy aspect of the subordinate's job. This almost guarantees that, in the higher ranks of the organization, the concentration of individuals with a weak hold on reality will tend to increase over time.

Loss of Reality at NASA

It is always difficult, and often impossible, to specify precisely where the loss of reality begins in an organization. This is because of the importance of the ego ideal in our mental lives and because of our willingness to project it into our important social arrangements. Fantasy, therefore, is almost always ready at hand to interfere with our perception of reality and it should never be entirely surprising when our performance falls short of the optimum. In NASA's case, for example, an earlier tragedy, when fire broke out as the first manned Apollo craft stood on the launchpad, killing all three astronauts, was attributed to complacency and sloppiness of the sort bred by engaging in fantasy (Hirsch and Trento, 1973).

However, a quantum leap is taken when the fantasy, rather than being a disorganized, unconscious tendency that we fall into, becomes instead the organization's official doctrine and the organization's processes end up being structured around it. I call this the *institutionalization of the fiction* (Schwartz, 1989, 1990).

Typically, the institutionalization of the fiction begins with a bad decision made by the organization in the normal course of doing business. To maintain its image of itself as a perfect organization, the organization begins the redirection of its processes toward the justification of that bad decision. Further decisions will have the original bad decision built into them as a premise and therefore will themselves be bad decisions. The "why" of these decisions becomes "indiscussable" (Argyris and Schön, 1974). From a psychoanalytic point of view, the process of such redirection must be made unconsciously, because in the organization ideal decisions are simply good decisions and do not need to be made to look like good decisions. And as this goes on, the organization not only loses touch with reality, but even loses touch with the fact that it has lost touch with reality.

NASA is useful as an illustration of this because it is possible to identify precisely the point at which the justification of a bad decision came to be conscious policy and reality began to be lost as a result. NASA's original bad decision was the complex undertaking to maintain the grandiose ambitions that the organization had developed for manned space flight, even when it became clear that the funding for this grandiose agenda would not be forthcoming. But this is so only in a general sense. Specifically, the bad decision manifested itself in the form of an overt, conscious management thrust that they termed *success-oriented management*.

Success-oriented management differed from traditional NASA practice in that previous engineering was accomplished from the bottom up, in the sense that components were developed and perfected separately before being combined into a whole. In success-oriented management, however, engineering took place from the top down. As a remarkable article in *Science* (Smith, 1979, p. 910), written seven years before the *Challenger* explosion, put it: "The key to NASA's approach is success-oriented management, a strategy which is simply the inverse of Murphy's law; it assumes that everything will go right. As one official put it, 'It means you design everything to cost and then pray.'"

As I have said, when self-idealization has removed the original bad decision from criticism, further decisions will have it built into them as a premise and they will, in their own turn, be faulty. Thus: "Rather than cautiously — and expensively — test each engine component separately, NASA's main contractor . . . merely constructed everything to novel design, bolted it all together, and — with fingers crossed — turned on the power. At least five major fires resulted. . . . Fires have severely damaged a fuel pump, the engines themselves, the test orbiters to which they were attached, the insulation on an external fuel tank, and the test stand in which the engines sat" (Smith, 1979, p. 911). And: "Concomitant with a strategy that predicts success is a decision not to build spare parts. The engine testing program was delayed for months while the test stand was rebuilt. Malfunctions have been laboriously traced to flaws that might have been detected individually. Instead, every time a part failed, an entire engine was jeopardized" (Smith, 1979, p. 911).

But from the standpoint of the development of organizational decay, the increasing tendency of specific decisions to be flawed is perhaps less important than the increasing strains that the flaws in the decisions impose on those who are required to justify them. For this justification means that those who do it must abandon reality and begin to live more and more in fantasy.

In other words, the adoption of "success-oriented management" was a bad decision. And since actions in organization build on other actions, the sequelae of the bad decision would tend to be other bad decisions. But without self-idealization, the bad decisions would have been seen to be bad decisions.

Then their bad consequences could have been limited to some extent. But NASA's policy was evidently more than this, as is hinted in the use of the term *success-oriented*. Evidently, NASA's policy not only involved top-down engineering as a design and construction strategy, but included the doctrine that NASA employees had to believe in it as a design and construction strategy. It was this that forced the abandonment of reality.

As Smith (1979, p. 910, my italics) says: "The intention of the strategy . . . was to 'eliminate parallel and possibly redundant development and test hardware,' keeping expenses to an absolute minimum. But in NASA's hands, success-oriented management has led to wholesale deferrals of difficult work, embarrassing accidents, expensive redesigns, erratic staffing, weakening of specifications, *and the illusion that everything was running well.*" And: "Under the influence of success-oriented management, NASA officials perhaps began to confuse prediction with reality. NASA suffered from a 'technological hubris,' said a Senate aide. Managers became overconfident that technological breakthroughs would materialize to save the situation" (Smith, 1979, p. 912).

As I have suggested, when the process of decay begins, and as the organization shifts its functioning from coping with reality to presenting an idealization of itself, this is reflected in a reorientation of personnel policies favoring and supporting this shift. As this transformation takes place, the management of the organization is represented less and less by individuals who have a firm sense of reality, and becomes more a product of individuals who are more comfortable with fantasy. Thus, people will be hired and promoted or fired and isolated on the basis of their capacity to accommodate and enhance this process of fantasy generation.

For example, Trento (1987, p. 179) describes the process by which the Centaur, an upper-stage vehicle that many astronauts thought of as a "flying bomb," was approved by NASA management: "Lovelace succeeded in selecting the Centaur over the solid-fueled IUS because NASA was in full transition. The old-liners from the Apollo days were all but gone. . . . Lovelace convinced the shuttle managers in Houston to support Centaur.

For Lilly it was an amazing turnaround for the manned-flight people at Houston. '. . . They completely came around [as if] all the safety problems had been solved . . . and everything was fine, and no problems,' Lilly says sarcastically."

While this process is taking place, one may observe a shift in the ways in which management deals with information that conflicts with the organization ideal. Many organizations, I have suggested, have the fantasy of the organization ideal as an unconscious backdrop into which it is always possible to fall. But in healthy organizations, discrepant information is accepted as legitimate and is discussed, even if it is not received warmly. In the decaying organization it is suppressed and its bearers are stigmatized. Trento (1987, p. 121) quotes NASA veteran John Naugle to the effect that this transformation took place during the administration of Nixon appointee James Fletcher: "Up until that era there, I never worried about saying what I felt. I always felt my bosses . . . while they might not agree with me, they might slap me down, they might quarrel with me, but they were not going to throw me out just because I brought them bad news. And somewhere between the time Fletcher came on board and the time he left, I no longer felt that way."

Inevitably, the loss of reality affects not only management's orientation toward the external world, but also its orientation toward the internal processes of the organization. The increasing difficulty employees have in dealing with the world is seen as reflecting badly on them, indicating their unsuitability as participants in perfection. The work that they have to do to cope with reality must be kept from management, and the fact that they have kept it from management will have to be kept from management. As the decay process proceeds, then, management has less and less of a sense of what is going on within the organization.

This process was revealed starkly in NASA's response to the Cook memorandum. Richard C. Cook, a budget analyst for NASA, was assigned to assess the impact of any problems with the solid rocket boosters (SRBs). In a memorandum written on July 23, 1985, he warned that flight safety was being compromised by erosion of the seal O-rings and that failure would be catastrophic. After the explosion of the shuttle *Challenger* in January 1986, he wrote another memo, referring back to his first. This was leaked to the Rogers Commission, and Cook was called to testify on February 11. The Rogers Commission, which still maintained the idealization of NASA common at that time, was dismissive toward Cook and called NASA witnesses to refute his charges.

These officials were unanimous in their contention that the concerns Cook raised about the O-rings had been thoroughly investigated by more competent personnel and found baseless. More important for our purposes was the way in which they showed themselves out of touch with what their own engineering personnel believed and were worried about. In their mind, perfect open communication existed between them and their subordinates. But in fact, management and their subordinates were living in two different worlds. Here, for example, is part of the testimony of David Winterhalter, acting director of NASA's shuttle propulsion division: "And I pride, I prided myself on our division to be particularly good team workers. We have our differences, we work 'em out. . . . At no time . . . during that period did any of my people come to me, give any indication that they felt like there was any, any safety of flight problems in their area" ("Key Sections . . . ," 1986, p. B11). Two days later the commission heard: "Today, L. Michael Weeks, deputy associate administrator for space flight, the space agency's second-ranking shuttle official, said that the climate at the agency actually encouraged individuals two or three levels below him to speak their minds on safety concerns. He said that working-level engineers 'don't hesitate to tell Mike Weeks anything' and 'quite often will argue right on the spot at a significant meeting with me or with Jesse,' a reference to Jesse W. Moore, the top shuttle official" (Boffey, 1986, p. B4).

But when the *New York Times* gave Cook a chance to respond, this was his account:

> Richard C. Cook said that propulsion engineers at the National Aeronautics and Space Administration "whispered" in his ear ever since he arrived last

July that the seals were unsafe and even "held their breath" when earlier shuttles were launched.

Mr. Cook said he based his warning memorandum last July on conversations with engineers in the agency's propulsion division who were concerned about erosion of the rocket's safety seals. "They began to tell me that some of these things were being eaten away," he said, "and rather innocently I asked, 'What does that mean?' They said to me, almost in a whisper in my ear, that the thing could blow up," he continued. "I was shocked." In his July memorandum, Mr. Cook explained, "I was simply paraphrasing what this engineering group was telling me. I was not making it up that flight safety was being compromised and the results could be catastrophic. I didn't put it in my memorandum, but one of them said to me, 'When this thing goes up, we hold our breath'" [Boffey, 1986, p. B4].

Cook went on to give his opinion of how this blockage of information takes place. In a scenario that will be familiar to us, he pointed toward the pressure felt by lower personnel to support the image of organizational infallibility:

Cook said that, in meetings called by the shuttle program managers, a middle-level engineer with safety concerns is "just a little guy."

"You aren't going to find an engineer with 20 years' experience and a livelihood to protect stand up and say, 'Excuse me, but we might have an explosion on the next shuttle flight because the O-rings might break.' It's just not going to happen. If some[one] did get up, he would quickly be branded a nay-sayer," Mr. Cook said. "I never said a word in these meetings. I was a nobody, more junior than the veteran engineers. And there is always the nagging thought in the engineers' minds that, 'Gee, we may be wrong. Maybe nothing will happen'" [Boffey, 1986, p. B4].

In the end, what perhaps best demonstrates the psycho-pathology of this phenomenon is that all the while this process of decay was happening, the ethos of the organization became, not increasingly wary and concerned about the compromises that had been made, but more and more manic and convinced of its omnipotence. Thus, NASA increasingly developed a culture in which it saw itself as infallible, a culture so powerful within the organization that numerous observers commented on it following the disaster. Senator and former astronaut John Glenn, interviewed on the news program "This Week with David Brinkley" on June 8, 1986, said: "Well, I think there has been, and I think back in the days when I was in the program, I think there was a can-do attitude, a go-for-it attitude, and safety was paramount. Bob Gilruth, when we first got in the program, told us back in those days, 'You know, any time you have a question about safety, let me know and we'll stop, we'll change, we'll do additional tests, we'll do whatever.' And I think that can-do attitude, perhaps at least with some people at NASA . . . was replaced by a can't-fail attitude, and I think that's unfortunate that crept into the program."

And Eugene Cernan, another former astronaut, said on the same program, "I think they were just caught up with the fact that, 'Hey, we're infallible. We can't help but succeed.'" Indeed, it seems to me that it was this shift toward a culture of infallibility, a clear "manic defense" (Klein, 1975) that, more than anything else, establishes the decline of NASA as a phenomenon that requires a psychoanalytic explanation.

In the end, one can see this culture of infallibility, based on the belief in the organization ideal, in the specific decision taken to launch the *Challenger*. For the fact is that the decision was taken in the face of overwhelming engineering evidence that it would be dangerous to launch. The performance of the O-ring seals had a history of frequent near-failure. The cold conditions could not help but make the situation worse. Not one engineer supported the launch and, indeed, the Morton-Thiokol management team could not bring itself to approve the launch until they "took off their engineering hat" (Presidential Commission, 1986).

Yet not only did NASA management decide to launch the *Challenger*, but those responsible for the decision did not even give any indication to their own superiors that there had been a disagreement over the issue and, indeed, even after the explosion, continued to defend it as correct (Schwartz, 1987b). There does not seem to me to be any possible explanation for this *sangfroid* except the assumption that NASA officials believed that they, as NASA, the organization ideal, having made the decision to launch, had made it correctly.

The Loss of the Superego and Organizational Decay

This analysis shows a continuity between the NASA that launched the *Challenger* and the NASA that emerged after so many months of trying to reform itself. The pattern of commitment to grandiosity remained the same. This raises the question of why NASA was unable to reform itself, having had such a tremendous base of resources within American society to bring it back to health. The answer, it seems to me, is that American society was afflicted with the same pathology that caused NASA's decay in the first place. Indeed, perhaps that decay was only a more visible aspect of a broader process taking place within the whole of American society.

If psychoanalytic theory reveals the dynamics of the organizational decay process, it also points to a dynamic that counteracts the process of decay. This is the dynamic of the superego.

In Freud's ([1923] 1961) analysis of the traditional pattern of male socialization, the male child's return to the mother is blocked by the father. The boy must become "like" the father in order to fuse with someone like the mother and attain the ego ideal. Becoming like the father is a matter of identifying with the father's sense of what he, in his turn, is "supposed to" be and of undertaking to punish himself with guilt for deviations from these obligations, instead of having these deviations punished by the father. In this way, the child acquires a superego.

What is critical in this formulation, as far as it applies to the analysis of organizational decay, is the understanding that the child accepts the responsibility *to do something* in order to attain the ego ideal. He is not entitled to be the center of a loving world just because he is who he is. Some form of action has to be taken. The dynamic of becoming worthwhile, therefore, creates a psychological meaning for engaging the world with full regard to its reality, independence, and recalcitrance. The process of superego development is not always successful; however, without a sufficiently developed superego, the tendency toward decay through increasing immersion in fantasy becomes irresistible.

I have argued elsewhere (Schwartz, 1988) that the superego disappeared from the imagery that the United States was using to envision its manned space flight program and, through it, itself. From a symbol of the single-combat warrior, who would do battle with the Soviets and save the nation, the symbol of manned flight regressed to come to represent Disneyland-in-space, a sphere of children at play, free from danger, and with no obligations to fulfill. A society that saw itself in this way—denying the necessity of accomplishment for the attainment of the ego ideal—would not have the psychological base necessary to fulfill the technological demands that space flight imposes. The world it had created, as in the world of the child, had replaced technology with magic.

If this analysis is correct it is easy to see why NASA could not reform itself. It is because within the society as a whole, the superego has lost its meaning and the engagement of reality has lost its affective base. I suggest that a society that collectively believes that people have no obligation to do anything that they do not want to do, that nobody should have to achieve anything in order to "be somebody," that anybody who does not "have it all" must have had it taken away from them, cannot organize a viable space program—or very much else, for that matter.

References

Argyris, C., and Schön, D. A. *Theory in Practice: Increasing Professional Effectiveness.* San Francisco: Jossey-Bass, 1974.

Boffey, P. M. "Analyst Who Gave Shuttle Warning Faults 'Gung-Ho,' 'Can-Do' Attitude," *New York Times,* Feb. 14, 1986, p. B4.

Broad, W. J. "Higher Estimate for Maintaining Station in Space."
    New York Times, July 11, 1990a, pp. A1, B6.
Broad, W. J. "Space Station Must Be Altered to Reduce Work,
    NASA Says." *New York Times,* July 21, 1990b, pp. 1, 8.
Broad, W. J. "Troubles Raising Questions About Space Agency."
    New York Times, July 1, 1990c, p. 16.
Cernan, E. Interview on "This Week with David Brinkley," ABC
    Television, June 8, 1986.
Chasseguet-Smirgel, J. *The Ego Ideal: A Psychoanalytic Essay on
    the Malady of the Ideal.* (P. Burrows, trans.) New York: Nor-
    ton, 1985.
Chasseguet-Smirgel, J. *Sexuality and Mind: The Role of the Father
    and Mother in the Psyche.* New York: New York University
    Press, 1986.
Freud, S. "Group Psychology and the Analysis of the Ego." In
    J. Strachey (ed. and trans.), *The Standard Edition of the Com-
    plete Psychological Works of Sigmund Freud.* Vol. 18. London:
    Hogarth Press, 1955. (Originally published 1921.)
Freud, S. "On Narcissism: An Introduction." In J. Strachey (ed.
    and trans.), *The Standard Edition of the Complete Psychological
    Works of Sigmund Freud.* Vol. 14. London: Hogarth Press,
    1957. (Originally published 1914.)
Freud, S. "The Ego and the Id." In J. Strachey (ed. and trans.),
    *The Standard Edition of the Complete Psychological Works of Sig-
    mund Freud.* Vol. 19. London: Hogarth Press, 1961. (Origi-
    nally published 1923.)
Glenn, J. Interview on "This Week with David Brinkley," ABC
    Television, June 8, 1986.
Hirsch, R., and Trento, J. J. *The National Aeronautics and Space
    Administration.* New York: Praeger, 1973.
"Key Sections of Testimony at Hearing of Shuttle Catastrophe."
    New York Times, Feb. 12, 1986, pp. B10, B11.
Klein, M. "A Contribution to the Psychogenesis of Manic-
    Depressive States." In M. Klein, *Love, Guilt, and Repara-
    tion and Other Works, 1921–1945.* London: Hogarth Press,
    1975.
Klein, S. M., and Ritti, R. R. *Understanding Organizational Be-
    havior.* (2nd ed.) Boston: Kent, 1984.

Presidential Commission on the Space Shuttle Challenger Accident. *Report of the Presidential Commission on the Space Shuttle Challenger Accident.* Washington, D.C.: U.S. Government Printing Office, June 6, 1986.

Sartre, J.-P. *Being and Nothingness.* New York: Philosophical Library, 1953.

Schwartz, H. S. "Antisocial Actions of Committed Organizational Participants: An Existential Psychoanalytic Perspective." *Organization Studies,* 1987a, *8* (4), 327–340.

Schwartz, H. S. "On the Psychodynamics of Organizational Disaster: The Case of the Space Shuttle Challenger." *Columbia Journal of World Business,* 1987b, *22* (1), 59–67.

Schwartz, H. S. "On the Psychodynamics of Organizational Totalitarianism." *Journal of Management,* 1987c, *13* (1), 45–54.

Schwartz, H. S. "The Symbol of the Space Shuttle and the Degeneration of the American Dream." *Journal of Organizational Change Management,* 1988, *1* (2), 5–20.

Schwartz, H. S. "Organizational Disaster and Organizational Decay: The Case of the National Aeronautics and Space Administration." *Industrial Crisis Quarterly,* 1989, *3* (4), 319–334.

Schwartz, H. S. *Narcissistic Process and Corporate Decay: The Theory of the Organization Ideal.* New York: New York University Press, 1990.

Smith, R. J. "Shuttle Problems Compromise Space Program." *Science,* 1979, *206* (23), 910–914.

Trento, J. J. *Prescription for Disaster: From the Glory of Apollo to the Betrayal of the Shuttle.* New York: Crown, 1987.

PART FIVE

Organizational Consultation and Change

13

---•◆•◆•◀━━

Understanding
the Dynamics Between
Consulting Teams
and Client Systems

James Krantz
Thomas North Gilmore

Consultants are faced with the need to frame problems and design interventions on the basis of extremely limited data about their client systems. (The discussion here is mostly concerned with social consultation, that is, understanding and intervening in the social system. However, the distinction between technical and social consultation is far from distinct because both require human collaboration. Designing and implementing even the most technical of interventions depends on the receptivity of the client system, an effective implicit theory of the social system, and an appropriate problem formulation. Often, the acceptance of a "technical" frame in the presenting problem is itself a form of collusion between client and consultant to steer away from more difficult, anxiety-laden aspects of a problematic situation.) Information is distorted and efforts toward change are often undermined by implicit and unrecognized forces that emerge in the course of an intervention. Rice (1963, p. 274) illustrates this point: "What appears on the surface as a simple organizational problem may often be found to have underlying

it deep-seated and largely unrecognized emotional conflicts. . . .
A solution to the overt problem may not provide relief; indeed
it may exacerbate the underlying difficulties by removing a
symptom, attention to which has provided a defence against the
anxiety of having to face the real causes. In the extreme, a client
may well wish to keep the overt problem alive and unsolved as
a means of containing the anxiety inherent in its solution."

The misunderstandings that grow out of these forces can
surface in all phases of an intervention, starting with the way
in which a client's presenting problem shapes the initial formulation. No amount of sophistication in the execution of an intervention can overcome an error in problem definition, what
Mitroff and Featheringham (1974) call *Type III error*. And throughout the initiative the interventionist's understanding, and therefore his or her ability to act purposefully, are subject to distor-
tion by unrecognized and important aspects of the client system.

Yet how is one to identify these latent, often hidden features? Interventionists have developed a variety of technologies
to help them inquire systematically into the settings they are
attempting to alter. Self-report methods and survey instruments
have proved useful for gaining access to certain types of data.
However, they are of limited use in revealing those dimensions
of organizational life that are beyond the awareness of the informants (Nisbet and Wilson, 1977; Salancik and Pfeffer, 1977).
And these forces are often the most formidable barriers to successful projects.

To understand these dynamics, consultants must use more
interpretative methods, trying to piece together data that yield a
deeper understanding of the organization's culture and critical
latent features (Weiss, 1968). Such data can be found in a variety
of ways as one listens with the "third ear" to the client system.

Our contention is that the roles assigned to the consultant, or the intragroup dynamics induced in the consulting team,
reproduce important and unconscious dynamics of the client system. Properly understood, this reproduction process provides
invaluable data for understanding critical aspects of the client
system and can therefore enhance the consultant's ability to work
effectively.

In this chapter, we identify a theoretical construct developed in the object relations school of psychoanalytic thinking that appears to explain the phenomena with which we are concerned. We also review, with the help of case studies, a variety of ways in which this process has been observed. The first case is an example of how an individual consultant can be inducted into a certain relational system that, when understood clearly, provides the clue to designing a more effective intervention. The second is an example of how dynamics in the client system unconsciously shaped the working relationship between two consultants, and their relationship with the client, and how the resulting team dynamics were used to understand the client system's developmental needs more deeply. The last case examines ways in which projective identification affected a consulting team engaged with a large information services company. Finally, we discuss the implications of this formulation for the organization of consultancies and the ways it can inform the interventionist's approach.

Theoretical Background

The theoretical foundation for understanding implicit communication has evolved out of the object relations school of psychoanalysis. In particular, it rests on a process known as projective identification, first described by Melanie Klein (1975b). The process *simultaneously* involves a type of psychological defense against unwanted feelings or fantasies, a mode of communication, and a type of human relationship (Ogden, 1982).

The unconscious transfer of information occurring in projective identification is a two-phase process. It begins with the denial and rejection of feelings inherent in a person's unconscious image (fantasy) of a situation. The person therefore alters an uncomfortable experience by imagining that part of it is an attribute of someone or something else, rather than of himself or herself.

In the second phase of projective identification, the recipient of the attribution or projection is essentially inducted into the originator's scheme of things. He or she is subtly pressured into thinking, feeling, and behaving in a manner congruent with the feelings or thoughts projected by the other.

Thus, while projective identification is a type of *defense*, in the sense of unconsciously serving to insulate the projector from an aspect of his or her experience, it is also a mode of *communication*, in the sense that the feelings that are congruent with one's own inner image are induced in another, creating a sense of "being understood by or at one with the other" (Ogden, 1982).

The impact of projective identification on the therapist-patient interaction is profound and has been studied extensively by researchers exploring how a wide range of countertransference feelings and responses stem from the relationship itself rather than strictly from the therapist's own background. Through the mechanism of projective identification, the patient can actually induce the *therapist* to experience the denied aspect.

As Bion (1959, p. 149) describes it, the therapist is inducted into the patient's inner image of the world: "The analyst feels he is being manipulated so as to be playing a part, no matter how difficult to recognize, in someone else's fantasy." This link between internal intrapsychic process and the interpersonal dimension has provided the foundation for understanding important aspects of group and organizational life. Bion's (1959) pioneering studies of groups examined how a type of collusive, shared group mentality evolves through the collective use of projective identification. Jaques (1955) and Menzies (1960) used this framework for understanding how adults in group and institutional settings use projective identification to cope with complex feelings that arise in the course of ordinary social relations.

Projective identification enables us to understand a wide range of group and institutional phenomena. As various group members, subgroups, or organizational sectors come to symbolize or represent some unwanted aspect, they can serve as repositories for certain projected elements and are then induced to enact these feelings or fantasies. Frequently observed patterns of role differentiation (Gibbard, Hartman, and Mann, 1974; Wells, 1990), such as role suction (Redl, 1963; Horwitz, 1983), in which groups pressure a member into a needed role, and scapegoating (Jaques, 1955; Gibbard, Hartman, and Mann,

1974; Dunphy, 1974), are comprehensible in terms of projective identification.

How the recipient of this process responds has a crucial impact on the experience of the sender. If the recipient simply enacts the role he or she is assigned, then a tacit, collusive agreement is established in which the original meaning of the unwanted feelings or fantasies is reinforced and the sender's defense against thinking about them is confirmed.

Thus, the recipient (or possibly scapegoat) assumes, or even accentuates, the characteristics attributed to him or her and thereby confirms the repugnance others feel for that (disowned) aspect of themselves. Perhaps a group member embodies a role assigned by the group, such as the rebellion leader. Or possibly the therapist unconsciously becomes the sadistic parent of the patient's inner world by attempting one punishing interpretation after another.

If, on the other hand, the recipient can gain mastery over the process through understanding it, the process of projective identification can be usefully transformed into thought and symbolization (Segal, 1981; Ogden, 1982). In other words, meaning can be made of it. Psychotherapeutic literature devotes much discussion to the best ways to "contain" and transform the process into a useful experience for the patient (Ogden, 1982; Malin and Grotstein, 1986; Searles, 1963). In failing to do so, the therapist loses rich data concerning the patient's internal world. We want to consider here the ability to capture and use these data in an organizational context.

Projective identification, while it can produce dramatic events, is also an important part of ordinary social relations. It has been related, for example, to the capacity for empathy (Klein, 1975a). Projecting parts of the self into others and then identifying with them enables one individual to feel understood by another (Wells, 1990; Ogden, 1982; Winnicott, 1965). This sense of feeling understood is an important part of any helping alliance, whether in a therapeutic context or other confidant-type relationship, such as organizational consulting.

The way projective identification works in the consulting relationship is little understood or studied by consultants.

Two assumptions are necessary in order to gain understanding by mapping this concept onto the client-consultant relationship. One is that the same ongoing projective process that shapes the organizational social field also produces the organization's inability to address the problems or challenges for which it calls in an outside consultant. A typical instance of this is the defensive maneuver by which a manager denies his or her own responsibility for a situation and projects it onto others. Another instance is the way in which mutually maintained splitting and projective identification produce mistrust, suspicion, and adversarial relations between subgroups—labor and management, for example—and concomitantly a diminished ability to collaborate toward mutually acceptable solutions.

The same projective process that shapes the social field is inherent in the client's tacit understanding of the setting and relatedness to it. Relatedness here refers to the client's image or mental picture of the situation (Senge, 1990; Lawrence, 1979; Money-Kyrle, 1961) rather than to the situation itself. On the group level it refers to the shared understanding of a problematic situation.

The second assumption is that by engaging with the organization, the consultant or action research team enters the same social field, with all its distortions and shared constructs. In working with a consultant to clarify and understand a challenging or problematic situation, the client conveys a personal interpretation of the situation to the consultant, including those aspects of the problem that the client is denying to himself or herself (Bain, 1976). Thus the same projective process that shapes the client system will shape the interventionist's experience of the organization.

Given these two assumptions, we can see that of the myriad ways in which consultants come to understand the situation, both explicit and tacit, the projective process in the consultant-client relationship provides a key insight. It is a channel of communication that contains otherwise hidden information—data about the situation unavailable via more ordinary means of inquiry.

Several active researchers have observed and written about

projective identification in their work. Bain (1976, pp. 655–656) suggests that the "denied aspect of the presenting problem, i.e., the personal link that connects presenter and problem, is at first projected into the role that is desired for the consultant." His analysis is concerned with the presenting problem and the need for the consultant to examine the latent meaning of the presenting problem by understanding the role assigned to the consultant as a critical window into the client's unconscious understanding of the problem. How the consultant is made to feel about the problem and what the consultant is made to feel wanted for are the data for this analysis.

Other researchers have noticed that the dynamics of the research and consulting teams tend to reflect those of the host organization, without explicitly discussing the dynamic mechanism of projective identification. A group of researchers (Alderfer, 1977; Smith, 1984) has developed the concept of parallel processes, which refers to any apparent resonances between two engaged social systems. This concept is more general than projective identification because it includes a wide variety of conscious and unconscious mechanisms. Nonetheless, they often appear to be discussing the same phenomena we discuss in this chapter.

Still other researchers hover around the concept or describe it without using technical psychoanalytic terms. Smith (1984) mentions how "covert dynamics in one system can get played out, in parallel form by another system with which it interacts." Steele (1975) suggests that the emotional process of the client group can be observed by looking at the ways in which the consulting team's interactions have changed. In describing attempts to bring about labor-management cooperation systems, Walsh (1983) notes how readily client systems induce internal strife in consulting teams, labeling the dynamic *consultant splitting*. Most recently, Hirschhorn (1988) provides several illuminating case descriptions of the impact of projective identification on the consultant.

Now let us turn to three examples of how projective identification has influenced our own work with client systems and in particular how it has offered invaluable data for providing effective intervention.

Case Illustrations

This section illustrates the operation of projective identification in our consulting experience. We begin with the process as it unfolded with a single consultant, then with two consultants, and finally with a team of three. In the first case, the awareness on the consulting side of the relationship came, unfortunately, predominately after the completion of the consulting assignment. As a result, valuable information about the client organization, about which they themselves were unaware, was not brought into the work. In the second and third cases, the teams became aware of this process during the consultation and used the knowledge as the basis for the ongoing work with the organization.

Case A: Strategic Planning Workshop

The deputy director of a major city department requested the assistance of a consultant at a senior staff retreat. The aims were to set goals and review key tasks in each of the major divisions. The participants were the commissioner, the deputy, and the three division heads. At the initial interview, the deputy expressed considerable anxiety about the commissioner's volatility and his "personality or style" in dealing with the rest of the team. However, the deputy asked the consultant to stay away from these issues and to keep the group focused on goals and tasks.

    The consultant began the work by developing a questionnaire on goals, tasks, and team relationships that each participant would complete prior to the session. While preparing the document he began to feel increasingly anxious and caught in the middle between the commissioner and the others. During interviews with the commissioner, the consultant felt the commissioner was confiding thoughts about the others that he had not yet communicated directly to them. When with the others, the consultant was filled with their concerns about whether or not the commissioner would "blow up" if they were honest about the issues. A meeting of all parties was set prior to the retreat, but "inadvertently" the commissioner had not been notified and was not in attendance. The consultant, as a result, met with the commissioner several hours later, serving again as a go-between on the especially hot issues of how working relationships might be addressed during the retreat.

At the session itself, the commissioner failed to begin the meeting as he had agreed he would, instead rambling on about matters irrelevant to the task at hand. The time was slipping away and participants began to signal the consultant to control the commissioner and get him to start the session. As the consultant's anxiety mounted, he eventually signaled the commissioner to begin.

Let us now examine this case, drawing on the framework that we presented earlier. The deputy was presenting a technical problem about facilitating a strategic planning workshop. The "denied aspect of the presenting problem" was projected onto the consultant: the overfunctioning of this deputy in managing the relationships of the directors with the commissioner and the avoidance of the difficult relationship issues. Note that the deputy was not unaware of the commissioner's volatility and the interpersonal problems. What was projected were his links to those issues, his own contribution to the repetitive patterns. The consultant then acted out the projections by playing the go-between role and by managing the commissioner's behavior at the workshop. The consultant began to feel responsible and to overfunction with regard to these relationships issues — the second step in the process of projective identification. By enacting the projection rather than understanding it, the consultant lost an opportunity to intervene constructively in the real problems facing the group.

The session produced goal statements and lists of tasks, but left in place the dysfunctional relationships that were the real problem. Without better working alliances, the follow-through on the workshop was predictably poor. Rice (1949, p. 179) describes the danger for the specialist in "human relations" of aspiring to "a technocratic role, so that not only is his continued employment as a technician justified, but also so that technocracy itself may serve as a defense against some of the difficulties involved in any real attempt to resolve the problems for the solution of which he has ostensibly been introduced."

One of the dangers of working alone in complex emotional systems is the heightened difficulty of seeing when the above processes are operative. In this case, but unluckily too late, the consultant was able to see the major patterns and did get help from a colleague in understanding the feelings that were being projected onto him and their relationship to the central issues the work group faced.

Case B: Juvenile Justice Agency

In this case a pair of consultants participated in an ongoing change effort with a large juvenile justice agency. The aim of the consultancy was to assist a recently appointed commissioner in formulating new directions for the organization, in developing a strategy for implementation, and in building the necessary working relationships and competencies into the organization. The agency consisted of three major divisions: a secure detention center, an after-care program, and a nonsecure network of group homes. Each had historically functioned in relative isolation from one another. A major initiative of the new commissioner was to link the divisions more effectively around a shared mission that integrated child-care functions and security concerns. Furthermore, she began to develop a case-management system that would both increase accountability for services and focus staff on each child.

Within the context of this case, we will explore how the dynamics of the consulting partners mirrored those in the system and provided us with useful information about the client system. Once we were able to understand this correspondence we were able to guide our interventions favorably.

The consulting partners worked originally with the senior staff on agencywide strategic planning issues. As the scope of work began to include more implementation issues, the major operating units were also offered consulting resources for their work. Of the two consultants, the team leader, Tom, worked principally with the commissioner and headquarters staff. The other, Jim, was assigned to work with key operating units, most notably the secure detention function. This deployment allowed for particular identification of different consultants with different units and levels of the organization.

One of the central issues early in the work was the relationship of the commissioner with the director of the secure detention facility (called "Elmwood" here). While the relationship between a commissioner and his or her wardens is key in all correctional organizations, this one was particularly sensitive because the facility accounted for almost 75 percent of the agency's budget. Furthermore, they were interdependent in two important senses. First, the administration's political vulnerability and its reputation to the outside world rested largely on what happened (or did not happen) at Elmwood. Second, the extensive changes that this commissioner undertook had to be accomplished, to a large degree, in that setting.

Thus, the relationship was already charged and, by the time of our arrival, had been turbulent. One of the major issues between the commissioner and the Elmwood director was that the director's planning work was underdeveloped. The commissioner framed the problem as follows: "For us, to learn how better to help her; for her, to learn how to use us so that her work gets better so that it's more likely to fly — so that she does not have to do it four times. . . . We picked unit reorganization because [the detention director] wanted to do it, but it's taken us six weeks to get the necessary materials and we've lost the interesting aspects of the conversation, decentralization, etc., in the process."

The extensive development effort required considerable written work and documentation in order to sell the unit reorganization to central control agencies outside the department. Somehow the commissioner felt unable to get the level and quality of work she needed to accomplish the tasks on her own level; she was disappointed and discouraged with the situation and felt ineffectual.

The idea of unit reorganization had emerged from the director of Elmwood as part of her agenda in getting control over the facility. During the agencywide planning sessions it had been conceptually linked to the case-management agenda. The unit reorganization would decentralize authority to the units and make them more accountable for the total experience of the young people in detention.

The consulting pair became involved in this initiative at a meeting of the commissioner, accompanied by two other key members of headquarters staff, with the director of Elmwood and two of her staff members. The commissioner chaired the meeting, flanked by her two deputies. At the other end of the table sat the director and her assistants. The two consultants sat in the middle on either side of the table. The meeting was a difficult one. The commissioner began by listing questions that had to be thought through, and the institutional staff began to present data. It quickly became clear that the different parties had different expectations of the meeting. The information was confused and presented in a format that ruled out testing some of the alternatives on the table. The institutional staff appeared confused as to whether they were expected to develop a desired unit reorganization or simply fashion a feasible plan within the many existing constraints of budget and personnel categories. By the close of the meeting, it was agreed that the institutional staff would take the key questions back and develop a specific proposal. The consultants were offered and accepted as a resource for this work, given their knowledge about organizational design issues. Thus, we received our assignment within an initial framing of the problem as a technical organizational issue. As discussed in the following section, this framing was crucially shaped by the patterns of projection within the agency that we had accepted in ways we only came to understand as we began to work on the redesign effort.

We joined the detention facility executive team in a day-long planning session to assist in the development of the unit design. The chief consultant was Jim, the team member assigned to work with Elmwood; Tom, though director of the overall team, took a support role on this assignment. The day went quite well, with a creative design emerging from the discussions.

On leaving, the consultants agreed to write a summary note on the day describing the design ideas and their organizational implications, with Jim taking responsibility for producing the note. Two days later, Tom became anxious about the note and sent Jim a draft document he had written himself, leaving several sections blank for pieces Jim was still to write, but substantially developing the document and its organization. Jim became resentful and pointedly reminded Tom of the original delegation to him of the work with Elmwood in general and this task in particular. He asked for his delegation to be reconfirmed; he would take the notes as input but would develop the document in the way he felt was best, which he did.

A day later, reflecting on this awkward exchange, the two consultants began to see how they had been enacting an important dynamic within the client system. Tom, the director of the team and the person most closely aligned with the commissioner, felt he was being given an unpalatable choice—to delegate completely (perhaps to the point of abdication) or to do the job himself. There did not appear to be a middle collaborative ground, especially with Jim (the subordinate consultant aligned most closely with the director) in the lead role and Tom acting as a resource.

The resonance of this with the picture conveyed to us in our work with the commissioner helped us make sense of our experiences. Inside the organization, the director of detention felt that the authority to do her assignment in the way she felt best was undercut by the "impatient" participation of the commissioner. The commissioner was sending mixed signals about the responsibility for the reorganization of Elmwood. She respected the competence and leadership of the institution, but needed to be involved in the design of the change. Yet the either-or style of collaboration evolving on that boundary made her participation impossible without seeming like a "vote of no confidence."

This enactment of the client system dynamic within the consulting pair and our ability to recognize that this was not simply an issue in our own work relationship (our ability to recognize it was partly because it seemed so out of character to us) helped us understand a major issue. From initially accepting this assignment as a technical design issue, we had come to understand, through our containing and interpreting the projections into the consulting partnership, that the issue *really* concerned difficulties of collaboration across a hierarchical boundary.

Making sense of projected data involves avoiding the enactment of the pattern and transforming it into thought that can be used in the subsequent work. First, though we agreed to write up notes of the meeting as consultants to the director of Elmwood, we made sure that they were not in a form that could be submitted as a ghostwritten report. This would have been colluding with the unconscious purpose of our being deployed by the commissioner to "fix" the problem of poor staffing and planning work from the facility. Second, we presented our understandings (based on this and other pattern data) at a meeting with the commissioner and her top staff.

We maintain that these points could not have been diagnosed by questionnaires or other additional means because neither the commissioner nor the director of detention was conscious of how their struggle over authority on shared projects affected one another. While both were concerned about difficulties in the relationship, they were unaware of how the framing of issues as technical (that is, organizational design) was a defensive avoidance of confronting disturbing social system issues. Indeed, our experience of working with Elmwood staff was that they were far more technically competent when thinking among themselves than when working across the boundary, when they were rendered ineffectual by the dynamics of the mutual projections.

In this instance, we were able to present our thinking effectively to the clients and support their work on this issue. However, such data do not always have to be interpreted and represented to the client. Often their major impact is in simply shaping the decisions the consultants make on their side of the boundary regarding deployment of their resources, such as reshaping the focus of the consultants' diagnostic inquiry, leading them to reframe intervention efforts, or causing them to alter tactics to avoid being inducted unconsciously into unhelpful roles.

Another episode involving the same clients illuminates a somewhat more substantive difficulty that interfered with the sophisticated collaborative work needed to undertake the change efforts. One ongoing tension between the Elmwood managers and the headquarters executives was over the degree to which matters of safety and security had to be attended to before major changes in the service areas could be undertaken. The struggles over this issue appeared to be quite manifest, since discussion of the problems involved were held in a number of arenas. On the surface, there was a basic agreement that key safety and security issues warranted priority attention.

Yet the conversations between Tom and Jim on this issue left an unsatisfying feeling, particularly for Jim. On examination, Jim did not feel his position was understood, though both Jim and Tom had been acting as though a shared understanding had evidently been reached. As part of the work in making sense of this type of data, Jim wrote a memorandum to Tom: "One is the question of just how different are the HQ versus Elmwood priorities regarding safety issues? You thought the differences were exaggerated and I think differently. Obviously we have absorbed something from the system here, and it is something that I think is interfering with collaboration."

On the hypothesis that this too reflected an unconscious systemic dynamic, we investigated and discovered that a similar dynamic was influencing work on the Elmwood-headquarters boundary.

These episodes, and several others reflecting different issues, revealed a pattern of difficulty in the field–central office working alliance. In a working note to the commissioner, we presented the issue of headquarters-field relationships as a central problem. On reflection, the difference between the two consultants here mirrored a rich set of institutional tensions. Underlying and amplifying the interpersonal struggles over delegation, accountability, and dependency were historic intergroup and institutional tensions grounded in sociocultural and socioeconomic factors. Headquarters was traditionally "white," middle-class, and highly educated, while Elmwood was "black" and was composed of staff who were less educated and who were identified with the children. Just as the relationship between the commissioner and her director served as a microcosm for these institutional and cultural tensions, so the relationship between Jim and Tom became a "container" for the anxiety-laden, disturbing aspects of these deeper issues to the extent that they shaped the interpersonal collaboration between the commissioner and the director.

We offered as evidence our experience both in transactions with the client and within our own team as we had come to represent the different parts of the organization. While we did not develop our position on the basis of these experiences alone, they were instrumental in our ability to guide our own inquiry into the organization and to shape our understanding of the subtle specifics and local complexities of the very generic issues often confronting such institutions.

Other issues came to light through examination of our own internal team dynamics as well. Though many have proved less helpful in our work with the client system, our insights into these issues have been very useful to our team's capacity to collaborate well together. As Steele (1977) suggests, anxiety-laden aspects of the client organization appear in the form of regressed consulting team dynamics. Working to understand how this occurs can free the consulting team from maintaining the rigid, constricted roles that emerge under conditions of projective identification and thereby enhance its own collaborative capabilities, enabling it to work more effectively with a client system.

Case C: An Information Services Company

A large information services company engaged consultants to help it implement a newly forged strategic plan, which reorganized the firm from a traditional functional orientation to a product-line approach. Implementing the plan would require extensive structural and cultural development. The team consisted of three consultants. The lead consultant established a link with the primary client within the system, the COO, who had recently been hired with this strategic development in mind. A second senior consultant worked initially with the CEO. The team's junior consultant was assigned to work with the director of the major product line that accounted for almost half the revenue. This director had also competed for the COO's position.

As the consultation unfolded, the senior executive group was enthusiastically engaged with the development work. The consultants, particularly the lead consultant, were regarded with great respect. Their work was at times idealized, as if it was the magical solution to implementing this strategic plan.

At the same time a rift emerged within the consulting team between the two senior consultants and the more junior member (Bill), who was aligned with the product-line director. Increasingly, Bill felt himself excluded from team conversations and sensed that the others devalued his work. They, on the other hand, became increasingly critical of his work and felt that it was not integrated into the overall development effort. The "fault line" around which this conflict emerged concerned how to integrate business planning on the operational level substantively with the strategic planning at the executive levels.

As the conflict crystallized, the junior consultant began to feel that the others had an unexpressed contempt and disregard for the "nitty gritty" of operations. The senior consultants, in turn, felt that Bill was unintentionally colluding with the director by getting overly involved in the psychosocial issues of the unit while avoiding the complex structural and operational questions involved in implementing the strategic plan at the division level. Each member of the consulting team had the sense of being caught in a perplexing unconscious dynamic that was making it difficult to work together and particularly difficult to vitalize the executive-operational boundary.

When we review the conflict two interesting hypotheses emerge. One is that the team was enacting the unexpressed, tacit doubts about the strategic plan as a tool for guiding operations. In other words, to some degree, for the executive level the plan was serving as a socially maintained defense to foster the notion of coherence, purposefulness, and controlled direction for this very complex, fragmented system. The consulting team's difficulty in integrating the operational planning and development with the strategic plan reflected the system's unaddressed failure, that is, to create the links between levels to make the strategic plan a true guide for operations. The defensive idealization of the lead consultant similarly reflected the splitting process that underlay the fantasies about the strategic plan.

A second, correlated process concerned the relationship between the newly hired COO and the director. The director, who had not been chosen for the COO's post, was skeptical of the plan's performance markers and many of the assumptions on which the overall plan was based. In deploying Bill to work

with the director, the team was also unconsciously enacting the
COO's wish to get the director "on board" with the use of consultation. The director's resistance to using his consultant predictably mirrored his resistance to accepting his new boss and
to joining with the new boss's vision. The atypically critical and
punitive dynamic that emerged at times in the consulting team
enacted the COO's frustration with his own transition and his
anger with the director of his major product line.

Implications

The implications of attending to issues of projective identification extend throughout a consultation from the first encounter
with a client through the termination of the relationship. The
consultative relationship brings a consultant into contact with
many dimensions and levels of a client system. Often, effective
work requires attending to the deeper processes and levels and
their impact on the more manifest problems consultants are
generally asked to address. The turbulent conditions with which
organizations must now contend increasingly put strategic questions into the forefront (Kanter, 1989). The need for active, ongoing adaptation to changing circumstances puts organizations
under pressure to innovate and regularly realign themselves.
Dealing with issues on this level inevitably requires change efforts
to grapple with deeper dimensions of organizational life and confronts consultants with the perplexing, often seemingly irrational,
behavior that accompanies such change efforts. Consequently,
consultants will increasingly need the conceptual machinery to
address the underlying, unconscious dimensions of the consulting
relationship.

The impact of projections from the client system and consultants' vulnerability to being induced into clients' unconscious
patterns are infrequently discussed in consulting literature, where
they are often written about as "pathologies" (Steele, 1975, p.
117) rather than as rich sources of information about the unconscious dimensions of the client's organization. They are important for a single consultant but become particularly complex
and rich when a team of consultants is involved.

Consultants are often called in because of distortions in the social field that render the client organization unable to investigate freely and address effectively its own difficulties. The projective processes at the root of these distortions stem from anxieties inherent in difficult or threatening situations. Frequently, maintaining these distortions involves the avoidance of responsibility by individuals, groups, or organizations and the projection of responsibility for failure into others.

In the understandable wish to join successfully with the client organization, the consultant tries to be helpful and sympathetic. If this is done uncritically, he or she runs the very grave risk of colluding with the distorted image of the situation that the client conveys. The pull to identify with the client is strong, especially in the early stages, when the alliance is so fragile. Yet in doing so, and becoming an uncritical mirror of the client's projective process, the consultant can easily help undermine the conditions necessary for organizational change and development. Alternatively, attention to projective identification as a process can increase a consultant's ability to join with a client and establish the feelings of being understood that are necessary to begin work. In one instance, for example, one author experienced utter incompetence and ineffectiveness with a group of third-year pediatric residents who were meeting to discuss their new leadership roles. At the second session, the consultant interpreted his experiences and what he had been made to feel at the first session as a reflection of what it was like to be a leader in their setting. As a result, a working alliance was established because the group felt he understood their culture and the challenges they faced.

With consultant teams, different members may be selected as targets for different aspects of the presenting situation. For example, in the juvenile justice setting, one consultant was mobilized by the grandiosity themes in the system and was actively suggesting the use of idealized design as a structured process, while at the same time the other consultant was influenced by the rigidity, the depression, and the difficulty of the site. Again, with the information services company, the junior consultant "contained" the client system's doubts about the value of the idealized strategic plan to guide operations. If understood, these projections in the consulting team can increase its ability to decipher some of the inner tensions of the host organization. If they are simply enacted, they stymie the ability of the consultants to think and act, just as they have the client organization.

One typical problem that can be understood in terms of projective identification is the tendency for consultants to over-function. Projection of massive competence and responsibility into the consultant, when enacted collusively by the consultant, serves to impoverish further the client system's ability to address important issues. The anxieties that underlie organizational problems and the fantasies that can be evoked in efforts to ad-dress them can easily lead to a primitive splitting process in which the consultant is idealized as a potential savior and the organi-zation itself is devalued. The interplay of this dynamic with the substantive issues under consideration provides a critical win-dow into the deeper dimensions of what the consultant is, in fantasy, being expected to do. With projective identification, the recipient of the projection, in whom parts of the sender are lodged, is no longer felt to be a separate person. In terms of the consulting relationship, this process can pull the consultant powerfully into and out of roles that are much more appropri-ate for actual members of the organization. The overfunction-ing consultant often takes on a kind of executive staff role that unintentionally reinforces fantasies of internal incompetence and efforts to sidestep responsibility for difficult actions.

In terms of the management of intervention efforts, one important implication of this discussion is the need for consul-tant teams (and individuals via supervision) to create occasions to work on these dynamics. Sometimes, as with the informa-tion services company, projective dynamics can only be discov-ered when a consulting team seeks out consultation itself. The first requirement is paying careful attention to one's feelings dur-ing work episodes with clients and accepting these experiences as valid data about the social field. The capacity to work produc-tively with projective processes in real time is to a very large extent a function of the consultant's self-understanding. For ex-ample, the key interaction described in the juvenile justice agency did not arise from any scheduled focus on team interactions, but erupted as friction in the work relationship of two consultants; it was only later understood in the context of the work.

One difficulty in discerning the presence of mirrored dynamics arises from the natural tendencies that each individual brings to consulting. For instance, one consultant may have a personal tendency toward overfunctioning, another toward underfunctioning. When they enter a system, this inclination in each will tend to be activated by congruent strains in the system. The difficulty is then to distinguish what is induced by the work with the client from what is naturally present in each person as a simple function of individual personalities.

Two points are particularly useful as guideposts or warning signs in understanding these situations. Experiencing oneself as somewhat "out of character," or acting in ways that seem slightly odd, is indicative of unconscious communication from the client system. An example of this, once again, was in the information services company, when the two team members experienced an uncharacteristic difficulty with collaboration as well as an unusual inability to discuss it openly. Hornstein (1980) offers a list of indicators of what he terms *counterreactions,* such as depressed feelings, repeated carelessness over arrangements, gossiping, and anxiety over the stakes of the consultancy.

However, we have also found in client systems an uncanny ability to tap into and to use preexisting tendencies and differences within the consultants. With consultant teams, different members may be selected as targets for different aspects of the presenting situation. As we mentioned earlier, at the beginning of the juvenile justice project, one consultant was particularly receptive to the commissioner's grand hopes for transformation and another was particularly sensitive to the difficulties and barriers to such change. This splitting in the client system around these issues was projected into the consultant team and served to amplify a long-standing, preexisting difference between the two consultants over organizational intervention methods. Distinguishing what is valid information about the client system under such conditions can be difficult.

Learning to understand the impact of projective identification in the consulting relationship can be a vital source of information about the client system's unconscious functioning and about how to work more effectively. If ignored, however, projective identification creates forces that can easily lead consultants to work along pathways that unintentionally collude with their client system's defensive self-understanding or can readily induce consultants into potentially destructive roles. By using the insights developed in psychoanalytic practice in the arena of organizational consultation, consultants are provided with an invaluable window into the unconscious dimensions of a client system. Using this tool requires self-reflection and puts the consultant-client relationship squarely in the center of diagnostic and intervention efforts.

References

Alderfer, C. P. "Group and Intergroup Relations." In J. R. Hackman and J. L. Suttle (eds.), *Improving Life and Work: Behavioral Sciences Approaches to Organizational Change.* Santa Monica, Calif.: Goodyear, 1977.

Bain, A. "Presenting Problems in Social Consultancy." *Human Relations,* 1976, *29* (7), 643–657.

Bion, W. R. *Experiences in Groups, and Other Papers.* London: Tavistock, 1959.

Dunphy, D. "Phases, Roles, and Myths in Self-Analytic Groups." In G. S. Gibbard, J. J. Hartman, and R. D. Mann (eds.), *Analysis of Groups: Contributions to Theory, Research, and Practice.* San Francisco: Jossey-Bass, 1974.

Gibbard, G. S., Hartman, J. J., and Mann, R. D. (eds.). *Analysis of Groups: Contributions to Theory, Research, and Practice.* San Francisco: Jossey-Bass, 1974.

Hirschhorn, L. *The Workplace Within: Psychodynamics of Organizational Life.* Cambridge, Mass.: MIT Press, 1988.

Hornstein, H. A. "Turning Barriers into Benefits: Searching for Consultants' Biases and Their Impact on Relationships with Clients." In W. W. Burke and L. D. Goodstein (eds.), *Trends and Issues in OD: Current Theory and Practice.* San Diego, Calif.: University Associates, 1980.

Horwitz, L. "Projective Identification in Dyads and Groups." *International Journal of Group Psychotherapy*, 1983, *33* (3), 259–275.

Jaques, E. "Social Systems as a Defence Against Persecutory and Depressive Anxiety." In M. Klein, P. Heimann, and R. E. Money-Kyrle (eds.), *New Directions in Psychoanalysis.* London: Tavistock, 1955.

Kanter, R. M. *When Giants Learn to Dance — Mastering the Challenges of Strategy, Management, and Careers in the 1990s.* New York: Simon & Schuster, 1989.

Klein, M. "On Identification." In *Envy and Gratitude and Other Works, 1946–1963.* New York: Delacorte Press/Seymour Laurence, 1975a.

Klein, M. "Notes on Some Schizoid Mechanisms." In *Envy and Gratitude and Other Works, 1946–1963.* New York: Delacorte Press/Seymour Laurence, 1975b.

Lawrence, G. (ed.). *Exploring Individual and Organizational Boundaries.* New York: Wiley, 1979.

Malin, A., and Grotstein, J. S. "Projective Identification in the Therapeutic Process." *International Journal of Psychoanalysis,* 1986, *47,* 26–31.

Menzies, I. "A Case Study in the Functioning of Social Systems as a Defence Against Anxiety: A Report on a Study of the Nursing Service of a General Hospital." *Human Relations,* 1960, *13,* 95–121.

Mitroff, I., and Featheringham, T. R. "Systematic Problem Solving and the Error of the Third Kind." *Behavioral Science,* 1974, *19* (6), 383–393.

Money-Kyrle, R. *Man's Picture of his World: A Psychoanalytic Study.* London: Duckworth, 1961.

Nisbet, R., and Wilson, T. "Telling More Than We Can Know: Verbal Reports on Mental Processes." *Psychological Review,* 1977, *83* (3), 231–259.

Ogden, T. H. *Projective Identification and Psychotherapeutic Technique.* New York: Aronson, 1982.

Redl, F. "Group Emotion and Leadership." *Psychiatry,* 1963, *5,* 573–596.

Rice, A. K. "The Role of the Specialist in the Community." *Human Relations,* 1949, *2,* 176–187.

Rice, A. K. *The Enterprise and Its Environment.* London: Tavistock, 1963.

Salancik, G., and Pfeffer, J. "An Examination of Need Satisfaction Models of Job Satisfaction." *Administrative Science Quarterly,* 1977, *22* (3), 427–456.

Searles, J. F. "Tranference Psychosis in the Psychotherapy of Schizophrenia." *International Journal of Psychoanalysis,* 1963, *44*, 249–281.

Segal, H. *The Work of Hanna Segal.* New York: Aronson, 1981.

Senge, P. *The Fifth Discipline: The Art and Practice of the Learning Organization.* New York: Doubleday/Currency, 1990.

Smith, K. "Toward a Conception of Organizational Currents." *Group and Organization Studies,* 1984, *9* (2), 285–312.

Steele, F. *Consulting for Organizational Change.* Amherst: University of Massachusetts Press, 1975.

Steele, F. *Organizational Consultation.* Reading, Mass.: Addison-Wesley, 1977.

Walsh, J. "Cityville, USA: Learning from Adversity." In N. Herrick (ed.), *Improving Government.* New York: Praeger, 1983.

Weiss, R. "Issues in Holistic Research." In S. Becker, B. Geer, P. Riesman, and R. Weiss (eds.), *Institutions and the Person: Papers Presented to Everett C. Hughes.* Chicago: Aldine, 1968.

Wells, L. "The Group as a Whole: A Systemic Socioanalytical Perspective on Group Relations." In J. Gillette and M. McCollom (eds.), *Groups in Context: A New Perspective in Group Relations.* Reading, Mass.: Addison-Wesley, 1990.

Winnicott, D. W. *The Maturational Processes and the Facilitating Environment.* New York: International Universities Press, 1965.

14

The Psychodynamics of Upheaval: Intervening in Merger and Acquisition Transitions

Roderick Gilkey

More than twenty years have passed since Harry Levinson (1970) published his classic article "A Psychologist Diagnoses Merger Failures." In this paper Levinson argued that although merger derailments are blamed on financial and technical problems, these failures actually result from psychological factors unrecognized and unmanaged by corporate leaders. He urged executives to try to gain a better understanding of their motives, needs, and fundamental assumptions before pursuing such ventures. Unfortunately, despite the acuity of his insights, Levinson's cautionary advice seems to have gone largely unheeded. Mergers and acquisitions are still designed with business and financial fit as primary considerations, while psychological and cultural issues are usually secondary concerns. Since Levinson's article appeared, the volume and size of mergers and acquisitions have increased steadily. The flurry of activity has been accompanied by a rate of failure that is regrettably predictable. By numerous accounts, over 60 percent of these transactions fail to meet expectations (Balloun, 1985). In one study, two-thirds

of the mergers and acquisitions failed to produce earnings equivalent to certificates of deposit (Magnet, 1984). These dismal
results lead us to ask why so little has been learned over the
past two decades about successfully managing such ventures.

Psychological Dilemmas in the Postmerger Environment

Economic theory and principles of rational self-interest do little
to explain why the level of merger activity is so high despite
the low rates of return. A more promising avenue of inquiry
is offered by a psychoanalytic perspective that addresses the invisible and unconscious dynamics underlying merger activity.
Previous efforts to describe the psychological factors affecting
postmerger performance have been either very general, often
failing to address unconscious dynamics, or very specific, focusing only on selected psychodynamic themes. This chapter attempts to identify the broad array of psychological dilemmas
present in a postmerger environment, while addressing the underlying psychodynamic causes of those difficulties, by using
a framework suggested by Erik Erikson (1963). He described
the progression of human development as a series of eight predictable stages, each consisting of a normative conflict or developmental crisis that must be resolved before the individual
can move on to the next stage (see Table 14.1).

This schema provides a comprehensive map for understanding the broad array of developmental issues and unconscious conflicts that human beings must master as they mature,
and it also provides a valuable model for identifying and understanding some of the major psychodynamic upheavals caused
by a corporate merger. Mergers and acquisitions, like any major
change, disrupt individual and organizational equilibrium. Old
psychological contracts are broken, loyalties and informal networks are undermined, and a sense of purpose and direction
is often lost. Erikson has noted that the stress associated with
major disruptions in life routine can create a regression in which
all of the conflicts associated with earlier life need to be
renegotiated. The dysfunctional levels of stress associated with
corporate upheavals can precipitate severe regressions. For example, an employee coping with the demands of a newly merged

corporation and with new management must first deal with the issue of basic trust. The most predictable normative conflict facing such employees is the reacquisition of basic trust in a turbulent environment that is more likely to reinforce their sense of basic mistrust. Regrettably, many mergers fail to deal effectively with the psychological requirements of employees and thus do not help the organization move through the predictable sequence of psychosocial conflicts that follow these major upheavals. In failing to reestablish employees' capacities for basic trust, autonomy, and initiative (the first three strengths identified by Erikson's model), these ventures frequently flounder. They are unable to overcome the regressive impact of such major reorganization and restore the strengths and commitments of their employees.

In the sections that follow, the psychological dilemmas associated with postmerger stress will be discussed in the sequence suggested by Erikson's model. This chapter assumes that such a radical reorganization creates a dramatic regression in the lives of both individuals and organizations and forces them to deal with the earliest psychological conflicts associated with growth and development.

The data for this chapter were gathered as part of a two-year study that focused on successful postmerger management practices. Over 100 interviews were conducted with a diverse range of individuals, including CEOs, board members, key executives, investment bankers, management consultants, and merger and acquisition lawyers. The merger of Allied and Signal corporations represented some of the best transition/integration efforts we observed in postmerger environments. The overall findings of both this research and a related study of family dynamics in postmerger organizations have been reported elsewhere (McCann and Gilkey, 1988; Fulmer and Gilkey, 1988). These studies serve as the basis for the observations that follow.

Basic Trust Versus Basic Mistrust

In the developmental sequence suggested by Erikson, we can chart the predictable sequence of conflicts associated with the regression brought on by a merger or acquisition. The issue of

Table 14.1. Normative Conflict and Human Development.

Normative Conflict	Potential Intervention
1. Basic Trust Versus Basic Mistrust	Provide clear communication and detailed information about the transition process and the task forces that are involved. Communicate realistic expectations and avoid overly optimistic reassurances and promises that cannot be kept. Address issues of job security as realistically and promptly as possible.
2. Autonomy Versus Doubt and Shame	Define roles quickly and provide opportunities for participation in the merger transition process whenever possible. Promote the venture and the value it can create for everyone. Begin clarifying expectations to give people a benchmark against which to operate.
3. Initiative Versus Guilt	Help survivors deal with guilt by providing clear information about the decision-making processes and strategic objectives, so that there is a way for them to understand why they are a part of the new venture (and why others may have had to leave). Communicate a vision in sufficient detail to allow employees to take on an active role in managing the merger. Continue clarifying roles and provide linkages (clear reporting relationships) to the transition team.
4. Industry Versus Inferiority	Restate the vision, including the rationale for the merger. State clear guidelines and expectations about how to succeed in the new organization. Communicate an intermediate vision, how people should manage in the meantime—in the chaotic period between "no longer" and "not yet."
5. Identity Versus Identity Confusion	Clarify the roles, expectations, and structures that will exist in the postmerger environment. Help employees identify career paths and understand the promotional system and the performance appraisal process. Provide clear feedback of how individual employees are doing and what they need to be doing to continue their successful participation.

6. Intimacy Versus Isolation

Clarify the importance of individual contributions of employees to the overall venture. Specify as much as possible the ways in which they are valued members in the new order. Avoid arrogance and partisan politics while emphasizing a collaborative approach — for example, you belong here, you are one of us.

7. Generativity Versus Stagnation

Help the organization and employees further develop a sense of their mission and the most effective strategies for realizing it. Clarify the most important priorities and highest values of the firm, and what employees can do to best serve both.

8. Integrity Versus Despair

Communicate the sense of value you place in past as well as present contributions. Link your recognition of those accomplishments to the future vision of the company.

basic trust versus basic mistrust is primary. Employees at all
levels want to know whether the new environment will be at
least as predictable, stable, and benevolent as the previous one.
Until these issues are resolved, the contributions and commitments of employees will be tentative and conditional. These dynamics may well underlie what has been described by terms such
as *postmerger drift* (Pritchett, 1985) and *psychological quit* (Greenhalgh, 1980), where employees are physically present at work
but unable or unwilling to devote themselves effectively to the
tasks at hand. Without a fundamental psychological substrate
of trust and hope, the ability of employees to recover from the
disruptive effects of such major reorganizations can be severely
impaired.

The disruption of this most fundamental sense of security and well-being exacerbates the general sense of loss that
occurs after a merger. Such loss reactions are normal and expected, but if they are not well managed they can lead to pro-
tracted periods of dysfunctional depression. In his study of
depression, Sigmund Freud ([1917] 1957) distinguished between
mourning, a normative condition of sadness and grief following a loss, and melancholia, a pathological condition extending
beyond a normal period of grief and producing a highly dysfunctional detachment from life. In a postmerger environment,
the mourning process must be managed in a psychologically
effective and humane manner to avoid the more serious problems associated with depression. A natural and predictable
period of mourning follows major corporate change, and the
stronger the attachment and loyalty of employees, the greater
their need to mourn the loss of the old company and the previous
regime. Managers must facilitate the mourning process to assist
employees and to revitalize the organization. One corporation
that was very sensitive to these dynamics staged a mock funeral
to eulogize a product being phased out. Key individuals and
contributions were honored as part of the process of saying goodbye and mourning the passing of an era. There was a general
recognition that employees had suffered the loss of products in
which they had made significant emotional investments.

Levinson (1972) identifies four types of loss that occur during times of organizational upheaval. They include:

1. The loss of love, which in this context involves the loss of familiar work relationships, products, and work settings. In our field research we were told of an unexpected work stoppage at a recently acquired bank on the day the sign with the name of the old bank on it was replaced by one bearing the bank's new name. Members of the parent bank's transition team traveled to the branch to talk with employees and to help them deal with their unanticipated grief reaction to the loss of "their" sign, which had been a landmark in the center of their small community for decades.

2. The loss of support that occurs when ties to valued subordinates, superiors, and networks are disrupted. In one dramatic case a senior executive became severely depressed following a postmerger reorganization when three of her protégés were reassigned to another division of the company. Her emotional attachment to these younger managers and her personal investment in their development made her vulnerable to a profound grief reaction when they were unexpectedly removed from her division.

3. The loss of sensory input resulting from changes in the amount or type of information received by the individual. This loss of input creates confusion and counterproductive anxiety. In one case, a highly valued sales team resigned because members, having received no information about their new role in a recently merged company, assumed that they would be let go anyway.

4. The loss of the capacity to act, caused by loss of power when organizations are destabilized and individuals are displaced. One manager reported his consternation at seeing employees in one of his plants "wandering around in a daze . . . with no one seeming to be doing anything" several weeks after a particularly chaotic merger.

The inevitable sense of loss experienced during a merger is rooted in the deepest core of the personality. That core consists of the primary psychological attachments that create the capacity to trust, the basic strength that underlies all other psychological strengths. Failure to deal with the psychological issues can evoke primitive responses from the members of an organization who are reexperiencing anxieties and conflicts from the earliest stages of their lives. This phenomenon was described by Elliott Jaques (1976) when he wrote about paranoiagenic organizations, settings where increasing levels of stress are accompanied by decreasing flows of information so that paranoid symptoms appear. In these cases, the loss of information and supportive relationships appears to be responsible for the loss of trust and emergence of paranoid delusions in the organization. Such extreme cases point to the depth of crisis and regression that can be brought about by unmanaged organizational change.

Autonomy Versus Doubt and Shame

Accompanying the struggle for a renewed sense of trust is the predictable conflict over whether one can regain a sense of autonomy sufficient to overcome feelings of doubt and shame. The general confusion associated with merger transitions makes it difficult for people to maintain role clarity and continuity of involvement. Employees can lose the ability to function as autonomous contributors, resulting in a loss of self-esteem and increased feelings of personal doubt and shame. The normative struggles are intensified when the acquiring firm tries to exert excessive control and begins to operate in a crisis mode (Mirvis and Marks, 1986). This crisis mentality, and the anxiety that gives rise to it, is often a consequence of poor planning and execution during the initial phases of the merger. It is further exacerbated by the lack of sound transition planning and the absence of transition management structures and systems. Faced with potentially overwhelming confusion, disruption, and loss of control, executives often try to centralize their power as a part of a "defensive retreat." In operating as an isolated control center, they give themselves the illusion of being in charge by screening out anxiety-provoking (but often critical) information. The loss of information from below impairs the ability of these executives to cope with the turbulence. In addition, they can also try to gain control by seizing power and monopolizing the exercise of management prerogatives. The effects of such tactics are paradoxical, since top management gains a sense of control by disempowering other employees, who are then unable to act with efficacy. In the extreme, the management-by-crisis approach can create the very loss of control and precipitate the crisis it was attempting to prevent. Management interventions that undermine the ability of employees to assume responsibility and to act autonomously ultimately impede the developmental progression that must be made to overcome the losses in productivity and performance that are associated with reorganization.

Initiative Versus Guilt

Even successful mergers and acquisitions have the capacity to evoke strong feelings of debilitating unconscious guilt. The most obvious causes are related to the rationalizing, downsizing, and outplacement programs that frequently occur after a merger. Those individuals who are not affected are prone to suffer from "survivor's guilt" — to feel anxious and guilty about having passed through the crisis with impunity. As one manager stated, "I simply don't understand by what right I have remained here while so many good people have been forced out in this deal." This reaction is often seen in two groups of newcomers, the young talents who are brought in to be groomed for leadership positions in the new organization, and senior managers, who were retained because of their continued ability to contribute. Both groups share certain characteristics, including a high value to the organization, a painful awareness of the loss of their predecessors, and a sense that their good fortune may be arbitrary and ill-deserved and, at worst, gained through the misfortune of others. Young managers can be particularly vulnerable. One such individual joined a company after an acquisition and downsizing program had led to the outplacement of many senior people in her group. Of her early days in the organization, she recalled, "It was the most awkward experience I've ever had. I felt undeserving. I had just been hired and only weeks later survived the large downsizing when people many years my senior had been let go. Then I was promoted to group head. It was so uncomfortable I avoided calling my people together for more than two weeks."

An additional and deeper source of unconscious guilt evident in mergers and acquisitions is related to Oedipal issues. The presence of such dynamics is hardly surprising, since the language of mergers and acquisitions is very Oedipal; the images evoked by terms such as *suitors, white knights, black knights, greenmail,* and *poison pills* are more closely connected to romantic quests than to corporate transactions (Hirsch, 1987). The winners and losers of these dramatic encounters are reenacting romantic quests that have their origins in our early psychological development in the family, where we first encounter rivalrous competition for the affection of others.

In the struggles that are associated with merger and acquisition quests, success can easily come at the price of unconscious guilt. A poignant example of such dynamics involved a senior executive who entered treatment after he was asked by his company to run one of its newly acquired firms. His work was made very difficult by the strong-armed, condescending tactics of his own corporation. He felt that he had become an unwitting accomplice in a brutal exercise of power. At one point he reported a dream in which he was trying to rescue some small helpless people from a marauding bear. His associations with the dream centered on a time when he had let out of its cage a small wild animal, which had then bitten his younger brother. He felt pained by the destructive forces he saw unleashed. His work became a source of conflict and his guilt soon overran any real sense of accomplishment. He felt he was becoming burned out, and ultimately he resigned. Clearly, if an acquiring company treats its new employees in an insensitive and callous manner, it can inadvertently exacerbate guilt reactions and impair the performance of its critical leaders.

Industry Versus Inferiority

In a properly managed postmerger transition, employees are helped through a process that reaffirms their capacity for basic trust in the organization and its mission, restores their ability to act in an autonomous manner, and reactivates their desire to take initiative. The transition state following a merger helps restore the ability of both individuals and the organization to recover from the disorganizing and regressive effects of the merger. Transition task forces and other mechanisms designed to facilitate the change process restore psychological strengths. A general restabilization makes it possible to begin to execute plans developed during the transition period. This integration stage marks the beginning of a new phase of organizational restoration in which the anticipated gains will become evident. Psychodynamically, integration reestablishes the capacity of employees to act with a sense of industry and efficacy as opposed to a sense of inferiority. After the upheavals of the transition stage, this new phase brings forth the challenge of settling in to accomplish the real mission of the venture and to achieve measurable results. The challenges and questions addressed are more directly work related and strategic. Now that we are a functioning team with a sense of direction, can we accomplish our objectives?

The answer is in large part determined by the effectiveness of the previous period, the transition stage. If the transition process addresses the psychological needs of employees effectively, they will be able to devote themselves fully to the tasks at hand. If, however, the psychological aftershocks have not been managed, very basic issues — trust, autonomy, and initiative — will continue to be the focus, and the ability of employees to become effective contributors in the new environment will be impeded.

It is at this juncture, six to eight months after a merger or acquisition transaction has occurred, that the first clear indication of the success or failure of the venture is likely to be revealed. Because the causes of failure are not well understood, however, interventions are often misdirected. Organizations tend to become immersed in symptomatic behavior and activity that further detracts from their true objectives. Abraham Zaleznik (1989) describes the general tendency of organizations to become involved in what he called *psychopolitics*, where energy is directed toward managing unconscious anxiety about the workers' place in the firm rather than toward their actual performance. Employees and management can become focused on process instead of substance. To the extent that the transition process is undermanaged, the integration stage will be plagued by unresolved psychological and political issues that become a dominant agenda, detracting from the accomplishment of the firm's actual mission. These unresolved issues create further conflicts and anxieties that require sizable expenditures of energy. In extreme cases, the collective response of employees becomes symptomatic, diverting major corporate activities and functions from accomplishing real work toward alleviating unconscious anxiety. Observers such as Menzies (1960) and Jaques (1976) describe how social systems exist at two distinct levels—the manifest and consciously agreed-on level, where form and content are consistent with stated organizational purposes, and the latent and unconsciously derived level, where form and content are congruent with unstated and often disavowed objectives. These objectives often include managing unconscious anxiety and guilt, a highly problematic aftereffect of any merger.

An example of these difficulties can be seen in the case of two recently merged consumer products companies that held prolonged discussions about how to establish mechanisms and procedures to reconcile differences in the benefits programs and performance appraisal systems. Meanwhile organizational performance declined sharply, and the benefits administration department became chaotically dysfunctional. This case is an example of the effects of psychopolitics and of what Howard Baum (1987) refers to as the *invisible bureaucracy*. In his studies, Baum found that bureaucratic organizations tended to deal with unconscious conflicts and anxieties by activating a number of intrapsychic defenses. He noted their tendency to define organizational problems in technical rather than interpersonal or political terms to avoid the anxieties associated with more personal forms of conflict. Consequently, when technical expertise was mobilized in the service of defensive needs, the unconscious agenda to minimize anxiety often worked against the realistic need to take in more information and to consider alternative courses of action to solve political differences. These forms of unconscious defenses divert energy from the real task at hand by dealing with the unconscious needs of the employee (to find comfort or escape, for instance) instead of with the actual needs of the organization. In extreme cases, as Baum (1987, p. 26) notes, "apparently rational approaches to substantive problems may founder atop unconscious struggles over authority."

Clearly, the need to expend energy to deal with unresolved conflicts from earlier stages of the merger process detracts from the ability to perform optimally at later stages. The need of employees to resolve past problems and to cope with current challenges can be overwhelming and anxiety-provoking. Thus it is not surprising to find that both individuals and organizations can become symptomatic and dysfunctional, a situation that creates a secondary set of problems. As the decline in performance becomes evident, the sense of inferiority grows and the level of morale declines. In the case involving the impasse of two merged consumer products companies, an outside consultant was called in to assess the situation. When the members realized that they had immersed themselves in procedural issues at the expense of performance, they were shocked into a highly uncomfortable awareness, which unfortunately only exacerbated the sense of inferiority already present in the new company.

An organization's ability to execute its plans and achieve its objectives during the integration stage rests on the quality of its previous transition efforts. Similarly, the ability of employees to replace inferiority with a sense of industry also rests on that previous stage, which, if optimally managed, restores the basic psychological strengths that were tested during the postmerger process. The developmental progression of both individuals and organizations is cumulative.

Identity Versus Identity Confusion

The final consolidation of a merger occurs in the integration stage, when employees develop a shared sense of purpose and identity based on a synthesis of their past identities in their organizations. They convey a sense of being part of a winning team with shared ideals and collective goals. The unconscious bonds that develop during this stage allow employees to adapt to changing circumstances because they are now guided by an internalized sense of direction. They do not have to become absorbed by procedural or policy issues or impeded by questions about authority roles.

One of the most successful efforts to manage the identity crisis created by a merger was made by the Allied Corporation. Both its first major merger with Bendix and its later merger with Allied (to create the Allied-Signal Corporation) were regarded as models of effective transition management. For example, despite the media circus and evident chaos surrounding the Allied-Bendix merger, the venture emerged, in the words of *Fortune*'s Myron Magnet (1984, p. 44), as "a model of how to put two companies together." The efforts of Allied CEO Ed Hennessey created what was described as "one of the most successful transition management programs in modern corporate history." The success of this endeavor is largely attributable to Hennessey's decision to create a single transition management task force composed of representatives from both corporations. This decision reinforced the effort to develop a common corporate identity from two previously separate enterprises. The task force was structured to provide as broad a representation as possible of all of the major functions and business components. The goal was to draw on the best people, practices, and resources from both firms as they attempted to forge a common new identity.

During the five months the task force worked to develop plans to integrate the two firms, they had eleven preliminary objectives:

1. Begin channeling information to decision-makers.
2. Help form positive attitudes about the merger.
3. Communicate both internally and externally about the new company.
4. Define common terms to clarify communication and objectives.
5. Support any business unit requesting assistance.
6. Identify problems threatening the transition effort.

7. Identify policy differences that would impede the creation of the new organization.
8. Identify overlaps and duplications in staffing so recommendations could be made for downsizing.
9. Set timetables for each phase of the integration stage.
10. Organize task force members' specific activities so they had clear lines of authority and responsibility.
11. Deal with problems by identifying organizational options [McCann and Gilkey, 1988, p. 175].

These efforts not only promoted the development of a new corporate identity, but also addressed the underlying psychological dynamics described earlier, including the need to instill basic trust, clarify roles and expectations, facilitate the exercise of autonomy, and foster the use of initiative to deal with the challenges of merging the organizations.

Intimacy Versus Isolation

In Erikson's model, the term *intimacy* refers to an individual's newly emerging capacity for closeness and mutuality following the acquisition of a stable sense of personal identity in late adolescence. The organizational equivalent of this personal strength is the firm's enhanced capacity for teamwork and collaboration, evident in high-commitment organizations. The shared sense of purpose and direction, gained from the previous integration phase, provides the foundation for such high degrees of cooperation. At best, the various groups and teams that form are capable of reaching unexpected levels of synergy and achievement.

Freud's early investigations into this realm highlight the need to manage the psychological dynamics to foster the development of groups that share a strong identification with a leader and a mission. In submerging their individual aims to those of the group, members come to share an ego ideal or common set of internalized aspirations. From a psychological perspective, it is this focus on common ideals and purposes that allows groups to become more than simply aggregates of individuals. The bonding that occurs in effective groups is made possible by leaders.

Such leaders can emerge in a postmerger organization if the environment has been one that engenders trust, sponsors autonomy, and encourages initiative-taking. As one of the key figures in the postmerger task force at Allied-Signal observed, "We found that when we managed the transition process well we had a ready supply of highly motivated effective leaders available. I think our efforts helped sponsor many of them. These people emerged from the transition process stronger and more highly motivated than before — many of them as informal leaders." These leaders came from both Allied and Signal, as did the variety of teams that contributed to the success of the effort. The intimacy, enthusiasm, and collaboration observable in such organizations stand in strong contrast to the factionalism, divisiveness, and competition present in many postmerger environments, where a sense of isolation can easily prevail.

Generativity Versus Stagnation

Senior executives find that the opportunity to help create a new organization can be a fulfilling and rewarding experience. As one executive commented, "Putting this new organization together has been the most exhausting, exhilarating, and rewarding experience in my professional life!" This individual echoed the sentiments of many of his counterparts, who commented on the satisfaction they gained from overcoming the odds and successfully launching a new venture. The sense of satisfaction these individuals reported seemed to be based on the feelings of mastery and accomplishment they experienced as they saw their efforts to create something new come to fruition.

These positive outcomes are, however, uncommon. More typical are ventures that flounder and create a feeling of stagnation and failure. From a psychological vantage point, they reinforce the vulnerability of mid-career executives to feelings of obsolescence and even of uselessness and depression (Levinson, 1970). Failure to deal with the psychological challenges of a given stage, like all developmental failures, is a function of the difficulties in managing the previous phases. When a merger effort flounders and the two firms are unable to develop a shared sense of purpose and identity, the ensuing decline in performance and morale reinforces a sense of stagnation in both individuals and organizations.

The causes of such failures are of three general types: (1) strategic failures, where the basic idea of merging the companies is flawed because of fundamental differences in the operations or cultures of the firms; (2) inadequate postmerger transition management, which fails to deal with the psychological dynamics I have described; and (3) a failure to consolidate the merger. The latter difficulty is described by Andrew Pettigrew (1985) as one of the primary causes of poor outcomes. In this context, the rapidity with which the senior company pursues another merger opportunity can imperil its previous transaction. The strain on financial and human resources can easily exceed the capacity to manage another new venture successfully, and the previous merger also remains incomplete and adrift.

Integrity Versus Despair

In the most senior executive group it is possible that individual and organizational tasks will reinforce each other. The personal struggle of the executive to gain a sense of integrity over despair promotes a ready involvement in self-reflection that serves the interests of both the individual and the organization. In questioning the worth of their achievements and the validity of their assumptions, senior executives can add great value to the deliberations that go on in their corporate environments. The maturity and depth of perspective required to answer important personal questions can also be used to deal with critical questions about corporate mission and strategy. Ideally this maturity can add to the rigor of corporate debate, since more value-driven criteria for decision making are advanced by the most mature senior executives. Such ideal situations differ from reality, however, and prompt us to ask whether the current high failure rate of mergers reflects a more serious underlying crisis in leadership development. The inability to create and sustain viable value-adding corporate partnerships may reflect not so much a lack of business acumen as a failure to develop mature leaders who are capable of creating successful collaborative ventures that serve both individual and collective needs.

The ultimate criterion for the success of any venture is whether its sponsors would choose to do it again if given the opportunity. Those individuals and companies that can answer in the affirmative are capable of experiencing what Erikson described as *ego integrity* — a sense of assurance that, despite setbacks, successes have been sufficient to provide a sense of accomplishment and confidence. This confidence takes the form of belief in the soundness of one's endeavors and the trustworthiness of one's predecessors and successors. Such an affirmative spirit provides the links of continuity necessary to sustain individual and organizational life. In accepting both the limitations and benefits of their endeavors, such individuals possess what Erikson (1963, p. 269) calls "an emotional integration which permits participation by followership as well as acceptance of the responsibility of leadership." This identification with roles and responsibilities greater than their own permits individuals to transcend the limits of their own abilities. Their sense of dedication allows them to serve when necessary as leader-statesmen or servant-followers. In pursuing ego needs beyond their own, possessors of psychological integrity fulfill collective aspirations and promote the highest ideals. Perhaps few individuals attain such a station or play such a vital role, but organizations do well to try to develop an environment that nurtures these qualities in all employees.

The individual psychological dynamics that come into play after a merger constitute a crucial factor that requires understanding and intervention, but these individual dynamics do not occur in isolation. Significant social or social psychological forces are also at play. Among the most important of these are family dynamics. The language used in describing mergers and acquisitions provides important evidence about the unconscious meaning of these transactions. The language of the premerger environment is the language of romance, rivalry, and courtship. In contrast, with the consummation of the merger, the tone and content of the language used to describe significant relationships change. Although there may be fleeting references to a honeymoon period, the more staid language of marriage and commitment quickly replaces the language of romantic conquest.

To understand fully the psychodynamic aspects of postmerger environments we must address the family issues that emerge after the romance and drama of premerger courtship has passed.

Family Dynamics in Corporate Mergers

A research effort designed to learn more about the unconscious family dynamics associated with merger transitions involved interviewing more than 200 executives. Although the need to manage family dynamics during a merger was noted in Levinson's earliest work on the subject, the nature of these dynamics is only just beginning to be understood. Executives interviewed frequently referred to the problems of dealing with a blended family. This was instructive, because much of the thinking about family issues in merged corporate environments has focused on the difficulties of nuclear families. Blended families, or reconstituted families as they are sometimes called, where both parents have been married before, are usually more complex and difficult to manage than nuclear ones. The metaphor of the blended corporate family was first suggested by one executive who was part of a four-person team who started a small high-tech business during the 1970s. After five years, the company was acquired by a larger firm. During the past six years, this official has lived through three mergers with successively larger companies. He suggested: "Maintaining motivation after a merger involves looking for the right balance between corporate control and small business unit autonomy in a merged company. It's a little like trying to motivate a teenage stepchild. You've got to know what's important and not hassle too much or an adolescent will become completely demotivated and do nothing, or rebel and do something really bad. It is especially tough if you're not the natural parent and your values are both different and new."

The psychological challenges facing a blended corporation with multiple "family" histories are very different from those of nuclear corporations, which have not experienced such major reorganizations and still have direct links to their founders. The differences that distinguished the two types of firms included five dimensions: (1) the structure of the system, (2) the purpose of the system, (3) the tasks of the system, (4) the forces influencing managers, and (5) the forces impinging on the system. A summary of these conflicts and of the differences between nuclear and blended corporations appears in Table 14.2.

**Table 14.2. The Differences Between
Nuclear and Blended Corporations.**

Structural Issues	
Nuclear	Blended
People and systems have evolved with the organization.	Previous management systems and personnel exert continued influence on current employees.
Everyone has experienced the same management and management style.	Varied experiences of being managed by different leadership styles, systems, and personnel.
Employees belong to one major system.	Multiple systems are present.
Membership is clearly defined, based on historical continuity, selection procedures, and a formal organizational chart — a relatively closed system.	A more open system where personnel comes in from outside the organization in roles and relationships that are often initially unclear.
Relationships are clearly defined and reinforced by social networks and systems that offer rites of passage, rituals, and a common history and folklore that support the organization.	Bonds uniting people are sudden, often arbitrary, and ill-defined. There is no sense of historical continuity, body of shared experience, or ritual to support the formation of a bonding unit or culture.
Boundaries are clear and based on historical precedent.	Boundaries are fuzzy and there are no precedents.
Purpose of the System	
Nuclear	Blended
Clearly defined mission and strategy that come from within the company, from its own people, past and present.	Sense of mission and understanding of strategy are often unclear and come in part or whole from "outsiders."

Table 14.2. The Differences Between
Nuclear and Blended Corporations, Cont'd.

Tasks of the System

Nuclear	Blended
Consistent with the overall level of the organization's stage of development.	Often inconsistent and incongruent since different companies in different phases of development must address varying tasks in managing growth/maturity.
Definition of task flows from a central management system that has enjoyed continuity. Roles are defined.	Task definition comes from changed and multiple sources. Roles are defined.

Factors Influencing Managers

Nuclear	Blended
Because of strong internal traditions and shared experiences, "outside" managerial experience and relationships exert little influence over current performance.	Continuing contact with past systems, practices, and personnel can exert great influence and make the integration process more difficult.
Ideals from the past serve the interest of continuity during times of change.	Ideals from the past, to the extent they have been internalized and lived, are often distracting.
Career paths are stable and perceived as relatively predictable.	Career paths and plans are changed, thus raising concerns about fairness and future memberships.
Geographic location and the need to move seen as relatively predictable.	Location and moving are major, often realistic, concerns.
Patterns and systems for exerting influence are clear and established.	Employee influence systems are disrupted and significant forms or procedures for influencing the company are often lost, thus exacerbating all the previously cited difficulties (loyalty conflicts, loss of sense of purpose, and so on).
The levels of dissent, innovation, and risk taking are relatively clear.	The limits for "deviant" behavior not defined; risk-averse behavior usually prevails, although the system may inadvertently encourage behind-the-scenes rebellions.

Table 14.2. The Differences Between
Nuclear and Blended Corporations, Cont'd.

Forces That Impinge on the System	
Nuclear	Blended
External sources of influence on the system are arranged in stable and predictable patterns.	Influence and control are suddenly exerted by new players outside the organization, whose language, methods, and purposes are often unclear and unpredictable.
Locus of expertise is internal and relatively centralized.	Locus of expertise is more external, creating confusion about the locus and nature of power and influence in the system.
Stakeholders are defined and their agendas are usually known.	New stakeholders are present and their agendas are often unknown or unclear.

Managing the Blended Corporate Family

There are strong parallels between managing the blended family—given the presence of legal constraints, lawyers, ex-spouses, divergent family histories, rules, rituals, traditions, and ideals—and managing a corporate merger, in both type and scale. The lack of a shared history with a common vision of both past and future is one of the most difficult challenges that the newly blended corporation, like the blended family, must face. There are five major commonly occurring problems.

1. New Structure and Systems. In merged organizations, authority structures and systems of control are unclear and in flux, leading to confusion and anxiety. The lack of historical precedent means that such basic issues as the travel and entertainment policy, or even the more personal issue of dress or grooming standards, may need to be clarified or discussed. At a more fundamental level, the question "Who decides what?" must be addressed before equilibrium can be restored.

2. The Power of Outsiders. The fact that power is exercised by intermediaries and outsiders, who ordinarily play a more minor role in the company (if they have a role at all), exacerbates this problem. Like a newly blended family that may have to deal with judges, lawyers, psychiatrists, and social workers, a newly blended corporation has to conduct its business in an arena where investment bankers, brokers, and consultants all exert power and influence. In such an environment, the sources of expertise and authority become more decentralized and diffuse, which can undermine the effectiveness of the management system. Paul Sadler, a manager in an acquired corporation, disdainfully commented, "Whenever I have to get input from above to deal with a problem, I think about going directly to McKinsey, since those are the guys who are really calling the shots around here now. It was bad enough when you tried to get information from above and you'd have to wait around. Now you wait and when you hear something you're not even sure it's coming from your own organization!"

In addition, the appearance of "outsiders" from the acquiring company disrupts mentoring relationships and career paths, as new structures, demands, and competitors appear. The new managers can become resentful, much like a parent in a blended family who has to manage someone else's children. The resentment between new managers and employees is often mutual and is particularly likely to arise when the stronger party exercises power in an insensitive manner.

3. Territorial Battles. Previous alliances and power structures persist, often overriding or causing individuals to resist the new authority structure. The party in power before the marriage took place can easily invoke power again and use it to impede the unification of the family. Under such circumstances an informal organization can form, thwarting efforts to establish a more formal system of control. The new corporate family needs this control, however, to develop as a consistent and well-defined unit. Old loyalties and ties, when combined with sibling rivalry and intergenerational conflicts, can be an overwhelming barrier to unification and growth.

4. Boundary Delineation. Membership in the new family system is no longer clearly defined after a major reorganization. Since conflicts inevitably arise as the company defines its new identity, it is not possible to determine easily who is and who is not meeting the new criteria. Like adolescents in a family, long-term employees can experience the greatest difficulty in dealing with the new situation. The longer the individual's association with a particular group, the more likely it is that he or she will experience problems in disengaging and forming new attachments. It is therefore both understandable and ironic that some of the most loyal employees are most likely to become recalcitrant and unproductive in a new environment.

5. Start-Up Problems. The blended family must begin to work as a functional unit immediately after the merger, before sufficient historical precedent has developed to establish a smoothly operating system. In addition, there are no culturally transmitted rites of passage to assist in bridging the transition from separate to blended states.

Interventions for Blended Corporate Families

The interventions required to deal with blended family dynamics during a merger are similar to those needed to manage the individual psychological conflicts already described. Prompt communication, clarification, reassurance, and responsiveness are critical elements of effective transition management. There are a number of specific intervention strategies that can be used to alleviate the adjustment pains of employees in a blended corporate family. They are summarized in Table 14.3.

Despite the complexity of blended corporate families, predictable conflicts and dynamics can be identified and addressed.

Table 14.3. Summary of Blended Corporate
Family Problems and Interventions.

Problem	Intervention
New structure and systems	Reaffirm basic structure Clarify controls and reporting relationships Actively involve CEO and others to bridge/facilitate the transition Communicate actively
The power of outsiders	Create representative transition team Use participative management Apply "scheduled candor" Deal with an acquired company as if it were a partner in a merger Clarify general mission, strategy, and the role of external players
Territorial battles	Held transitional rites to provide social mechanisms to usher in the acceptance of the new state
The question of who fits in	Clarify job status, role, and reporting relationships Provide reassurance and feedback mechanisms Create positive new practices
Start-up problems	Build a new culture using key leadership figures, the media, and all available forms of communication Use management education to distribute information, socialize, and acculturate

1. New Structure and Systems. This normative crisis can be dealt with through a transition management program that quickly reaffirms basic structures and clarifies the control system and reporting relationships. Thus, for example, as soon as decisions are made about the "survivors" of a merger, the change in the organization should be announced so that each employee can begin to work out his or her new role and expectations. The new organization should then clarify roles and procedures

as quickly as possible. In those situations where more delibera-
tion is called for, the transition managers should make clear when
decisions will be made and announced.

Even when bad news has to be shared, a prompt announcement enables people to deal with the situation more effectively
than being forced to "wait for the other shoe to drop." Tony
Stone, general manager in the Electronics and Instrumentation
Sector at Allied, felt that "one of the major successes in Allied's
integration activities was the commitment to employees to [let
them] know about their status within two months of the merger
approval. Although some of the news was not positive, everybody from the corporate staff received written notices about [his
or her] future. Within nine months, the integration of the two
staffs was largely complete" (personal communication). Like
other blended families, blended corporate families need clear
interpretations of their situation so that members can gain an
intermediate vision of the future before the consolidation into
a functional unit takes place. When a company interprets and
clarifies the transition process and outlines the immediate steps
and inevitable uncertainties associated with each step, it can offer
support and prevent declining morale and postmerger drift.

2. The Power of Outsiders. This problem can be alleviated by
establishing a transition team composed of members from both
corporate staffs. Choosing individuals from both sides tends to
blunt the us-and-them perspective. The most carefully orchestrated merger and acquisition efforts attempt from the outset
to create a climate of mutuality and cooperation. According to
Ed Hennessey, CEO and chairman of Allied-Signal, who has
been involved in over 100 acquisitions, "If you are ever going
to make the people part work out, you have to treat the deal
as a merger, even, maybe especially, if it is an acquisition" (personal communication). This approach is not intended to be
manipulative; rather, it is an attempt to treat everyone with
respect and make all individuals feel a part of the new corporate
family as soon as possible.

At Allied-Signal these attempts were supported by what
was called "scheduled candor"; senior executives like Hennessey

made themselves available at various times, such as at senior manager seminars, to discuss openly the concerns of everyone present. Hennessey himself spoke with over 3,000 employees in various forums during the merger process.

3. Territorial Battles. Old loyalties persist long after the new organization has been established. Although it is easier to redefine jobs than to realign loyalties, in time both will happen. In the meantime, a struggle during which old allegiances and alliances continue to exert their influence in the political process may develop.

These conflicts can be alleviated by helping employees deal with the loss of the old order to which they were attached. Efforts to help employees with the mourning process described earlier can contribute to the restoration of their morale and their capacity to make new commitments.

Realigning commitments is generally easier in environments where the founding family members are not present. Although these individuals have an important symbolic role to play in ensuring continuity and continued commitment, they can unconsciously interfere with the processes needed to establish a more highly developed new organization. The employees' attachments to the previous organization and its leaders should not, however, be casually dismissed and disregarded; it is often imperative for the new management in a merger or acquisition to demonstrate its awareness of the contributions of its predecessors. In one very successful bank takeover, the acquiring bank instructed members of the transition team to spend time in the new bank talking with employees about what it was like to work for the bank (which was then privately held) before the change and to share in the exchange of stories and anecdotes about banking in the "old days." This effort was intended to provide support to people who had experienced a serious loss and who needed that loss to be acknowledged and understood by everyone. As the vice president of human resources in charge of the transition process stated, "It was important that all of us demonstrated some empathy and awareness, that we respected what they had accomplished in the bank, and also that we understood that sense of loss they were experiencing." Factionalism and divided loyalties are unavoidable parts of the normal progression after a merger; however, if the causes of these conflicts are understood and respected, managers can play a vital and constructive role in facilitating their eventual resolution.

4. Boundary Delineation. Since membership in the new family is not initially clear or ensured, a period of testing and negativism is a predictable feature of the blended corporate family. Some negativism is inevitable, but some is preventable if the proper clarifying and supportive interventions are made — such as when the firm announces quickly who will be staying and what their status will be. The next step is to provide extra reassurance. This practice was followed after the Allied-Bendix merger, when the majority of employees who were retained were offered increased responsibilities and higher salaries. After the process was completed, employee attitude surveys indicated that the morale of Bendix employees was actually higher than that of their Allied counterparts.

5. Start-Up Problems. Since there is insufficient time to develop a culture and history to support the new corporation, transitional ideologies and mediating structures have to be developed. Strong communication efforts, sponsored, if not spearheaded, by the CEO, seem to be a preferred mode of dealing with this problem in the most successful mergers. In the case of Allied-Signal, Ed Hennessey oversaw the production of a film that was shown to several thousand employees in an effort to develop a common understanding of, or ideological perspective on, the historical events in which they were participating. This self-conscious attempt to develop a common history and to build a new culture is a necessary part of the transition process for the blended corporate family. A variety of means are available for developing a common new culture. Among them is the use of management training to further the socialization and acculturation process.

Several firms have successfully used massive training and education programs to bring about a cultural change that emphasized common objectives and shared values. In addition to the information and education offered, seminars provide an opportunity for managers to meet their counterparts from different parts of the merged organization.

Whereas all of these interventions draw on the internal resources of the firms, numerous roles can also be played by outside consultants to facilitate the transition effort. Experienced consultants can help merging firms identify the psychological conflicts that will emerge and help mobilize the internal resources of the firms to deal with them. They can play a vital role as interpreters, using their experience and critical detachment to see the psychological dynamics more clearly than the participants. They can correctly diagnose the causes of postmerger problems and avoid superficial interventions that address only the symptoms of underlying problems.

The failure to anticipate and manage the psychological upheavals of a postmerger environment can derail the best-conceived strategic design. Experience suggests that attempts to achieve elusive synergies by merging the financial and operational capacities of two firms are unlikely to work without effective transition management to address the human factors. Two crucial arenas of human involvement must be addressed. First, in the premerger phase it is necessary for leaders to be critically aware of the personal motives and needs that impel them to pursue the high-risk strategies of mergers and acquisitions. Second, in the postmerger phase it is imperative that corporate leaders anticipate the predictable individual and familial dynamics that will be played out in the course of the process. Skillful planning in the initial strategic phase is unlikely to overcome poor execution in the transition phase, when the psychological forces described here must be understood and managed in a thoughtful and sensitive manner.

References

"Acquiring Without Smothering," *Fortune,* Nov. 12, 1984, pp. 22–28.

Balloun, J. *The Acquisition Management Framework.* McKinsey and Company, 1985.

Baum, H. S. *The Invisible Bureaucracy.* New York: Oxford University Press, 1987.

Erikson, E. *Childhood and Society.* (2nd ed.) New York: Norton, 1963.

Freud, S. "Mourning and Melancholia." In J. Strachey (ed. and trans.), *The Standard Edition of the Complete Psychological Works of Sigmund Freud.* Vol. 14. London: Hogarth Press, 1957. (Originally published 1917.)

Fulmer, R., and Gilkey, R. "Blended Corporate Families: Management and Organization Development." *Academy of Management Executive,* 1988, *2* (4), 275–283.

Greenhalgh, L. "A Process Model of Organizational Turnover: The Relationship with Job Security as a Case in Point." *Academy of Management Review,* 1980, *5* (2), 299–303.

Hirsch, P. *Pack Your Own Parachute.* Reading, Mass.: Addison-Wesley, 1987.

Jaques, E. *A General Theory of Bureaucracy.* London: Heinemann, 1976.

Levinson, H. "A Psychologist Diagnoses Merger Failures." *Harvard Business Review,* 1970, *48,* 20–28.

Levinson, H. "Easing the Pain of Personal Loss." *Harvard Business Review,* 1972, *50,* 80–88.

McCann, J., and Gilkey, R. *Joining Forces: Creating and Managing Successful Mergers and Acquisitions.* Englewood Cliffs, N.J.: Prentice-Hall, 1988.

Magnet, M. "Help! My Company Has Just Been Taken Over." *Fortune,* July 9, 1984, pp. 44–51.

Menzies, I. "A Case Study in the Functioning of Social Systems as a Defence Against Anxiety: A Report on a Study of the Nursing Service of a General Hospital." *Human Relations,* 1960, *13,* 95–121.

Mirvis, P., and Marks, M. "Merger Syndrome: Management by Crisis." *Mergers and Acquisitions,* 1986, *20* (3), 70–76.

Pettigrew, A. *The Awakening Giant: Continuity and Change at ICI.* New York: Oxford University Press, 1985.

Pritchett, P. *After the Merger: Managing the Shockwaves.* New York: Dow Jones Irwin, 1985.

Zaleznik, A. "Real Work." *Harvard Business Review,* 1989, *89,* 57–64.

15

Changing Organizations and Individuals: Psychoanalytic Insights for Improving Organizational Health

Isabel Menzies Lyth

Otto Fenichel (1945) once stated that social institutions arise through the efforts of individuals to satisfy their needs but that the institutions then become external realities, comparatively independent of the individuals, that affect the personality structure of the individuals, temporarily or permanently. Fenichel was using the term *institution* in a wide sense to include customs, practices, and the culture of society as well as the organizations in which consultants work. I shall be using the term mainly in the latter sense.

Institutions have an extraordinary capacity to sustain their most important characteristics over long periods of time, even when significant changes have taken place in the environment, in the demands on them, and in the resources available to meet those demands. Individuals who establish the institution or who join it later must somehow adapt themselves to "fit in," since their chance of basically changing the institution is more limited. Consultancy, however, may help in this process.

The main way in which individuals adapt is through introjective identification, one of the major processes by which

361

children develop and form their personalities. The possibility of change by introjective identification is retained throughout life, even for mature adults. On entering an institution, individuals must take in and identify with the main characteristics of the institution if they want to remain there. If they cannot do this, and so fail to become sufficiently like the institution and the other members, they will find themselves under overt or covert pressure to leave. They may find the effort and the effects of trying to adapt too stressful and leave of their own accord.

The Negative Impact of Institutions on Mental Health

I will give some examples from institutions whose influence on their members was detrimental to their mental health and to their growth and maturation. The first is from a study of the nursing service of a general teaching hospital in London (Menzies Lyth, 1988). In this institution, the level of stress among the nurses was extremely high. At first glance, this seemed hardly surprising. Nurses are in constant contact with people who are physically ill, injured, or dying. They are confronted with the reality of suffering and death as few other people are. Their work involves tasks that, by ordinary standards, are distasteful, disgusting, and frightening. Intimate physical contact with patients arouses strong libidinous and erotic feelings that may be hard to control. The nurses' feelings are strong and mixed: pity, compassion, and love; guilt and anxiety; hatred and resentment of the patients who arouse such strong feelings; envy of the care given to the patients. Nurses also have to cope with the feelings of patients and relatives and other nurses. The feelings are deep, powerful, and primitive, picking up and drawing strength from many memories and fantasies, both conscious and unconscious. However, this did not seem sufficient to explain the high level of stress in this particular nursing service. This raised the question of why the nursing service and the nurses had not come to terms more effectively with their work situation and their stress.

Among the needs that people have of institutions is their use as a defense against anxiety. This leads to the development of socially structured defense systems that arise through an attempt by individuals to externalize and give substance to their characteristic psychic defense mechanisms. A social defense system thus develops over time as the result of collusive interaction and agreement, often unconscious, between members of the organization. When facing powerful and primitive anxieties, like nurses do, people tend to regress in terms of the defenses used. This seemed to be what had happened in the nursing service.

For example, such regressed defenses appeared in the sometimes manic denial of the suffering of patients and relatives and, indeed, of the nurses themselves. The nurse-patient relationship was in a sense fragmented by the work organization, in which all the nurses looked after all the patients indiscriminately. The work took the form of multiple indiscriminate caretaking, so that close, intimate, and lengthy contact between them was limited. There were attempts to "depersonalize" both patient and nurse and to deny the significance of the individual, by emphasizing uniformity and by putting people into categories that defined their rights, privileges, and responsibilities regardless of their own needs or capacities. Attempts were made to avoid the stress of decision making by eliminating the need for decisions as far as possible by ritualization and by constant checking and counterchecking. Tasks and responsibilities tended to be located at an inappropriately elevated hierarchical level and/or entrusted to people whose capabilities far exceeded those needed for the job they were doing. This was a complicated interacting and interdependent system of defenses, which, however, had in common the attempt to deal with anxiety by avoiding it or trying to eliminate situations that might stimulate it. The system made little provision for confronting anxiety and working it through, the only way in which a real increase in the capacity to cope with it and personal maturation would take place. As a social defense system, it was ineffectual in containing anxiety. Returning to Fenichel, the social defense system that the nurses had to identify with and operate if they stayed in the service was immature and regressed. Moreover, the effect of the system on personality was to inhibit maturation and growth. This situation was not peculiar to the hospital studied. It was also characteristic of nurse training schools at the time. Here it is interesting to note that 30 to 40 percent of student nurses did not complete their training. Those who stayed were on the whole those most able to incorporate the system. Furthermore, a significant number of those who left were the more mature students who could not or would not do so. Thus the system became self-perpetuating. Those who remained accepted it and continued it. Those who did not accept it and would have wanted to change it left.

My second example comes from a study in a day nursery conducted by my colleagues Alastair Bain and Lynn Barnett to which I was a consultant (Bain and Barnett, 1982). In their study, Bain and Barnett described the discontinuity of care provided by even a single caretaker in a traditionally run day nursery. The children's intense needs for individual attention tended to mean that they did not allow the nurse to pay attention to any one child for any length of time. Other children pulled at her skirt, wanted to sit on her lap, and would push away the child who was receiving attention. The predominant pattern of relationships between adults and children was experienced as a series of discontinuities of attention, a nurse momentarily directing her attention from one child to another. The children and their claim on her attention were seen as part of a series of disconnected episodes.

A follow-up study of these children into school showed them to have identified with and to be operating that model, a model of episodic and discontinuous attention, forming a series of episodic and discontinuous relationships with their world through fleeting superficial attachments, episodic discontinuous play activities, and difficulty in sustaining continuous attention in school. I called this the *butterfly phenomenon,* the child flitting apparently aimlessly from person to person and activity to activity.

Children are, of course, more malleable and more susceptible to institutional influence than adults, although the general point holds throughout the age groups. And, sadly, unlike the "refugees" from nursing, children did not usually have the option of leaving the nursery and escaping from its adverse effects on personality development.

The Potential of Psychoanalysis
for Improving Organizational Health

Fortunately, such situations are not inevitable. In particular, it is sometimes possible through the use of institutional consultancy to change the institution in such a way as to improve the mental health of its members, as happened in both the preceding examples. The improvement in the hospital was minimal, but in the day nursery it was considerable. Children going to school after the consultancy showed little evidence of the "butterfly phenomenon." My main concern here is not with those comparatively few members of an institution who are psychiatrically ill, but rather with raising the level of mental health throughout the membership and facilitating further growth and maturation. Incidentally, a side effect of such development would be a decrease in the incidence of actual mental breakdown.

In institutional consultancy, consultants owe a great debt to psychoanalysis. We see our aim as facilitating a change in institutions that will not only benefit the institution per se, but that will incidentally improve the mental health of individual members. Sociotherapy can have a psychotherapeutic effect. Psychoanalysis was in itself a major breakthrough in improving the mental health of individuals, the clinical setting being the first significant "institution" devoted to doing so.

Psychoanalysis provides insights into the human personality and object relationships together with the conviction of the significance of the unconscious mind for experience and behavior. From Freud and later psychoanalytic research, we have come to understand the particular importance of anxiety and related defenses both to the mental health of the individual and to the functioning of institutions and the health of their members. Psychoanalysis has contributed a great deal to our knowledge of the environmental conditions that further mental health, from young babies with their mothers in their families to adults in larger institutions. Health improves as defenses are modified or abandoned and replaced by better adaptations and sublimations. Of great significance also is the growing appreciation of both transference and countertransference and, from that, the use of ourselves as an invaluable resource in understanding what is going on between our clients and ourselves and in the client institution. In institutions, it is important to make contact with the implicit as well as the unconscious. By implicit, I mean things that are quite conscious in individuals but kept secret or shared with only a few others, sometimes only outside the institution. The implicit is thus not immediately available for work. Whether unconscious or implicit, we share with psychoanalysis the task of seeking out and making manifest the hidden factors that impede healthy development.

In this context, I am reminded of the title of a paper I have never written: "Self-Diagnosis and Prescription as a Defense Against Institutional Change." This comes about when clients themselves tell us what the problem is and what they expect us to do about it. Usually the prescription implies minimal involvement in the core of the institution and often, indeed, doing something right outside. Thus, clients try to avoid change that they anticipate would be catastrophic (Bion, 1970), even if it is potentially beneficial, because it means disruption of established modes of behavior, traditional attitudes, and established relationships. It is part of our responsibility as consultants to explore the situation, revise the diagnosis, and facilitate appropriate change in the core of the institution. In doing so, consultancy becomes like psychoanalysis.

For example, the Tavistock Institute was hired by the London Fire Brigade Committee. Their diagnosis was that the brigade was suffering from a manpower shortage and needed more recruits. Our given task, the prescription, was to devise a recruitment campaign that would ensure sufficient numbers of appropriate recruits (Menzies Lyth, 1989). There really was a manpower shortage, but when we looked into the situation with the men and women of the brigade, we found that the problem stemmed mainly from the loss of existing staff who found conditions of work in the brigade unduly stressful and unsatisfying. If this loss could be reduced there would not have been much problem in getting enough good recruits. But dealing with the loss would have meant a considerable modification in the whole way the brigade operated. Sadly, in this case, the committee, which was itself far removed from and largely ignorant of the conditions of work within the brigade, could not face our diagnosis and prescription. I believe we could have worked with the brigade itself, if we had been able to gain the necessary access.

Alas, people never learn. The British government has just spent a vast sum on a recruitment campaign for nurses that produced very few recruits. The shortage of nurses is truly desperate, but the remedy lies in reducing wastage by modifying the core of the work situation, not in enticing new recruits who are soon likely to leave themselves. I am sad and perhaps rather ashamed that I predicted in about 1960 that if something basic was not done about the working conditions for nurses, exactly the situation that now exists would arise (Menzies Lyth, 1988). However, we have not yet found a way of doing anything about it.

My colleague Alastair Bain (1982) had a similar experience when he was asked to deal with several problems in a computer firm, including high wastage, low productivity, and general worker dissatisfaction. The operatives themselves told him what they thought was wrong, that is, generally rather dreary working conditions. Their own prescription was more flexible hours, being allowed to chat with each other as in an ordinary office job, free tea and coffee, more holidays — things to make life more comfortable. Bain was quite unconvinced that this was the substance of the matter. From further exploration a rather terrible picture emerged: loss of the sense of self or fears of this, loss of awareness of what was going on around them although they continued to function, feeling like automatons or like the machines they worked on, irritation, boredom, alienation, depersonalization. This was much more convincing and led to the need for action in the job situation itself, not just additional fringe benefits. Bain's work led to a major reorganization of the work situation that completely changed the operatives' experience, and incidentally increased productivity and decreased wastage.

Mistaken self-diagnosis and related unrealistic prescriptions occur over and over again. The fact that the remedies have not worked in the past does not seem to deter people from repeatedly trying them and each time attributing some magic to them: "This time it really will work." This way of looking at things is very true of nursing. Improved training courses to achieve higher status and more pay have been tried over and over again. In the meantime, the job of nursing itself has not been appreciably upgraded to match the upgraded training. The discrepancy between the level of training and the level of the job has thus been increased. The nurses' complaints about their jobs remain much the same and wastage remains excessive. The remedies do not touch the core of the problem and are repeatedly ineffectual.

Bain's case demonstrates what I think often happens in such a situation. The defensive maneuvers are indicative. There is a focus of deep anxiety and distress in the institution associated with despair about being able to tackle the situation directly. The defensive system collusively set up against these feelings consists, first, in fragmenting the core problem so that it no longer exists in recognizable form in the minds of those concerned. The fragments are then embodied in aspects of the ambience of the work situation that are honestly but wrongly experienced as the problem about which something needs to be done—usually by someone else. Responsibility is also projected. Hope for a real remedy only exists if the fragments can be reintegrated and the core problem recognized again and confronted.

Psychoanalytically Oriented Methods

We are indebted to psychoanalysis and particularly to Freud himself for technical help and for models of working that both facilitate the exploration that may lead to more effective diagnosis and show how, having made the diagnosis, we can work with our clients to tackle the problem at the heart of the matter.

From Freud's technical papers we learn much that is relevant to our own work. Derivatives from the psychoanalytic clinical method give us our own most useful tools (Freud, [1911–1915] 1958). Freud recommends evenly suspended attention — a very open mind. His point is that we should try not to direct our attention to anything in particular to avoid premature selection and prejudgment of the issues. That would block our receptivity to what might emerge as being significant. If one can hold to that attitude one can hope that gradually the meaning of what one's clients are showing one may evolve.

Later psychoanalysts have learned the value of this attitude and have clarified it further. Bion (1970), for example, recommends eschewing memory and desire, that is, not deliberately summoning up conscious memories of what has previously happened — even if only yesterday. Dismissing such memories from one's mind leaves one's mind free for the spontaneous emergence of memories, rather like dreams, evoked by what the clients are telling us in the here and now, memories more likely to be relevant to the understanding of the current situation. Similarly, desires for the clients or the progress of the work, or for that matter for oneself, may seriously interfere with helping the clients to find their own way through to change that is appropriate to their circumstances and resources. We, too, can sometimes be caught in the trap of false diagnosis and unrealistic prescriptions.

The strain of working in this way is as considerable for the consultant as it is for the psychoanalyst. One has deliberately knocked away one's traditional props: memory, consciously set objectives, and theory. Consequently, one exists for a great deal of one's working time in a state of ignorance, uncertainty, and doubt, often not knowing for the moment where one's clients stand, or oneself, a state that may be profoundly frightening to one's belief in one's own competence to understand and help one's clients. One needs faith that there is light at the end of the tunnel even when there may not seem to be much hope.

This experience is compounded by being repetitive. If one is lucky, or perhaps skillful, and holds to ignorance, meaning may evolve — some partial understanding and some idea of how to proceed. But this will serve usually to show how much more of the unknown still surrounds us and how far there is still to go. It sometimes feels unrelenting. Our clients themselves may precipitate us farther into the unknown if they accept our partial interpretation of the situation and are prepared and able to go on.

Nor need we suppose that our clients will necessarily accept or like our rather strange way of working, especially those who want, or are used to, the kind of "expert" who will give them a definitive answer quickly rather than help them evolve a solution for themselves. So we may have to teach them how to use us, work with their resistance, and support them through the early distrust and frustration aroused by our methods. Furthermore, in working through these problems with our clients we will also be helping them to see the value of learning to work in a similar way themselves: not to make prejudgments about relevance, for example, but to cast the net wide; not to be overinfluenced by such common attitudes as loyalty to colleagues, tact, and discretion, often used as defenses against engaging in difficult explorations. For instance, it took some time to help the staff in the hospital where I worked to understand that an unwritten rule — that one did not talk about colleagues in their absence even, or especially, when the absence itself was a key issue — was defensive and obstructive.

One is coming close to helping one's clients toward free association, though today neither consultants nor psychoanalysts would think it of much use to ask people to free associate. Rather, one has to work to remove resistance to free speech and help the clients to appreciate its value. One can also give permission and offer oneself as a model.

In the first nursing study, although the set problem was the deployment of student nurses to practical training and nursing services in the hospital, we asked our respondents to discuss any features of their nursing experience that seemed significant to them. The discussions were quite discursive and helped to put the deployment problem into the wider context of institutional anxieties and defenses. Clients can learn to work this way. This will be even more relevant in the later stages of a project when one is sharing data and interpretations, working through resistance to acceptance, correcting or modifying one's own interpretations if necessary, and working toward change.

The interpretative method we use to further such work again owes much to psychoanalysis: making the unconscious and implicit explicit, working with resistance to unwelcome insights, helping our clients to think more freely and laterally, using transference and countertransference and at times interpreting them, helping clients to modify their defenses, exploring important projection systems, and helping them move toward significant change and sustaining them through the difficulty and stress of implementing it. This is challenging and rewarding for both clients and consultants. This is analysis.

In institutional terms, Bain (1982) has described this analysis as tripartite—work culture analysis, role analysis, and structure analysis. All three types of analysis prove on examination to owe a great deal to insights from psychoanalysis. This is most obvious in work culture analysis, which deals with attitudes and beliefs, traditions, patterns of relationships, the context within which work takes place. But analysis of roles and structure show that they also are permeated with content and dynamics with which psychoanalysts are also familiar. For example, institutionally sustained projection systems, anxieties, and defenses contribute to role definition, to role relationships, and so to structure. These are quite as influential in the experience and personality structure of members as work culture. The three types of analysis are theoretically separable but in practice are and must be carried out together.

There is the danger in institutional consultancy that only one or two types of analysis may be used. Quite frequently, consultants, particularly in "humane" institutions, only undertake work culture analysis, commonly described as sensitivity or support groups for staff, aimed at increasing their sensitivity to their clients and themselves. Psychoanalysts and members of related professions who are not also social scientists are prone to do this. The objectives of this work are not too difficult to achieve within the groups themselves; the group members both want and are quite able to become more sensitive. But they usually return to a work situation where roles and structure have not been modified. This may make it impossible for them to deploy their new insights in action. A nurse cannot be more sensitive and intimately related to her patients when a nursing system based on multiple indiscriminate caretaking prevents her from ever really getting to know them well.

Nonpsychoanalytically oriented consultants may carry out only role and structure analysis and suggest changes that cannot be implemented effectively because parallel changes in work culture have not been achieved. In fact, in many of these cases attention to work culture might well have shown that the suggested changes in role and structure were inappropriate. This is what appears to have happened in the British Health and Social Services, where repeated consultancy seems to have produced little significant benefit.

In either case, the consultancy is likely to prove ineffectual and the hoped-for benefits will not materialize. The clients are disappointed, frustrated, disillusioned. The consultants and what they stand for may be discredited.

To return now to the change process in institutions and to a point I raised earlier, there is another parallel with psychoanalysis. The initiative for taking action, as insights and meaning evolve, lies with clients just as it does with patients. The consultants' responsibility is to be available to collaborate in this task, to help clarify objectives and plan change and to bear the stress of carrying it out.

This is, I am sure, established practice among psychoanalytically oriented consultants, although it is by no means accepted by all consultants. Some make their diagnostic explorations and send reports to their clients, often blueprints of what they think should be done. They then leave the clients to do what they can, dodging out of what may well be the most stressful part of the consultancy. This is an important aspect of the failure of consultancy in many cases, contributing especially to the relative failure of consultancy in the British Health and Social Services. It would be unthinkable to assess patients, give them detailed reports about their psychopathology and instructions as to what they should do about it, and send them away to carry out the instructions on their own. I would find it just as unthinkable to treat clients that way.

My final point in drawing the parallels between psychoanalysis and consultancy practice concerns termination: the difficult questions of when termination is appropriate and how it should be accomplished. The point at which termination is appropriate concerns more than simply what the institution has gained from the consultancy, in particular that the problems tackled in the joint work have reached resolution and that one can be reasonably certain that the gains will be sustained. One would also hope that the clients have learned a way of tackling problems that will survive when the consultants have left and that can be applied to new tasks and problems as they arise. This is particularly important in present-day society, where there is great and immediate need for continual institutional change to match rapidly changing circumstances. A crucial aspect of management is the management of innovation (Rice, 1965). As consultants we can help increase such management skills. This is in some ways analogous to the capacity for self-analysis one hopes patients will develop and continue to use to meet the new situations they will confront.

Sustaining the learning requires that the process of termination be carried out effectively. In psychoanalytic terms, this could be described as helping to establish the consultant and the consultancy method as a "good object" within the client so that they continue to be used consciously and unconsciously as a resource when needed.

One important requirement is that the consultant and the client have time to work through together what termination means. A process of mourning is appropriate and needs to be facilitated: to face anger about deprivation of the consultant's further help, to work through anticipatory anxiety about being left on one's own, to face feelings about the loss of people who are withdrawing, to speculate and fantasize about whether some sort of continued relationship might be appropriate institutionally or personally, and if so what. Nor are the feelings all on the side of the client. The loss of a rewarding project, and of the friends one's clients almost inevitably become, may also be hard for the consultant. The consultant too needs to be able to work this through in order to be able to help the client mourn.

However, perhaps one should not push the analogies with psychoanalysis too far. There are differences, too, between psychoanalytic and consultancy practice, some of which are to the consultants' advantage, some to their disadvantage.

It is more difficult to sustain analytic anonymity in consultancy; one has to mix socially to some extent with clients or even with their families. Maintaining the balance between social and professional relationships can be difficult. Holding a neutral position between different members and groups in the institution can also be difficult. These factors greatly complicate both transference and countertransference and require great sensitivity from the consultant. However, those difficulties may be mitigated by the fact that the consultant need not, often cannot, work alone. Consultancy is not quite so lonely as psychoanalysis. Fellow consultants are invaluable in helping sort out transference and countertransference. Working with others also gives added richness to the interpretation of data, bringing different perspectives and different field experiences to bear. Freud discouraged the taking of notes during sessions since it would interfere with free-floating attention. But one consultant may work with free-floating attention while the other takes notes, inevitably selectively. Together they may produce a better record of the complex data we handle.

One may also have to write reports for a client, for those who provide research funds or for publication, as the psychoanalyst does not. How does one avoid the consequences of sending blueprint-type reports? I think only by reporting first verbally to clients and working through the report with them before writing so that the report becomes a distillation of work already done. This is also necessary in order to get agreement for publication. This is very stressful and time consuming. It may in the end mean, frustratingly, that one cannot publish. The Tavistock Institute is a graveyard of unpublished reports. But I am sure there is no way around this.

Measuring the Health of Institutions

In concluding this chapter I would like to return to Fenichel (1945) and the view that institutions affect the personality structures of their members temporarily or permanently. I think that our work in consultancy supports this view. As the institution changes, so also do the members—their attitudes, their behavior, their relationships with the institution and with each other. These changes can become fixed and may be carried outside the institution as well. The success of a consultancy may be judged in two interrelated ways. First, it may be judged by the success of the institution itself: Has it become more effective in carrying out the task it was set up to do? Has productivity gone up? If it is a humane institution like a school, hospital, or children's home, has the care given become better and more realistic, and has it led to real growth and maturation in those who are cared for? The second concerns the staff members of the institution. Have there been changes for the better in their personalities? Has the quality of mental health improved? Have the members grown and matured? The connection between the two criteria is to some extent circular. An institution is likely to become more task-efficient if the members grow and mature, orient themselves more realistically to their own part in the common task, and cooperate in a more healthy way with others also involved in the common task. From the other side, efficient task performance is itself rewarding: It reduces anxiety and guilt and the defenses against them that stem from bad task performance; it increases confidence and self-esteem. Task-effective institutions tend to be healthy for their members, and vice versa.

There are some fairly simple measures of institutional health: productivity, if that can be simple to measure, and others that used to be known at the Tavistock Institute as *morale indicators,* for example, labor turnover, absenteeism, and sickness rates. These give some indication of the mental health of members, of their satisfaction or dissatisfaction, the strength of the need to escape from a situation that is too stressful, perhaps to save themselves from breakdown. Going to conferences might be another such measure in some institutions. For example, a senior civil servant at a Leicester conference indicated that part of his motive for being there was to get away from an almost intolerable work situation for a time so that he could go back and cope again. These measures are also some indication of the loyalty that members feel toward the institution and their esteem for it. Institutions that may otherwise be judged unhealthy tend to show high figures on all the indices.

Other measures of mental health are more complicated, but the evidence on an intuitive level is unmistakable when one gets to know the members. There is no mistaking the high level of anxiety and the inadequate defenses among nurses and the danger to their growth and maturation. Likewise, there was no mistaking the confusion, disorientation, and low self-esteem of the men and women of the London Fire Brigade. Similarly, one is aware when members of an institution are confident about the institution and themselves, enjoy being there, feel they are valued, and feel themselves to be growing and developing. It is gratifying for us consultants to watch one kind of situation change into another as our work develops. For example, in a study done at the Royal National Orthopaedic Hospital (Menzies Lyth, 1988), the staff themselves noticed it, as shown in a typical remark by a senior nurse: "This has been the most definitive learning experience in my whole life." The atmosphere and the people change, changes that are also marked by the morale indicators.

A great deal of my own work in recent years has been in institutions caring for children, where the main objective was to improve the standard of care. In the Royal National Orthopaedic Hospital we were particularly concerned to develop a care method that would mitigate or prevent the classic bad effects of hospitalization on personality development and mental health, as described in the early hospital studies of the Robertsons (Robertson, 1970). A follow-up study of the children and families showed that none of the children suffered from the effects of hospitalization described by the Robertsons.

At the Cotswold Community, which cared for very disturbed and often-delinquent boys from disturbed families, the results were not so encouraging; the task was much more difficult. But, nevertheless, the improvements in the boys' personalities and in their subsequent life performance were significantly better than those of similar boys cared for in other communities that operated on a different model of care.

These results were impressive, but perhaps more impressive were the beneficial side effects for other people. The adults concerned also grew and matured as the care system changed, often involving them in more challenging but more rewarding work and stretching their capacities as they had never been stretched before. Most apparent was the change in the young nursery nurses in the Orthopaedic Hospital as they took on increasingly difficult tasks, for example in family support, and through case assignment came more directly into contact with the children's and families' distress and their own. Senior nurses were often understandably anxious lest the changes were imposing too much strain on the nursery nurses. They need not have worried; the nurses took to the new tasks like ducks to water and thrived on them. I have already mentioned how senior nurses felt. Other adults who spent time in the unit also grew, particularly the children's mothers. Their confidence and skill in their mothering increased, as did attachment to their child. In fact, implicit in devising a better care system for the children was to help the adults become better models for the children to identify with. Role and structure changes gave the adults more authority and responsibility, which helped the adults mature and made them better models for identification. As before, one may note that better task performance in child care went hand in hand with maturation in the staff providing the care.

Finally, one can begin to establish principles, or theories, about what constitutes a healthy institution that performs well and furthers the mental health of its members. Each institution has to be helped to implement the principles in its own way, with its own tasks, problems, and resources. These principles match quite closely the criteria for a healthy personality as derived from psychoanalysis. They include avoiding dealing with anxiety by the use of regressed defenses; more use of adaptations and sublimation; the ability to confront and work through problems; opportunities for people to deploy their capacities to their fullest, no more or less than they are able to; opportunity to operate realistic control over their life in the institution while being able to take due account of the needs and contributions of others; independence without undue supervision; and visible relation between effort and rewards, not only financial. But having outlined the principles, one forgets them in the field, in the here-and-now relationship with clients. The principles evolve over and over again in the work; they cannot be imposed. The principles are not so new. Implementing them is what is so difficult, and I suppose that to date our failures have been as great as, or greater than, our successes. We have been more successful when we have worked in rather small self-contained units where face-to-face contact is easy.

What has proved much more difficult, and what we still have much to learn about, is working with very large organizations and multiple organizations that are subject to a great deal of central control and aim at uniformity. One can build a model in a subinstitution such as the Orthopaedic Hospital, but how does one transfer the learning to other hospitals? How does one get beyond a central committee to the operating units, as in the London Fire Brigade? I think this is a serious problem now and for the future.

References

Bain, A. *The Baric Experiment.* Occasional Paper No. 4. London: Tavistock, 1982.

Bain, A., and Barnett, L. *The Design of a Day Care System in a Nursery Setting for Children Under Five.* Occasional Paper No. 8. London: Tavistock, 1982.

Bion, W. R. *Attention and Interpretation.* London: Tavistock, 1970.

Fenichel, O. *The Psychoanalytic Theory of Neurosis.* New York: Norton, 1945.

Freud, S. "Papers on Technique." In J. Strachey (ed. and trans.), *The Standard Edition of the Complete Psychological Works of Sigmund Freud.* Vol. 12. London: Hogarth Press, 1958. (Originally published 1911–1915.)

Menzies Lyth, I. *Containing Anxiety in Institutions: Selected Essays.* Vol. 1. London: Free Association Books, 1988.

Menzies Lyth, I. *The Dynamics of the Social: Selected Essays.* Vol. 2. London: Free Association Books, 1989.

Rice, A. K. *Learning for Leadership.* London: Tavistock, 1965.

Robertson, J. *Young Children in Hospital.* London: Tavistock, 1970.

16

Struggling with the Demon: Confronting the Irrationality of Organizations and Executives

Manfred F. R. Kets de Vries

On April 14, 1925, Freud wrote to the novelist Stefan Zweig that the "fundamental task of psychoanalysis . . . was to 'struggle with the demon [of irrationality] in a sober way'" (Gay, 1988, p. xvii). Freud, as a conquistador of the human mind, viewed himself very much as a destroyer of illusions about human nature. And he has been quite successful in assuming that particular role, having acquired a place in the pantheon of science together with luminaries such as Copernicus, Newton, Darwin, and Einstein. His insights into the behavior of humankind have profoundly affected our way of looking at the world. None of the social sciences has remained untouched by his discoveries. The various contributions in this volume demonstrate the extent to which his ideas have pervaded organizational studies and the world of work.

As an example, building on Freud's insights, Abraham Zaleznik (1990, p. 228) suggests that "you should realize that thinking with psychoanalysis as a frame of reference puts you in a position of despising pretense." Zaleznik makes a plea for understanding what really happens within organizations and dwells on the need to transcend "the infinite variety of ways people have of obscuring and obfuscating what is real" (p. 228).

Demystifying the Myth of Irrationality

In one way or another all the contributors to this book can be considered breakers of illusions. By taking a clinical approach to organizational analysis, these management scholars have laid to rest the myth of organizational rationality. Their contributions give us true insights into human nature. They demonstrate the extent to which irrational acts and behavior affect organizational life, while simultaneously "wrestling with Freud's demon," stripping away the veneer from these irrational activities. They make us aware that things that at first glance may seem mystifying actually have an underlying rationale. This is the real paradox of choosing the clinical paradigm as an investigative method. Knowing how to apply this particular body of psychoanalytic knowledge and concepts has added another dimension to our way of looking at things. These specific models of the mind have helped us in the process of "making sense."

An analysis based solely on the observation of surface manifestations will only take the observer so far. The recognition that certain phenomena that are beyond direct awareness can nevertheless profoundly affect the outcome of specific decisions cannot help but change our attitudes tremendously. By viewing these surface manifestations as transformations of deep, difficult-to-access structures, the various contributors to this book expand our understanding of the functioning of organizational life and executive behavior.

We have to probe the inner world of executives if we want to understand organizational behavior. It is extremely difficult to make sense of an executive's motives, needs, and attitudes without understanding the role that fantasy, conflict, and defense play in the individual's intrapsychic and interpersonal world. An orientation that recognizes the role of unconscious motivation, the presence of intrapsychic conflict, and the impact of early developmental processes on later behavior will have an enriching effect on more traditional theories of individual and organizational functioning.

As the chapters in this book show, the application of clinical concepts to the analysis of organizational relationships and the use of theory-based typologies facilitate ways of intervention and prediction that reach far beyond the scope of more traditional theories. At the same time, the clinical approach to organizational analysis has led to a general sobering up, the realization that there are no magic solutions for organizational intervention and change. Changing people and organizations is not an instant affair. It requires an elaborate process of working through — a mourning process of coming to grips with what these changes signify (Kets de Vries and Miller, 1984). People who promise quick-fix solutions are playing a delusional game. There is a world of difference between identifying symptoms and analyzing and treating the real nature of a problem.

Although the various contributors to this book have broadly delineated the boundaries of the theories and conceptualizations that define the clinical paradigm, there is much more work to be done. Psychoanalytic theory is itself in the middle of a dramatic period of transformation and change, and many new ideas have come to the fore. In particular, there have been many developments in the areas of object relations theory, hermeneutics, elaborations about the concept of self, and the role of narcissism in everyday life. Findings from infant observation, ethology, family process theory, cognition, neurophysiology, cybernetics, and information systems theory are being integrated into psychoanalytic theory and practice. Advances in methodology and technology permit the retrieval of more reliable quantitative and qualitative data concerning affective, cognitive, and physiological developmental processes. Moreover, to complicate things further, a large number of scholarly contributions to psychoanalytic thought are coming from people trained in the philosophy of science, history, sociology, anthropology, biography, psycholinguistics, and literary criticism.

Converging Views

Given its current state of ferment, the challenge for psychoanalysis is how to utilize these emerging models in a synergetic manner and apply them to the study of organizations and their occupants. Laurence J. Gould, Harry Levinson, and Laurent Lapierre take an important step forward by showing us how to employ many of these conceptualizations. They also indicate some of the directions in which these theories may take us. All three make a strong case for basing psychoanalytically oriented models of organizational analysis on clinical observations. The "sites" differ, however, varying from being centered around an individual, some kind of group event, a specific project, an all-inclusive organizational diagnosis, or a feature film, to a work of fiction.

In Chapter One, Gould raises some important questions concerning the applicability of psychoanalytic methodology to the work setting. Given the need for techniques and interventions that are analogous to clinical methods, he speculates about the kinds of modifications needed to make such an endeavor possible. In contrast, Lapierre introduces a more hermeneutic perspective to organizational analysis, while Levinson has a less philosophical and more pragmatic outlook on the systematic analysis of organizations. In that respect, his orientation has been greatly influenced by Karl Menninger's (1962, 1963) detailed work on diagnosis of the individual.

Abraham Zaleznik, Alain Noël, and I concentrate on the enigma of leadership and executive behavior, raising a number of intriguing questions about the intrapsychic world of executives. By applying clinical insights, each of us raises the curtain on the private theater of these people. However, it would be timely to look even more closely at the reasons why leaders do the things they do. Given the importance of leadership for the world in general, continuing investigation of its characteristics and vicissitudes is needed. In particular, the insidious effects of power on a person's mind merit further exploration.

Another issue worth addressing is how the individual is affected by the process of deference that accompanies the rise to power. Leader-follower relationships are a whole subject in themselves. An important question in this context is whether there are other forces that influence the superior-subordinate interface, apart from the obvious transferential ones.

Finally, more work remains to be done in the area of leadership development. Of course, the first question we really have to ask ourselves in this context is what can be done in the area of leadership training. Considering the importance of early developmental experiences, perhaps the die has already been cast by the time the potential candidates for this kind of training arrive at the organization's door. It is important to explore what steps can be taken later in the career life cycle. On this point, Lapierre suggests one interesting way of applying psychoanalytically based methodology to leadership development.

The chapters by Susan C. Schneider, Michael A. Diamond, and Larry Hirschhorn and Donald R. Young shed greater light on the way groups really function. Their application of the clinical paradigm to regressive group behavior helps clear up the mystery surrounding this phenomenon. Many of the ideas about primitive group functioning derive from insights developed by Bion (1959). This begs the question, however, of further refining his theoretical framework, to go beyond the primitive defensive reactions that lie at its core.

In Chapter Nine, Hirschhorn and Young remind us of the way groups within organizations develop specific social defenses that may adversely affect organizational functioning. They draw on the influential work of Jaques (1955) and Menzies (1960), who describe how people transform primitive feelings of persecutory and depressive anxiety into various social defenses. The concept of social defense—a system of defenses that results from collusive interaction among the organization's participants—has become a promising avenue to understanding the existence of certain group-designated roles and tasks, and the way in which particular organizational structures develop.

That the concept of organizational culture and character has assumed an increasingly central position in management theory is nothing new. The most important contributing factors to this are developments such as deregulation and its aftermath, the merger and acquisition phenomenon, and the tendency of certain national cultures to be more competitive than others in the global marketplace.

Howell S. Baum, Howard S. Schwartz, and Danny Miller and I, each taking a somewhat different perspective, tackle the issue of corporate character. Miller and I, using the Weberian notion of "ideal" types, have tried to clarify the nature of the links between personality, leadership style, and corporate culture, structure, and strategy. With further refinements in the *Diagnostic and Statistical Manual of Mental Disorders* (the forthcoming *DSM-IV*) and developments in the psychoanalytic study of character (Kets de Vries and Perzow, 1991), additional revisions can be foreseen.

In his study of NASA, Schwartz lays the foundation for a better understanding of the role of the organization ideal in organizational functioning. This concept and the concept of organizational culture seem to be closely intertwined. More work, however, remains to be done in order to flesh out the exact nature of the interface. Another question worth exploring here is the relationship between character type and organization ideal. What must one look out for in different organizational cultures, given the emergence of specific organization ideals? Can one arrive at a typology of corporate culture based on the notion of organization ideal? Is it possible to operationalize the concept of organization ideal and use it as a diagnostic tool?

Baum provides another way of looking at organizational culture and understanding better the subjective experience of bureaucracy. In his analysis he goes far beyond the traditional investigations of bureaucracy, which tend to focus more on social structure. The emphasis on psychological structure, as well as on the defensive responses of organizational participants, is extremely helpful as an explanation of the "character" of bureaucracy.

These contributions on the subject of organizational character help move us toward a more sophisticated understanding of organizational culture. This is in sharp contrast to many other efforts. For example, "culture audits" turn out all too frequently to be extremely shallow endeavors. It is not enough to say that a particular corporation "has respect for the individual" or "values the customer," since this does not provide insight into the organization's character in any meaningful sense. We need to go beyond this sort of platitude and explore the underlying psychology of the firm.

The clinical paradigm allows these researchers to open a window on the very nature of organizational character. However, more research is needed. In a world in which the transnational corporation is becoming more and more important, the relationship between corporate culture and national culture warrants further exploration. Perhaps, viewed through the clinical microscope, the slippery concept of national culture may be somewhat easier to handle. Obvious questions to be addressed are why people in different cultures diverge in their attitudes toward authority and power, why structure and hierarchy are so important to specific cultural groups, and whether cultures differ in preferred leadership style.

As the many case vignettes and organizational interventions throughout the book demonstrate, organizational consultation and change can very much benefit from the clinical paradigm. Isabel Menzies Lyth, Roderick Gilkey, and James Krantz and Thomas North Gilmore discuss the advantages of using clinical concepts in consultation. The proliferation of the quick-fix type of consultancy has made the education of more clinically trained consultants a high priority. Menzies Lyth's description of a special type of action research, whereby consultants and their clients engage in a collaborative effort in problem solving, goes a long way in that direction.

As a diagnostic tool, the notion of parallelism has been highlighted. Analogous to the clinical encounter, where specific patient-therapist interaction patterns may repeat themselves in the therapist-supervisor dialogue, is the interface between clients and consultants. These findings have implications for the composition of consulting teams and their particular modus operandi.

Of course, the notion of parallelism is closely related to what are now quite familiar clinical concepts, such as projective identification and countertransference. It should be said, however, that the outlook of clinicians toward countertransference has come a long way. From being viewed initially as a hindrance to the therapeutic process, countertransference is now seen as an invaluable source of new information. Krantz and Gilmore show us how useful an understanding of this process can be in an organizational setting.

Some of the most topical issues in management are the phenomena of mergers, acquisitions, and strategic alliances. Until now, attention has typically been paid to the financial aspects of the merger and acquisition process. But the human side of this process is neglected at the negotiators' peril—as the failure of a considerable number of these deals to produce the anticipated financial results reveals. The further costs that are incurred in terms of human suffering are incalculable. Gilkey demonstrates how clinical concepts can be put to good use in easing the inevitable transition pains that accompany such alliances.

However, our understanding of these phenomena is only in its infancy. Much more research is needed if we are to become more proficient in handling some very important questions, such as the following: How do we find out if there is real cultural compatibility between the respective parties? How should we handle the premerger negotiations? When should the process be aborted? And how can we facilitate the process of transition?

Other Areas of Exploration

Management is an enormous field of study, and for reasons of space this book is unable to cover all the areas where the clinical approach can make a contribution. There are, of course, many potential areas of application outside the scope of this book that can benefit greatly from the clinical paradigm. One obvious example is individual and organizational stress. Clinical observations are a sine qua non if we want to understand which factors contribute to stress. In this context, it is worth addressing the question of how organizations become "stress carriers." What creates high-stress organizations? What can organizations and individuals do to reduce the level of stress? How can people become more stress resistant? Unfortunately, there are no easy answers to these questions.

Another general field where the clinical paradigm can be put to good use is that of career. By providing insight into a person's "inner theater"—paying attention to the content of parapraxes, fantasies, daydreams, and dreams—the clinical approach can help us to better understand the reasons behind certain career decisions. Many other questions can be raised in this context. For example, what kind of events have a determining effect on major career decisions? What leads people to make dramatic career changes? What roles do mentors play in guiding individuals in their careers? What makes a person plateau or burn out?

The clinical paradigm provides us with the conceptual tools we need to understand the various challenges that all of us face at different stages of the life cycle. Not the least of these is the nature of the continuous interface between an individual's private and public life. How does the individual's private life affect his or her public life, and vice versa? What kind of spillovers can occur? The nature of these interrelationships has to be addressed.

One significant arena where private and public life tend to overlap is in the family business. It is easy to forget the importance of family businesses to the national economy of most countries. Although estimates vary, it has been suggested that 80 to 90 percent of all businesses in most European countries and the United States are family controlled. Given the type of upheaval that so often plagues a family business, consultants trained in the clinical approach will be ideally positioned to provide assistance. Typical problems encountered in the troubled family business are parent-offspring conflict, sibling rivalry, and difficulties surrounding succession. The founder of the enterprise, the original entrepreneur, is not infrequently a difficult person to get along with. His or her leadership style — which may have been very effective in the start-up phase — may no longer be appropriate when a company has attained a certain size. Some form of intervention might be needed to help maintain its continuing growth and development record. Without some kind of clinical training, it can often be very difficult for consultants to make sense of the "irrational" aspects of much entrepreneurial behavior.

Another underdeveloped area where a clinical outlook can make a difference is the study of gender relationships in the workplace. This also brings us to the role of sexuality. Unfortunately, like sex in Victorian England, the role of sexuality in organizations has been pushed underground to a great extent. Organizations seem to prefer to view themselves as sexual "neuters"; there is a preponderant myth that sexuality plays no part in organizational life. A cursory glance at most management text-books supports this supposition, since the word *sexuality* is usually nowhere to be found in their indexes. Nevertheless, the sexual dimension has a major role in organizations. Sexuality is an all-pervasive force in organizational life, affecting the type of imagery we develop about an organization as well as the nature of moti-vation and power relationships. At the same time, the way sex-uality operates within an organization is often very subtle. By paying attention to the kind of stereotyping and joking behavior prevalent in an organization, the consultant can frequently get a handle on the nature of problematic gender relationships.

Another topic usually neglected in organizational litera-ture is the emotional environment of an organization. Some or-ganizations seem to strive to create an environment in which people work without passion; it is as if no form of affect or en-thusiasm is permitted to sully the atmosphere. In this context, I have previously written about the alexithymic personality (Kets de Vries, 1989). This characterizes the type of person who has an extreme reality-based cognitive style, an impoverished fan-tasy life, a paucity of inner emotional experiences, a tendency to engage in stereotypical interpersonal behavior, and speech remarkable for its iteration of endless, trivial, repetitive details. To what extent do organizations attract or develop this kind of personality? What is it like to work for an alexithymic boss? How do organizations manage the feelings of their employees? What effect does "emotional management" have on the individ-ual's mental health? Will it result in feelings of alienation and depersonalization? What other symptoms appear? There has been some research in this area (see, for example, Hochschild, 1983), but the psychological implications need further development.

A major challenge for executives today is how to keep their organizations creative and innovative. If the creative process is not nurtured and maintained, organizations will very quickly lose their competitive edge and falter. It is therefore critical for executives to understand the nature of the creative individual and the process of creativity.

Clinical observation of creative individuals shows that the process of creativity tends to work side by side with underlying conflict. Creativity is the beneficial end result of the transformations of archaic narcissism. Mastery of psychic trauma, problems concerning body image and self-image, and the experiences of death, grief, and loss often play a crucial part in the lives of truly creative people. Many creative individuals are engaged in an intricate, symbolic process of reparation, motivated by an urgent need to restore the body's completeness and to recapture in one form or another the lost or destroyed object. This need for some form of reparation, to come to grips with the chaos within, affects the capacity for feeling, thinking, symbolization, and imagination. With respect to both individuals and organizations, there is a growing belief that the clinical paradigm can make a major contribution to the understanding of the creative process and the conditions that foster creativity and innovation.

Conclusion

These are only a few topics among many that could profit from the application of the clinical paradigm. Naturally, as the field of management evolves, other topics will be added. I anticipate that this book will stimulate further thought and inquiry, taking the clinical paradigm as general Weltanschauung. We have gone on an adventurous journey that to many more traditional scholars of management may appear quite exotic. Despite my awareness of the uneasiness that this approach might generate, I hope that the contributions to this book will show skeptics the added value of following our route.

John Maynard Keynes once described economics as the "dismal science," while Sigmund Freud called psychoanalysis the "impossible profession." I am in the strange position of having a background in both disciplines, and I strongly believe that the combination of these two apparent negatives will have a very positive, synergetic end result.

References

Bion, W. R. *Experiences in Groups, and Other Papers.* London: Tavistock, 1959.

Gay, P. *Freud: A Life for Our Time.* New York: Norton, 1988.

Hochschild, A. R. *The Managed Heart.* Berkeley: University of California Press, 1983.

Jaques, E. "Social Systems as a Defence Against Persecutory and Depressive Anxiety." In M. Klein, P. Heimann, and R. E. Money-Kyrle (eds.), *New Directions in Psychoanalysis.* London: Tavistock, 1955.

Kets de Vries, M.F.R. "Alexithymia in Organizational Life: The Organization Man Revisited." *Human Relations,* 1989, *42* (12), 1079–1093.

Kets de Vries, M.F.R., and Miller, D. *The Neurotic Organization: Diagnosing and Changing Counterproductive Styles of Management.* San Francisco: Jossey-Bass, 1984.

Kets de Vries, M.F.R., and Perzow, S. *Handbook of Character Studies.* New York: International Universities Press, 1991.

Menninger, K. *A Manual for Psychiatric Case Study.* New York: Grune & Stratton, 1962.

Menninger, K. *The Vital Balance.* New York: Viking Press, 1963.

Menzies, I. "A Case Study in the Functioning of Social Systems as a Defence Against Anxiety: A Report on a Study of the Nursing Service of a General Hospital." *Human Relations,* 1960, *13,* 95–121.

Zaleznik, A. *Executive's Guide to Motivating People.* Chicago: Bonus Books, 1990.

Name Index

391

Subject Index

A

Ablis, CEO of, 126–127

Accidents: approaches to investigating, 238–240; auditing, 237–238

Acquisitions. *See* Mergers and acquisitions

Action: capacity for, 337; organizational, 59

Activity essence, and strategy formation, 153–156, 158

Activity patterns, and strategy formation, 149–151, 152, 154, 158

Affiliation, and group membership, 192–193, 195

Aging, of CEOs, 130, 138

Aggressor, identification with, 195, 206, 207

Alexthymia, and unconscious fantasy, 74, 388

Allied-Bendix, merger of, 344, 358

Allied-Signal Corporation, merger of, 333, 344–345, 346, 356–357, 358

Ambiguity, of authority and responsibility, 267, 275–277

Ambivalence, in preoccupations, 157

American Psychiatric Association, 245, 246, 247, 250, 258, 261, 384

Annihilation anxiety, and group membership, 196, 198–199, 201, 209, 210

Anxiety, social defenses against, 215–240

Apollo program, impact of, 287, 293, 295

Apple Computers, CEO of, 132–133

Asia, competition from, 101

Atlantis, problems with, 286

Attitudes, organizational, 59–60

Autocratic group, culture of, 197, 205–207, 211–212

Authority: ambiguity of, 267, 275–277; autonomous, 268; concept of, 71; creating, on outside, 275–280; denoted, 274; and leadership compact, 107; and politicization, 113–114; unresolved conflicts about, 127

Autonomy: of authority, 268; and boundaries, 185; and strategy formation, 159, 160

Autonomy versus doubt and shame: interventions for, 334; in mergers, 338–339

Avoidant style: culture of, 251–252; and need for detachment, 257–258

B

Bendix, in merger, 344, 358

blended corporations: family metaphor for, 349–350; interventions for, 354–359; managing, 351–354; and nuclear corporations, 350–352

Boundaries: aspects of managing,

397

Separateness, sense of, 99–100

Settings, of organizations, 48, 49–50

Sexuality: research needed on, 387–388; in workplace, 6–13, 17, 270–275, 281–282

Shame: autonomy versus, 334, 338–339; in bureaucracies, 271, 279–280

Signal, in merger, 333, 344–345, 346, 356–357, 358

Signifiers, and semantics of desire, 14

Social defenses: and anxiety of working, 215–240; background on, 215–216; and hero role, 227, 228–236; and organizational health, 362–363; presenting situation of, 216–223; and psychodynamics of safety, 223–228; splitting as, 219–225, 227, 236–237; summary on, 236–240

Social structures: and institutionalized groups, 201–203; manifest and latent levels of, 342; of organizations, 265–266

Splitting: and group membership, 198, 199, 201, 203; at oil refinery, 219–225, 227, 236–237; of perceptions of parents, 80; in projective identification, 312, 313, 326, 327; and safety, 225–226

Stagnation, generativity versus, 335, 346–347

Start-up problems, in blended corporations, 354, 355, 358–359

Stop & Shop, leadership of, 114–115

Strategic planning workshop, projective identification in, 314–316

Strategy formation: and activity essence, 153–156, 158; and activity patterns, 149–151, 152, 154, 158; aspects of unconscious processes in, 140–166; background on, 140–142; CEOs described for, 144–148; clues to, 142–144; and contacts, nature of, 151–153, 154, 158; and Magnificent Obsessions, 159–163; from manifest to latent interpretations of,

148–161; preoccupations and, 157–161; and subordinates, 156; uncovering, 162

Structure and systems, in blended corporations, 352–353, 355–356

Subjectivity: and leadership, 74–75; of researcher-authors, 77–79

Success: and ego ideal, 289; as management orientation, 293–295

Superego, loss of, 300–301

Support, loss of, in mergers, 337

Switzerland, Vocatron in, 6–13

Sycophancy, and transference, 127–128

T

Tasks: and boundaries, 178–179, 181–182; patterns of, 48

Tavistock Institute of Human Relations: and organizational health, 366–367, 374, 375; and psychoanalytic framework, 29, 32, 33, 39

Teamwork, and intimacy issues, 345. *See also* Groups

Termination, by consultants, 62–68, 372–373

Territorial battles, in blended corporations, 353–354, 355, 357–358

Texas Instruments, and managerial mystique, 108

Texts: case study of analyzing, 6–13; and dynamics of leadership, 76, 79, 89; of organizations, 5–6, 10, 11, 13–18; rules of interpretation for, 16–18; and semantics of desire, 13–15

Thematic unity: in interpretation, 16–17; and strategy formation, 143

Therapy of the group, 31

Transference: in bureaucracies, 267, 268; and CEOs, 124–128; concept of, 15, 124; and helplessness, 234, 235; made explicit, 34; mirroring, 125, 205, 211; persecutory, 199, 211; and textual analysis, 14–15, 17

Transition: in groups, 209–212; in mergers, 331–360